Physics
FOR OCR

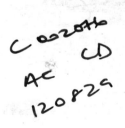

TOWER HAMLETS
POPLAR HIGH STREET
LONDON E14 0AF
Tel: 0207 510 7763

Gurinder Chadha
David Sang

CAMBRIDGE
UNIVERSITY PRESS

CAMBRIDGE UNIVERSITY PRESS
Cambridge, New York, Melbourne, Madrid, Cape Town, Singapore, São Paulo, Delhi

Cambridge University Press
The Edinburgh Building, Cambridge CB2 8RU, UK

www.cambridge.org
Information on this title: www.cambridge.org/9780521738309

© Cambridge University Press 2009

First published 2009

Printed in the United Kingdom at the University Press, Cambridge

A catalogue record for this publication is available from the British Library

ISBN 978-0-521-73830-9 paperback with CD-ROM

ACKNOWLEDGEMENTS
Project management: Sue Kearsey
Page layout, illustration and preparation of interactive PDFs: HL Studios, Long Hanborough
Front cover photograph: Region around the Horsehead Nebula in the constellation of Orion/Royal Observatory, Edinburgh/AAO/Science Photo Library

Contents

Contents

Introduction

Cambridge OCR Advanced Sciences

The new *Cambridge OCR Advanced Sciences* course provides complete coverage of the revised OCR AS and A2 Level science specifications (Biology, Chemistry A and Physics A) for teaching from September 2008. There are two books for each subject – one covering AS and one covering A2. Some material has been drawn from the existing *Cambridge Advanced Sciences* books; however the majority is new.

The course has been developed in an innovative format, featuring Cambridge's new interactive PDFs on CD-ROM in the back of the books, and free access to a dedicated website. The CD-ROM provides additional material, including detailed objectives, hints on answering questions, and extension material. It also provides access to web-based e-learning activities to help students visualise abstract concepts, understand calculations and simulate scientific processes.

The books contain all the material required for teaching the specifications, and can be used either on their own or in conjunction with the interactive PDFs and the website.

In addition, *Teacher Resource CD-ROMs* with book PDFs plus extra material such as worksheets, practical activities and tests, are available for each book. These CD-ROMs also provide access to the new *Cambridge OCR Advanced Sciences* Planner website with a week-by-week adaptable teaching schedule.

Introduction to Physics 2 for OCR – the physics A2 text

This book covers the entire OCR A2 Physics A specification for first examination in 2010. Chapters 1 to 7 correspond to Unit G484, The Newtonian World. Chapters 8 to 19 correspond to Unit G485, Fields, Particles and Frontiers of Physics. The content of the chapters closely matches the sequence of modules and sections as laid out in the specification. Each chapter ends with a summary. The summary includes all the definitions, principles and concepts required by the specification.

The book builds on the material covered in *Physics 1 for OCR*. The language is kept simple, to improve accessibility for all students, while still maintaining scientific rigour throughout. Care is taken to introduce and use all the specialist terms that students need for the specification. In the text, key terms are highlighted in bold. The glossary at the end of the book carefully defines these terms so that they match with the expectation of the OCR examiners.

The depth and breadth of treatment of each topic is pitched at the appropriate level for OCR A2 students. The accompanying CD-ROM also contains some extension material that goes a little beyond the requirements of the specification, which should engage and stretch the more able students.

Some of the text and illustrations are based on material from the endorsed text *Physics 2*, which covered the earlier OCR specification, while some is completely new. All of it has been scrutinised and revised, to match the specification and examination papers for G484 and G485. In addition to the main content in each chapter, there are also How Science Works boxes. These describe issues or events related to physics that have been included as learning outcomes in the specification. The How Science Works boxes also explore the impact of scientific enquiry on individuals and society.

Self-assessment questions (SAQs) in each chapter provide opportunities to check understanding and to make links back to earlier work. Some SAQs are marked, with a blue, vertical bar, as 'stretch-and-challenge' SAQs. These questions are less atomistic and may be open-ended. In examinations, such questions will often target the higher grades. Past examination questions at the end of each chapter allow students to practise answering exam-style questions. The answers to these, along with exam-style mark schemes and hints on answering questions, are found on the accompanying CD-ROM. Many of the SAQs and end-of-chapter questions require the student to think back to work done during their AS course or during other parts of the A2 specification. So they help students to make links between different areas of physics and therefore to address the synoptic aspects of the A2 physics course. These 'synoptic' questions are marked with the following icon.

Acknowledgements

We would like to thank the following for permission to reproduce images:

Cover, p. 184 Royal Observatory, Edinburgh/AAO/Science Photo Library; p. 1 © Bernhard Classen/Alamy; pp. 2, 3, 10b, 53, 66, 67r, 68, 82, 86, 105, 109, 127, 130, 158, 213b, extension 1.1 Andrew Lambert Photography/Science Photo Library; pp. 5, 36, 103 Images Colour Library; p. 8 MSSSO, ANU/Science Photo Library; p. 9 © ImageState/Alamy; p.10t Kieran Doherty/Reuters/Popperfoto; p. 11 I Virginia Regt. USA; extension 1.3a, p. 187 Lawrence Berkeley Laboratory/Science Photo Library; pp. 14, 45 Science Photo Library; p. 18 © TMPhoto/Alamy; p. 25 © Ben Pipe/Alamy; pp. 31, 280, 281 NASA/Science Photo Library; p. 33 Roger G. Howard; p.43l © NASA Images/Alamy; p. 43r Royal Astronomical Society/Science Photo Library; p. 52 Kim Taylor/Bruce Coleman Collection; p. 58 Gurinder Chadha; p. 67l UPI/Corbis; p. 69l © Bettmann/CORBIS; p. 69r Simon Fraser/Science Photo Library; p. 74l Philippe Plailly/Science Photo Library; p. 74r Science Museum/Science & Society Picture Library; p. 96 Segre Collection/American Institute of Physics/Science Photo Library; pp. 104, 226l Sheila Terry/Science Photo Library; p.120 Alex Bartel/Science Photo Library; p. 133 Science Source/Science Photo Library; p. 134 European Space Agency/Science Photo Library; p. 139 Sean Gallup/Getty Images; p. 144 Bill Longchore/Science Photo Library; p. 153 Pasquale Sorrentino/Science Photo Library; p. 172 David Hay Jones/Science Photo Library; pp. 178, 179 University of Cambridge, Cavendish Laboratory; p. 188 Adam Hart-Davis/Science Photo Library; p. 193 US Navy/Science Photo Library; p. 195l © Travel Ink/JET/Life File; p. 195r David Austen/Bruce Coleman Collection; p. 201 Martin Bond/Science Photo Library; p. 204 US Department of Energy/Science Photo Library; p. 206 Jean-Loup Charmet/Science Photo Library; p. 211 N Feather/Science Photo Library; p. 213t Leslie Garland Picture Library/Alamy; p. 219 James King-Holmes/Science Photo Library; p. 226r Mauro Fermariello/Science Photo Library; pp. 227t, 256 AJ Photo/Hop Americain/Science Photo Library; p. 227b Edward Kinsman/Science Photo Library; p. 232 Du Cane Medical Imaging Ltd/Science Photo Library; p. 233 Zephyr/Science Photo Library; p. 234, 254 Gustoimages/Science Photo Library; p. 235 Michelle Del Guercio/Science Photo Library; p. 238l © Mark A. Johnson/Alamy; p. 238r RVI Medical Physics, Newcastle/Simon Fraser/Science Photo Library; p. 241 CNRI/Science Photo Library; p. 243 Wellcome Dept. of Cognitive Neurology/Science Photo Library; p. 244 Geoff Tompkinson/Science Photo Library; p. 247l Alfred Pasieka/Science Photo Library; p. 247r Sovereign, ISM/Science Photo Library; p. 250 Ian Hooten/Science Photo Library; p. 256l Professor AT Elliott, Department of Clinical Physics and Bioengineering, University of Glasgow; p. 261 NASA/ESA/STScI/R. Windhorst & S. Driver, ASU/Science Photo Library; p. 262 Chris Butler/Science Photo Library; p. 263 Matthew Bate/Science Photo Library; p. 264 Mark Garlick/Science Photo Library; p. 265l NASA/ESA/STScI/Science Photo Library; p. 265r Physics Today Collection/American Institute of Physics/Science Photo Library; p. 270 Hale Observatories/Science Photo Library; p. 277 NASA/ESA/STScI/R. Williams, HDF Team/Science Photo Library; p. 278 David A. Hardy/Science Photo Library; p. 279 Emilio Segre Visual Archives/American Institute of Physics/Science Photo Library; extension 10.1 Reprinted by permission of The Random House Group Ltd; extension 16.1 Dr M. Phelps & Dr J. Mazziotta et al/Neurology/Science Photo Library; extension 17.1 Dr Najeeb Layyous/Science Photo Library.

We would like to thank OCR for permission to reproduce exam questions.

Chapter 1

Momentum

Fun – and physics – on screen

If you play computer games (Figure 1.1) you will be familiar with the way in which characters move about the screen. Cars accelerate and decelerate rapidly as they chase each other around. A character flying through the air will follow a curved path under the influence of gravity. Human figures may be given bulging muscles so that they can leap and punch with enormous force, but their motion usually obeys the laws of physics.

The programmers who produce these games know Newton's laws of motion, and these laws are built into the software. However, there is often some subtle cheating going on. For example, the strength of gravity may be reduced so that characters can jump higher and spend longer moving through the air. Objects may be made springier than is possible in reality, so that landings are softer and collisions are bouncier. The trick is that users of the games should not notice these effects.

It would look wrong if a character were to jump straight up in the air and then suddenly move sideways or stop for a long time in mid-air (as sometimes happens in cartoons). Our experience of the world gives us an intuitive grasp of how things move and it is unlikely that we would accept games where objects moved in impossible ways.

The same is true when we watch or play sports such as football or tennis. We learn to predict where the ball will go when it has been kicked or hit. We may be surprised when a skilful player makes the ball swerve through the air – perhaps they are able to use the force that arises when a spinning ball interacts with the air – but we know that the laws of physics are still being obeyed.

In this chapter, we will explore how the idea of momentum can allow us to predict how objects move after colliding (interacting) with each other. In Chapter 2, we will see how Newton's laws of motion can be expressed in terms of momentum.

Figure 1.1 Playing a computer game – the software relies on the laws of physics.

The idea of momentum

Snooker players can perform some amazing moves on the table, without necessarily knowing Newton's laws of motion – see Figure 1.2. However, the laws of physics can help us to understand what happens when two snooker balls collide or when one bounces off the side cushion of the table.

Here are some examples of situations involving collisions:

- two cars collide head-on
- a fast-moving car runs in to the back of a slower car in front
- a rugby player performs a tackle on the legs of an opponent

Figure 1.2 If you play snooker often enough, you will be able to predict how the balls will move on the table. Alternatively, you can use the laws of physics to predict their subsequent motion.

- a hockey stick strikes a ball
- a comet or an asteroid collides with a planet as it orbits the Sun
- the atoms of the air collide constantly with each other, and with the walls of their surroundings
- electrons that form an electric current collide with the vibrating ions that make up a metal wire
- two distant galaxies collide over millions of years.

From these examples, we can see that collisions are happening all around us, all the time. They happen on the microscopic scale of atoms and electrons, they happen in our everyday world, and they also happen on the cosmic scale of our universe.

Modelling collisions

Springy collisions

Figure 1.3a shows what happens when one snooker ball collides head-on with a second, stationary ball. The result can seem surprising. The moving ball stops dead. The ball initially at rest moves off with the same velocity as that of the original ball. To achieve this, a snooker player must observe two conditions:

- The collision must be head-on. (If one ball strikes a glancing blow on the side of the other, they will both move off at different angles.)
- The moving ball must not be given any spin. (Spin is an added complication which we will ignore in our present study, although it plays a vital part in the game of snooker.)

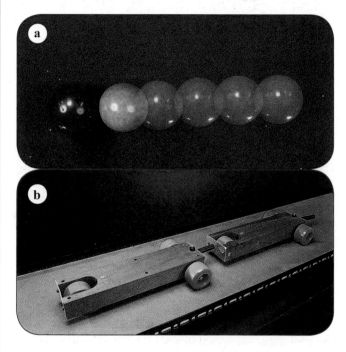

Figure 1.3 a One snooker ball hits another head-on. **b** You can do the same thing with two trolleys in the laboratory.

You can mimic the collision of the snooker balls in the laboratory, using two identical trolleys, as shown in Figure 1.3b. The moving trolley has its spring-load released, so that the collision is springy. As one trolley runs into the other, the spring is at first compressed, and then it pushes out again to set the second trolley moving. The first trolley comes to a complete halt. The 'motion' of one trolley has been transferred to the other.

You can see another interesting result if two moving identical trolleys collide head-on. If the collision is springy, both trolleys bounce backwards. If a fast-moving trolley collides with a slower one, the fast trolley bounces back at the speed of the slow one, and the slow one bounces back at the speed of the fast one. In this collision, it is as if the velocities of the trolleys have been swapped.

Sticky collisions

Figure 1.4 shows another type of collision. In this case, the trolleys have adhesive pads so that they stick together when they collide. A sticky collision like this is the opposite of a springy collision like the ones described above.

Figure 1.4 If a moving trolley sticks to a stationary trolley, they both move off together.

If a single moving trolley collides with a single stationary one, they both move off together. After the collision, the speed of the combined trolleys is half that of the original trolley. It is as if the 'motion' of the original trolley has been shared between the two. If a single trolley collides with a double one (twice the mass), they move off with one-third of the original velocity.

From these examples of sticky collisions, you can see that, when the mass of the trolley increases as a result of a collision, its velocity decreases. Doubling the mass halves the velocity, and so on.

SAQ

1 Here are two collisions to picture in your mind. Answer the question for each.
   a Ball A, moving towards the right, collides with stationary ball B. Ball A bounces back; B moves off slowly to the right. Which has a greater mass, A or B?
   b Trolley A, moving towards the right, collides with stationary trolley B. They stick together, and move off slower than half A's original speed. Which has the greater mass, A or B?

> Answer

Defining linear momentum

From the examples discussed above, we can see that two quantities are important in understanding collisions:

- mass m of the object
- velocity v of the object.

These are combined to give a single quantity, called the **linear momentum** (or simply momentum) p of an object. The momentum of an object is defined as the product of the mass of the object and its velocity. Hence:

$$\text{momentum} = \text{mass} \times \text{velocity}$$
$$p = mv$$

The unit of momentum is kg m s^{-1}. There is no special name for this unit in the SI system. Momentum is a vector quantity because it is a product of a vector quantity (velocity) and a scalar quantity (mass). Momentum has both magnitude and direction. Its direction is the same as the direction of the object's velocity.

In the earlier examples, we described how the 'motion' of one trolley appeared to be transferred to a second trolley, or shared with it. It is more correct to say that it is the trolley's momentum that is transferred or shared. (Strictly speaking, we should refer to linear momentum, because there is another quantity called angular momentum, which is possessed by spinning objects.)

Like energy, we find that momentum is also conserved. We have to consider objects which form a **closed system** – that is, no external force acts on them. The principle of **conservation of momentum** states that:

Within a closed system, the total momentum in any specified direction remains constant.

The principle of conservation of momentum can also be expressed as follows:

For a closed system, in any specified direction:
total momentum of objects before collision
= total momentum of objects after collision

A group of colliding objects always has as much momentum after the collision as it had before the collision. This principle is illustrated in Worked example 1.

Worked example 1

In Figure 1.5, trolley A of mass 0.80 kg travelling at a velocity of $3.0\,\mathrm{m\,s^{-1}}$ collides head-on with a stationary trolley B. Trolley B has twice the mass of trolley A. The trolleys stick together and have a common velocity of $1.0\,\mathrm{m\,s^{-1}}$ after the collision. Show that momentum is conserved in this collision.

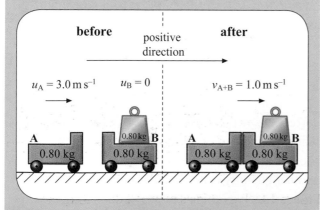

Figure 1.5 The state of the trolleys A and B, before and after the collision.

continued

Step 1 Make a sketch using the information given in the question. Notice that we need two diagrams to show the situations before and after the collision. Similarly, we need two calculations – one for the momentum of the trolleys before the collision and one for their momentum after the collision.

Step 2 Calculate the momentum before the collision:

momentum of trolleys before collision
$$= m_A \times u_A + m_B \times u_B$$
$$= (0.80 \times 3.0) + 0$$
$$= 2.4\,\mathrm{kg\,m\,s^{-1}}$$

The trolley B has no momentum before the collision, because it is not moving.

Step 3 Calculate the momentum after the collision:

momentum of trolleys after collision
$$= (m_A + m_B) \times v_{A+B}$$
$$= (0.80 + 1.60) \times 1.0$$
$$= 2.4\,\mathrm{kg\,m\,s^{-1}}$$

So, both before and after the collision, the trolleys have a combined momentum of $2.4\,\mathrm{kg\,m\,s^{-1}}$. Momentum has been conserved.

SAQ

2 Calculate the momentum of each of the following objects:
  a A 0.50 kg stone travelling at a velocity of $20\,\mathrm{m\,s^{-1}}$.
  b A 25-tonne bus travelling at $20\,\mathrm{m\,s^{-1}}$ on a road. 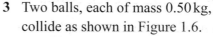 Hint
  c An electron travelling at $2.0 \times 10^7\,\mathrm{m\,s^{-1}}$. The mass of the electron is $9.1 \times 10^{-31}\,\mathrm{kg}$. Answer

3 Two balls, each of mass 0.50 kg, collide as shown in Figure 1.6. Show that their total momentum before the collision is equal to their total momentum after the collision. Hint / Answer

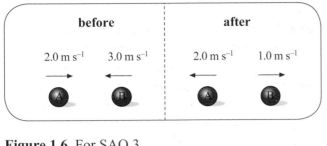

Figure 1.6 For SAQ 3.

Understanding collisions

The cars in Figure 1.7 have been badly damaged by a collision. The front of a car is designed to absorb the impact of the crash. It has a 'crumple zone', which collapses on impact. This absorbs most of the kinetic energy that the car had before the collision. It is better that the car's kinetic energy should be transferred to the crumple zone than to the driver and passengers.

Figure 1.7 The front of each car has crumpled in, as a result of a head-on collision.

Motor manufacturers make use of test labs to investigate how their cars respond to impacts. When a car is designed, the manufacturers combine soft, compressible materials that absorb energy with rigid structures that protect the car's occupants. Old-fashioned cars had much more rigid structures. In a collision, they were more likely to bounce back and the violent forces involved were much more likely to prove fatal.

Two types of collision

When two objects collide, they may crumple and deform. Their kinetic energy may also disappear completely and they come to a halt. This is an example of an inelastic collision. Alternatively, they may spring apart, retaining all of their kinetic energy. This is a perfectly elastic collision. In practice, in most collisions, some kinetic energy is transformed into other forms (e.g. heat or sound) and the collision is inelastic. Previously we described the collisions as being 'springy' or 'sticky'. We should now use the correct scientific terms **perfectly elastic** and **inelastic**.

We will look at examples of these two types of collision and consider what happens to linear momentum and kinetic energy in each.

A perfectly elastic collision

Two identical objects A and B, moving at the same speed but in opposite directions, have a head-on collision, as shown in Figure 1.8. This is a perfectly elastic collision. Each object bounces back with its velocity reversed.

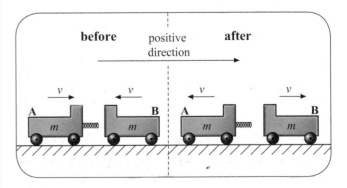

Figure 1.8 Two objects may collide in different ways: this is an elastic collision. An inelastic collision of the same two objects is shown in Figure 1.9.

You should be able to see that, in this collision, both momentum and kinetic energy are conserved. Before the collision, we have an object A of mass m moving to the right at speed v and an object B of mass m moving to the left at speed v. Afterwards, we have the same, but now object A is moving to the left, and object B is moving to the right.

Mathematically, we can express this as follows:

Before the collision

Object A

mass $= m$

velocity $= v$

momentum $= mv$

Object B

mass $= m$

velocity $= -v$

momentum $= -mv$

The object B has negative velocity and momentum because it is travelling in the opposite direction to object A.

Therefore we have:

total momentum before collision
$$= \text{momentum of A} + \text{momentum of B}$$
$$= mv + (-mv) = 0$$

total kinetic energy before collision
$$= \text{KE of A} + \text{KE of B}$$
$$= \tfrac{1}{2}mv^2 + \tfrac{1}{2}mv^2 = mv^2$$

The magnitude of the momentum of each object is the same. Momentum is a vector quantity and we have to consider the directions in which the objects travel. The combined momentum is zero. On the other hand, kinetic energy is a scalar quantity and direction of travel is irrelevant. Both objects have the same kinetic energy and therefore the combined kinetic energy is twice the kinetic energy of a single object.

After the collision
Both objects have their velocities reversed, and we have:

total momentum after collision
$$= (-mv) + mv = 0$$

total kinetic energy after collision
$$= \tfrac{1}{2}mv^2 + \tfrac{1}{2}mv^2 = mv^2$$

So the total momentum and the total kinetic energy are unchanged. They are both conserved in a perfectly elastic collision such as this.

An inelastic collision

In Figure 1.9, the same two objects collide, but this time they stick together after the collision and come to a halt. Clearly, the total momentum and the total kinetic energy are both zero after the collision, since neither mass is moving. We have:

	Before collision	After collision
momentum	0	0
kinetic energy	mv^2	0

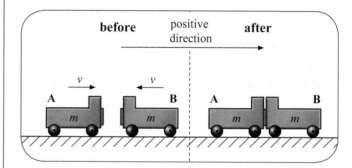

Figure 1.9 An inelastic collision between two identical objects.

Again we see that momentum is conserved here. However, kinetic energy is not conserved. It is lost because work is done in deforming the two objects.

In fact, *momentum is always conserved* in all collisions. There is nothing else into which momentum can be converted. Kinetic energy is usually not conserved in a collision, because it can be transformed into other forms of energy – sound energy if the collision is noisy, and the energy involved in deforming the objects (which usually ends up as heat – they get warmer). Of course, the total amount of energy remains constant as prescribed by the principle of conservation of energy.

SAQ

4 Copy the table below, choosing the correct words from each pair.

Type of collision	Momentum	Kinetic energy	Total energy
perfectly elastic	conserved / not conserved	conserved / not conserved	conserved / not conserved
inelastic	conserved / not conserved	conserved / not conserved	conserved / not conserved

Answer

Solving collision problems

We can use the idea of conservation of momentum to solve numerical problems, as illustrated by Worked example 2.

Worked example 2

In the game of bowls, a player rolls a large ball towards a smaller, stationary ball. A large ball of mass 5.0 kg moving at 10.0 m s^{-1} strikes a stationary ball of mass 1.0 kg. The smaller ball flies off at 10.0 m s^{-1}.

a Determine the final velocity of the large ball after the impact.

b Calculate the kinetic energy 'lost' in the impact.

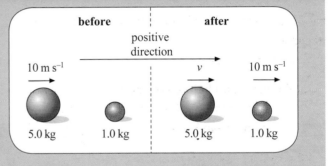

Step 1 Draw two diagrams, showing the situations before and after the collision. Figure 1.10 shows the values of masses and velocities; since we don't know the velocity of the large ball after the collision, this is shown as v. The direction from left to right has been assigned 'positive direction'.

Step 2 Using the principle of conservation of momentum, set up an equation and solve for the value of v:

total momentum before collision
        = total momentum after collision

$$(5.0 \times 10) + (1.0 \times 0) = (5.0 \times v) + (1.0 \times 10)$$

$$50 + 0 = 5.0v + 10$$

$$v = \frac{40}{5.0} = 8.0 \,\text{m s}^{-1}$$

So the speed of the large ball decreases to 8.0 m s^{-1} after the collision. Its direction of motion is unchanged – the velocity remains positive.

Figure 1.10 When solving problems involving collisions, it is useful to draw diagrams showing the situations before and after the collision. Include the values of all the quantities that you know.

Step 3 Knowing the large ball's final velocity, calculate the change in kinetic energy during the collision:

total KE before collision
        $= \frac{1}{2} \times 5.0 \times 10^2 + 0 = 250 \,\text{J}$

total KE after collision
        $= \frac{1}{2} \times 5.0 \times 8.0^2 + \frac{1}{2} \times 1.0 \times 10^2 = 210 \,\text{J}$

KE 'lost' in the collision
        $= 250 \,\text{J} - 210 \,\text{J} = 40 \,\text{J}$

This lost kinetic energy will appear as heat energy (the two balls get warmer) and as sound energy (we hear the collision between the balls).

SAQ

5 Figure 1.11 shows two identical balls A and B about to make a head-on collision. After the collision, ball A rebounds at a speed of 1.5 m s^{-1} and ball B rebounds at a speed of 2.5 m s^{-1}. The mass of each ball is 4.0 kg.

[Hint]

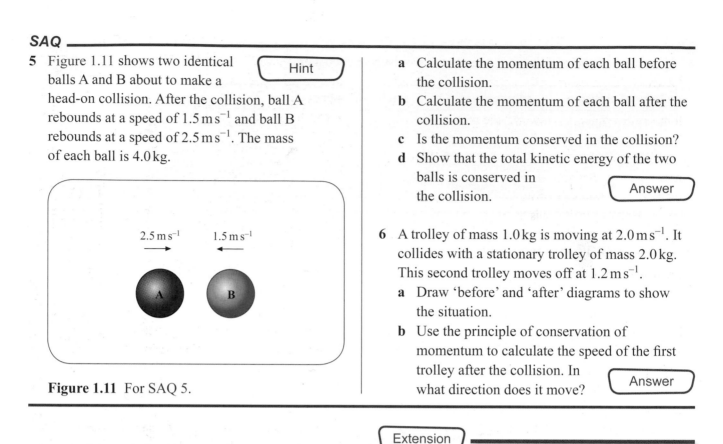

2.5 m s^{-1} 1.5 m s^{-1}

A   B

Figure 1.11 For SAQ 5.

a Calculate the momentum of each ball before the collision.
b Calculate the momentum of each ball after the collision.
c Is the momentum conserved in the collision?
d Show that the total kinetic energy of the two balls is conserved in the collision.

[Answer]

6 A trolley of mass 1.0 kg is moving at 2.0 m s^{-1}. It collides with a stationary trolley of mass 2.0 kg. This second trolley moves off at 1.2 m s^{-1}.
a Draw 'before' and 'after' diagrams to show the situation.
b Use the principle of conservation of momentum to calculate the speed of the first trolley after the collision. In what direction does it move?

[Answer]

[Extension]

Momentum in space

We can learn a lot about momentum by looking at how things move in space. When Comet Shoemaker–Levy collided with the planet Jupiter in 1994 (Figure 1.12), it transferred its momentum (and much of its kinetic energy) to the planet. The course of Jupiter in its orbit was slightly altered as a result. Some scientists are concerned that a similar fate could befall the Earth. They have suggested that a series of telescopes should be set up to monitor the skies for any signs of danger. Nuclear missiles might be used to deflect any threatening comets.

The Space Shuttle is used to transport astronauts up to orbiting space stations. The Shuttle docks with the space station, and this is a form of collision. The Shuttle must dock very gently, or it will push the space station out of its orbit. Docking is like a collision; if the Shuttle is travelling fast when it docks, it will transfer a lot of momentum to the space station. A change in momentum means a change in velocity, so the space station will change speed and move off in a different direction.

Figure 1.12 In 1994, Comet Shoemaker–Levy collided with Jupiter. The comet's momentum was transferred to the planet, causing a small change in Jupiter's orbit round the Sun. This photograph was taken by an Earth-based observatory 13 minutes after the impact of one major fragment of the comet.

continued

The astronaut shown in Figure 1.13 is on a 'space walk'. A cable tethers him to the Shuttle. To return to the craft, he pulls on the tether. This gives him some momentum towards the spacecraft, and he moves gently back to it.

Where does this momentum come from? Has it been created out of nothing? The astronaut gives himself momentum towards the spacecraft by tugging on the tether. At the same time, his tug pulls on the spacecraft and causes it to accelerate towards him. The spacecraft gains momentum towards the astronaut. These two momenta must be equal and opposite, so that their sum is zero; otherwise the astronaut really will have created momentum out of nothing. The astronaut has a small mass, and moves relatively quickly towards the spacecraft. The spacecraft's mass is much greater, and so its velocity must be much smaller.

Here is another momentum problem for an astronaut. Suppose he is working with tools on the outside of the craft, and then realises that his tether has snapped. How can he get back to the craft?

He wants to have some momentum towards the spacecraft, so he must create some momentum away from it as well. The solution is to throw one of his tools out into space. It has momentum away

Figure 1.13 Astronauts often carry out 'space walks', when they leave the shuttle to work outside. They have a tether so that they don't drift off into space.

from the spacecraft, so he has momentum towards the spacecraft.

Fortunately, astronauts now usually wear backpacks with 'Manned Manoeuvring Units' attached. These are rocket-powered units which allow the astronaut to move around. The rocket blasts a jet of gas into space; this gives the astronaut momentum in the opposite direction.

SAQ

7 An astronaut of mass 100 kg is adrift in space. He is 10.0 m from his spacecraft. To get back, he throws a spanner of mass 1.0 kg directly away from the craft at a speed of $5.0\,\mathrm{m\,s^{-1}}$.

  a Explain why he moves back towards the spacecraft.

  b Calculate how long it will take him to reach the spacecraft. *Answer*

8 A ball of mass 0.40 kg is thrown at a wall. It strikes the wall with a speed of $1.5\,\mathrm{m\,s^{-1}}$ perpendicular to the wall and bounces off the wall with a speed of $1.2\,\mathrm{m\,s^{-1}}$.

  Explain the changes in momentum and energy which happen in the collision between the ball and the wall. Give numerical values where possible. *Answer*

Explosions and crash-landings

The rockets shown in Figure 1.14 rise high into the sky. As they start to fall, they send out showers of chemical packages, each of which explodes to produce a brilliant sphere of burning chemicals. Material flies out in all directions to create a spectacular effect.

Does an explosion create momentum out of nothing? The important point to note here is that the burning material spreads out equally in all directions. Each tiny spark has momentum, but for every spark, there is another moving in the opposite direction, i.e. with opposite momentum. Since momentum is a vector quantity, the total amount of momentum created is zero.

At the same time, kinetic energy is created in an explosion. Burning material flies outwards; its kinetic energy has come from the chemical potential energy stored in the chemical materials before they burn.

Figure 1.14 These exploding rockets produce a spectacular display of bright sparks in the night sky.

An explosion in the laboratory

You can investigate momentum in explosions using trolleys, as shown in Figure 1.15. When the spring-load of the trolley on the left is released, the trolleys are pushed apart in a one-dimensional explosion. The spring-load stores elastic potential energy when it is compressed; this gives the trolleys kinetic energy when it is released, like the chemical potential energy stored in explosives. Now look at Worked example 3.

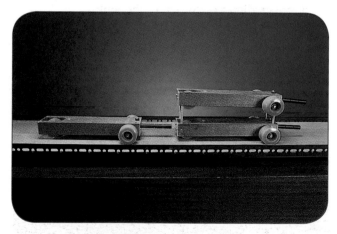

Figure 1.15 These trolleys move apart when the spring-load is released.

Worked example 3

Consider the one-dimensional explosion between two trolleys, A and B. Trolley A has half the mass of trolley B, and moves at a speed of $2.0\,\mathrm{m\,s^{-1}}$ after the explosion. Calculate the speed and the direction of trolley B.

You can probably guess the answer: the mass of B is twice that of A, so it will move at half the speed. Here is how to show this mathematically.

Step 1 In an explosion, momentum is conserved. Therefore:

total momentum before explosion
= total momentum after explosion

Before the explosion, the trolleys were not moving:

total momentum before explosion = 0

After the explosion, both trolleys are moving:

total momentum after explosion
$= m_A \times v_A + m_B \times v_B$

So we must have:

$$m_A \times v_A + m_B \times v_B = 0$$

$$m_A \times v_A = -(m_B \times v_B)$$

$$\frac{m_A}{m_B} = -\frac{v_B}{v_A}$$

Step 2 Use the data from the question. We have:

$$\frac{m_A}{m_B} = 0.5 \quad \text{and} \quad v_A = 2.0\,\mathrm{m\,s^{-1}}$$

Hence:

$$0.5 = -\frac{v_B}{2.0}$$

$$v_B = -(0.5 \times 2.0) = -1.0\,\mathrm{m\,s^{-1}}$$

Notice how the minus sign appears when we rearrange the equation. This shows that trolley B has a negative velocity; it is moving in the opposite direction to trolley A. Its speed is, as we guessed, half that of trolley A.

More fireworks

A roman candle fires a jet of burning material up into the sky. This is another type of explosion, but it doesn't send material in all directions. The firework tube directs the material upwards. Has momentum been created out of nothing here?

Again, the answer is no. The chemicals have momentum upwards, but at the same time, the roman candle pushes downwards on the Earth. An equal amount of downwards momentum is given to the Earth. Of course, the Earth is massive, and we don't notice the tiny change in its velocity which results. In a similar way, when a gun is fired, a relatively small mass (the bullet) moves rapidly away in one direction; the gun is pushed back into the shoulder of the person who fired it. This is known as the recoil of the gun. Figure 1.16 shows a cannon as it is fired.

(We have already considered some examples of 'explosions' like this on page 9: the astronaut throwing a tool to get back to the spacecraft is relying on recoil, as does a rocket-powered backpack for moving about in space.)

Figure 1.16 When a cannon like this was fired, the gun-crew had to keep clear as the cannon recoiled.

Down to Earth

If you push a large rock over a cliff, its speed increases as it falls. Where does its momentum come from? And when it lands, where does its momentum disappear to?

The rock falls because of the pull of the Earth's gravity on it. This force is its weight and it makes the rock accelerate towards the Earth. Its weight does

work and it gains kinetic energy. It gains momentum downwards. Something must be gaining an equal amount of momentum in the opposite (upward) direction. It is the Earth, which starts to move upwards as the rock falls downwards. As before, the mass of the Earth is so great that its change in velocity is small, far too small to be noticeable.

When the rock hits the ground, its momentum becomes zero. At the same instant, the Earth also stops moving upwards. The rock's momentum cancels out the Earth's momentum. At all times during the rock's fall and crash-landing, momentum has been conserved.

If a rock of mass $60\,\mathrm{kg}$ is falling towards the Earth at a speed of $20\,\mathrm{m\,s^{-1}}$, how fast is the Earth moving towards it? Figure 1.17 shows the situation. The mass of the Earth is $6.0\times10^{24}\,\mathrm{kg}$. We have:

total momentum of Earth and rock = 0

Hence:

$$(60\times20)+(6.0\times10^{24}\times v)=0$$
$$v=-2.0\times10^{-22}\,\mathrm{m\,s^{-1}}$$

The minus sign shows that the Earth's velocity is in the opposite direction to that of the rock.

The Earth moves very slowly indeed. In the time of your fall, it will move much less than the diameter of the nucleus of an atom!

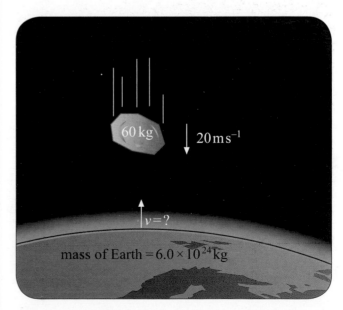

Figure 1.17 One way to make the Earth move.

SAQ

9 Discuss whether momentum is conserved in each of the following situations:

   a A star explodes in all directions – a supernova.

   b You jump up from a trampoline. As you go up, your speed decreases; as you come down again, your speed increases.

         ⬚ Answer

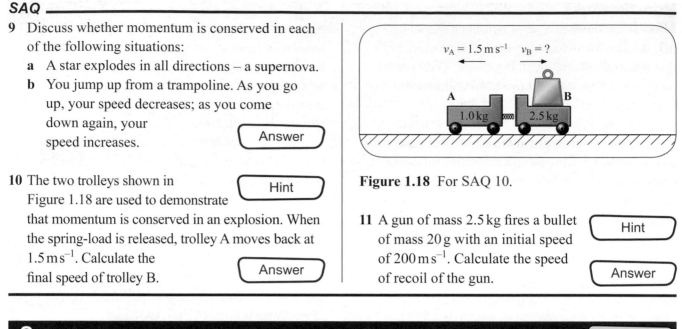

Figure 1.18 For SAQ 10.

10 The two trolleys shown in Figure 1.18 are used to demonstrate that momentum is conserved in an explosion. When the spring-load is released, trolley A moves back at $1.5\,\text{m s}^{-1}$. Calculate the final speed of trolley B.

         ⬚ Hint

         ⬚ Answer

11 A gun of mass 2.5 kg fires a bullet of mass 20 g with an initial speed of $200\,\text{m s}^{-1}$. Calculate the speed of recoil of the gun.

         ⬚ Hint

         ⬚ Answer

Summary

⬚ Glossary

- Linear momentum is the product of mass and velocity:

    momentum = mass × velocity $p = mv$

- Principle of conservation of momentum:
  For a closed system, in any specified direction, the total momentum before an interaction (e.g. collision) is equal to the total momentum after the interaction.

- In all interactions or collisions, momentum and total energy are conserved.

- Kinetic energy is conserved in a perfectly elastic collision.

- Kinetic energy is not conserved in an inelastic collision. In such a collision, kinetic energy is transformed into other forms of energy (e.g. heat or sound). Most collisions are inelastic.

Questions

1 **a** Define *linear momentum*. [1]

   b Explain why momentum is a vector quantity. [1]

   c A car of mass 900 kg starting from rest has a constant acceleration of 3.5 m s^{-2}. Calculate its momentum after travelling a distance of 40 m. [4]

   d The diagram below shows two identical objects about to make a head-on collision. The objects stick together during the collision. Determine the final speed of the objects. State the direction in which they move.

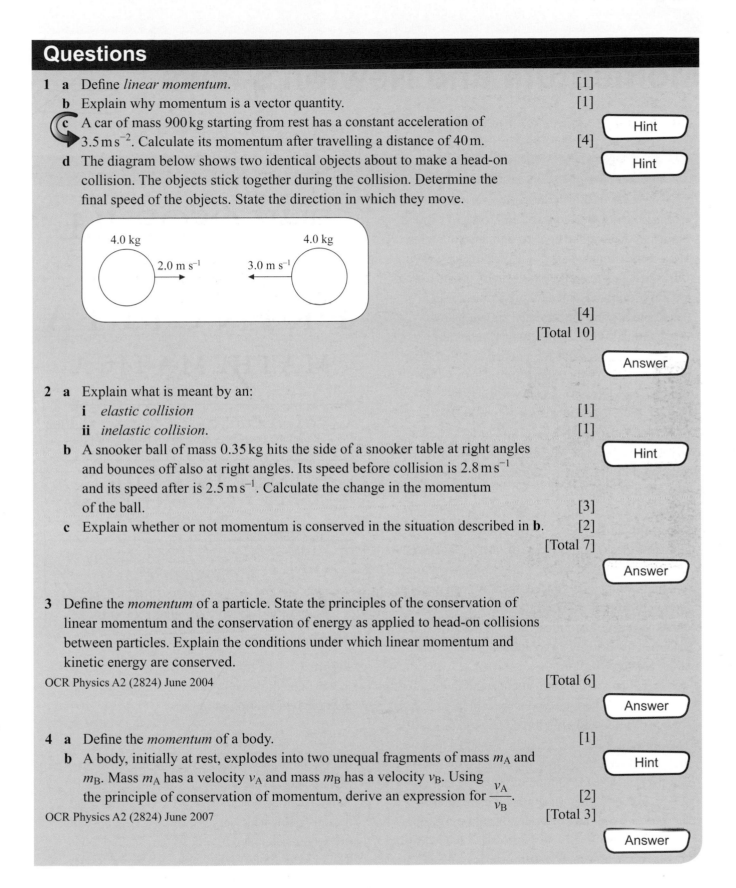

[4]

[Total 10]

2 **a** Explain what is meant by an:

   i *elastic collision* [1]

   ii *inelastic collision.* [1]

   b A snooker ball of mass 0.35 kg hits the side of a snooker table at right angles and bounces off also at right angles. Its speed before collision is 2.8 m s^{-1} and its speed after is 2.5 m s^{-1}. Calculate the change in the momentum of the ball. [3]

   c Explain whether or not momentum is conserved in the situation described in **b**. [2]

[Total 7]

3 Define the *momentum* of a particle. State the principles of the conservation of linear momentum and the conservation of energy as applied to head-on collisions between particles. Explain the conditions under which linear momentum and kinetic energy are conserved.

OCR Physics A2 (2824) June 2004 [Total 6]

4 **a** Define the *momentum* of a body. [1]

   b A body, initially at rest, explodes into two unequal fragments of mass m_A and m_B. Mass m_A has a velocity v_A and mass m_B has a velocity v_B. Using the principle of conservation of momentum, derive an expression for $\dfrac{v_A}{v_B}$. [2]

OCR Physics A2 (2824) June 2007 [Total 3]

Hint

Hint

Answer

Hint

Answer

Answer

Hint

Answer

Chapter 2

Momentum and Newton's laws

e-Learning

Objectives

Isaac Newton's big ideas

The big ideas of physics are often very simple; that is to say, it takes only a few words to express them and they can be applied in many situations. However, 'simple' does not usually mean 'easy'. Concepts such as force, energy and voltage, for example, are not immediately obvious. They usually took someone to make a giant leap of imagination to first establish them. Then the community of physicists spent decades worrying away at them, refining them until they are the fundamental ideas which we use today.

Take Isaac Newton's work on motion. He published his ideas in a book commonly known as the *Principia* (see Figure 2.1); its full title translated from Latin is *Mathematical Principles of Natural Philosophy*.

The *Principia* represents the results of twenty years of thinking. Newton was able to build on Galileo's ideas (as discussed in *Physics 1*) and he was in correspondence with many other scientists and mathematicians. Indeed, there was an ongoing feud with Robert Hooke as to who was the first to come up with certain ideas. Among scientists, this is known as 'priority', and publication is usually taken as proof of priority.

Newton had to develop an understanding of the idea of 'force'. Perhaps you were told in your early studies of science that 'a force is a push or a pull'. That doesn't tell us very much. Newton's idea was that forces are interactions between bodies and that they change the motion of the body that they act on. Forces acting on an object can produce acceleration. For an object of constant mass, this acceleration is directly proportional to the net force acting on the object. That is much more like a scientific definition of force.

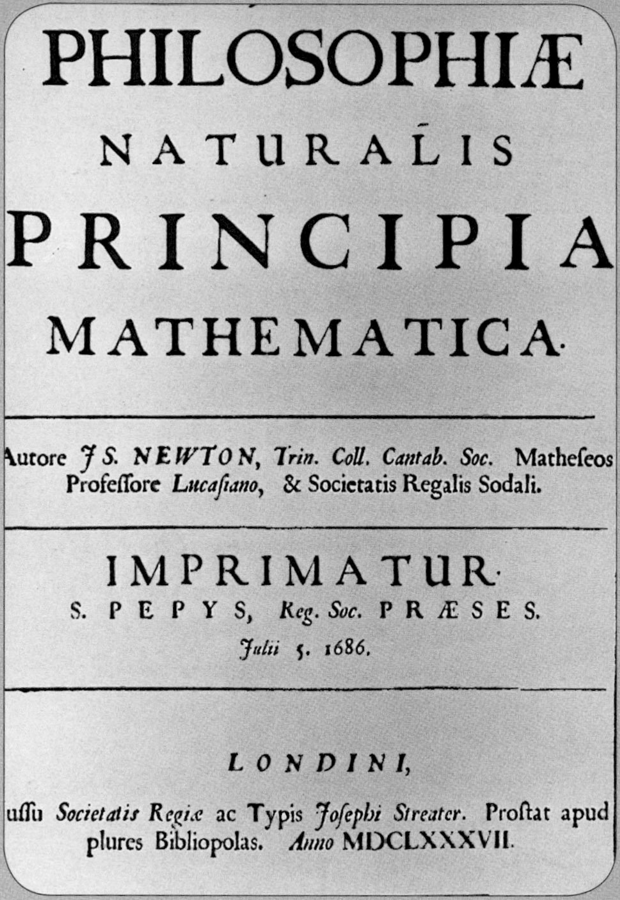

PHILOSOPHIÆ
NATURALIS
PRINCIPIA
MATHEMATICA.

Autore *J S.* NEWTON, *Trin. Coll. Cantab. Soc.* Matheſeos Profeſſore *Lucaſiano*, & Societatis Regalis Sodali.

IMPRIMATUR.
S. PEPYS, *Reg. Soc.* PRÆSES.
Julii 5. 1686.

LONDINI,

uſſu *Societatis Regiæ* ac Typis *Joſephi Streater*. Proſtat apud plures Bibliopolas. *Anno* MDCLXXXVII.

Figure 2.1 The title page of Newton's *Principia* in which he outlined his theories of the laws that governed the motion of objects.

Newton presented his ideas to the Royal Society in London in the form of three volumes in 1686–87. The Society agreed to publish them, thus establishing Newton's priority. Unfortunately, the Society had recently published a large illustrated volume about fish which had failed to sell, so they had no funds available. Edmond Halley provided the necessary money from his own pocket.

Understanding motion

In *Physics 1*, we looked at how to describe motion (kinematics) and how to explain motion in terms of forces (dynamics). We briefly touched on Newton's laws of motion. We can get further insight into these laws by thinking about them in terms of momentum.

Newton's first law of motion

In everyday speech, we sometimes say that something has momentum when we mean that it has a tendency to keep on moving of its own free will. An oil tanker is difficult to stop at sea, because of its momentum. We use the same word in a figurative sense: 'The election campaign is gaining momentum.' This idea of keeping on moving is just what we discussed in connection with **Newton's first law** of motion:

An object will remain at rest or keep travelling at constant velocity unless it is acted on by an external force.

An object travelling at constant velocity has constant momentum. Hence the first law is really saying that the momentum of an object remains the same unless the object experiences an external force.

Newton's second law of motion

Newton's second law of motion links the idea of the net force acting on an object and its momentum. A statement of Newton's second law is:

The net force acting on an object is directly proportional to the rate of change of the linear momentum of that object. The net force and the change in momentum are in the same direction.

Hence:

net force ∝ rate of change of momentum

This can be written as:

$$F \propto \frac{\Delta p}{\Delta t}$$

where F is the net force and Δp is the change in momentum taking place in a time interval of Δt.

(Remember that the Greek letter delta, Δ, is a shorthand for 'change in …', so Δp means 'change in momentum'.) The change in momentum and force are both vector quantities, hence these two quantities must be in the same direction.

The unit of force (the newton N) is defined to make the constant of proportionality equal to one, so we can write the second law of motion mathematically as:

$$F = \frac{\Delta p}{\Delta t}$$

If the forces acting on an object are balanced, there is no resultant or net force and the object's momentum will remain constant. If a net force acts on an object, its momentum (velocity and/or direction) will change. The equation above gives us another way of stating **Newton's second law** of motion:

The net force acting on an object is equal to the rate of change of its momentum. The net force and the change in momentum are in the same direction.

Worked example 1 shows how to use this equation.

Worked example 1

Calculate the average force acting on a 900 kg car when its velocity changes from 5.0 m s⁻¹ to 30 m s⁻¹ in a time of 12 s.

Step 1 Write down the quantities given:

$m = 900$ kg   initial velocity $u = 5.0$ m s⁻¹
$\Delta t = 12$ s

Step 2 Calculate the initial momentum and the final momentum of the car.

momentum = mass × velocity

initial momentum
$$= mu = 900 \times 5.0 = 4500 \text{ kg m s}^{-1}$$

final momentum
$$= mv = 900 \times 30 = 27\,000 \text{ kg m s}^{-1}$$

continued

Step 3 Use Newton's second law of motion to calculate the average force on the car:

$$F = \frac{\Delta p}{\Delta t} = \frac{27\,000}{4500} = 1875\,\text{N} \approx 1900\,\text{N}$$

The average force acting on the car is about 1.9 kN.

A special case of Newton's second law of motion

Imagine an object of constant mass m acted upon by a net force F. The force will change the momentum of the object. According to Newton's second law of motion, we have:

$$F = \frac{\Delta p}{\Delta t} = \frac{mv - mu}{t}$$

where u is the initial velocity of the object, v is the final velocity of the object and t is the time taken for the change in velocity.

The mass m of the object is a constant; hence the above equation can be rewritten as:

$$F = m\left[\frac{v - u}{t}\right]$$

Worked example 2 shows how to use this equation. The term in brackets is the acceleration a of the object. Therefore a special case of Newton's second law is:

$$F = ma$$

Worked example 2

If you squirt water out of a hosepipe, the water gains momentum. You feel a force pushing back on you – a kind of recoil. If you let go of the hosepipe, it will move backwards. (Fire-fighters have to be strong to hold their hoses, because they are squirting large masses of water at high speed and this produces a very large recoil force.)

Figure 2.2 shows a hosepipe squirting water at a rate of 6.0 kg per second. The water moves through the pipe at $1.2\,\text{m s}^{-1}$, and leaves the nozzle at $15\,\text{m s}^{-1}$. Calculate the force F needed to push the water forwards.

Step 1 We will consider a time interval Δt of 1.0 s. In this time, 6.0 kg of water leaves the hosepipe. We have:

$$\Delta t = 1.0\,\text{s} \qquad m = 6.0\,\text{kg}$$
$$u = 1.2\,\text{m s}^{-1} \qquad v = 15\,\text{m s}^{-1}$$

Step 2 Use Newton's second law to determine the force F.

$$F = \frac{\Delta p}{\Delta t} = m\left(\frac{v - u}{t}\right)$$

$$F = 6.0 \times \left(\frac{15 - 1.2}{1.0}\right) = 82.8\,\text{kg m s}^{-2} \approx 83\,\text{N}$$

The force F accelerating the water out from the hosepipe is equal to 83 N and you will also feel a force equal to 83 N pushing back on you. Note that the final units are kg m s^{-2}, which is the same as N.

15 m s⁻¹

1.2 m s⁻¹

Figure 2.2 Water accelerates as it emerges from the hosepipe.

We have already met this equation in *Physics 1*. In Worked example 1, you could have determined the average force acting on the car using this simplified equation for Newton's second law of motion. Remember that the equation $F = ma$ is a special case of $F = \dfrac{\Delta p}{\Delta t}$ which only applies when the mass of the object is constant. There are situations where the mass of an object changes as it moves, for example a rocket, which burns a phenomenal amount of chemical fuel as it accelerates upwards.

SAQ

1   A car of mass 1000 kg is travelling at a velocity of $10\,\mathrm{m\,s^{-1}}$. It accelerates for 15 s, reaching a velocity of $24\,\mathrm{m\,s^{-1}}$. Calculate:
   a   the change in the momentum of the car in a period of 10 s
   b   the average force acting on the car as it accelerates.

2   A ball is kicked by a footballer. The average force on the ball is 240 N, and the impact lasts for a time interval of 0.25 s.
   a   Calculate the change in the ball's momentum.
   b   State the direction of the change in momentum.

3   Water pouring from a broken pipe lands on a flat roof. The water is moving at $5.0\,\mathrm{m\,s^{-1}}$ when it strikes the roof. The water hits the roof at a rate of $10\,\mathrm{kg\,s^{-1}}$. Calculate the force of the water hitting the roof. (Assume that the water does not bounce as it hits the roof. If it did bounce, would your answer be greater or smaller?)

Newton's third law of motion

What happens when you hit a nail with a hammer? The hammer exerts a force on the nail and the nail exerts an equal but opposite force on the hammer – you can feel this force. The same happens when you clap your hands. Each hand experiences a force from the other hand. The forces on each hand are equal in size and opposite in direction.

Newton's third law of motion is often quoted as 'every action has an equal and opposite reaction', but this is not a helpful way of stating this important law. Newton's third law of motion is to do with interacting objects. These could be two magnets attracting or repelling each other, two electrons repelling each other, etc.

Imagine yourself hanging from a tree and you let go. The Earth exerts a force on you – this is your weight. You and the Earth are two interacting objects. You also exert an equal but opposite force on the Earth. If the Earth pulls you down with a force of 700 N, then you also exert an upward force of 700 N on the Earth. Your falling acceleration is much larger than that of the Earth. This is because your mass is tiny compared with that of the Earth. The Earth is about 10^{23} times as massive as you!

So **Newton's third law** of motion is as follows:

> When two bodies interact, the forces they exert on each other are equal and opposite.

As mentioned above, the two forces are often referred to as *action* and *reaction*. This can be a bit deceptive. It suggests that one body exerts a force on another (the action force), and this causes an equal and opposite force to act on the first body (the reaction). In fact, both forces happen at the same time; it isn't a case of one causing the other.

Picture holding two magnets, one in each hand. You gradually bring them towards each other (Figure 2.3a) so that they start to attract each other. Each feels a force pulling it towards the other. The two forces are the same size, even if one magnet is stronger than the other. Indeed, one magnet could be replaced by an unmagnetised piece of steel and they would still attract each other equally.

If you release the magnets, they will gain momentum as they are pulled towards each other. One gains momentum to the left while the other gains equal momentum to the right.

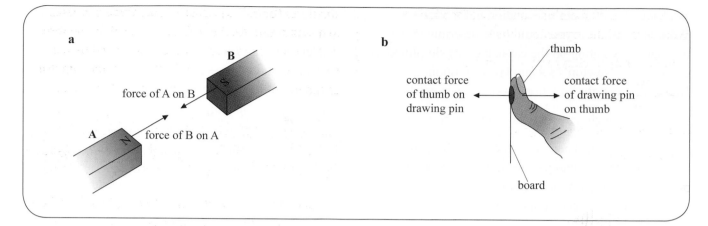

Figure 2.3 a Newton's third law states that the forces these two magnets exert on each other must be equal and opposite. **b** The contact force of the thumb on the drawing pin is equal and opposite to the contact force of the drawing pin on the thumb.

The two forces described by Newton's third law of motion:

- act on different bodies
- are equal in magnitude
- are opposite in direction
- are of the same type.

Here, 'of the same type' means both magnetic, or both gravitational, or both electrical, etc. Figure 2.3b shows the contact forces which act when you push a drawing pin into a board. (The contact forces between two surfaces arise because of electrical repulsion between the billions of electrons that orbit atomic nuclei.) The two contact forces are equal and opposite; one acts on the person's thumb, the other on the drawing pin.

Notice that pairs of forces like this do not 'cancel each other out'. They are not a pair of *balanced* forces because they act on *different* objects. If you were to draw a free body diagram of the thumb in Figure 2.3b, only the contact force pointing to the right would be shown.

Impulse of a force

Figure 2.4 shows a golf ball as it is struck by a club. The head of the club was moving at over $40\,\mathrm{m\,s^{-1}}$ at the time of impact, and the photograph was made using a stroboscopic light whose flash lasted just one-millionth of a second. You can see that, while the club is in contact with the ball, the ball is squashed by the force of the impact.

Figure 2.4 During the time that the club is in contact with the ball, it transfers momentum to the ball.

The force of the club on the ball makes the ball fly off. Any golfer knows that the bigger the force, the faster the ball will move, that is, the more momentum will be transferred from the club to the ball. The ball also has greater momentum if the contact time between the club and the ball is longer.

So both the size of the force and the time for which it acts affect the momentum of the ball. Consider another example. A driver wants to make her car go faster. She presses on the accelerator; this increases the unbalanced force on the car. Pressing harder gives a bigger force so that the car reaches a higher velocity. Pressing the accelerator for longer also results in a higher final velocity.

We can use Newton's second law of motion to make sense of the examples above:

force = rate of change of momentum

$$F = \frac{\Delta p}{\Delta t}$$

Rearranging this equation gives:

$$F \times \Delta t = \Delta p$$

or

$$F \times \Delta t = mv - mu$$

The product of force and time is equal to the change of momentum of the object. That is:

force × time = change in momentum

The quantity 'force × time', or simply $F\Delta t$, is defined as the **impulse** of the force. So we have:

impulse of force = change in momentum

The unit of impulse is the newton second (N s). This is the same as the unit of momentum, hence we have:

$$1\,\text{N s} = 1\,\text{kg m s}^{-1}$$

If a constant force F acts on a body for time Δt, we need simply calculate $F \times \Delta t$ to find its impulse and hence the change in the body's momentum. However, it is often the case that a force is not constant. The club hitting the golf ball is an example. At the first instant of impact, the force of the club on the ball is

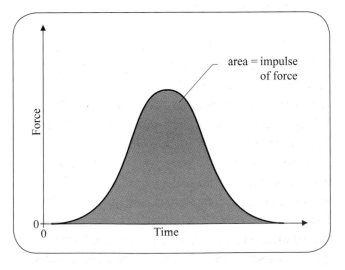

Figure 2.5 A force against time graph showing how the force on a golf ball varies as it is struck by a club.

small. As the ball squashes up, the force increases to a maximum. As the ball leaves the club, the force decreases back to zero. This is represented by the graph shown in Figure 2.5. In this case, the impulse of the force is given by the area under the graph:

impulse of force
    = area under a force against time graph

Worked example 3 and Worked example 4 show how to use these equations for impulse.

Worked example 3

A car of mass 600 kg is travelling at a velocity of $10\,\text{m s}^{-1}$. The driver accelerates so that a net force of 200 N acts on the car for a period of 12 s. Calculate the impulse of this force and hence determine the final velocity of the car.

Step 1 Calculate the impulse of the force:

impulse = force × time

impulse = $200 \times 12 = 2400\,\text{N s}$

Step 2 Since impulse = change in momentum, we can write

change in momentum = $2400\,\text{kg m s}^{-1}$

(Remember the unit 'N s' is equivalent to the unit 'kg m s^{-1}'.)

Step 3 We know the car's mass and initial velocity, so we can determine the final velocity of the car using:

change in momentum = $mv - mu$

$$2400 = 600v - (600 \times 10)$$

Rearranging this equation gives:

$$600v = 2400 + 6000$$
$$= 8400$$
$$v = \frac{8400}{600} = 14\,\text{m s}^{-1}$$

Worked example 4

A golf ball is struck by a club. The graph shown in Figure 2.6 shows how the force on the ball varies during the impact.

Calculate the impulse of the force.

The mass of the ball is 45 g. Calculate the final velocity of the ball as it leaves the club.

Step 1 The force on the ball is not constant. You have to determine the impulse of the force from the area under the force against time graph. This is a triangle, and area = $\frac{1}{2}$ base × height.

Hence:

impulse of force = area under graph

$$= \frac{1}{2} \times 8.0 \times 10^{-3} \times 450$$

$$= 1.8\,\text{N s}$$

Step 2 We can now use 'impulse of force = change in momentum' ($F\Delta t = \Delta p$) to determine the final velocity of the ball.

The ball is initially at rest – its initial momentum is zero. The change in the momentum of the ball must therefore be equal to the final momentum. Therefore:

$F\Delta t = \Delta p$

$1.8 = 0.045v$

$v = \dfrac{1.8}{0.045} = 40\,\text{m s}^{-1}$

The final velocity of the ball as it leaves the club is $40\,\text{m s}^{-1}$.

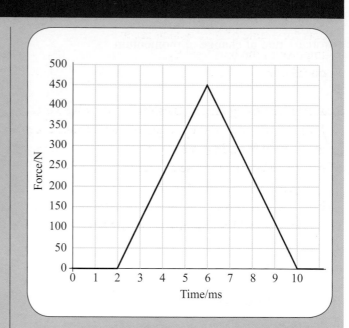

Figure 2.6 An idealised graph showing the variation of force on a golf ball with time when it is struck by a golf club.

An alternative method for determining the area under the graph is to count squares. The sides of each square of the graph grid are:

base = $1\,\text{ms} = 1 \times 10^{-3}\,\text{s}$

height = $50\,\text{N}$

So the area of each square represents an impulse of $50 \times 10^{-3}\,\text{N s}$.

Total number of squares = 36

(This is found by adding up whole squares and bits of squares.)

Hence:

impulse = $36 \times 50 \times 10^{-3}\,\text{N s} = 1.8\,\text{N s}$

For a regularly shaped graph like the one shown in Figure 2.6, it is simpler to calculate the area. However, for irregularly shaped graphs, the method of counting squares may be useful.

SAQ

4   The braking force acting on a car is 400 N and acts for a time of 3.5 s. Calculate the impulse of the braking force on the car. **Answer**

5   A stone of weight 2.5 N falls vertically downwards for 3.0 s. The two forces acting on the falling stone are its weight and air resistance.

a   Calculate the impulse of the force of gravity during this period of 3.0 s.

b   The average air resistance acting on the falling stone is 0.80 N. Calculate the impulse of this force on the stone.

c   Determine the increase in the momentum of the stone at the end of the 3.0 s period. **Answer**

6   Look at Worked example 3 on the accelerating car. You can determine the final velocity of the car by an alternative route. Calculate the acceleration of the car and then use one of the equations of motion to calculate the final velocity of the car. **Hint** **Answer**

7   A golf ball has a mass of 0.046 kg. The final velocity of the ball after being struck by a golf club is $50\,\mathrm{m\,s^{-1}}$. The golf club is in contact with the ball for a time of 1.3 ms. Calculate the average force exerted by the golf club on the ball. **Hint** **Answer**

8   A rocket of mass $2.0 \times 10^5\,\mathrm{kg}$ is initially stationary. It lifts off the ground and, after 10 s, it is travelling at a velocity of $50\,\mathrm{m\,s^{-1}}$. During this short time interval of 10 s, the mass of the rocket does not change significantly.

a   Calculate the impulse of the force on the rocket.

b   Calculate the resultant force acting on the rocket. **Answer**

9   Look at Worked example 4. Figure 2.6 shows that the force varies from 0 N to 450 N. A reasonable estimate for the average force on the ball is half of the maximum force.

a   From the graph, estimate the time for which the club is in contact with the golf ball.

b   Hence determine the impulse of the force on the golf ball. Compare your answer with the value found by counting squares. **Answer**

Newton's laws and the conservation of momentum

Newton's second and third laws can help us to understand why momentum is conserved in all interactions.

Figure 2.7 shows two trolleys pushing each other apart – a kind of one-dimensional explosion. At first the trolleys are stationary, so their total momentum is zero. When the spring mechanism is released, each trolley pushes on the other.

● According to Newton's third law, the forces acting on each trolley have the same magnitude F but act in opposite directions.

● The forces also act for the same time Δt – the time during which the trolleys remain in contact.

● So the impulse of each force ($F\Delta t$) is equal in magnitude but opposite in direction.

● The impulse of the force acting on each trolley is equal to its change in momentum (Δp).

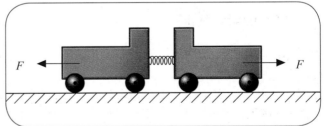

Figure 2.7 These trolleys move apart when the spring-load is released. Each exerts an equal but opposite force on the other. The impulses of the forces are also equal but opposite.

● We can conclude that:

change in momentum of one trolley
= − change in momentum of other trolley

In other words, if one trolley *gains* momentum in an interaction, then the other trolley *loses* an equal amount of momentum. The total change of momentum for the two trolleys is zero. Hence momentum has been conserved in this interaction. So the principle of conservation of momentum is a logical consequence of Newton's second and third laws.

SAQ

10 A car of mass 800 kg is travelling along a level road at a constant velocity of $6.0\,\text{m}\,\text{s}^{-1}$. A net force of 120 N in the direction of travel acts on the car for a period of 10 s.
  a Calculate the impulse of the force on the car.
  b Calculate the change in momentum of the car and hence its final velocity after 10 s.

c Use one of the equations of motion to determine the distance travelled by the car in this 10 s period.

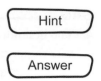

11 A body of mass 1000 kg, initially stationary, is acted on by a net force of 20 N for 2.0 minutes.
  a At the end of 2.0 minutes, determine the increase in the velocity of the body and the increase in its kinetic energy.
  b Determine the acceleration of the body, the distance travelled in 2.0 minutes and the work done by the force on the body.
  c Use your answers from **a** and **b** to explain how the work done on the body is related to the increase in its kinetic energy.

Answer

Extension

Summary

Glossary

● Newton's first law of motion states that:
An object will remain at rest or keep travelling at constant velocity unless it is acted on by an external force.

● Newton's second law of motion states that:
The net force acting on an object is equal to the rate of change of its momentum. The net force and the change in momentum are in the same direction.

● Newton's third law of motion states that:
When two bodies interact, the forces they exert on each other are equal and opposite.

● The net force acting on a body is equal to the rate of change of its momentum:

net force = rate of change of momentum   or $F = \dfrac{\Delta p}{\Delta t}$

● The equation $F = ma$ is a special case of Newton's second law of motion when mass m remains constant.

● The impulse of a force is defined as the product of the force F acting on an object and the time Δt for which it acts.

impulse = force × time   or   impulse = $F\Delta t$

● For a varying force, the impulse is equal to the area under the force against time graph.

● The impulse of a force is equal to the change in momentum of a body:

impulse = change in momentum   or   impulse = Δp

Questions

1 This question is about kicking a football.

a The graph shows how the force F applied to a ball varies with time t whilst it is being kicked horizontally. The ball is initially at rest.

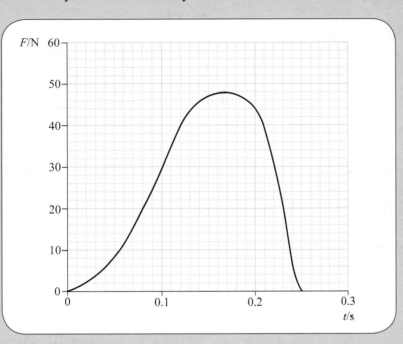

i Use the graph to find:
  1 the maximum force applied to the ball
  2 the time the boot is in contact with the ball. [1]
ii The mean force multiplied by the time of contact is called the impulse delivered to the ball. Use the graph to estimate the impulse delivered to the ball. [2]

b The mass of the ball is 0.50 kg. Use your answers to a to calculate:
  i the maximum acceleration of the ball [2]
  ii the final speed of the ball [2]
  iii the kinetic energy of the ball after the kick. [2]

c The ball hits a wall with a speed of 14 m s^{-1}. It rebounds from the wall along its initial path with a speed of 8.0 m s^{-1}. The impact lasts for 0.18 s. Calculate the mean force exerted by the ball on the wall. [3]

OCR Physics A2 (2824) June 2005 [Total 12]

Hint

Hint

Answer

continued

2 This question is about pressing a red hot bar of steel into a sheet in a rolling mill.

a A bar of steel of mass 500 kg is moved on a conveyor belt at $0.60 \, \text{m s}^{-1}$. Calculate the momentum of the bar, giving a suitable unit for your answer. [2]

b From the conveyor belt, the bar is passed between two rollers, shown in the diagram. The bar enters the rollers at $0.60 \, \text{m s}^{-1}$. The rollers flatten the bar into a sheet with the result that the sheet leaves the rollers at $1.8 \, \text{m s}^{-1}$.

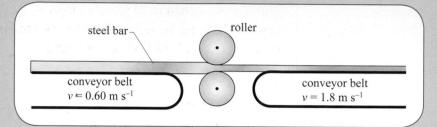

i Explain why there is a resultant horizontal force on the bar at the point immediately between the rollers. [2]

ii In which direction does this force act? [1]

iii The original length of the bar is 3.0 m. Calculate the time it takes for the bar to pass between the rollers. [1]

iv Calculate the magnitude of the resultant force on the bar during the pressing process. [3]

OCR Physics A2 (2824) June 2006   [Total 9]

Hint

Answer

3 A car of mass 1100 kg is travelling at $24 \, \text{m s}^{-1}$. The driver applies the brakes and the car decelerates uniformly and comes to rest in 20 s.

a Calculate the change in momentum of the car. [2]

b Calculate the braking force on the car. [2]

c Determine the braking distance of the car. [3]

[Total 7]

Answer

Chapter 3

Circular motion

Objectives

Describing circular motion

Many things move in circles. Here are some examples:

- the wheels of a car or a bicycle
- the Earth in its (approximately circular) orbit round the Sun
- the hands of a clock
- a spinning DVD in a laptop
- the drum of a washing machine.

Sometimes, things move along a path that is part of a circle. For example, a car may travel around a bend in the road which is an arc of a circle (Figure 3.1).

Figure 3.1 Two examples of circular motion: the racing car's wheels spin around the axles, and the car follows a curved path as it speeds round the bend.

Circular motion is different from the straight-line motion that we have discussed previously in our study of kinematics and dynamics in *Physics 1*. However, we can extend these ideas of dynamics to build up a picture of circular motion.

Around the clock

The second hand of a clock moves steadily round the clock-face. It takes one minute for it to travel all the way round the circle. There are 360° in a complete circle and 60 seconds in a minute. So the hand moves 6° every second. If we know the angle θ through which the hand has moved from the vertical (12 o'clock) position, we can predict the position of the hand.

In the same way, we can describe the position of any object as it moves around a circle simply by stating the angle θ of the arc through which it has moved from its starting position. This is shown in Figure 3.2.

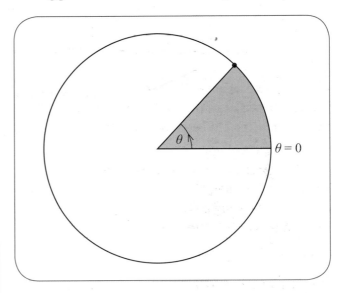

Figure 3.2 To know how far an object has moved round the circle, we need to know the angle θ.

The angle θ through which the object has moved is known as its **angular displacement**. For an object moving in a straight line, its position was defined by its displacement x, the *distance* it has travelled from its starting position. The corresponding quantity for circular motion is angular displacement θ, the *angle* of the arc through which the object has moved from its starting position.

SAQ

1 a By how many degrees does the angular displacement of the hour hand of a clock change each hour?

b A clock is showing 3.30. Calculate the angular displacements in degrees from the 12.00 position of the clock to
i the minute hand
ii the hour hand.

Answer

Angles in radians

When dealing with circles and circular motion, it is more convenient to measure angles and angular displacements in units called radians rather than in degrees.

If an object moves a distance s around a circular path of radius r (Figure 3.3a), its angular displacement θ in **radians** is defined as follows:

$$\text{angle (in radians)} = \frac{\text{length of arc}}{\text{radius}}$$

or
$$\theta = \frac{s}{r}$$

Since both s and r are distances measured in metres, it follows that the angle θ is simply a ratio. It is a dimensionless quantity. If the object moves twice as far around a circle of twice the radius (Figure 3.3b), its angular displacement θ will still be the same.

$$\theta = \frac{\text{length of arc}}{\text{radius}} = \frac{2s}{2r} = \frac{s}{r}$$

When we define θ in this way, its units are radians rather than degrees. How are radians related to degrees? If an object moves all the way round the circumference of the circle, it moves a distance of $2\pi r$. We can calculate its angular displacement in radians:

$$\theta = \frac{\text{circumference}}{\text{radius}} = \frac{2\pi r}{r} = 2\pi$$

Hence a complete circle contains 2π radians. But we can also say that the object has moved through 360°. Hence:

$$360° = 2\pi\,\text{rad}$$

Similarly, we have:

$$180° = \pi\,\text{rad} \qquad 90° = \frac{\pi}{2}\,\text{rad}$$

$$45° = \frac{\pi}{4}\,\text{rad} \qquad \text{and so on}$$

Defining the radian

An angle of one radian is defined as follows (see Figure 3.4):

> One **radian** is the angle subtended at the centre of a circle by an arc of length equal to the radius of the circle.

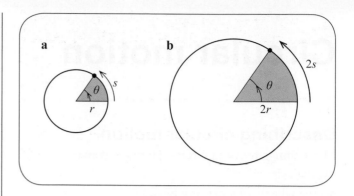

Figure 3.3 The size of an angle depends on the radius and the length of the arc. Doubling both leaves the angle unchanged.

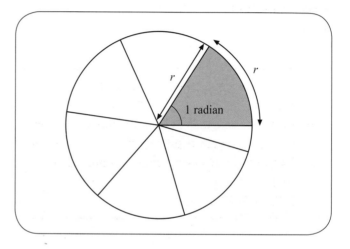

Figure 3.4 The length of the arc is equal to the radius when the angle is 1 radian.

An angle of 360° is equivalent to an angle of 2π radians. We can therefore determine what 1 radian is equivalent to in degrees.

$$1\ \text{radian} = \frac{360}{2\pi}$$

or 1 radian $\approx 57.3°$

If you can remember that there are $2\pi\,\text{rad}$ in a full circle, you will be able to convert between radians and degrees:

- to convert from degrees to radians, multiply by $\dfrac{2\pi}{360°}$ or $\dfrac{\pi}{180°}$

- to convert from radians to degrees, multiply by $\dfrac{360°}{2\pi}$ or $\dfrac{180°}{\pi}$.

Now look at Worked example 1.

Worked example 1

If $\theta = 60°$, what is the value of θ in radians?

$\theta = 60°$

360° is equivalent to 2π radians. Therefore:

$$\theta = \frac{60 \times 2\pi}{360}$$

$$= \frac{\pi}{3} = 1.05 \, \text{rad}$$

(Note that it is often useful to express an angle as a multiple of π radians.)

SAQ

2　a　Convert the following angles from degrees into radians: 30°, 90°, 105°.

　　b　Convert these angles from radians to degrees: 0.5 rad, 0.75 rad, π rad, $\frac{\pi}{2}$ rad.

　　c　Express the following angles as multiples of π radians:
　　　30°, 120°, 270°, 720°.

[Answer]

Steady speed, changing velocity

If we are to use Newton's laws of motion to explain circular motion, we must consider the *velocity* of an object going round in a circle, rather than its *speed*.

There is an important distinction between speed and velocity: **speed** is a scalar quantity, but **velocity** is a vector quantity, with both magnitude and direction. We need to think about the direction of motion of an orbiting object.

Figure 3.5 shows how we can represent the velocity of an object at various points around its circular path. The arrows are straight and show the direction of motion at a particular instant. They are drawn as tangents to the circular path. As the object travels through points A, B, C, etc., its speed remains constant but its direction changes. Since the direction of the velocity v is changing, it follows that v itself (a vector quantity) is changing as the object moves in a circle.

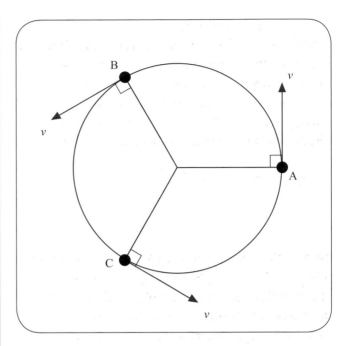

Figure 3.5 The velocity v of an object changes direction as it moves along a circular path.

SAQ

3　Explain why all the arrows in Figure 3.5 are drawn the same length.

[Answer]

4　A toy train travels at a steady speed of $0.2 \, \text{m s}^{-1}$ around a circular track (Figure 3.6).

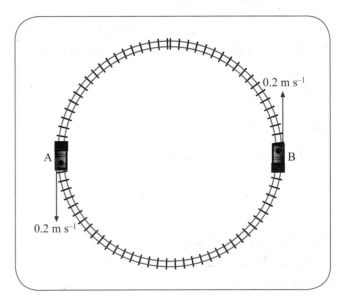

Figure 3.6 A toy train travelling around a circular track.

A and B are two points diametrically opposite to one another on the track.

a Determine the change in the speed of the train as it travels from A to B.

b Determine the change in the velocity of the train as it travels from A to B.

Centripetal forces

When an object's velocity is changing, it has acceleration. In the case of uniform circular motion, the acceleration is rather unusual because, as we have seen, the object's speed does not change but its velocity does. How can an object accelerate and at the same time have a steady speed?

One way to understand this is to think about what Newton's laws of motion can tell us about this situation. **Newton's first law** states that an object remains at rest or in a state of uniform motion (at constant speed in a straight line) unless it is acted on by an external force. In the case of an object moving at steady speed in a circle, we have a body whose velocity is not constant; therefore, there must be a resultant (unbalanced) force acting on it.

Now we can think about various situations where objects are going round in a circle and try to find the force that is acting on them.

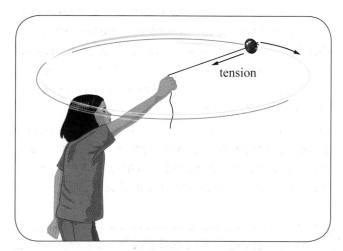

Figure 3.7 Whirling a conker.

- Consider a conker on the end of a string. Imagine whirling it in a horizontal circle above your head (Figure 3.7). To make it go round in a circle, you have to pull on the string. The pull of the string on the conker is the unbalanced force, which is constantly acting to change the conker's velocity as it orbits your head. If you let go of the string, suddenly there is no tension in the string and the conker will fly off at a tangent to the circle.

- Similarly, the Earth as it orbits the Sun has a constantly changing velocity. Newton's first law suggests that there must be an unbalanced force acting on it. That force is the gravitational pull of the Sun. If the force disappeared, we would travel off in a straight line.

In both of these cases, you should be able to see why the direction of the force is as shown in Figure 3.8. The force on the object is directed towards the centre of the circle. We describe each of these forces as a **centripetal force** – that is, directed towards the centre.

It is important to note that the word *centripetal* is an adjective. We use it to describe a force that is making something travel along a circular path. It does not tell us what causes this force, which might be gravitational, electrostatic, magnetic, frictional or whatever.

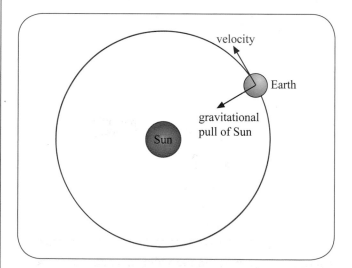

Figure 3.8 The gravitational pull of the Sun provides the centripetal force that keeps the Earth in its orbit.

SAQ

5 In each of the following cases, state what provides the centripetal force:

   a the Moon orbiting the Earth

   b a car going round a bend on a flat, rough road

   c the weight on the end of a swinging pendulum.

6 A car is travelling along a flat road. Explain why it cannot go around a bend if the road surface is perfectly smooth. Suggest what might happen if the driver tries turning the steering wheel.

Answer

Vector diagrams

Figure 3.9a shows an object travelling along a circular path, at two positions in its orbit. It reaches position B a short time after A. How has its velocity changed between these two positions?

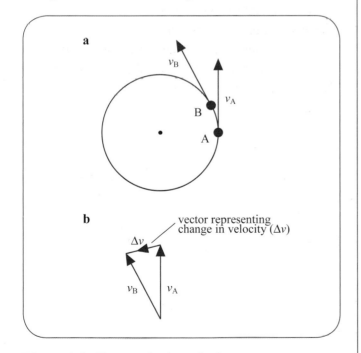

Figure 3.9 Changes in the velocity vector.

The change in the velocity of the object can be determined using a vector triangle. This vector triangle in Figure 3.9b shows the difference between the final velocity v_B and initial velocity v_A. The change in the velocity of the object between the points B and A is shown by the smaller arrow labelled

Δv. Note that the change in the velocity of the object is (more or less):

- at right angles to the velocity at A
- directed towards the centre of the circle.

The object is accelerating because its velocity changes. Since acceleration is the rate of change of velocity

$$a = \frac{\Delta v}{\Delta t}$$

it follows that the acceleration of the object must be in the same direction as the change in the velocity – towards the centre of the circle. This is not surprising because, according to $F = ma$, the acceleration a of the object is in the same direction as the centripetal force F.

Acceleration at steady speed

Now that we know that the centripetal force F and acceleration are always at right angles to the object's velocity, we can explain why its speed remains constant. If the force is to make the object change its speed, it must have a component in the direction of the object's velocity; it must provide a push in the direction in which the object is already travelling. However, here we have a force at 90° to the velocity, so it has no component in the required direction. (Its component in the direction of the velocity *is* $F \cos 90° = 0$.) It acts to pull the object around the circle, without ever making it speed up or slow down.

You can also use the idea of work done to show that the speed of the object moving in a circle remains the same. The work done by a force is equal to the product of the force and the distance moved by the object in the direction of the force. The distance moved by the object in the direction of the centripetal force is zero; hence the work done is zero. If no work is done on the object, its kinetic energy must remain the same and hence its speed is unchanged.

SAQ

7 An object follows a circular path at a steady speed. Describe how each of the following quantities changes as it follows this path: speed, velocity, kinetic energy, momentum, centripetal force, centripetal acceleration. (Refer to both magnitude and direction, as appropriate.)

Answer

Thinking like Newton

Isaac Newton devised an ingenious 'thought experiment' that allows us to think about circular motion, particularly in connection with objects orbiting the Earth. Consider a large cannon on some high point on the Earth's surface, capable of firing objects horizontally. Figure 3.10 shows what will happen if we fire them at different speeds.

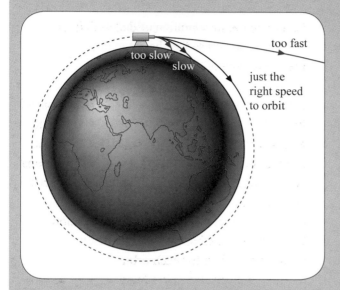

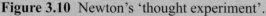

Figure 3.10 Newton's 'thought experiment'.

If the object is fired too slowly, gravity will pull it down towards the ground and it will land at some distance from the cannon. A faster initial speed results in the object landing further from the cannon.

Now, if we try a bit faster than this, the object will travel all the way round the Earth. We have to get just the right speed to do this. As the object is pulled down towards the Earth, the curved surface of the Earth falls away beneath it. The object follows a circular path, constantly falling under gravity but never getting any closer to the surface.

If the object is fired too fast, it travels off into space, and fails to get into a circular orbit. So we can see that there is just one correct speed to achieve a circular orbit under gravity.

Note that we have ignored the effects of air resistance – that's easy to do in a thought experiment. The term 'thought experiment' (or *Gedankenexperiment* in German) was first used by Hans Christian Oersted in about 1812. Scientists have often made use of such an approach when developing their theories. The idea is to start with a hypothesis (an idea to be tested). Then ask the question, 'If the hypothesis is true, what would happen if we could do such-and-such…?' The experiment is not carried out, but the likely results show whether the hypothesis is possible or not.

Famous examples of thought experiments from physics include Galileo's Leaning Tower of Pisa experiment and Schrödinger's cat (an example from quantum physics). An internet search for 'thought experiments' will lead you to more examples.

Calculating force and acceleration

If an object having a particular mass m is to travel in an orbit of radius r and at speed v, there is a particular value of centripetal force F needed to keep it in orbit. The force F must depend on m, v and r. You can investigate the relationship between these quantities in the 'whirling conker' experiment.

Here is the equation for the centripetal force F:

$$\text{centripetal force, } F = \frac{mv^2}{r}$$

If you think about whirling a conker on a string, you should be able to see that the relationships between force, mass and speed are reasonable. A conker of greater mass will require a greater force. When it is moving faster you will also require a greater force. However, you may not find it obvious that to make it go at the same speed in a bigger circle will require a smaller force, but that is how it behaves.

Newton's second law of motion

Now that we have an equation for centripetal force, we can use **Newton's second law** of motion to deduce an equation for centripetal acceleration. If we write this law as $a = F/m$, we find:

$$\text{centripetal acceleration, } a = \frac{v^2}{r}$$

Remembering that an object accelerates in the direction of the resultant force on it, it follows that both F and a are in the same direction, towards the centre of the circle.

Strictly speaking, it is more correct to think of the relationship between centripetal force and acceleration the other way round. We should say that the acceleration is given by:

$$a = \frac{v^2}{r}$$

and then use:

$$F = ma$$

to deduce that:

$$F = \frac{mv^2}{r}$$

Extension ───────────────────

Calculating orbital speed

We can use the equation for a to calculate the speed that an object must have to orbit the Earth under gravity, as in Newton's thought experiment. The necessary centripetal force mv^2/r is provided by the Earth's gravitational pull mg.

Hence:

$$mg = \frac{mv^2}{r}$$

$$g = \frac{v^2}{r}$$

where $g = 9.81 \, \mathrm{m\,s^{-2}}$ is the acceleration of free fall close to the Earth's surface. The radius of its orbit is equal to the Earth's radius, approximately 6400 km. Hence, we have:

$$9.81 = \frac{v^2}{(6.4 \times 10^6)}$$

$$v = \sqrt{9.81 \times 6.4 \times 10^6} = 7.92 \times 10^3 \, \mathrm{m\,s^{-1}}$$

Thus if you were to throw or hit a ball horizontally at almost 8 km s⁻¹, it would go into orbit around the Earth.

SAQ ────────────────────────

8 Calculate how long it would take a ball to orbit the Earth once, just above the surface, at a speed of $7920 \, \mathrm{m\,s^{-1}}$. (The radius of the Earth is 6400 km.)

 Hint

Answer

9 A stone of mass 0.20 kg is whirled round on the end of a string of length 30 cm. The string will break when the tension in it exceeds 8.0 N. Calculate the maximum speed at which the stone can be whirled without the string breaking.

Answer

10 Helen Sharman, the first Briton in space, worked in the Mir space station (Figure 3.11). This had a mass of 20 900 kg, and orbited the Earth at an average height of 350 km, where the gravitational acceleration is $8.8 \, \mathrm{m\,s^{-2}}$. The radius of the Earth is 6400 km. Calculate:
   a the centripetal force on the space station
   b the speed at which it orbited
   c the time taken for each orbit
   d the number of times it orbited the Earth each day.

Answer

Figure 3.11 The Mir space station orbiting Earth over Australia.

11 A stone of mass 0.40 kg is whirled round on the end of a string 0.50 m long. It makes three complete revolutions each second. Calculate:
   a its speed
   b its centripetal acceleration
   c the tension in the string.

Hint

 Answer

Summary

- Angles can be measured in radians. An angle of 2π rad is equal to 360°.

- An object moving at a steady speed along a circular path has uniform circular motion.

- The angular displacement θ is a measure of the angle through which an object moves in a circle.

- An object moving in a circle is not in equilibrium; it has a net force acting on it.

- The net force acting on an object moving in a circle is called the centripetal force. This force is directed towards the centre of the circle and is at right angles to the velocity of the object.

- The magnitude of the centripetal force F acting on an object of mass m moving at a speed v in a circle of radius r is given by:

$$F = \frac{mv^2}{r}$$

- An object moving in a circle has a centripetal acceleration a given by:

$$a = \frac{v^2}{r}$$

Questions

1 The electric motor in a washing machine rotates the drum containing the clothes by means of a rubber belt stretched around two pulleys, one on the motor shaft and the other on the drum shaft, as shown in the diagram.

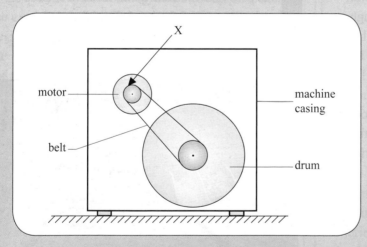

    a The motor pulley of radius 15 mm rotates at 50 revolutions per second. Calculate:
       i the speed of the belt   [2]
       ii the centripetal acceleration of the belt at point X.   [2]
    b When the motor speed is increased, the belt can start to slip on the motor
      pulley. Explain why the belt slips.   [2]

OCR Physics A2 (2824) January 2007   [Total 6]

Hint

Answer

continued

2 a Describe what is meant by *centripetal force*. [1]

b The diagram shows a toy of mass 60 g placed on the edge of a rotating turntable.

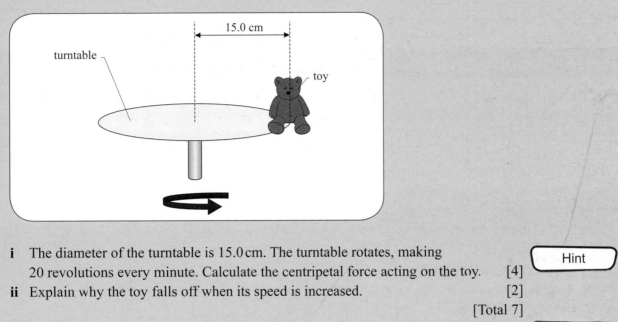

i The diameter of the turntable is 15.0 cm. The turntable rotates, making 20 revolutions every minute. Calculate the centripetal force acting on the toy. [4]

ii Explain why the toy falls off when its speed is increased. [2]

[Total 7]

Hint

Answer

3 One end of a string is secured to the ceiling and a metal ball of mass 50 g is tied to its other end. The ball is initially at rest in the vertical position. The ball is raised through a vertical height of 70 cm (see diagram). The ball is then released. It describes a circular arc as it passes through the vertical position.

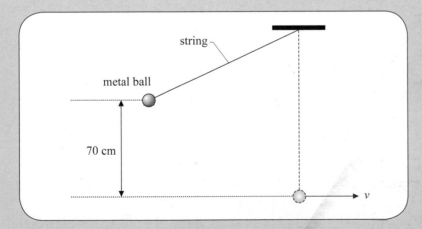

The length of the string is 1.50 m.

a Ignoring the effects of air resistance, determine the speed *v* of the ball as it passes through the vertical position. [3]

b Calculate the tension *T* in the string when the string is vertical. [4]

c Explain why your answer to **b** is not equal to the weight of the ball. [2]

[Total 9]

Hint

Answer

Chapter 4

Gravitational fields

Objectives e-Learning

Ideas about gravity

In Chapter 3, we considered the motion of objects moving in circular paths, including objects orbiting under the influence of gravity. But what is gravity? How can we describe it, and how can we explain it?

We live our lives with the constant experience of gravity. We know that things fall when we let go of them. We know that we will return to the ground if we jump up in the air or from an aircraft (Figure 4.1). We can live quite happily without thinking about why this is so. Once we start thinking about the force of gravity, which makes things fall, we may come up with some odd ideas.

Figure 4.1 Skydivers balance the forces of gravity and air resistance.

Young children take it for granted that things fall. They are mystified if you ask them to explain it. They also take it for granted that things stay where they are on the ground; they don't think it necessary to talk about two balanced forces. Surely gravity disappears as soon as something stops falling?

You have learned that a stationary object as shown in Figure 4.2 has two forces acting on it: the force of gravity (its weight) and the normal contact force exerted by the ground. A child does not have

this mental picture, but these forces really do exist, as they would discover if they put their fingers underneath a large weight!

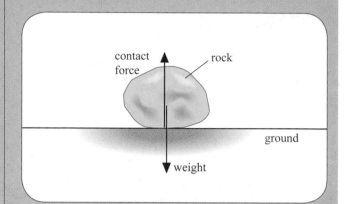

Figure 4.2 Two balanced forces act on this stationary object.

Weighty thoughts

Children learn at school that there is a force called *gravity*, which holds us on to the Earth's surface. So, what causes this gravitational pull of the Earth? Try asking some children. Here are some of the ideas that they may come up with – many adults have similar ideas.

'Gravity is made by the Earth spinning. If it stopped spinning, we would all fall off.'

'If the Earth spun faster and faster, we would all fall off' (Figure 4.3).

'Gravity is caused by the Earth's atmosphere pressing down on us.'

'If you dropped something on the Moon, it would just float about, because there is no air.'

'There is a giant magnet inside the Earth. It attracts us to the Earth.'

continued

Figure 4.3 Hold on to the pole if you don't want to fall off!

Gravity is not caused by the Earth's rotation, but it is true that, if the Earth spun a lot faster, gravity might not be strong enough to hold us on. Nor is gravity caused by the atmosphere. Perhaps this idea comes from seeing astronauts in orbit above the Earth's atmosphere ('in space'), where they appear to be weightless. On the Moon, gravity is weaker than on the Earth, so objects fall more slowly and astronauts can jump higher.

Isaac Newton (1642–1727) tried to understand the force of gravity. In particular, he wondered whether the Earth's gravitational pull was confined to the Earth's surface, or whether it extended into space – as far as the Moon. Previously, it had been suggested that the Moon was held in its orbit around the Earth by magnetic attraction. After all, it was known that the Earth is magnetic, and that magnetic forces act at a distance.

Newton rejected this theory, partly on the grounds that the Sun is very hot and magnets lose their magnetism when they are heated. Instead, he suggested that it is the *mass* of a body that causes it to attract other bodies. Objects close to the Earth's surface fall towards the ground because their mass is attracted by the mass of the Earth. The Moon continues in its orbit round the Earth because their two masses attract each other (Figure 4.4).

Newton's great achievement was to relate the falling of an apple to the ground to the 'falling' of the Moon as it orbits the Earth.

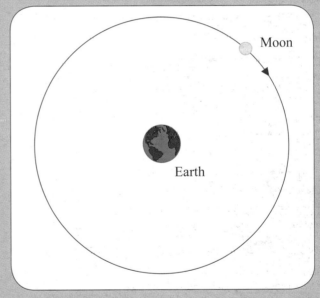

Figure 4.4 The Moon orbits the Earth. There is an attractive gravitational force acting on the Moon due to its mass and the mass of the Earth.

Gravitational forces and fields

The Earth's gravitational force extends well beyond its surface. The Moon stays in its orbit, at a distance of about 400 000 km away, because of the Earth's gravitational pull. The Earth orbits the Sun at a distance of 150 000 000 km because of the gravitational force between them.

According to Newton, all masses create a gravitational field in the space around them. This field gives rise to a force on any object having mass placed in this field. The Moon orbits the Earth because it experiences a gravitational force due to the Earth's gravitational field.

We can represent the Earth's gravitational field by drawing field lines, as shown in Figure 4.5. (You will be familiar with this type of representation when drawing the magnetic field patterns of magnets.) The field lines show two things:

- The arrows on the field lines show us the direction of the gravitational force on a mass placed in the field.
- The spacing of the field lines indicates the strength of the gravitational field – the farther apart they are, the weaker the field.

The drawing of the Earth's gravitational field shows that all objects are attracted towards the centre of the Earth. This is true even if they are below the surface of the Earth. The gravitational force gets weaker as you get farther away from the Earth's surface – this is shown by the greater separation between the field lines. The Earth is almost a uniform spherical mass – it bulges a bit at the equator. The gravitational field of the Earth is as if its entire mass was concentrated at its centre. As far as any object beyond the Earth's surface is concerned, the Earth behaves as a **point mass**.

Figure 4.6 shows the Earth's gravitational field closer to its surface. The gravitational field in and around a building on the Earth's surface shows that the gravitational force is directed downwards everywhere and (because the field lines are parallel and evenly spaced) the strength of the gravitational field is the same at all points in and around the building. This means that your weight is the same everywhere in this gravitational field. Your weight does not get significantly less when you go upstairs.

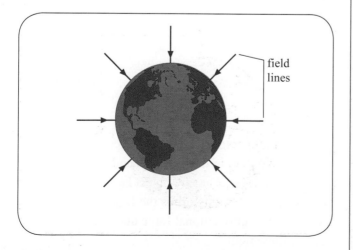

Figure 4.5 The Earth's gravitational field is represented by field lines.

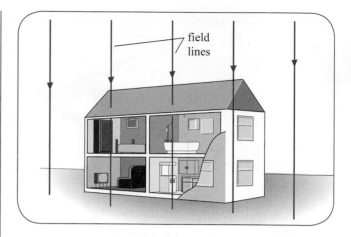

Figure 4.6 The Earth's gravitational field is uniform on the scale of a building.

We describe the Earth's gravitational field as *radial*, since the field lines diverge (spread out) radially from the centre of the Earth. However, on the scale of a building, the gravitational field is *uniform*, since the field lines are equally spaced.

Jupiter is a more massive planet than the Earth and so we would represent its gravitational field by showing more closely spaced field lines.

Newton's law of gravitation

Newton used his ideas about mass and gravity to suggest a law of gravitation for two point masses (Figure 4.7). He considered two point masses M and m separated by a distance r. Each point mass attracts the other with a force F. (According to Newton's third law of motion, the point masses interact with each other and therefore exert equal but opposite forces on each other.) A statement of **Newton's law of gravitation** is shown below.

> Any two point masses attract each other with a force that is directly proportional to the product of their masses and inversely proportional to the square of their separation.

Note that the law refers to 'point masses' – you can alternatively use the term 'particles'. Things are more complicated if we think about solid bodies which occupy a volume of space. Each particle of one body attracts every particle of the other body and we would have to add all these forces together to work out the

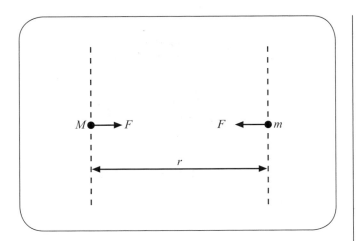

Figure 4.7 Two point masses separated by distance r.

force each body has on the other. Newton was able to show that two uniform spheres attract one another with a force which is the same as if their masses were concentrated at their centres (provided their radii are much smaller than their separation).

According to Newton's law of gravitation, we have:

force ∝ product of the masses   or $F \propto Mm$

force ∝ $\dfrac{1}{\text{distance}^2}$ or $F \propto \dfrac{1}{r^2}$

Therefore:

$$F \propto \frac{Mm}{r^2}$$

To make this into an equation, we introduce the gravitational constant G. We also need a minus sign to show that the force is attractive.

$$F = -\frac{GMm}{r^2}$$

The gravitational constant G has an experimental value of $6.67 \times 10^{-11} \, \text{N}\,\text{m}^2\,\text{kg}^{-2}$. The equation above can also be applied to spherical objects (such as the Earth and the Moon) provided we remember to measure the separation r between the centres of the objects.

Let us examine this equation to see why it seems reasonable.

First, each of the two masses is important. Your weight (the gravitational force on you) depends on your mass and on the mass of the planet you happen to be standing on.

Second, the further away you are from the planet, the weaker its pull. Twice as far away gives one-

quarter of the force. This can be seen from the diagram of the field lines in Figure 4.8. If the distance is doubled, the lines are spread out over four times the surface area, so their concentration is reduced to one-quarter. This is called an inverse square law – you may have come across a similar law for radiation such as light or gamma-rays spreading out uniformly from a point source.

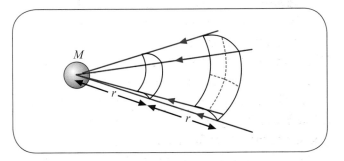

Figure 4.8 Field lines are spread out over a greater surface area at greater distances, so the strength of the field is weaker.

As already mentioned, the minus sign represents the fact that the force is attractive. The radial distance r is measured outwards from the attracting body; the force F acts in the opposite direction, and so our sign convention requires that F is negative.

We measure distances from the centre of mass of one body to the centre of mass of the other (Figure 4.9). We treat each body as if its mass was concentrated at one point. The two bodies attract each other with equal and opposite forces, as required by

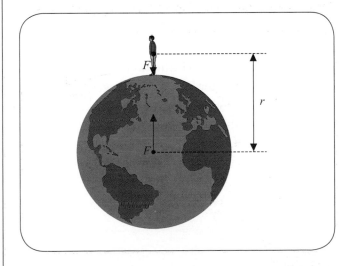

Figure 4.9 A person and the Earth exert equal and opposite attractive forces on each other.

Newton's third law of motion. The Earth pulls on you with a force (your weight) directed towards the centre of the Earth; you attract the Earth with an equal force, directed away from its centre and towards you. Your pull on an object as massive as the Earth has little effect on it. The Sun's pull on the Earth, however, has a very significant effect.

SAQ

1 Calculate the gravitational force of attraction between:
   a two objects separated by a distance of 1.0 cm and each having a mass of 100 g
   b two asteroids separated by a distance of 4.0×10^9 m and each having a mass of 5.0×10^{10} kg
   c a satellite of mass 1.4×10^4 kg orbiting the Earth at a distance of 6800 km from the Earth's centre. (The mass of the Earth is 6.0×10^{24} kg.)

   (Answer)

2 Estimate the gravitational force of attraction between two people sitting side-by-side on a park bench. How does this force compare with the gravitational force exerted on each of them by the Earth, i.e. their weight?

   (Answer)

(Extension)

Gravitational field strength g

We can describe how strong or weak a gravitational field is by stating its **gravitational field strength**. We are used to this idea for objects on or near the Earth's surface. The gravitational field strength is the familiar quantity g. Its value is approximately $9.81\ \mathrm{m\,s^{-2}}$. The weight of a body of mass m is mg.

To make the meaning of g clearer, we should write it as $9.81\ \mathrm{N\,kg^{-1}}$. That is, each 1 kg of mass experiences a gravitational force of 9.81 N.

The gravitational field strength g at any point in a gravitational field is defined as follows:

The gravitational field strength at a point is the gravitational force exerted per unit mass on a small object placed at that point.

This can be written as an equation:

$$g = \frac{F}{m}$$

where F is the gravitational force on the object and m is the mass of the object. Gravitational field strength has the unit $\mathrm{N\,kg^{-1}}$. This is also equivalent to $\mathrm{m\,s^{-2}}$.

We can use the definition above to determine the gravitational field strength for a point (or spherical) mass. The force between two point masses is given by:

$$F = -\frac{GMm}{r^2}$$

The gravitational field strength g due to the mass M at a distance of r from its centre is thus:

$$g = \frac{F}{m} = -\frac{GM\cancel{m}}{r^2\cancel{m}}$$

or

$$g = -\frac{GM}{r^2}$$

Since force is a vector quantity, it follows that gravitational field strength is also a vector. We need to give its direction as well as its magnitude in order to specify it completely. The field strength g is not a constant; it decreases as the distance r increases. The field strength obeys the inverse square law with distance. The field strength will decrease by a factor of four when the distance from the centre is doubled. Close to the Earth's surface, the magnitude of g is about $9.81\ \mathrm{N\,kg^{-1}}$. Even if you climbed Mount Everest, which is 8.85 km high, the field strength will only decrease by 0.3%.

So the gravitational field strength g at a point depends on the mass M of the body causing the field, and the distance r from its centre (see Worked example 1).

Gravitational field strength g also has units $m\,s^{-2}$; it is an acceleration. Another name for g is 'acceleration of free fall'. Any object that falls freely in a gravitational field has this acceleration, approximately $9.81\,m\,s^{-2}$ near the Earth's surface. In Chapter 3 of *Physics 1* you learned about how to determine an experimental value for g, the local gravitational field strength.

Worked example 1

The Earth has radius 6400 km. The gravitational field strength on the Earth's surface is $9.81\,N\,kg^{-1}$. Use this information to determine the mass of the Earth and its mean density.

Step 1 Write down the quantities given.

$r = 6.4 \times 10^6\,m$
$g = 9.81\,N\,kg^{-1}$

Step 2 Use the equation $g = -\dfrac{GM}{r^2}$ to determine the mass of the Earth.

$g = -\dfrac{GM}{r^2}$

$9.81 = \dfrac{6.67 \times 10^{-11} \times M}{(6.4 \times 10^6)^2}$ (we ignore the negative sign)

mass of Earth $= M = \dfrac{9.81 \times (6.4 \times 10^6)^2}{6.67 \times 10^{-11}}$

$= 6.0 \times 10^{24}\,kg$

Step 3 Use the equation $\text{density} = \dfrac{\text{mass}}{\text{volume}}$ to determine the density of the Earth.

The Earth is a spherical mass. Its volume can be calculated using $\frac{4}{3}\pi r^3$.

$\text{density} = \rho = \dfrac{M}{V} = \dfrac{6.0 \times 10^{24}}{\frac{4}{3} \times \pi \times (6.4 \times 10^6)^3}$

$\approx 5500\,kg\,m^{-3}$

	Mass/kg	Radius/ km	Distance from Earth/km
Earth	6.0×10^{24}	6400	–
Moon	7.4×10^{22}	1740	3.8×10^5
Sun	2.0×10^{30}	700 000	1.5×10^8

Table 4.1 Data for SAQs 3–9.

SAQ

You will need the data in Table 4.1 to answer these questions.

3 Mount Everest is approximately 9.0 km high. Calculate how much less a mountaineer of mass 100 kg (including backpack) would weigh at its summit, compared to her weight at sea level. Would this difference be measurable with bathroom scales?　　Hint　Answer

4 a Calculate the gravitational field strength:
 i close to the surface of the Moon
 ii close to the surface of the Sun.
 b Suggest how your answers above help to explain why the Moon has only a thin atmosphere, while the Sun has a dense atmosphere.　Answer

5 a Calculate the Earth's gravitational field strength at the position of the Moon.
 b Calculate the force the Earth exerts on the Moon. Hence determine the Moon's acceleration towards the Earth.　Answer

6 Jupiter's mass is 320 times that of the Earth and its radius is 11.2 times the Earth's. The Earth's surface gravitational field strength is $9.81\,N\,kg^{-1}$. Calculate the gravitational field strength close to the surface of Jupiter.　Answer

7 The Moon and the Sun both contribute to the tides on the Earth's oceans. Which has a bigger pull on each kilogram of seawater, the Sun or the Moon?

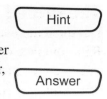

8 Astrologers believe that the planets exert an influence on us, particularly at the moment of birth. (They don't necessarily believe that this is an effect of gravity!)

   a Calculate the gravitational force on a 4.0 kg baby caused by Mars when the planet is at its closest to the Earth at a distance of 100 000 000 km. Mars has mass 6.4×10^{23} kg.

   b Calculate the gravitational force on the same baby due to its 50 kg mother at a distance of 0.40 m.

9 There is a point on the line joining the centres of the Earth and the Moon where their combined gravitational field strength is zero. Is this point closer to the Earth or to the Moon? Calculate how far it is from the centre of the Earth.

Orbiting under gravity

For an object orbiting a planet, such as an artificial satellite orbiting the Earth, gravity provides the centripetal force which keeps it in orbit (Figure 4.10). This is a simple situation as there is only one force acting on the satellite – the gravitational attraction of the Earth. The satellite follows a circular path because the gravitational force is at right angles to its velocity

From Chapter 3, you know that the centripetal force F on a body is given by:

$$F = \frac{mv^2}{r}$$

Consider a satellite of mass m orbiting the Earth at a distance r from its centre at a constant speed v. Since it is the gravitational force between the Earth and the satellite which provides this centripetal force, we can write:

$$\frac{GMm}{r^2} = \frac{mv^2}{r}$$

Figure 4.10 The gravitational attraction of the Earth provides the centripetal force on an orbiting satellite.

where M is the mass of the Earth. (There is no need for a minus sign here as the gravitational force and the centripetal force are both directed towards the centre of the circle.)

Rearranging gives:

$$v^2 = \frac{GM}{r}$$

This equation allows us to calculate, for example, the speed at which a satellite must travel to stay in a circular orbit. Notice that the mass of the satellite m has cancelled out. The implication of this is that all satellites, whatever their masses, will travel at the same speed in a particular orbit. You would find this very reassuring if you were an astronaut on a space walk outside your spacecraft (Figure 4.11). You would travel at the same speed as your craft, despite the fact that your mass is a lot less than its mass. The equation above can be applied to the planets of our Solar System – M becomes the mass of the Sun.

Now look at Worked example 2.

Figure 4.11 During this space walk, both the astronaut and the spacecraft travel through space at over $8\,\text{km s}^{-1}$.

Worked example 2

The Moon orbits the Earth at an average distance of $384\,000\,\text{km}$ from the centre of the Earth. Calculate its orbital speed. (The mass of the Earth is $6.0\times10^{24}\,\text{kg}$.)

Step 1 Write down the known quantities.

$$r = 3.84\times10^8\,\text{m} \qquad M = 6.0\times10^{24}\,\text{kg} \qquad v = ?$$

Step 2 Use the equation $v^2 = \dfrac{GM}{r}$ to determine the orbital speed v.

$$v^2 = \frac{GM}{r}$$

$$v^2 = \frac{6.67\times10^{-11}\times6.0\times10^{24}}{3.84\times10^8}$$

$$v^2 = 1.04\times10^6$$

$$v = 1020\,\text{m s}^{-1} \approx 1.0\times10^3\,\text{m s}^{-1}$$

So the Moon travels around its orbit at a speed of roughly $1\,\text{km s}^{-1}$.

SAQ

10 Calculate the orbital speed of an artificial satellite travelling $200\,\text{km}$ above the Earth's surface. (The radius of Earth is $6.4\times10^6\,\text{m}$ and its mass is $6.0\times10^{24}\,\text{kg}$.)

Answer

The orbital period

It is often more useful to consider the time taken for a complete orbit, the orbital **period** T. Since the distance around an orbit is equal to the circumference $2\pi r$, it follows that:

$$v = \frac{2\pi r}{T}$$

We can substitute this in the equation for v^2 on page 42. This gives:

$$\frac{4\pi^2 r^2}{T^2} = \frac{GM}{r}$$

and rearranging this equation gives:

$$T^2 = \left(\frac{4\pi^2}{GM}\right)r^3$$

This equation shows that the orbital period T is related to the radius r of the orbit. The square of the period is directly proportional to the cube of the radius ($T^2 \propto r^3$). This is an important result. It was first discovered by Johannes Kepler (Figure 4.12), who analysed the available data for the planets of the Solar System. It was an empirical law (one based

Figure 4.12 Johannes Kepler devised mathematical laws to describe the motion of the planets in our Solar System.

solely on experiment) since he had no theory to explain why there should be this relationship between T and r. It was not until Isaac Newton formulated his law of gravitation that it was possible to explain the relationship, which is known as Kepler's third law of planetary motion:

> The square of the period T of a planet is directly proportional to the cube of its distance r from the Sun – that is, $T^2 \propto r^3$.

Explaining Kepler's law was one of the greatest triumphs of Newton's law of gravitation.

Table 4.2 shows values of T and r for the four planets of the Solar System that are closest to the Sun. (These are considerably more accurate than the values that Kepler had available to him.) The values of T^2 (y-axis) and r^3 (x-axis) are plotted in Figure 4.13. The gradient of this graph can be used to determine the mass M of the Sun, as follows. Comparing

$$T^2 = \left(\frac{4\pi^2}{GM}\right) r^3$$

to the equation for a straight line through the origin $y = mx$, we find the gradient of the line is equal to

$$\left(\frac{4\pi^2}{GM}\right)$$

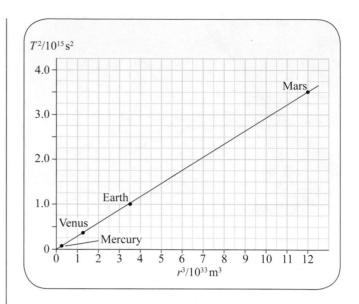

Figure 4.13 A graph to show the validity of Kepler's law for the four planets (data from Table 4.2).

Therefore:

$$\text{gradient} = \left(\frac{4\pi^2}{GM}\right) = 3.0 \times 10^{-19}\,\text{s}^2\,\text{m}^{-3}$$

Hence:

$$M = \frac{4\pi^2}{G \times \text{gradient}}$$

$$= \frac{4\pi^2}{(6.67 \times 10^{-11} \times 3.0 \times 10^{-19})}$$

$$= 2.0 \times 10^{30}\,\text{kg}$$

Now look at Worked example 3.

Planet	r/m	T/s	r^3/m^3	T^2/s^2
Mercury	5.8×10^{10}	7.6×10^6	2.0×10^{32}	5.8×10^{13}
Venus	1.1×10^{11}	1.9×10^7	1.3×10^{33}	3.6×10^{14}
Earth	1.5×10^{11}	3.2×10^7	3.4×10^{33}	1.0×10^{15}
Mars	2.3×10^{11}	5.9×10^7	1.2×10^{34}	3.5×10^{15}

Table 4.2 Orbital data for the four planets closest to the Sun.

Moon	r/m	T/days
Io	4.2×10^8	1.77
Europa	6.7×10^8	3.55
Ganymede	1.1×10^9	7.2
Callisto	1.9×10^9	16.7

Table 4.3 The moons of Jupiter discovered by Galileo. The orbital periods are given in Earth-days.

Figure 4.14 A composite photograph of Jupiter and its four Galilean moons.

Worked example 3

The mean distance between the Sun and the Earth is known as 1 astronomical unit (AU). The planet Uranus orbits at a distance of 19.2 AU. Calculate the orbital period of Uranus in Earth-years.

Step 1 Write down the information about the Earth and Uranus.

Earth: $r = 1.0$ AU $T = 1$ year
Uranus: $r = 19.2$ AU $T = ?$

Step 2 Use Kepler's third law to determine the orbital period for Uranus.

Kepler's third law is $T^2 \propto r^3$.

Therefore $\dfrac{T^2}{r^3} = $ constant

and we can write:

$$\frac{T^2}{r^3} \text{ for Uranus} = \frac{T^2}{r^3} \text{ for Earth}$$

$$\frac{T^2}{19.2^3} = \frac{1.0^2}{1.0^3}$$

$$T = \sqrt{19.2^3} \approx 84 \text{ years}$$

Note that you can use Kepler's law with any system of units – you just need to be consistent.

SAQ

11 Jupiter has many moons (Figure 4.14). The four largest moons were discovered by Galileo Galilei in 1610 and others have been discovered since. Table 4.3 shows the orbital periods and radii of the Galilean moons.

   a Use these data to show that they follow Kepler's law of planetary motion ($T^2 \propto r^3$).

   b Use the average value of $\dfrac{T^2}{r^3}$ to determine the mass of Jupiter.

   c The American astronomer Edward Emerson Barnard observed a fifth moon, Amalthea, in 1892. Its orbital period is 0.50 days. Calculate the radius of its orbit around Jupiter.

   Answer

Orbiting the Earth

The Earth has one natural satellite – the Moon – and many thousands of artificial satellites – some spacecraft and a lot of debris. Each of these satellites uses the Earth's gravitational field to provide the centripetal force that keeps it in orbit. In order for a satellite to maintain a particular orbit, it must travel at the correct speed. This is given by the equation on page 42:

$$v^2 = \frac{GM}{r}$$

It follows from this equation that the closer the satellite is to the Earth, the faster it must travel. If it travels too slowly, it will fall down towards the Earth's surface. If it travels too quickly, it will move out into a higher orbit.

SAQ

12 A satellite orbiting a few hundred kilometres above the Earth's surface will experience a slight frictional drag from the Earth's (very thin) atmosphere. Draw a diagram to show how you would expect the satellite's orbit to change as a result. How can this problem be overcome if it is desired to keep a satellite at a particular height above the Earth?

Hint

Answer

Elliptical orbits

As you probably know, and as Kepler discovered, the planets do not orbit the Sun in perfectly circular orbits. Rather, they follow elliptical paths. An ellipse is a particular mathematical form, an elongated circle (a circle is simply one form of ellipse). A planet following an elliptical path is not at a constant distance from the Sun. As it moves further from the Sun, it travels more slowly; it then speeds up as it 'falls' closer to the Sun. The planetary orbits are not very elongated; they are close to being circular.

Kepler didn't know, but the planets' elliptical orbits are a consequence of the inverse square law of gravitation, discovered by Newton. Robert Hooke (of Hooke's law fame) was a constant critic of Newton. The two men competed to claim priority on many different ideas and observations. History has supported many of Newton's claims, but he didn't always get things right.

Hooke issued a challenge to Newton: if gravity follows an inverse square law, what shape should the planets' orbits have? Newton drew a sketch showing that the orbits would either be circular, or the planets would spiral in towards the Sun. Hooke was jubilant. He had already deduced that the orbits would be elliptical.

Observing the Earth

Artificial satellites have a variety of uses. Many are used for making observations of the Earth's surface for commercial, environmental, meteorological and military purposes. Others are used for astronomical observations, benefiting greatly from being above the Earth's atmosphere. Still others are used for navigation, telecommunications and broadcasting.

Figure 4.15 shows two typical orbits. A satellite in a circular orbit close to the Earth's surface and passing over the poles, completes about 16 orbits in 24 hours. As the Earth turns below it, the satellite 'sees' a different strip of the Earth's surface during each orbit. A satellite in an elliptical orbit has a more distant view of the Earth.

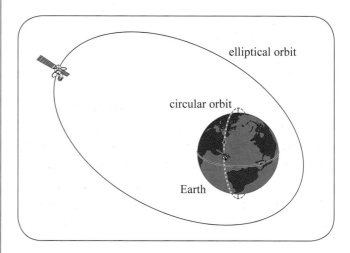

Figure 4.15 Satellites orbiting the Earth.

Geostationary orbits

A special type of orbit is one in which a satellite is positioned so that, as it orbits, the Earth rotates below it at the same rate. The satellite remains above a fixed point on the Earth's surface. This kind of orbit is called a **geostationary orbit**. This idea was first suggested in 1945 by the engineer and science fiction writer Arthur C. Clarke. He proposed setting up a series of communications satellites in a 'Clarke belt' above the equator. These would allow telecommunications signals to leap-frog around the world.

We can determine the distance of a satellite in a geostationary orbit using the equation:

$$T^2 = \left(\frac{4\pi^2}{GM}\right) r^3$$

For a satellite to stay above a fixed point on the equator, it must take exactly 24 hours to complete one orbit (Figure 4.16). We know:

$$G = 6.67 \times 10^{-11} \, \mathrm{N \, m^2 \, kg^{-2}}$$

$$T = 24 \text{ hours} = 86\,400 \, \mathrm{s}$$

$$M = 6.0 \times 10^{24} \, \mathrm{kg}$$

Hence:

$$r^3 = \frac{GMT^2}{4\pi^2} = \frac{6.67 \times 10^{-11} \times 6.0 \times 10^{24} \times (86400)^2}{4\pi^2}$$

$$= 7.66 \times 10^{22} \, \mathrm{m^3}$$

$$r = \sqrt[3]{7.66 \times 10^{22}} = 4.23 \times 10^7 \, \mathrm{m}$$

So, for a satellite to occupy a geostationary orbit, it must be at a distance of 42 300 km from the centre of the Earth and at a point directly above the equator. Note that the radius of the Earth is 6400 km, so the orbital radius is 6.6 Earth radii from the centre of the Earth (or 5.6 Earth radii from its surface). Figure 4.16 has been drawn to give an impression of the size of the orbit.

Parking in space

A geostationary orbit is sometimes known as a 'parking orbit'. There are over 300 satellites in such orbits. They are used for telecommunications (transmitting telephone messages around the world) and for satellite television transmission. A base station on Earth sends the TV signal up to the satellite, where it is amplified and broadcast back to the ground. Satellite receiver dishes are a familiar sight; you will have observed how, in a neighbourhood, they all point towards the same point in the sky. Because the satellite is in a geostationary orbit, the dish can be fixed. Satellites in any other orbits move across the sky so that a tracking system is necessary to communicate with them. Such a system is complex and expensive, and too demanding for the domestic market.

Geostationary satellites have a lifetime of perhaps ten years. They need a fuel supply to maintain them in the correct orbit, and to keep them pointing correctly towards the Earth. Eventually they run out of fuel and need to be replaced.

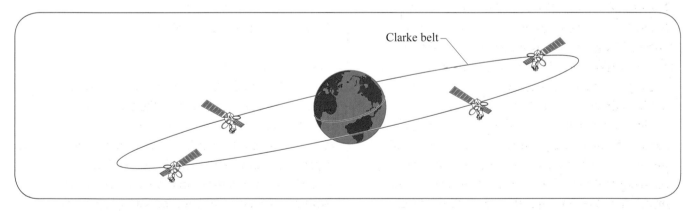

Figure 4.16 Geostationary satellites are parked in the 'Clarke belt', high above the equator. This is a perspective view; the Clarke belt is circular.

SAQ

13 For any future mission to Mars, it would be desirable to set up a system of three or four geostationary (or 'martostationary') satellites around Mars to allow communication between the planet and Earth. Calculate the radius of a suitable orbit around Mars.
   Mars has mass 6.4×10^{23} kg and a rotational period of 24.6 hours.

> Hint

> Answer

14 Although some international telephone signals are sent via telecommunications satellites in geostationary orbits, most are sent along cables on the Earth's surface. This reduces the time delay between sending and receiving the signal. Estimate this time delay for communication via a satellite, and explain why it is less significant when cables are used.
   You will need the following:
   - radius of geostationary orbit = 42 300 km
   - radius of Earth = 6400 km
   - speed of electromagnetic waves in free space $c = 3.0 \times 10^8$ m s^{-1}

> Answer

Summary

> Glossary

- The force of gravity is an attractive force between any two objects due to their masses.

- The gravitational field strength g at a point is the gravitational force exerted per unit mass on a small object placed at that point – that is:

$$g = \frac{F}{m}$$

- The external field of a uniform spherical mass is the same as that of an equal point mass at the centre of the sphere.

- Newton's law of gravitation states that:
  Any two point masses attract each other with a force that is directly proportional to the product of their masses and inversely proportional to the square of their separation.

- The equation for Newton's law of gravitation is: $F = -\dfrac{GMm}{r^2}$

- The gravitational field strength at distance r from a point or spherical mass M is given by: $g = -\dfrac{GM}{r^2}$

- On or near the surface of the Earth, the gravitational field is uniform, so the value of g is approximately constant. Its value is equal to the acceleration of free fall.

- The orbital period of a satellite is the time taken for one orbit.

- The orbital period can be found by equating the gravitational force $\dfrac{GMm}{r^2}$ to the centripetal force $\dfrac{mv^2}{r}$.

- Kepler's third law of planetary motion relates the orbital period T to the orbital radius r: $T^2 \propto r^3$.

- The orbital speed of a planet or satellite can be determined using the equation: $v^2 = \dfrac{GM}{r}$

- Geostationary satellites have an orbital period of 24 hours and are used for telecommunications transmissions and for television broadcasting.

Questions

1   In a distant galaxy, the planet Odyssey is orbited by two
   small moons Scylla and Charybdis, labelled O, S and C
   respectively in the diagram. The distances of the moons from
   the centre of the planet are 5R and 4R, where R is the radius
   of the planet.

   a   Copy the diagram and draw a gravitational field
      line of the planet passing through moon S.   [1]

   b   The radius R of the planet is 2.0×10^7 m. The
      gravitational field strength g at its surface is
      $40 \, \text{N kg}^{-1}$.

      i   Write down a formula for the gravitational
         field strength g at the surface of the planet
         of mass M.   [1]

      ii   Use the data above to show that the gravitational
         field strength at S is $1.6 \, \text{N kg}^{-1}$.   [2]

      iii   Show that the gravitational field strength at C is $2.5 \, \text{N kg}^{-1}$.   [1]

      iv   Using an average value of g, estimate the increase ΔE in gravitational
         potential energy of a small space vehicle of mass 3.0×10^3 kg when it
         moves from the orbit of C to the orbit of S.   [3]

   c   Calculate the orbital period of S. Assume that the gravitational effects of
      the two moons on each other are negligible in comparison to the
      gravitational force of O.   [4]

OCR Physics A2 (2824) June 2007   [Total 12]

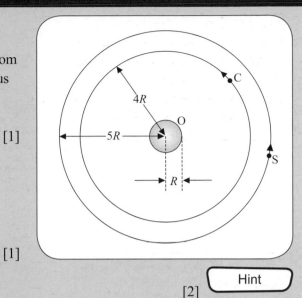

Hint

Hint

Answer

2   a   The diagram shows a graph of the variation of the gravitational field strength g of
      the Earth with distance r from its centre.

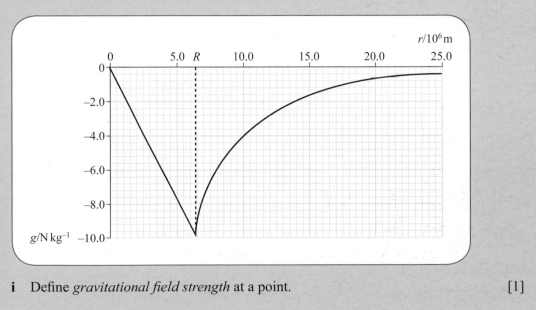

   i   Define *gravitational field strength* at a point.   [1]

continued

ii Write down an algebraic expression for the gravitational field strength g at the surface of the Earth in terms of its mass M, its radius R and the universal gravitational constant G. [1]

iii Use data from the diagram and the value of G to show that the mass of the Earth is 6.0×10^{24} kg. [2]

Hint

iv State which feature of the graph in the diagram indicates that the gravitational field strength at a point below the surface of the Earth, assumed to be of uniform density, is proportional to the distance from the centre of the Earth. [1]

v Calculate the two distances from the centre of the Earth at which $g = 0.098 \, \text{N} \, \text{kg}^{-1}$. Explain how you arrived at your answers. [4]

b A spacecraft on a journey from the Earth to the Moon feels no resultant gravitational pull from the Earth and the Moon when it has travelled to a point 0.9 of the distance between their centres. Calculate the mass of the Moon, using the value for the mass of the Earth in a iii. [3]

Hint

OCR Physics A2 (2824) June 2006 [Total 12]

Answer

3 a Define *gravitational field strength* at a point in a gravitational field. [1]

b The diagram shows how the gravitational field strength g varies with distance r from the <u>centre</u> of the planet of radius 2.0×10^7 m.

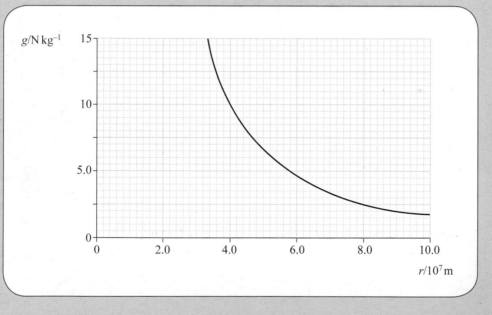

i Use the diagram to write down the value of g in $\text{N} \, \text{kg}^{-1}$ at a height of 4.0×10^7 m above the <u>surface</u>. [1]

Hint

continued

    ii Write down an algebraic expression for g at a distance r from the centre of the planet. The planet can be treated as a point mass of magnitude M situated at its centre. [1]

    iii The value of g at the surface is $40\,\mathrm{N\,kg^{-1}}$. Use this information and your answer to **ii** to check, by a suitable calculation, your answer to **i**. [2]

OCR Physics A2 (2824) June 2005   [Total 5]

Answer

4 A binary star is a pair of stars which move in circular orbits around their common centre of mass. For stars of equal mass, they move in the same circular orbit, shown by the dotted line in the diagram. In this question, consider the stars to be point masses situated at their centres at opposite ends of a diameter of the orbit.

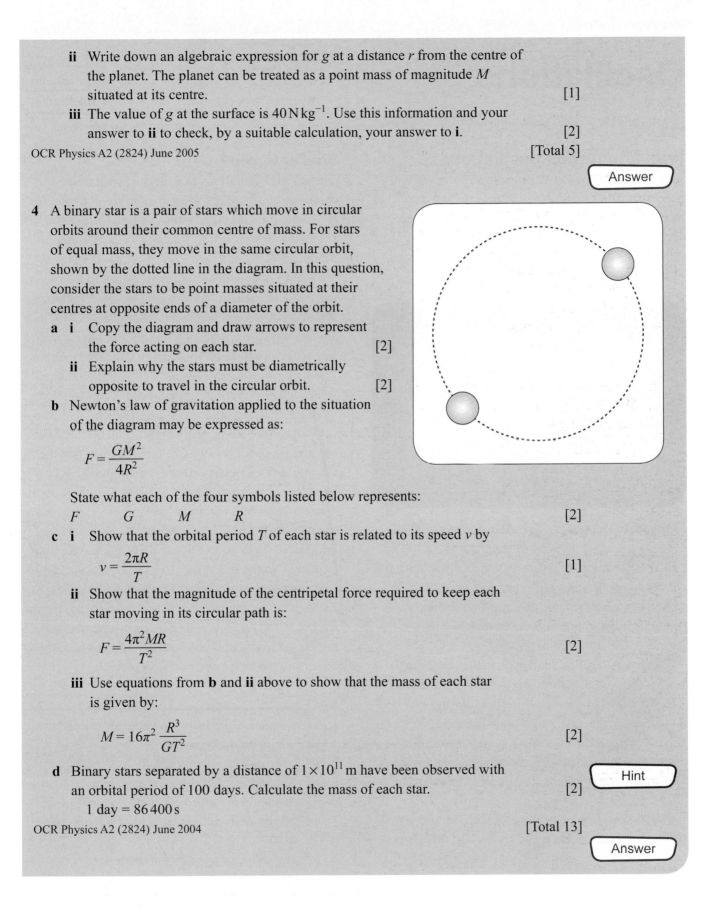

  a **i** Copy the diagram and draw arrows to represent the force acting on each star. [2]

    ii Explain why the stars must be diametrically opposite to travel in the circular orbit. [2]

  b Newton's law of gravitation applied to the situation of the diagram may be expressed as:

$$F = \frac{GM^2}{4R^2}$$

State what each of the four symbols listed below represents:

    F G M R [2]

  c **i** Show that the orbital period T of each star is related to its speed v by

$$v = \frac{2\pi R}{T}$$

[1]

    ii Show that the magnitude of the centripetal force required to keep each star moving in its circular path is:

$$F = \frac{4\pi^2 MR}{T^2}$$

[2]

    iii Use equations from **b** and **ii** above to show that the mass of each star is given by:

$$M = 16\pi^2 \frac{R^3}{GT^2}$$

[2]

  d Binary stars separated by a distance of $1 \times 10^{11}\,\mathrm{m}$ have been observed with an orbital period of 100 days. Calculate the mass of each star. [2]

Hint

    1 day = $86\,400\,\mathrm{s}$

OCR Physics A2 (2824) June 2004   [Total 13]

Answer

Chapter 5

Oscillations

Objectives

Free and forced oscillations

A bird in flight flaps its wings up and down (Figure 5.1). An aircraft's wings also vibrate up and down, but this is not how it flies. The wings are long and thin, and they vibrate slightly because they are not perfectly rigid. Many other structures vibrate – bridges when traffic flows across, buildings in high winds.

Figure 5.1 The wings of a bird oscillate as it flies.

A more specific term than vibration is **oscillation**. An object **oscillates** when it moves back and forth repeatedly, on either side of some equilibrium position. If we stop the object from oscillating, it returns to the equilibrium position.

We make use of oscillations in many different ways – for pleasure (a child on a swing), for music (the vibrations of a guitar string), for timing (the movement of a pendulum or the vibrations of a quartz crystal). Whenever we make a sound, the molecules of the air oscillate, passing the sound energy along. The atoms of a solid vibrate more and more as the temperature rises.

These examples of oscillations and vibrations may seem very different from one another. In this chapter, we will look at the characteristics that are shared by all oscillations.

Free or forced?

The easiest oscillations to understand are free oscillations. If you pluck a guitar string, it continues to vibrate for some time after you have released it. It vibrates at a particular frequency (the number of vibrations per unit time). This is called its **natural frequency** of vibration, and it gives rise to the particular note that you hear. Change the length of the string, and you change the natural frequency. In a similar way, the prongs of a tuning fork have a natural frequency of vibration, which you can observe when you strike it on a cork. Every oscillator has a natural frequency of vibration, the frequency with which it vibrates freely after an initial disturbance.

On the other hand, many objects can be forced to vibrate. If you sit on a bus, you may notice that the vibrations from the engine are transmitted to your body, causing you to vibrate with the same frequency. These are not free vibrations of your body; they are forced vibrations. Their frequency is not the natural frequency of vibration of your body, but the forcing frequency of the bus.

In the same way, you can force a metre ruler to oscillate by waving it up and down; however, its natural frequency of vibration will be much greater than this, as you will discover if you hold one end down on the bench and twang the other end (Figure 5.2).

SAQ

1 State which of the following are free oscillations, and which are forced:
   a the wing beat of a mosquito
   b the movement of the pendulum in a grandfather clock
   c the vibrations of a cymbal after it has been struck
   d the shaking of a building during an earthquake.

Answer

Figure 5.2 A ruler vibrating freely at its natural frequency.

Observing oscillations

Many oscillations are too rapid or too small for us to observe. Our eyes cannot respond rapidly enough if the frequency of oscillation is more than about 5 Hz (five oscillations per second); anything faster than this appears as a blur. In order to see the general characteristics of oscillating systems, we need to find suitable systems that oscillate slowly. Here are three suitable situations to look at.

A mass–spring system

A trolley, loaded with extra masses, is tethered by identical springs in between two clamps (Figure 5.3). Displace the trolley to one side and it will oscillate back and forth along the bench. Listen to the sound of the trolley moving. Where is it moving fastest? What happens to its speed as it reaches the ends of its oscillation? What is happening to the springs as the trolley oscillates?

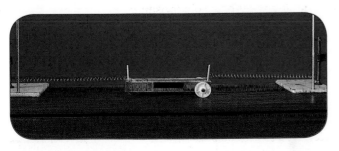

Figure 5.3 A trolley tethered between springs will oscillate freely from side to side.

A long pendulum

A string, at least 2 m long, hangs from the ceiling with a large mass fixed at the end (Figure 5.4). Pull the mass some distance to one side, and let go. The pendulum will swing back and forth at its natural frequency of oscillation. Try to note the characteristics of its motion. In what ways is it similar to the motion of the oscillating trolley? In what ways is it different?

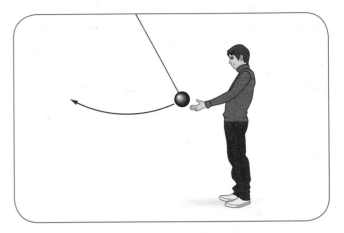

Figure 5.4 A long pendulum oscillates back and forth.

A loudspeaker cone

A signal generator, set to a low frequency (say, 1 Hz), drives a loudspeaker so that it vibrates (Figure 5.5). You need to be able to see the cone of the loudspeaker. How does this motion compare with that of the pendulum and the mass–spring system? Try using a higher frequency (say, 100 Hz). Use an electronic stroboscope flashing at a similar frequency to show up the movement of the cone. (It may help to paint a white spot on the centre of the cone.) Do you observe the same pattern of movement?

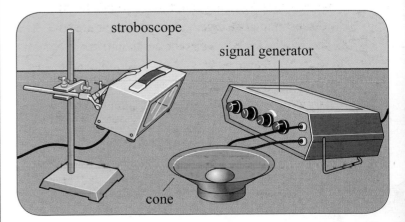

Figure 5.5 A loudspeaker cone forced to vibrate up and down.

SAQ

2 If you could draw a velocity against time graph for any of these oscillators, what would it look like? Would it be a curve like the one shown in Figure 5.6a, or triangular (saw-toothed) like the one shown in Figure 5.6b?

Answer

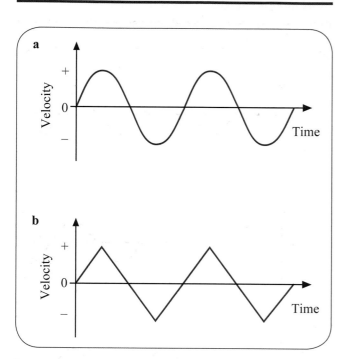

Figure 5.6 Two possible velocity against time graphs for vibrating objects.

Describing oscillations

All of these examples show the same pattern of movement. The trolley accelerates as it moves towards the centre of the oscillation. It is moving fastest at the centre. It decelerates as it moves towards the end of the oscillation. At the extreme position, it stops momentarily, reverses its direction and accelerates back towards the centre again.

Amplitude, period and frequency

Many oscillating systems can be represented by a displacement against time graph like that shown in Figure 5.7. The displacement varies in a smooth way on either side of the midpoint. The shape of this graph is a sine curve, and the motion is described as *sinusoidal*.

Notice that the displacement changes between positive and negative values, as the object moves through the equilibrium position. The maximum displacement from the equilibrium position is called the **amplitude** of the oscillation.

The displacement against time graph can also be used to find the period and frequency of the oscillation. The **period** T is the time for one complete oscillation. Note that the oscillating object must go from one side to the other and back again (or the equivalent). The **frequency** f is the number of oscillations per unit time, and so f is the reciprocal of T:

$$\text{frequency} = \frac{1}{\text{period}} \quad \text{or} \quad f = \frac{1}{T}$$

The equation above can also be written as:

$$\text{period} = \frac{1}{\text{frequency}} \quad \text{or} \quad T = \frac{1}{f}$$

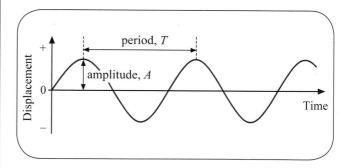

Figure 5.7 A displacement against time graph to show the meanings of amplitude and period.

SAQ

3 From the displacement against time graph shown in Figure 5.8, determine the amplitude, period and frequency of the oscillations represented.

Hint

Answer

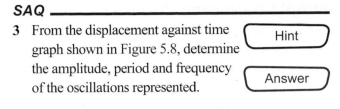
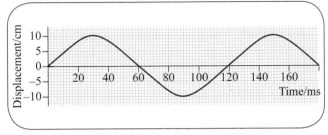

Figure 5.8 A displacement against time graph for an oscillator.

Phase

The term **phase** describes the point that an oscillating mass has reached within the complete cycle of an oscillation. It is often important to describe the **phase difference** between two oscillations. The graph of Figure 5.9a shows two oscillations which are identical except for their phase difference. They are out of step with one another. In this example, they have a phase difference of one-quarter of an oscillation. Phase difference can be measured as a fraction of an oscillation, in degrees or in radians (see Worked example 1).

SAQ

4 a Figure 5.9b shows two oscillations which are out of phase. By what fraction of an oscillation are they out of phase?

b Why would it not make sense to ask the same question about Figure 5.9c?

Answer

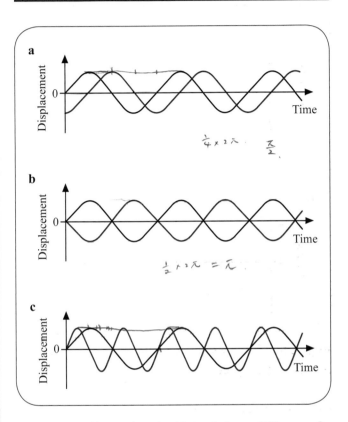

Figure 5.9 Illustrating the idea of phase difference.

Worked example 1

Figure 5.10 shows displacement against time graphs for two identical oscillators. Calculate the phase difference between the two oscillations. Give your answer in degrees and in radians.

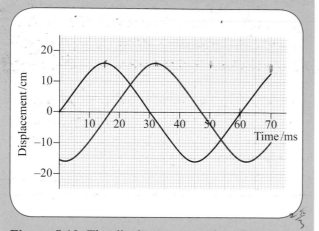

Figure 5.10 The displacement against time graphs of two oscillators with the same period.

Step 1 Measure the time interval t between two corresponding points on the graphs.

$t = 17\,\text{ms}$

Step 2 Determine the period T for one complete oscillation.

$T = 60\,\text{ms}$

Step 3 Now you can calculate the phase difference as a fraction of an oscillation.

phase difference = fraction of an oscillation

Therefore:

phase difference $= \dfrac{t}{T} = \dfrac{17}{60} = 0.283$ oscillation

Step 4 Convert to degrees and radians.

There are 360° and 2π rad in one oscillation.

phase difference $= 0.283 \times 360° = 102° \approx 100°$

phase difference $= 0.283 \times 2\pi\,\text{rad} = 1.78\,\text{rad}$
$\approx 1.8\,\text{rad}$

Simple harmonic motion

There are many situations where we can observe the special kind of oscillations called **simple harmonic motion** (s.h.m.). Some are more obvious than others. For example, the vibrating strings of a musical instrument show s.h.m. When plucked or bowed, the strings move back and forth about the equilibrium position of their oscillation. The motion of the tethered trolley in Figure 5.3 and of the pendulum in Figure 5.4 is also s.h.m. (Simple harmonic motion is defined in terms of the acceleration and displacement of an oscillator – see page 62.)

Here are some other, less obvious, situations where simple harmonic motion can be found.

- When a pure (single tone) sound wave travels through air, the molecules of the air vibrate with s.h.m.
- When an alternating current flows in a wire, the electrons in the wire vibrate with s.h.m.
- There is a small alternating electric current in a radio or television aerial when it is tuned to a signal, in the form of electrons moving with s.h.m.
- The atoms that make up a molecule vibrate with s.h.m. (see for example the hydrogen molecule in Figure 5.11a).

Oscillations can be very complex, with many different frequencies of oscillation occurring at the same time. Examples include the vibrations of

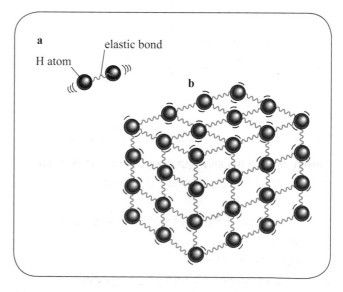

Figure 5.11 We can think of the bonds between atoms as being springy; this leads to vibrations in **a** a molecule of hydrogen and **b** a solid crystal.

machinery, the motion of waves on the sea, and the vibration of a solid crystal formed when atoms, ions or molecules bond together (Figure 5.11b). It is possible to break down a complex oscillation into a sum of simple oscillations, and so we will focus our attention in this chapter on s.h.m. with only one frequency. We will also concentrate on large-scale mechanical oscillations, but you should bear in mind that this analysis can be extended to the situations mentioned above, and many more besides.

The requirements for s.h.m.

If a simple pendulum is undisturbed, it is in equilibrium. The string and the mass will hang vertically. To start it swinging (Figure 5.12), it must be pulled to one side of its equilibrium position. The forces on the mass are unbalanced and so it moves back towards its equilibrium position. The mass swings past this point and continues until it comes to rest momentarily at the other side; the process is then repeated in the opposite direction. Note that a complete oscillation is from right to left and back again.

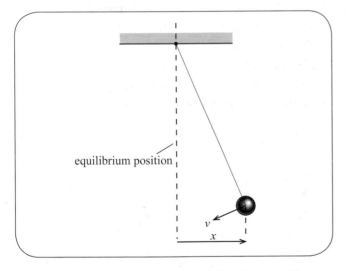

Figure 5.12 This swinging pendulum has positive displacement x and negative velocity v.

The three requirements for s.h.m. of a mechanical system are:

1 a mass that oscillates
2 a position where the mass is in equilibrium (conventionally, displacement x to the right of this position is taken as positive; to the left it is negative)

3 a restoring force that acts to return the mass to its equilibrium position; the restoring force F is directly proportional to the displacement x of the mass from its equilibrium position and is directed towards that point.

SAQ

5 Identify the features of the motion of the simple pendulum that satisfy the three requirements for s.h.m.

       Answer

6 Explain why the motion of someone jumping up and down on a trampoline is not simple harmonic motion. (Their feet lose contact with the trampoline during each bounce.)

       Answer

The changes of velocity in s.h.m.

As the pendulum swings back and forth, its velocity is constantly changing. As it swings from right to left (as shown in Figure 5.12) its velocity is negative. It accelerates towards the equilibrium position and then decelerates as it approaches the other end of the oscillation. It has positive velocity as it swings back from left to right. Again, it is has maximum speed as it travels through the equilibrium position and decelerates as it swings up to its starting position.

This pattern of acceleration – deceleration – changing direction – acceleration again is characteristic of simple harmonic motion. There are no sudden changes of velocity. In the next section we will see how we can observe these changes and how we can represent them graphically.

Graphical representations of s.h.m.

If you set up a trolley tethered between springs (Figure 5.13) you can hear the characteristic rhythm of s.h.m. as the trolley oscillates back and forth. By adjusting the mass carried by the trolley, you can achieve oscillations with a period of about two seconds.

The motion sensor allows you to record how the displacement of the trolley varies with time. Ultrasonic pulses from the sensor are reflected by the card on the trolley and the reflected pulses are detected. This 'sonar' technique allows the sensor to determine the displacement of the trolley. A typical screen display is shown in Figure 5.14.

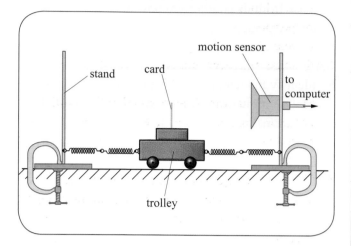

Figure 5.13 A motion sensor can be used to investigate s.h.m. of a spring–trolley system.

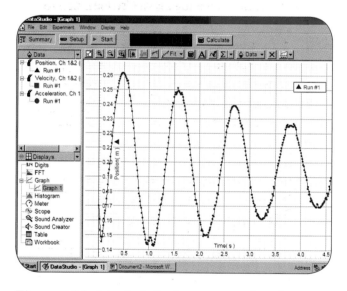

Figure 5.14 A typical displacement against time graph generated by a motion sensor.

The computer can then determine the velocity of the trolley by calculating the rate of change of displacement. Similarly, it can calculate the rate of change of velocity to determine the acceleration.

Idealised graphs of displacement, velocity and acceleration against time are shown in Figure 5.15. We will examine these graphs in sequence to see what they tell us about s.h.m. and how the three graphs are related to one another.

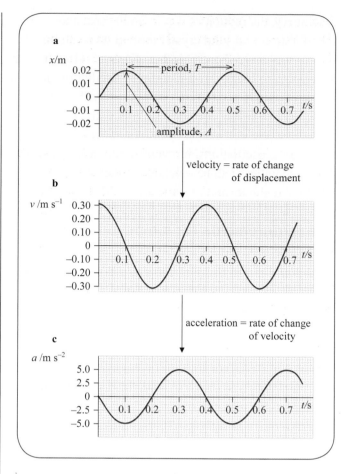

Figure 5.15 Displacement, velocity and acceleration against time graphs for s.h.m.

Displacement x against time t graph

The displacement of the oscillating mass varies according to the smooth curve shown in Figure 5.15a. Mathematically, this is a sine curve; its variation is described as *sinusoidal*. Note that this graph allows us to determine the amplitude A and the period T of the oscillations. In this graph, the displacement x of the oscillation is shown as zero at the start, when t is zero. We have chosen to consider the motion to start when the mass is at the midpoint of its oscillation (equilibrium position) and is moving to the right. We could have chosen any other point in the cycle as the starting point, but it is conventional to start as shown here.

Velocity *v* against time *t* graph

The velocity *v* of the oscillator at any time can be determined from the gradient of the displacement against time graph:

$$v = \frac{\Delta x}{\Delta t}$$

Again, we have a smooth curve (Figure 5.15b), which shows how the velocity *v* depends on time *t*. The shape of the curve is the same as for the displacement against time graph, but it starts at a different point in the cycle. When time $t = 0$, the mass is at the equilibrium position and this is where it is moving fastest. Hence the velocity has its maximum value at this point. Its value is positive because at time $t = 0$ it is moving towards the right.

Acceleration *a* against time *t* graph

Finally, the acceleration *a* of the oscillator at any time can be determined from the gradient of the velocity against time graph:

$$a = \frac{\Delta v}{\Delta t}$$

This gives a third curve of the same general form (Figure 5.15c), which shows how the acceleration *a* depends on time *t*. At the start of the oscillation, the mass is at its equilibrium position. There is no resultant force acting on it so its acceleration is zero. As it moves to the right, the restoring force acts towards the left, giving it a negative acceleration. The acceleration has its greatest value when the mass is displaced furthest from the equilibrium position. Notice that the acceleration graph is 'upside-down' compared with the displacement graph. This shows that:

acceleration ∝ − displacement

or

$$a \propto -x$$

In other words, whenever the mass has a positive displacement (to the right), its acceleration is to the left, and vice versa.

SAQ

7 Use the graphs shown in Figure 5.15 to determine the values of the following quantities:
  a amplitude
  b period
  c maximum velocity
  d maximum acceleration.

8 State at what point in an oscillation the oscillator has zero velocity but positive acceleration.

9 Look at the *x* against *t* graph of Figure 5.15a. When $t = 0.1\,$s, what is the gradient of the graph? State the velocity at this instant.

10 Figure 5.16 shows the displacement *x* against time *t* graph for an oscillating mass. Use the graph to determine the following quantities:
  a the velocity in cm s⁻¹ when $t = 0\,$s
  b the maximum velocity in cm s⁻¹
  c the acceleration in cm s⁻² when $t = 1.0\,$s.

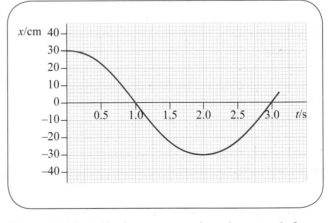

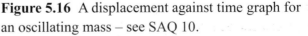

Figure 5.16 A displacement against time graph for an oscillating mass – see SAQ 10.

Frequency and angular frequency

The frequency f of s.h.m. is equal to the number of oscillations per unit time. As we saw earlier, f is related to the period T by

$$f = \frac{1}{T}$$

We can think of a complete oscillation of an oscillator or a cycle of s.h.m. as being represented by 2π radians. (This is similar to a complete cycle of circular motion, where an object moves round through 2π radians.) The phase of the oscillation changes by 2π rad during one oscillation. Hence, if there are f oscillations in unit time, there must be $2\pi f$ radians in unit time. This quantity is the **angular frequency** of the s.h.m. and it is represented by the symbol ω.

The angular frequency ω is thus related to frequency f by the following equation:

$$\omega = 2\pi f$$

Since $f = \frac{1}{T}$, the angular frequency ω is related to the period T of the oscillator by the equation:

$$\omega = \frac{2\pi}{T} \qquad \text{or} \qquad T = \frac{2\pi}{\omega}$$

In Figure 5.17, a single cycle of s.h.m. is shown, but with the x-axis marked with the phase of the motion in radians.

Extension _____

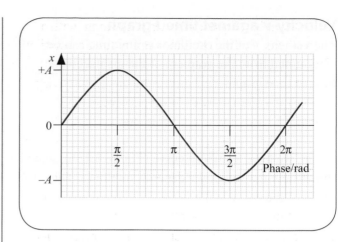

Figure 5.17 The phase of an oscillation varies from 0 to 2π during one cycle.

SAQ

11 An object moving with s.h.m. goes through two complete cycles in 1.0 s. Calculate:
   a the period T
   b the frequency f
   c the angular frequency ω.

Answer

12 Figure 5.18 shows the displacement against time graph for an oscillating mass. Use the graph to determine the following:
   a amplitude
   b period
   c frequency
   d angular frequency
   e displacement at A
   f velocity at B
   g velocity at C.

Hint

Answer

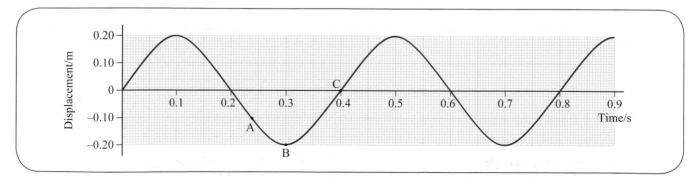

Figure 5.18 A displacement against time graph – see SAQ 12.

13 An atom in a crystal vibrates with s.h.m. with a frequency of 10^{14} Hz. The amplitude of its motion is 2.0×10^{-12} m.

  a Sketch a graph to show how the displacement of the atom varies during one cycle.

  b Use your graph to estimate the maximum velocity of the atom.

Hint

Answer

Equations of s.h.m.

The graph of Figure 5.15a shown earlier represents how the displacement of an oscillator varies during s.h.m. We have already mentioned that this is a sine curve. We can present the same information in the form of an equation. The relationship between the displacement x and the time t is as follows:

$$x = A \sin (2\pi f t)$$

where A is the amplitude of the motion and f is its frequency. Sometimes the same motion is represented using a cosine function, rather than a sine function:

$$x = A \cos (2\pi f t)$$

The difference between these two equations is illustrated in Figure 5.19. The sine version starts at $x = 0$; i.e. the oscillating mass is at its equilibrium position when $t = 0$. The cosine version starts at $x = A$, so that the mass is at its maximum displacement when $t = 0$.

Note that, in calculations using these equations, the quantity $(2\pi f t)$ is in radians. Make sure that your calculator is in radian mode for any calculation (see Worked example 2). The presence of the π in the equation should remind you of this.

Worked example 2

A pendulum oscillates with frequency 1.5 Hz and amplitude 0.10 m. If it is passing through its equilibrium position when $t = 0$, write an equation to represent its displacement x in terms of amplitude A, frequency f and time t. Determine its displacement when $t = 0.50$ s.

Step 1 Select the correct equation. In this case, the displacement is zero when $t = 0$, so we use the sine form:

$$x = A \sin (2\pi f t)$$

Step 2 Substitute values using the information given in the question: $A = 0.10$ m, $f = 1.5$ Hz. So:

$$x = 0.10 \sin (2\pi \times 1.5 \times t)$$
$$x = 0.10 \sin (3.0\pi t)$$

Step 3 To find x when $t = 0.50$ s, substitute for t and calculate the answer:

$$x = 0.10 \sin (2\pi \times 1.5 \times 0.50) = 0.10 \sin (4.713)$$
$$= -0.10 \text{ m}$$

This means that the pendulum is at the extreme end of its oscillation; the minus sign means that it is at the negative or left-hand end, assuming you have chosen to consider displacements to the right as positive.

(If your calculation above went like this: $x = 0.1 \sin (2\pi \times 1.5 \times 0.5) = 0.1 \sin (4.713)$ $= -8.2 \times 10^{-3}$ m, then your calculator was set to work in degrees, not radians.)

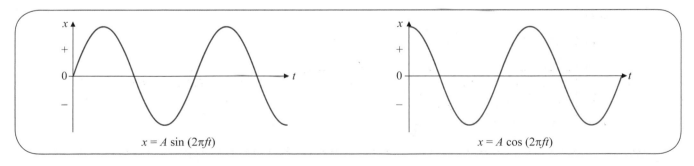

$x = A \sin (2\pi f t)$ $x = A \cos (2\pi f t)$

Figure 5.19 These two graphs represent the same simple harmonic motion. The difference in starting positions is related to the sine and cosine forms of the equation for x as a function of t.

SAQ

14 The vibration of a component in a machine is represented by the equation:

$$x = 3.0 \times 10^{-4} \sin(240\pi t)$$

where the displacement x is in metres. Determine the **a** amplitude, **b** frequency and **c** period of the vibration.

 Answer

15 A trolley is at rest, tethered between two springs. It is pulled 0.15 m to one side and, when time $t = 0$, it is released so that it oscillates back and forth with s.h.m. The period of its motion is 2.0 s. Write an equation for its displacement x at any time t (assume that the motion is not damped by frictional forces). Sketch a displacement against time graph to show two cycles of the motion, giving values where appropriate. Answer

Acceleration and displacement

In s.h.m., an object's acceleration depends on how far it is displaced from its equilibrium position. The greater the displacement x, the greater the acceleration a. In fact, a is proportional to x. We can write the following equation to represent this:

$$a = -(2\pi f)^2 x$$

This equation shows that a is proportional to x; the constant of proportionality is $(2\pi f)^2$. The minus sign shows that, when the object is displaced to the *right*, the direction of its acceleration is to the *left*. The acceleration is always directed towards the equilibrium position.

It should not be surprising that frequency f appears in this equation. Imagine a mass hanging on a spring, so that it can vibrate up and down. If the spring is stiff, the mass will be accelerated more for a given displacement and its frequency of oscillation will be higher. The equation:

$$a = -(2\pi f)^2 x$$

helps us to define simple harmonic motion. The acceleration a is directly proportional to displacement x; and the minus sign shows that it is in the opposite direction.

Simple harmonic motion is defined as follows:

A body executes simple harmonic motion if its acceleration is directly proportional to its displacement from its equilibrium position, and is always directed towards the equilibrium position.

If a and x were in the same direction (no minus sign), the body's acceleration would increase as it moved away from the fixed point and it would move away faster and faster, never to return.

Figure 5.20 shows the acceleration a against displacement x graph for an oscillator executing s.h.m. Note the following:

- The graph is a straight line through the origin ($a \propto x$).
- It has a negative slope (the minus sign in the equation $a = -(2\pi f)^2 x$). This means that the acceleration is always directed towards the equilibrium position.
- The magnitude of the gradient of the graph is $(2\pi f)^2$.
- The gradient is independent of the amplitude of the motion. This means that the frequency f or the period T of the oscillator is independent of the amplitude and so a simple harmonic oscillator keeps steady time.

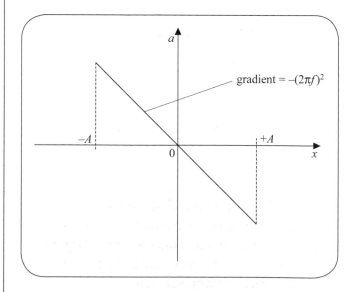

Figure 5.20 Acceleration a against displacement x graph for an oscillator executing s.h.m.

Maximum speed of an oscillator

If an oscillator is executing simple harmonic motion, it has maximum speed when it passes through its equilibrium position. This is when its displacement x is zero. The maximum speed v_{max} of the oscillator depends on the frequency f of the motion and on the amplitude A. The maximum speed is given by:

$$v_{max} = (2\pi f)A$$

According to this equation, for a given oscillation:

$$v_{max} \propto A$$

A simple harmonic oscillator has a period that is independent of the amplitude. A greater amplitude means that the oscillator has to travel a greater distance in the same time – hence it has a greater speed.

The equation also shows that:

$$v_{max} \propto f$$

Increasing the frequency means a shorter period. A given distance is covered in a shorter time – hence it has a greater speed.

Have another look at Figure 5.15. The period of the motion is 0.40 s and the amplitude of the motion is 0.02 m. The frequency f can be calculated as follows:

$$f = \frac{1}{T} = \frac{1}{0.40} = 2.5 \text{ Hz}$$

We can now use the equation $v_{max} = (2\pi f)A$ to determine the maximum speed v_{max}:

$$v_{max} = (2\pi f)A = (2\pi \times 2.5) \times 2.0 \times 10^{-2}$$

$$v_{max} \approx 0.31 \text{ m s}^{-1}$$

This is how the values on Figure 15.5b were calculated.

SAQ

16 A mass secured at the end of a spring moves with s.h.m. The frequency of its motion is 1.4 Hz.

   a Write an equation of the form $a = -(2\pi f)^2 x$ to show how the acceleration of the mass depends on its displacement.

   b Calculate the acceleration of the mass when it is displaced 0.050 m from its equilibrium position.

   Answer

17 A short pendulum oscillates with s.h.m. such that its acceleration a (in m s^{-2}) is related to its displacement x (in m) by the equation $a = -300x$. Determine the frequency of the oscillations.

   Answer

18 The pendulum of a grandfather clock swings from one side to the other in 1.00 s. Calculate:

   a the period of its motion

   b the frequency

   c the angular frequency.

   d Write an equation of the form $a = -(2\pi f)^2 x$ to show how the acceleration of the pendulum weight depends on its displacement.

   Answer

19 A trolley of mass m is fixed to the end of a spring. The spring can be compressed and extended. The spring has a force constant k. The other end of the spring is attached to a vertical wall. The trolley lies on a smooth horizontal table. The trolley oscillates when it is displaced from its equilibrium position.

   a Show that the motion of the oscillating trolley is s.h.m.

   b Show that the period T of the trolley is given by the equation

$$T = 2\pi \sqrt{\frac{m}{k}}.$$

   Answer

Big ideas in physics

This study of simple harmonic motion illustrates some important aspects of physics.

● Physicists often take a complex problem (such as, how do the atoms in a solid vibrate?) and reduce it to a simpler, more manageable problem (such as, how does a mass–spring system vibrate?). This is simpler because we know that the spring obeys Hooke's law, so that force is proportional to displacement.

continued

- Physicists generally feel happier if they can write mathematical equations which will give numerical answers to problems. The equation $a = -(2\pi f)^2 x$ which describes s.h.m. can be solved to give the sine and cosine equations we have considered above.
- Once physicists have solved one problem like this, they look around for other situations where they can use the same ideas all over again. So the mass–spring theory also works well for vibrating atoms and molecules, for objects bobbing up and down in water, and in many other situations.
- They also seek to modify the theory to fit a greater range of situations. For example, what happens if the spring doesn't obey Hooke's law? What happens if the vibrating mass experiences a frictional force as it oscillates? (The answer to this latter question appears later in this chapter.)

Your Advanced Physics course will help you to build up your appreciation of some of these big ideas – fields (magnetic, electric, gravitational), energy and so on.

Energy changes in s.h.m.

During simple harmonic motion, there is a constant interchange of energy between two forms: potential and kinetic. We can see this by considering the mass–spring system shown in Figure 5.21. When the mass is pulled to one side (to start the oscillations), one spring is compressed and the other is stretched. The springs store elastic potential energy. When the mass is released, it moves back towards the equilibrium position, accelerating as it goes. It has increasing kinetic energy. The potential energy stored in the springs decreases while the kinetic energy of the mass increases by the same amount (as long as there are no heat losses due to frictional forces). Once the mass has passed the equilibrium position, its kinetic energy decreases and the energy is transferred back to the springs. Provided the oscillations are undamped, the total energy in the system remains constant.

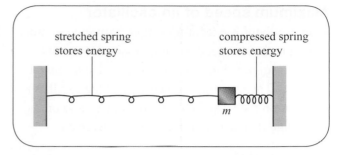

Figure 5.21 The elastic potential energy stored in the springs is converted to kinetic energy when the mass is released.

Energy graphs

We can represent these energy changes in two ways. Figure 5.22 shows how the kinetic energy and elastic potential energy change with time. Potential energy is maximum when displacement is maximum (positive or negative). Kinetic energy is maximum when displacement is zero. The total energy remains constant throughout. Note that both kinetic energy and potential energy go through *two* complete cycles during *one* period of the oscillation. This is because kinetic energy is maximum when the mass is passing through the equilibrium position to the left and to the right. The potential energy is maximum at both ends of the oscillation.

A second way to show this is to draw a graph of how potential energy and kinetic energy vary with displacement (Figure 5.23).

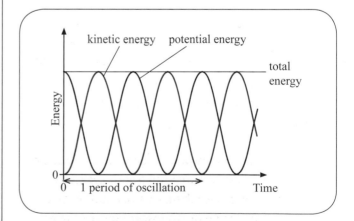

Figure 5.22 The kinetic energy and potential energy of an oscillator vary periodically, but the total energy remains constant if the system is undamped (see page 65).

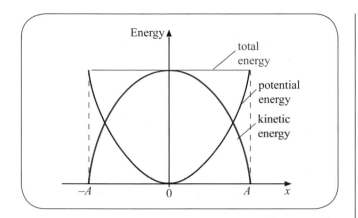

Figure 5.23 The kinetic energy is maximum at zero displacement; the potential energy is maximum at maximum displacement (A and $-A$).

The graph shows that:
- kinetic energy is maximum when displacement $x = 0$
- potential energy is maximum when $x = \pm A$
- at any point on this graph, the total energy (KE + PE) has the same value.

SAQ

20 To start a pendulum swinging, you pull it slightly to one side.

a What kind of energy does this transfer to the mass?

b Describe the energy changes that occur when the mass is released.

21 Figure 5.23 shows how the different forms of energy change with displacement during s.h.m. Copy the graph, and show how the graph would differ if the oscillating mass were given only half the initial input of energy.

22 Figure 5.24 shows how the velocity v of a 2.0 kg mass was found to vary with time t during an investigation of the s.h.m. of a pendulum. Use the graph to determine the following for the mass:

a its maximum velocity

b its maximum kinetic energy

c its maximum potential energy

d its maximum acceleration

e the maximum restoring force that acted on it.

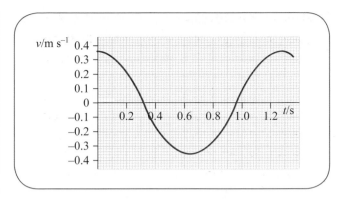

Figure 5.24 A velocity against time graph for a pendulum – see SAQ 22.

Damped oscillations

In principle, oscillations can go on for ever. In practice, however, the oscillations we observe around us do not. They die out, either rapidly or gradually. A child on a swing knows that the amplitude of her swinging will decline until eventually she will come to rest, unless she can put some more energy into the swinging to keep it going.

This happens because of friction. On a swing, there is friction where the swing is attached to the frame and there is friction with the air. The amplitude of the child's oscillations decreases as the friction transfers energy away from her to the surroundings.

We describe these oscillations as **damped**. Their amplitude decreases according to a particular pattern. This is shown in Figure 5.25.

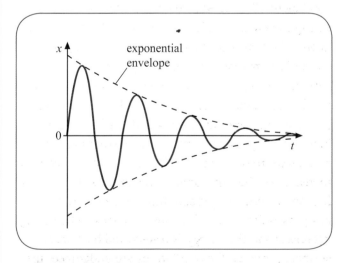

Figure 5.25 Damped oscillations.

The amplitude of damped oscillations does not decrease linearly. It decays exponentially with time. An exponential decay is a particular mathematical pattern that arises as follows. At first, the swing moves rapidly. There is a lot of air resistance to overcome, so the swing loses energy quickly and its amplitude decreases at a high rate. Later, it is moving more slowly. There is less air resistance and so energy is lost more slowly – the amplitude decreases at a lower rate. Hence we get the characteristic curved shape, which is the 'envelope' of the graph in Figure 5.25.

Notice that the frequency of the oscillations does not change as the amplitude decreases. This is a characteristic of simple harmonic motion. The child may swing back and forth once every two seconds, and this stays the same whether the amplitude is large or small.

Investigating damping

You can investigate the exponential decrease in the amplitude of oscillations using a simple laboratory arrangement (Figure 5.26). A hacksaw blade or other springy metal strip is clamped (vertically or horizontally) to the bench. A mass is attached to the free end. This will oscillate freely if you displace it to one side.

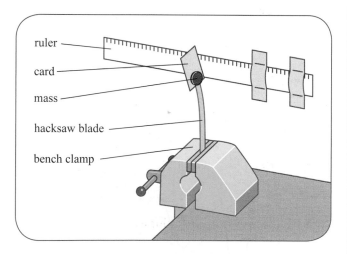
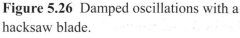

Figure 5.26 Damped oscillations with a hacksaw blade.

A card is attached to the mass so that there is significant air resistance as the mass oscillates. The amplitude of the oscillations decreases and can be measured every five oscillations by judging the position of the blade against a ruler fixed alongside.

A graph of amplitude against time will show the characteristic exponential decrease. You can find the 'half-life' of this exponential decay graph by determining the time it takes to decrease to half its initial amplitude (Figure 5.27).

By changing the size of the card, it is possible to change the degree of damping, and hence alter the half-life of the motion.

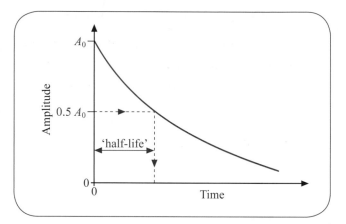
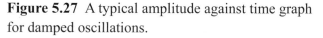

Figure 5.27 A typical amplitude against time graph for damped oscillations.

Energy and damping

Damping can be very useful if we want to get rid of vibrations. For example, a car has springs (Figure 5.28) which make the ride much more comfortable for us when the car goes over a bump. However, we wouldn't want to spend every car journey vibrating up and down as a reminder of the last bump we went over. So the springs are damped by the shock absorbers, and we return rapidly to a smooth ride after every bump.

Figure 5.28 The springs and shock absorbers in a car suspension system form a damped system.

Damping is achieved by introducing the force of friction into a mechanical system. In an undamped oscillation, the total energy of the oscillation remains constant. There is a regular interchange between potential and kinetic energy. By introducing friction, damping has the effect of removing energy from the oscillating system, and the amplitude and maximum speed of the oscillation decrease.

SAQ

23 a Sketch graphs to show how each of the following quantities changes during the course of a single complete oscillation of an undamped pendulum: kinetic energy, potential energy, total energy.

   b State how your graphs would be different for a lightly damped pendulum.

> Answer

Resonance

Resonance is an important physical phenomenon that can appear in a great many different situations. A dramatic example is the Tacoma Narrows bridge disaster (Figure 5.29). This suspension bridge in Washington State, USA, collapsed in a mild gale on 1 July 1940. The wind set up oscillating vortices of air around the bridge, which vibrated more and more violently until it broke up under the stress. The bridge had been in use for just four months; engineers learned a lot about how oscillations can build up when a mechanical structure is subjected to repeated forces.

Figure 5.29 The Tacoma Narrows bridge collapsed in 1940, a victim of resonant failure.

You will have observed a much more familiar example of resonance when pushing a small child on a swing. The swing plus child has a natural frequency of oscillation. A small push on each swing results in the amplitude increasing until the child is swinging high in the air.

Observing resonance

Resonance can be observed with almost any oscillating system. The system is forced to oscillate at a particular frequency. If the forcing frequency happens to match the natural frequency of oscillation of the system, the amplitude of the resulting oscillations can build up to become very large.

Barton's pendulums is a demonstration of this (Figure 5.30). Several pendulums of different lengths hang from a horizontal string. Each has its own natural frequency of oscillation. The 'driver' pendulum at the end is different; it has a large mass at the end, and its length is equal to that of one of the others. When the driver is set swinging, the others gradually start to move. However, only the pendulum whose length matches that of the driver pendulum builds up a large amplitude so that it is resonating.

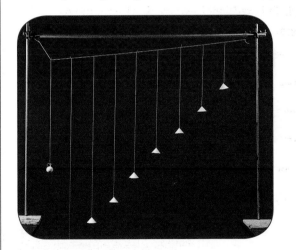

Figure 5.30 Barton's pendulums.

What is going on here? All the pendulums are coupled together by the suspension. As the driver swings, it moves the suspension, which in turn moves the other pendulums. The frequency of the matching pendulum is the same as that of the driver, and so it gains energy and its amplitude gradually builds up. The other pendulums have different natural frequencies, so the driver has little effect.

In a similar way, if you were to push the child on the swing once every three-quarters of an oscillation, you would soon find that the swing was moving backwards as you tried to push it forwards, so that your push would slow it down.

You can observe resonance for yourself with a simple mass–spring system. You need a mass on the end of a spring (Figure 5.31), chosen so that the mass oscillates up and down with a natural frequency of about 1 Hz. Now hold the top end of the spring and move your hand up and down rapidly, with an amplitude of a centimetre or two. Very little happens. Now move your hand up and down more slowly, close to 1 Hz. You should see the mass oscillating with gradually increasing amplitude. Adjust your movements to the exact frequency of the natural vibrations of the mass and you will see the greatest effect.

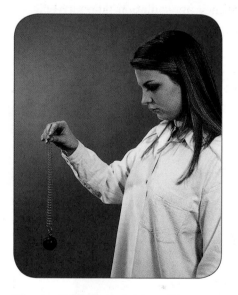

Figure 5.31 Resonance with a mass on a spring.

Defining resonance

For resonance to occur, we must have a system that is capable of oscillating freely. We must also have some way in which the system is forced to oscillate. When the forcing frequency matches the natural frequency of the system, the amplitude of the oscillations grows dramatically.

If the driving frequency does not quite match the natural frequency, the amplitude of the oscillations will increase, but not to the same extent as when resonance is achieved. Figure 5.32 shows how the amplitude of oscillations depends on the driving frequency in the region close to resonance.

In resonance, energy is transferred from the driver to the resonating system more efficiently than when resonance does not occur. For example, in the case of the Tacoma Narrows bridge, energy was transferred from the wind to the bridge, causing very large-amplitude oscillations.

The following statements apply to any system in resonance:

- its natural frequency is equal to the frequency of the driver
- its amplitude is maximum
- it absorbs the greatest possible energy from the driver.

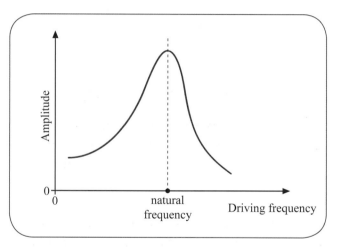

Figure 5.32 Maximum amplitude is achieved when the driving frequency matches the natural frequency of oscillation.

Resonance and damping

During earthquakes, buildings are forced to oscillate by the vibrations of the Earth. Resonance can occur, resulting in serious damage (Figure 5.33). In regions of the world where earthquakes happen regularly, buildings may be built on foundations that absorb the energy of the shock waves. In this way, the vibrations are 'damped' so that the amplitude of the oscillations cannot reach dangerous levels. This is an expensive business, and so far is restricted to the wealthier parts of the world.

increased, the amplitude of the resonant vibrations decreases. The resonance peak becomes broader. There is also an effect on the frequency at which resonance occurs, which becomes slightly lower for a lightly damped system.

Using resonance

As we have seen, resonance can be a problem in mechanical systems. However, it can also be useful. For example, many musical instruments rely on resonance.

Resonance is not confined to mechanical systems. It is made use of in, for example, microwave cooking. The microwaves used have a frequency that matches a natural frequency of vibration of water molecules (the microwave is the 'driver' and the molecule is the 'resonating system'). The water molecules in the food are forced to vibrate and they absorb the energy of the microwave radiation. The water gets hotter and the absorbed energy spreads through the food and cooks or heats it.

Magnetic resonance imaging (MRI) is increasingly used in medicine to produce images such as Figure 5.35, showing aspects of a patient's internal organs.

Figure 5.33 Resonance during the San Francisco earthquake of 1906 caused the collapse of many buildings. The steel structure of a partially built skyscraper remained intact.

Damping is thus useful if we want to reduce the damaging effects of resonance. Figure 5.34 shows how damping alters the resonance response curve of Figure 5.32. Notice that, as the degree of damping is

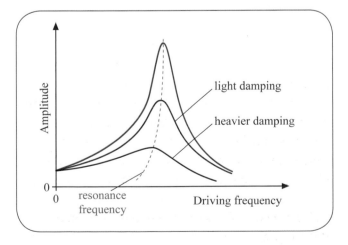

Figure 5.34 Damping reduces the amplitude of resonant vibrations.

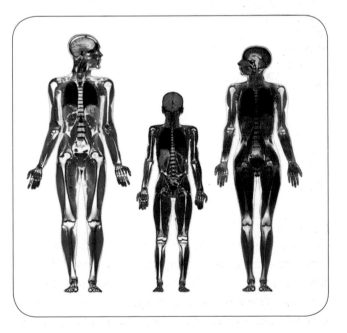

Figure 5.35 This magnetic resonance imaging (MRI) picture shows a man, a woman and a nine-year-old child. The image has been coloured to show up the bones (white), lungs (dark) and other organs. (See Chapter 16.)

Radio waves having a range of frequencies are used, and particular frequencies are absorbed by particular atomic nuclei. The frequency absorbed depends on the type of nucleus and on its surroundings. By analysing the absorption of the radio waves, a computer-generated image can be produced.

A radio or television also depends on resonance for its tuning circuitry. The aerial picks up signals of many different frequencies from many transmitters. The tuner can be adjusted to resonate at the frequency of the transmitting station you are interested in, and the circuit produces a large-amplitude signal for this frequency only.

SAQ

24 List three examples of situations where resonance is a problem, and three others where resonance is useful. In each case, state what the oscillating system is and what forces it to resonate.

(Answer)

Summary

(Glossary)

- Many systems, mechanical and otherwise, will oscillate freely when disturbed from their equilibrium position.

- Some oscillators have motion described as *simple harmonic motion* (s.h.m.). For these systems, graphs of displacement, velocity and acceleration against time are sinusoidal curves – see Figure 5.36.

- During a single cycle of s.h.m., the phase changes by 2π radians. The angular frequency ω of the motion is related to its period T and frequency f by the equations

$$\omega = \frac{2\pi}{T} \quad \text{and} \quad \omega = 2\pi f$$

- In s.h.m., displacement x can be represented as a function of time t by equations of the form:

$$x = A\sin(2\pi f t) \quad \text{and} \quad x = A\cos(2\pi f t)$$

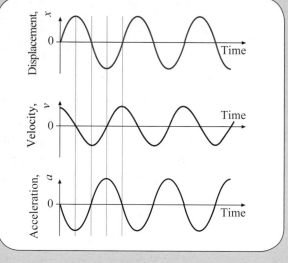

Figure 5.36 Graphs for s.h.m.

- A body executes simple harmonic motion if its acceleration is directly proportional to its displacement from its equilibrium position. The acceleration is always directed towards the equilibrium position.

- Acceleration a is related to displacement x by the equation $a = -(2\pi f)^2 x$.

- The maximum speed v_{max} is given by the equation $v_{max} = (2\pi f)A$.

- The frequency or period of a simple harmonic oscillator is independent of its amplitude.

- In s.h.m., there is a regular interchange between kinetic energy and potential energy.

- Resistive forces remove energy from an oscillating system. This is known as damping. Damping causes the amplitude to decay with time.

- When an oscillating system is forced to vibrate close to its natural frequency, the amplitude of vibration increases rapidly. The amplitude is maximum when the forcing frequency matches the natural frequency of the system; this is resonance.

- Resonance can be a problem, but it can also be very useful.

Questions

1 The external wing mirror of a large vehicle is often connected to the body of the vehicle by a long metal arm (Figure 1). The wing mirror assembly sometimes behaves like a mass on a spring, with the mirror oscillating up and down in simple harmonic motion about its equilibrium position. Figure 2 shows a typical oscillation.

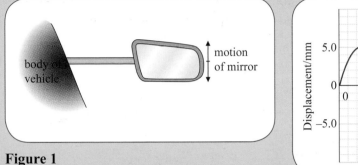

Figure 1

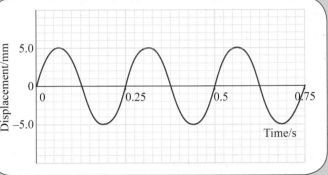

Figure 2

  a **i** Define *simple harmonic motion*. [2]

     ii Calculate the frequency of oscillation of the wing mirror. [2]

     iii Calculate the maximum acceleration of the wing mirror. [3]

  b With the vehicle at rest and the engine running slowly at a particular number of revolutions per second, the wing mirror oscillates significantly, whereas at other engine speeds the mirror hardly moves

     i Explain how this phenomenon is an example of resonance. [3]

     ii Suggest, giving a reason, <u>one</u> change to the motion of the mirror:

        1 for a mirror of greater mass [2]

        2 for a metal arm of greater stiffness. [2]

OCR Physics A2 (2824) June 2006   [Total 14]

> Hint

> Answer

2 This question is about a mass–spring system.

Figure 1 shows a mass attached to two springs. The mass moves along a horizontal tube with one spring stretched and the other compressed. An arrow marked on the mass indicates its position on a scale. Figure 1 shows the situation when the mass is displaced through a distance x from its equilibrium position. The mass is experiencing an acceleration a in the direction shown.

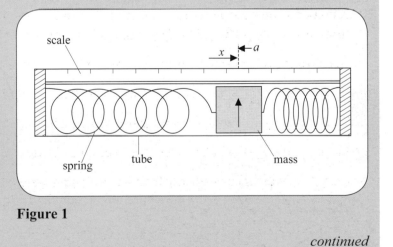

Figure 1

continued

Figure 2 shows a graph of the <u>magnitude</u> of the acceleration a plotted against the displacement x.

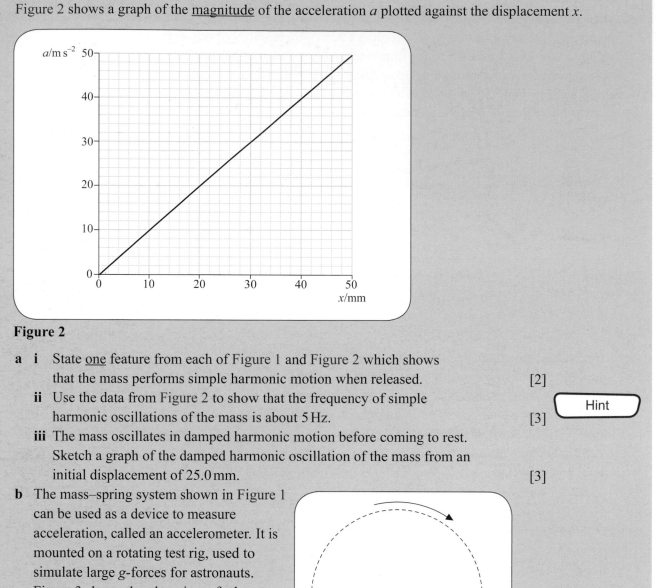

Figure 2

a **i** State <u>one</u> feature from each of Figure 1 and Figure 2 which shows
that the mass performs simple harmonic motion when released. [2]

   ii Use the data from Figure 2 to show that the frequency of simple
harmonic oscillations of the mass is about 5 Hz. [3]

   iii The mass oscillates in damped harmonic motion before coming to rest.
Sketch a graph of the damped harmonic oscillation of the mass from an
initial displacement of 25.0 mm. [3]

b The mass–spring system shown in Figure 1
can be used as a device to measure
acceleration, called an accelerometer. It is
mounted on a rotating test rig, used to
simulate large g-forces for astronauts.
Figure 3 shows the plan view of a long
beam rotating about axis A with the
astronaut seated at end B, facing towards
A. The accelerometer is parallel to the
beam and is fixed under the seat 10 m
from A.

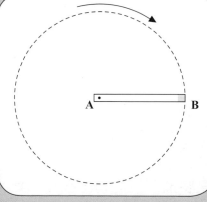

Figure 3

   i When the astronaut is rotating at constant speed, the arrow marked on
the mass has a constant deflection. Explain why. [2]

   ii Calculate the speed v of rotation of the astronaut when the deflection
is 50 mm. [3]

OCR Physics A2 (2824) January 2006

[Total 13]

Hint

Hint

Answer

continued

3 a The diagram shows a toy consisting of a light plastic aeroplane suspended from a long spring.

   i The aeroplane is pulled down 0.040 m and released. It undergoes a vertical harmonic oscillation with a period of 1.0 s. The oscillations are lightly damped. Sketch a graph of the displacement y of the aeroplane against time t from the moment of release to time $t = 4.0$ s. [3]

   ii The aeroplane is replaced by a heavier model made of the same plastic having the same fuselage but larger wings. State and explain two changes which this substitution will make to the displacement against time graph that you have drawn for part i. [4]

 b The top end of the spring in the diagram is then vibrated with a small constant amplitude. The motion of the aeroplane changes as the frequency of the oscillation of the top end of the spring is increased slowly from zero through resonance to 2.0 Hz.

   Explain the conditions for resonance to occur and describe the changes in the motion of the aeroplane as the frequency changes from zero to 2.0 Hz. [5]

OCR Physics A2 (2824) June 2005 [Total 12]

Hint

Answer

4 A mass oscillates on the end of a spring in simple harmonic motion. The graph of the acceleration a of the mass against its displacement x from its equilibrium position is shown in the graph.

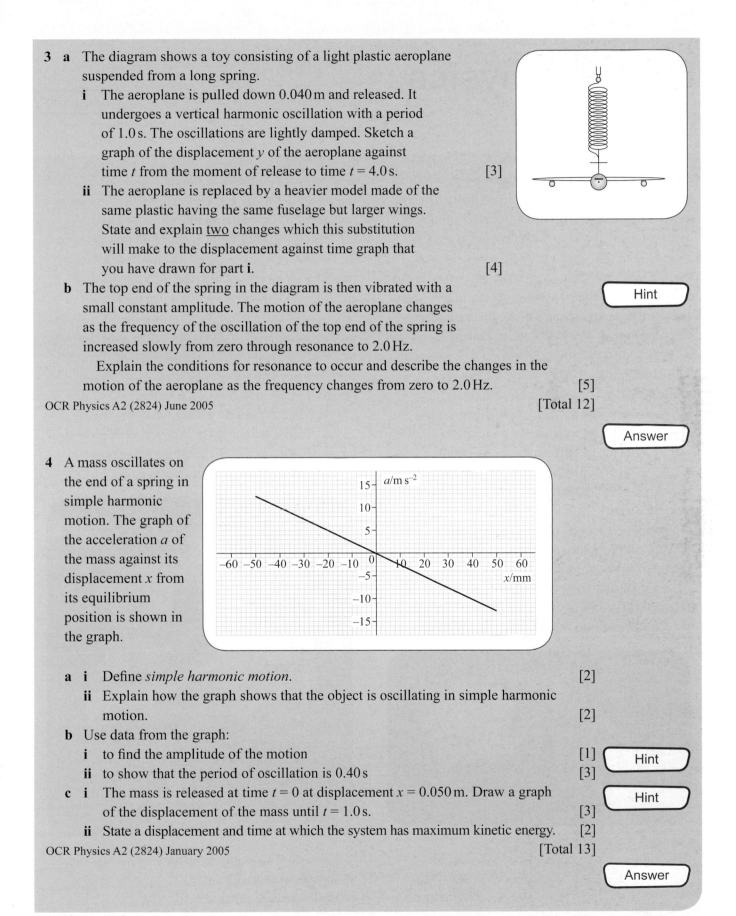

a i Define *simple harmonic motion*. [2]

   ii Explain how the graph shows that the object is oscillating in simple harmonic motion. [2]

 b Use data from the graph:

   i to find the amplitude of the motion [1]

   ii to show that the period of oscillation is 0.40 s [3]

 c i The mass is released at time $t = 0$ at displacement $x = 0.050$ m. Draw a graph of the displacement of the mass until $t = 1.0$ s. [3]

   ii State a displacement and time at which the system has maximum kinetic energy. [2]

OCR Physics A2 (2824) January 2005 [Total 13]

Hint

Hint

Answer

Chapter 6

Thermal physics

Objectives

Modelling the microscopic

In science, we use models. We try to explain many different phenomena using a few simple models – for example, the *wave model* is used to explain sound, light, the behaviour of electrons in metals, the energy levels of electrons in atoms and so on. In this chapter, we are going to look at the *particle model* of matter in order to see some of the different aspects of the behaviour of matter that it can explain.

We live in a macroscopic world. '*Macro*' means large, and our large-scale world includes rocks, trees, buildings, people and other animals, the atmosphere, planets and so on. We can simplify this complex world by focusing on particular materials – metals, stone, plastic, water, air. We can make measurements of many macroscopic properties of these materials – density, temperature, strength, viscosity, elasticity, pressure. However, in science, we are always looking for underlying explanations.

You will be familiar with a microscopic description of matter as being made up of particles. '*Micro*' means small, and these tiny particles may be atoms (Figure 6.1) or ions or molecules. By developing a simple picture of the way in which these particles behave, we can arrive at explanations of many of the macroscopic properties of matter listed above.

There is a great deal of satisfaction for a scientist in the way in which a simple microscopic model can explain a very diverse range of macroscopic phenomena. Nowadays we have techniques for showing up the particles from which matter is made, at least at the level of atoms and molecules. But bear in mind that many of these ideas were developed long before there was any possibility of 'seeing' atoms. In fact, until recently, a textbook like this might well have said that, because atoms are so small, there was no hope of ever seeing an individual atom. Inventions like the scanning tunnelling microscope (Figure 6.2) have changed all this.

Figure 6.2 This scanning tunnelling microscope is capable of showing details of the arrangement of atoms on a scale as small as 10^{-10} m.

Figure 6.1 This image, made using a scanning tunnelling microscope, shows atoms of gold (yellow/orange) on a graphite surface (green).

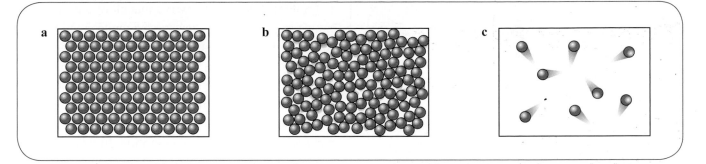

Figure 6.3 Typical arrangements of atoms in **a** a solid, **b** a liquid and **c** a gas.

The kinetic model

The model that we are going to use to describe matter is based on the following assumptions:

- Matter is made up of tiny particles – atoms or molecules.
- These particles tend to move about.

(The word '*kinetic*' means moving.)

For simplicity, we will refer to these particles as 'atoms'. We picture the atoms as small, hard spheres. Figure 6.3 shows the model for the three states of matter: solid, liquid and gas. We describe the differences between these three states in terms of three criteria:

- The *spacing* of the atoms – how far apart are they, on average?
- The *ordering* of the atoms – are they arranged in an orderly or a random way?
- The *motion* of the atoms – are they moving quickly, slowly or not at all?

You should be familiar with the idea that, as a material changes from solid to liquid to gas, there is a change from close spacing to greater spacing, from order to disorder, and from restricted motion to free, fast motion.

SAQ

1 Figure 6.3 illustrates how the kinetic model represents solids, liquids and gases. (These diagrams are two-dimensional representations only.) Explain how the diagrams represent the differences in spacing, ordering and motion of the atoms between the three states of matter.

Answer

Atoms of a gas

We picture the atoms of a gas as being fast-moving. They bounce off the walls of their container (and off each other) as they travel around at high speed. How do we know that these atoms are moving like this?

It is much harder to visualise the atoms of a gas than those of a solid, because they move about in such a disordered way, and most of a gas is empty space. The movement of gas particles was investigated in the 1820s, by a Scottish botanist, Robert Brown. He was looking at pollen grains under a microscope, and saw very small particles moving around inside the grains. He then saw the same motion in particles of dust in the air. It is easier in the laboratory to look at the movement of smoke grains in air.

Observing Brownian motion

The oxygen and nitrogen molecules that make up most of the air are far too small to see; they are much smaller than the wavelength of light. So we have to look at something bigger, to observe the effect of the air molecules. In this experiment (Figure 6.4), the smoke cell contains air into which a small amount of smoke has been introduced. The cell is lit from the side, and the microscope is used to view the smoke grains.

The smoke grains show up as tiny specks of reflected light, but they are too small to see any detail of their shape. What is noticeable is the way they move. If you can concentrate on a single grain, you will see that it follows a somewhat jerky and erratic path. This is a consequence of the repeated collisions between the smoke grain and the air molecules. The erratic motion of the smoke grain provides direct evidence that the air molecules must:

- be moving
- also have haphazard motion.

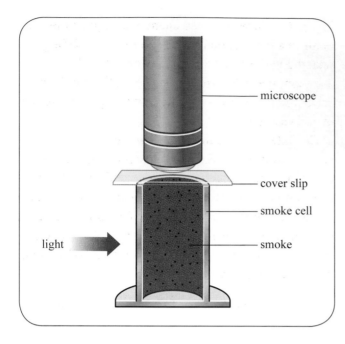

Figure 6.4 Experimental arrangement for observing Brownian motion.

Since the air molecules are much smaller than the smoke grain, we can deduce that they must be moving much faster than the smoke grain if they are to affect it in this way.

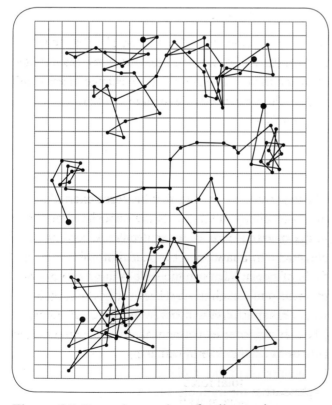

Figure 6.5 Brownian motion of pollen grains, as drawn by the French scientist Jean Perrin.

(Note that you may observe that all of the smoke grains in your field of view have a tendency to travel in one particular direction. This is a consequence of convection currents in the air. Also, you may have to adjust the focus of the microscope to keep track of an individual grain, as it moves up or down in the cell.)

Figure 6.5 shows the sort of path followed by a particle showing Brownian motion. In fact, this is from a scientific paper by the French physicist Jean Perrin, published in 1911. He was looking at the movement of a single pollen grain suspended in water. He recorded its position every 30 s; the grid spacing is approximately 3 μm. From this he could deduce the average speed of the grain and hence work out details of the movement of water molecules.

SAQ

2   Consider a smoke grain of mass M and speed V. It is constantly [Hint] buffeted by air molecules. The mass of a single air molecule is m and it has speed v. It is reasonable to assume that, on average, the smoke grain will have kinetic energy approximately equal to the kinetic energy of a single air molecule.

Show that, since $M \gg m$ (M is much greater than m), it follows that the air molecules must be moving much faster than the smoke grain ($v \gg V$). [Answer]

Fast molecules

For air at standard temperature and pressure (STP – 0 °C and 100 kPa), the average speed of the molecules is about $400 \, \text{m s}^{-1}$. At any moment, some are moving faster than this and others more slowly. If we could follow the movement of a single air molecule, we would find that, some of the time, its speed was greater than this average; at other times it would be less. The velocity (magnitude and direction) of an individual molecule changes every time it collides with anything else.

This value for molecular speed is reasonable. It is comparable to (but greater than) the speed of sound in air (approximately $330 \, \text{m s}^{-1}$ at STP). Very fast-moving particles can easily escape from the Earth's gravitational field. The required escape velocity is about $11\,km\,s^{-1}$. Since we still have an atmosphere, on average the air molecules must be moving much slower than this value.

Explaining pressure

A gas exerts pressure on any surface with which it comes into contact. Pressure is a macroscopic property, defined as the force exerted per unit area of the surface.

The pressure of the atmosphere at sea level is approximately 100 000 Pa. The surface area of a typical person is $2.0\,m^2$. Hence the force exerted on a person by the atmosphere is about 200 000 N. This is equivalent to the weight of about 200 000 apples! Fortunately, air inside the body presses outwards with an equal and opposite force, so we do not collapse under the influence of this large force.

We can explain the macroscopic phenomenon of pressure by thinking about the behaviour of the microscopic particles that make up the atmosphere.

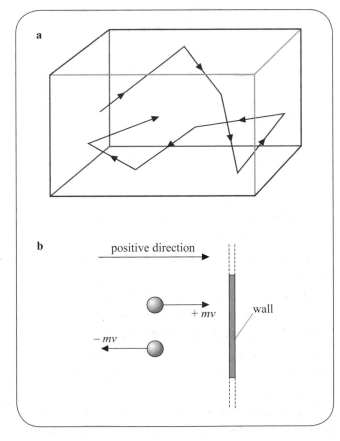

Figure 6.6 a The path of a single molecule in an otherwise empty box. **b** A collision of an individual molecule with the wall of the container; its change in momentum is $-2mv$.

Figure 6.6 shows the movement of a single molecule of air in a box. It bounces around inside, colliding with the various surfaces of the box. At each collision, it exerts a small impulse on the box. The pressure on the box is a result of the impulses exerted by the vast number of molecules in the box.

Consider a molecule of mass m travelling at right angles towards a wall of a container at a speed v. It makes an elastic collision with the wall and rebounds at a speed v (Figure 6.6b). This impact with the wall imparts a tiny force F to the wall. The force can be determined using Newtonian physics and the kinetic model. According to Newton's second law of motion, the force F is given by:

$$F = \text{rate of change of momentum of molecule}$$

or

$$F = \frac{\Delta p}{\Delta t}$$

The time between collisions with the opposite container walls is Δt. The change in momentum Δp of the molecule is:

$$\Delta p = \text{final momentum} - \text{initial momentum}$$

$$\Delta p = (-mv) - mv = -2mv$$

(Remember, momentum is a vector. The change in momentum is not just the difference in the magnitudes of the momentum. This will give a change of zero and this would mean a zero force on the wall!)

Therefore:

$$F = -\frac{2mv}{\Delta t}$$

The negative sign implies that the force exerted on the molecule by the wall is in the opposite direction to the initial velocity of the molecule. According to Newton's third law of motion, the molecule exerts a force of magnitude F on the wall. A large number of molecules make similar collisions with the container wall. This gives rise to a large total force on the wall. The pressure exerted on the wall due to the molecular collisions can be determined using:

$$\text{pressure} = \frac{\text{total force}}{\text{area of wall}}$$

Changes of state

Many solid materials, when heated, undergo a change of state. They first become a liquid, and then a gas. Some materials change directly from the solid state into a gas. (Some solids dissociate into simpler substances when heated, but we are not concerned here with such chemical changes.)

Figure 6.7 represents these changes of state at the molecular level. Consider first what happens when a solid melts. The atoms of the solid gain enough energy to break some of the bonds with their neighbours. They adopt a more disordered arrangement, and usually their average spacing increases. The atoms are more free to move around within the bulk of the material. The solid has melted.

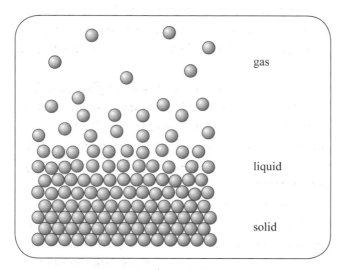

Figure 6.7 Changes of state.

As the liquid is heated further, the atoms become more disordered, further apart and faster moving. Eventually, at the boiling point, the atoms have sufficient energy to break free from their neighbours. They are now much further apart, moving rapidly about in a disordered state. The liquid has boiled to become a gas.

When a liquid boils at atmospheric pressure, its volume increases by a factor of about 1000. In the liquid state, the molecules were closely packed; now they are occupying 1000 times as much space. If the diameter of a single molecule is d, it follows that the average separation of molecules in the gas is about $10d$. It follows that about 99.9% of the volume of a gas is empty space.

The kinetic model we have described so far is very useful, but it cannot explain everything. It often has to be modified to explain particular observations. The change in density of ice when it melts is a case in point.

Our model suggests that, when a solid melts, the particles (atoms or molecules) from which it is made become slightly more disordered and further apart on average. We would thus expect a liquid to be less dense than the corresponding solid. This is generally the case, but there are exceptions. Ice is less dense than water, for example, and iron also expands when it freezes.

We have to modify the model. For water, we picture the molecules as being some shape other than spherical (Figure 6.8). When liquid water becomes solid ice, the particles pack in such a way that there is more empty space, and so the solid is less dense than the liquid.

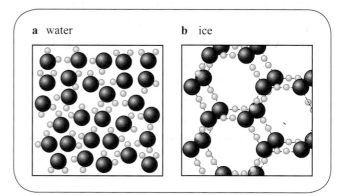

Figure 6.8 The molecules of water occupy less space **a** as a liquid than **b** as a solid. In ice the water molecules form a more regular 'hexagonal' arrangement.

Energy changes

Energy must be supplied to raise the temperature of a solid, to melt it, to heat the liquid and to boil it. Where does this energy go to? It is worth taking a close look at a single change of state and thinking about what is happening on the atomic scale.

Figure 6.9a shows a suitable arrangement. A test tube containing octadecanoic acid (a white, waxy substance at room temperature) is warmed in a water bath. At 80 °C, the substance is a clear liquid. The tube is then placed in a rack and allowed to cool. Its temperature is monitored, either with a thermometer or with a temperature probe and datalogger. Figure 6.9b shows typical results.

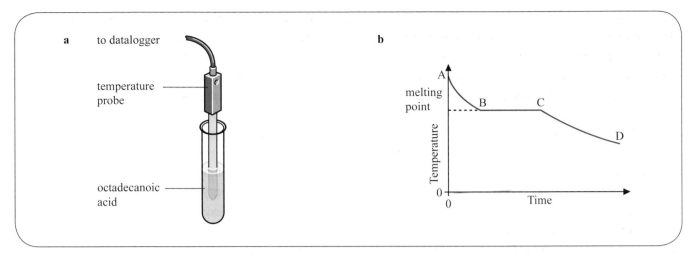

Figure 6.9 a Apparatus for obtaining a cooling curve, and **b** typical results.

The temperature drops rapidly at first, then more slowly as it approaches room temperature. The important section of the graph is the region BC. The temperature remains steady for some time. The clear liquid is gradually returning to its white, waxy solid state. It is essential to note that heat is still being lost even though the temperature is not decreasing, When no liquid remains, the temperature starts to drop again.

From the graph, we can deduce the melting point of octadecanoic acid. This is a technique used to help identify substances by finding their melting points.

Heating ice

In some ways, it is easier to think of the experiment above in reverse. What happens when we heat a substance?

Imagine taking some ice from the deep freeze. Put the ice in a well-insulated container and heat it at a steady rate. Its temperature will rise; eventually

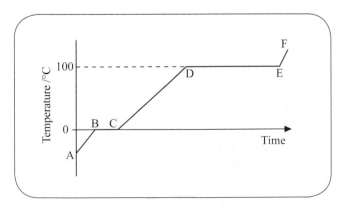

Figure 6.10 A temperature against time graph for water, heated at a steady rate.

we will have a container of steam. (Note that steam is an invisible gas; the 'steam' that you see when a kettle boils is not a gas but a cloud of tiny droplets of liquid water.)

Figure 6.10 shows the results we might expect if we could carry out this idealised experiment. Energy is supplied to the ice at a constant rate. We will consider the different sections of this graph in some detail, in order to describe where the energy is going at each stage.

We need to think about the kinetic and potential energies of the molecules. If they move around more freely and faster, their kinetic energy has increased. If they break free of their neighbours and become more disordered, their electrical potential energy has increased.

You know that the kinetic energy of a particle is the energy it has due to its motion. Figure 6.11 shows how the electrical potential energy of two isolated atoms depends on their separation. Work must be done (energy must be put in) to separate neighbouring atoms – think about the work you must do to snap a piece of plastic or to tear a sheet of paper. The graph shows that:

- the electrical potential energy of two atoms very close together is large and negative
- as the separation of the atoms increases, their potential energy also increases
- when the atoms are completely separated, their potential energy is maximum and has a value of zero.

Figure 6.13 Increasing the internal energy of a stone.

internal energy of the stone. The internal energy of a system (e.g. the heated stone) is defined as follows:

> The internal energy of a system is the sum of the random distribution of kinetic and potential energies of its atoms or molecules.

Molecular energy

Earlier in this chapter, where we studied the phases of matter, we saw how solids, liquids and gases could be characterised by differences in the arrangement, order and motion of their molecules. We could equally have said that, in the three phases, the molecules have different amounts of kinetic and potential energies.

Now, it is a simple problem to find the internal energy of some matter. We add up the kinetic and potential energies associated with all the molecules in the matter.

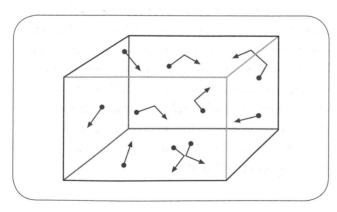

Figure 6.14 The molecules of a gas have both kinetic and potential energies.

For example, we consider the gas shown in Figure 6.14. There are ten molecules in the box; each has kinetic and potential energy, and we can work out what all of these are and add them together. The principle at least is simple, and this example should serve to explain what we mean by the internal energy of a gas.

Changing internal energy

There are two obvious ways in which we can increase the internal energy of some gas: we can heat it, or we can do work on it by compressing it.

- *Heating a gas* (Figure 6.15a)
  The walls of the container become hot and so its molecules vibrate more vigorously. The molecules of the cool gas strike the walls and bounce off faster. They have gained kinetic energy, and we say the temperature has risen.

- *Doing work on a gas* (Figure 6.15b)
  In this case, a wall of the container is being pushed inwards. The molecules of the cool gas strike a moving wall and bounce off faster. They have gained kinetic energy and again the temperature has risen. This explains why a gas gets hotter when it is compressed.

There are other ways in which the internal energy of a system can be increased; by passing an electric current through it, for example. However, doing work and heating are all we need to consider here.

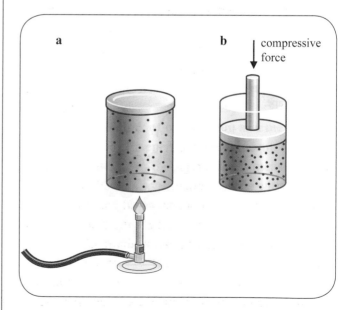

Figure 6.15 Two ways to increase the internal energy of a gas: **a** by heating it, and **b** by compressing it.

The meaning of temperature

Picture a beaker of boiling water. You want to measure its temperature, so you pick up a thermometer which is lying on the bench. The thermometer reads 20 °C. You place the thermometer in the water and the reading goes up… 30 °C, 40 °C, 50 °C. This tells you that the thermometer is getting hotter; energy is being transferred from the water to the thermometer.

Eventually, the thermometer reading reaches 100 °C and it stops rising. Because the reading is steady, you can deduce that energy is no longer being transferred to the thermometer and so its scale tells you the temperature of the water.

This simple, everyday activity illustrates several points:

- We are used to the idea that a thermometer shows the temperature of something with which it is in contact. In fact, it tells you *its own temperature*. As the reading on the scale was rising, it wasn't showing the temperature of the water. It was showing that the temperature of the thermometer was rising.
- Energy is transferred from a hotter object to a cooler one. The temperature of the water was greater than the temperature of the thermometer, so energy transferred from one to the other.
- When two objects are at the same temperature, there is no transfer of energy between them. That is what happened when the thermometer reached the same temperature as the water, so it was safe to say that the reading on the thermometer was the same as the temperature of the water.

From this, you can see that temperature tells us about the direction in which energy flows. If two objects are placed in contact (so that energy can flow between them), it will flow from the hotter to the cooler. Energy flowing from a region of higher temperature to a region of lower temperature is called **thermal energy**. (Here, we are not concerned with the mechanism by which the energy is transferred. It may be by conduction, convection or radiation.)

When two objects, in contact with each other, are at the same temperature, there will be no transfer of thermal energy between them. We say that they are in **thermal equilibrium** with each other – see Figure 6.16.

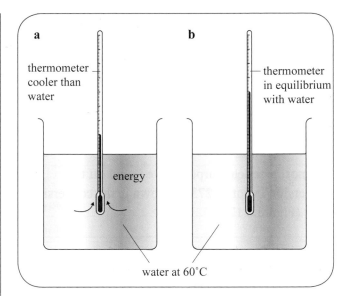

Figure 6.16 a Thermal energy is transferred from the hot water to the cooler thermometer because of the temperature difference between them. **b** When they are at the same temperature, there is no transfer of thermal energy and they are in thermal equilibrium.

The thermodynamic (Kelvin) scale

The Celsius scale of temperature is a familiar, everyday scale of temperature. It is based on the properties of water. It takes two fixed points, the melting point of pure ice and the boiling point of pure water, and divides the range between them into 100 equal intervals.

There is nothing special about these two fixed points. In fact, both change if the pressure changes or if the water is impure. The **thermodynamic scale**, also known as the Kelvin scale, is a better scale in that one of its fixed points, **absolute zero**, has a greater significance than either of the Celsius fixed points.

It is not possible to have a temperature lower than 0 K. Sometimes it is suggested that, at this temperature, matter has no energy left in it. This is not strictly true; it is more correct to say that, for any matter at absolute zero, it is impossible to *remove* any more energy from it. Hence absolute zero is the temperature at which all substances have the minimum internal energy. (The kinetic energy of the atoms or molecules is zero and their electrical potential energy is minimum.)

SAQ

You will need to use data from Table 6.2 to answer these questions.

6 Calculate the energy which must be supplied to raise the temperature of 5.0 kg of water from 20 °C to 100 °C.

Answer

7 Which requires more energy, heating a 2.0 kg block of lead by 30 K, or heating a 4.0 kg block of copper by 5.0 K?

Hint

Answer

8 A well-insulated 1.2 kg block of iron is heated using a 50 W heater for 4.0 min. The temperature of the block rises from 22 °C to 45 °C. Find the experimental value for the specific heat capacity of iron.

Hint

Answer

Ice, water, steam

Water is an unusual substance. We have already noted that it expands when it freezes – that is why ice floats on water. You can see from Table 6.2 that it also has an unusually high specific heat capacity. This means that water heats up and cools down relatively slowly. This makes water very suitable for the liquid in central heating systems.

Another consequence is that the sea cools down relatively slowly in the winter, compared to the land. Also it warms up relatively slowly in the summer. In the British Isles, we are surrounded by the sea, which helps to keep us warm in the winter and cool in the summer. In central Europe, far from the sea, temperatures fall more dramatically in the winter and rise higher in the summer. This is the origin of the difference between a maritime climate and a continental climate. If the sea was made of alcohol, the British climate would vary more between the seasons. You can probably imagine some other consequences!

Determining specific heat capacity c

How can we determine the specific heat capacity of a material? The principle is simple: supply a known amount of energy to a known mass of the material and measure the rise in its temperature. Figure 6.18 shows one practical way of doing this for a metal.

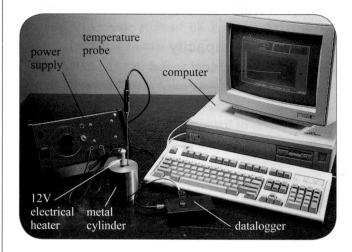

Figure 6.18 A practical arrangement for determining the specific heat capacity of a metal.

The metal is in the form of a cylindrical block of mass 1.00 kg. An electrical heater is used to supply the energy. This is because we can easily determine the amount of energy supplied – more easily than if we heated the metal with a Bunsen flame, for example. An ammeter and voltmeter are used to make the necessary measurements.

A thermometer or temperature sensor is used to monitor the block's temperature as it is heated. The block must not be heated too quickly; we want to be sure that the energy has time to spread throughout the metal.

The block should be insulated by wrapping it in a suitable material – this is not shown in the illustration. It would be possible in principle to determine c by making just one measurement of temperature change, but it is better to record values of the temperature as it rises and plot a graph of temperature θ against time t. The method of calculating c is illustrated in Worked example 2.

Worked example 2

An experiment to determine the specific heat capacity c of a 1.00 kg aluminium block is carried out; the block is heated using an electrical heater. The current in the heater is 4.17 A and the p.d. across it is 12 V. Measurements of the rising temperature of the block are represented by the graph shown in Figure 6.19. Determine a value for the specific heat capacity c of aluminium.

Step 1 Write down the equation that relates energy change to specific heat capacity:

$$E = mc\Delta\theta$$

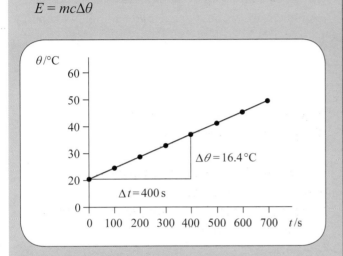

Figure 6.19 Temperature against time graph for an aluminium block as it is heated.

Step 2 Divide both sides by a time interval Δt:

$$\frac{E}{\Delta t} = mc\left[\frac{\Delta\theta}{\Delta t}\right]$$

The quantity $\dfrac{E}{\Delta t}$ is the rate at which energy is supplied, i.e. the power P of the heater. The quantity $\dfrac{\Delta\theta}{\Delta t}$ is the rate of rise of temperature of the block, i.e. the gradient of the θ against t graph. Hence:

$$P = m \times c \times \text{gradient}$$

Step 3 Calculate the power of the heater and the gradient of the graph.

$$\text{power} = \text{p.d.} \times \text{current}$$
$$P = VI = 12 \times 4.17 \approx 50 \, \text{W}$$

$$\text{gradient} = \frac{\Delta\theta}{\Delta t} = \frac{16.4}{400} = 0.041 \, °C \, s^{-1}$$

Step 4 Substitute values, rearrange and solve.

$$50 = 1.00 \times c \times 0.041$$

$$c = \frac{50}{1.00 \times 0.041} = 1220 \, J \, kg^{-1} \, K^{-1}$$

Sources of error

This experiment can give reasonably good measurements of specific heat capacities. As noted earlier, it is desirable to have a relatively low rate of heating, so that heat spreads throughout the block. If the block is heated rapidly, different parts may be at different temperatures.

Thermal insulation of the material is also vital. Inevitably, some energy will escape to the surroundings. This means that *more* energy must be supplied to the block for each degree rise in temperature and so the experimental value for the specific heat capacity will be too high. One way around this is to cool the block below room temperature before beginning to heat it. Then, as its temperature rises past room temperature, heat losses will be zero in principle, because there is no temperature difference between the block and its surroundings.

SAQ

9   At higher temperature, the graph shown in Figure 6.19 deviates increasingly from a straight line. Suggest an explanation for this.

Answer

10 In measurements of the specific heat capacity of a metal, energy losses to the surroundings are a source of error. Is this a systematic error or random error? Justify your answer.

Answer

11 In an experiment to measure the specific heat capacity of water, a student used an electrical heater to heat some water. His results are shown below. Calculate a value for the heat capacity of water. Comment on any likely sources of error.

mass of beaker = 150 g
mass of beaker + water = 672 g
current in the heater = 3.9 A
p.d. across heater = 11.4 V
initial temperature = 18.5 °C
final temperature = 30.2 °C
time taken = 13.0 min

12 A block of paraffin wax was heated gently, at a steady rate. Heating was continued after the wax had completely melted. The graph of Figure 6.20 shows how the material's temperature varied during the experiment.

  a For each section of the graph (AB, BC and CD), describe the state of the material.

  b For each section, explain whether the material's internal energy was increasing, decreasing or remaining constant.

  c Consider the two sloping sections of the graph. State whether the material's specific heat capacity is greater when it is a solid or when it is a liquid. Justify your answer.

Answer

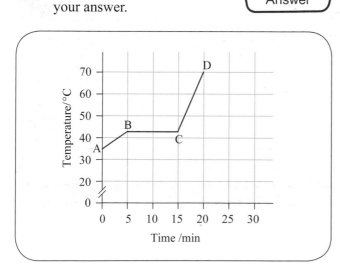

Figure 6.20 Temperature variation of a sample of wax, heated at a constant rate.

Extension

Specific latent heat

Energy must be supplied to melt or boil a substance. (In this case, there is no temperature rise to consider since the temperature stays constant during a change of state.) This energy is called latent heat.

> The specific latent heat of a substance is the energy required per kilogram of the substance to change its state without any change in temperature.

When a substance melts, this quantity is called the **specific latent heat of fusion**; for boiling, it is the **specific latent heat of vaporisation**. Worked example 3 shows how to calculate amounts of energy.

Worked example 3

The specific latent heat of vaporisation of water is 2.26 MJ kg^{-1}. Calculate the energy needed to change 2.0 g of water into steam at 100 °C.

Step 1 Use the specific latent heat of vaporisation of water to determine the energy needed to boil 1.0 kg of water.
  To change 1.0 kg (1000 g) of water into steam requires 2.26 MJ of energy.

Step 2 Determine the energy needed to change 2.0 g of water into steam.
  There are 1000 grams in a kilogram. So, for 2.0 g of water, the energy required is

$$\text{energy} = \frac{2.0}{1000} \times 2.26 \times 10^6 = 4520\,\text{J}$$

SAQ

13 The specific latent heat of fusion of water is 330 kJ kg^{-1}. Calculate the energy needed to change 2.0 g of ice into water at 0 °C. Suggest why the answer is much smaller than the amount of energy calculated in Worked example 3.

Answer

Summary

Glossary

- The kinetic model of matter allows us to explain behaviour (e.g. changes of state) and macroscopic properties (e.g. specific heat capacity and specific latent heat) in terms of the behaviour of molecules.

- The internal energy of a system is the sum of the random distribution of kinetic and potential energies associated with the atoms or molecules that make up the system.

- If the temperature of an object increases, there is an increase in its internal energy.

- Internal energy also increases during a change of state, but there is no change in temperature.

- Temperatures on the thermodynamic (Kelvin) and Celsius scales of temperature are related by:

$$T\,(\text{K}) = \theta\,(°\text{C}) + 273.15$$

$$\theta\,(°\text{C}) = T\,(\text{K}) - 273.15$$

- At absolute zero, all substances have a minimum internal energy.

- The word equation for the specific heat capacity of a substance is

$$\text{specific heat capacity} = \frac{\text{energy supplied}}{\text{mass} \times \text{temperature change}}$$

- The specific heat capacity of a substance is the energy required per unit mass of the substance to raise the temperature by 1 K (or 1 °C).

- The energy transferred in raising the temperature of a substance is given by $E = mc\Delta\theta$.

- The specific latent heat of a substance is the energy required per kilogram of the substance to change its state without any change in temperature.

Questions

1 A night storage heater can be considered as a stack of bricks which is warmed in the night by electric power and then cools down in the day heating a room. Calculate the energy given out by such a heater of mass 600 kg as it cools from 70 °C to 30 °C. The specific heat capacity of brick = $1.1 \times 10^3\,\text{J}\,\text{kg}^{-1}\,\text{K}^{-1}$. [3]

OCR Physics A2 (2824) June 2002 [Total 3]

Answer

continued

2 **a** **i** Explain the term *internal energy*. [2]

    ii Define the *specific heat capacity* of a body. [1]

  b Outline a method of measuring the specific heat capacity of aluminium. [4]

  c Consider a 2.0 kg block of aluminium. Assume that the heat capacity of aluminium is independent of temperature and that the internal energy is zero at absolute zero. Also assume that the volume of the block does not change over the range of temperature from 0 K to 293 K.

    Show that the internal energy of this block of aluminium at 20 °C is 540 kJ.

    (Specific heat capacity of aluminium = 920 J kg^{-1} K^{-1}.) [2]

OCR Physics A2 (2824) January 2006   [Total 9]

> Answer

3 This question is about the operation of an electrically operated shower.

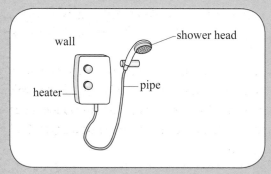

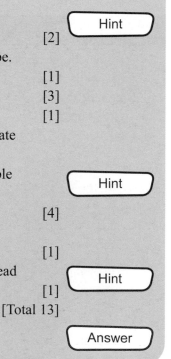

  a The water moves at constant speed through a pipe of cross-section 7.5×10^{-5} m^2 to a shower head (see the diagram above). The maximum mass of water which flows per second is 0.090 kg s^{-1}.

    i Show that the maximum speed of the water in the pipe is 1.2 m s^{-1}.

    (Density of water = 1000 kg m^{-3}.) [2]

> Hint

    ii The total cross-sectional area of the holes in the head is half that of the pipe. Calculate the maximum speed of the water as it leaves the shower head. [1]

    iii Calculate the magnitude of the force on the shower head. [3]

    iv State the direction of the force in **iii**. [1]

  b The water enters the heater at a temperature of 15 °C. At the maximum flow rate of 0.090 kg s^{-1}, the water leaves the shower head at a temperature of 27 °C.

    i Calculate the rate at which energy is transferred to the water. Give a suitable unit for your answer.

    (Specific heat capacity of water = 4200 J kg^{-1} K^{-1}.) [4]

> Hint

    ii Suggest a reason why the power of the heater must be greater than your answer to **b i**. [1]

    iii Calculate the maximum possible temperature of the water at the shower head when the flow rate is half of the maximum. [1]

> Hint

OCR Physics A2 (2824) January 2005   [Total 13]

> Answer

Chapter 7

Ideal gases

e-Learning

Objectives

Measuring gases

We are going to picture a container of gas, such as the box shown in Figure 7.1. There are four properties of this gas that we might measure: pressure, temperature, volume and mass. In this chapter, you will learn how these quantities are related to one another.

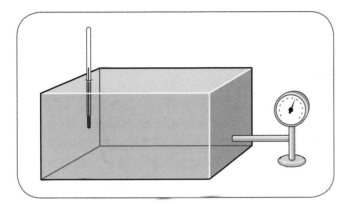

Figure 7.1 A gas has four measurable properties, which are all related to one another: pressure, temperature, volume and mass.

● *Pressure*

This is the force exerted normally per unit area by the gas on the walls of the container. We saw in Chapter 6 that this pressure is the result of molecular collisions with the walls of the container. Pressure is measured in pascals, Pa ($1\,Pa = 1\,N\,m^{-2}$).

● *Temperature*

This might be measured in °C, but in practice it is more useful to use the thermodynamic (Kelvin) scale of temperature. You should recall how these two scales are related:

$$T\,(K) = \theta\,(°C) + 273.15$$

● *Volume*

This is a measure of the space occupied by the gas. Volume is measured in m^3.

● *Mass*

This is measured in g or kg. In practice, it is more useful to consider the *amount* of gas measured in moles.

The mole is defined as follows:

> One mole of any substance is the amount of that substance which contains the same number of particles as there are in 0.012 kg of carbon-12.

(Here, 'particles' may be atoms, molecules, ions, etc.)

One mole of any substance is equal to the relative atomic or molecular mass of the substance measured in grams. For example, one mole of oxygen O_2 has a mass of about 32 g.

A mole of any substance (solid, liquid or gas) contains a standard number of particles (molecules or atoms). This number is known as the **Avogadro constant**, N_A. The experimental value for N_A is $6.02 \times 10^{23}\,mol^{-1}$. We can easily determine the number of atoms in a sample if we know how many moles it contains. For example:

2.0 mol of helium contains
$$2.0 \times 6.02 \times 10^{23} = 12.0 \times 10^{24}\text{ atoms}$$

10 mol of carbon contains
$$10 \times 6.02 \times 10^{23} = 6.02 \times 10^{24}\text{ atoms}$$

We will see later that, if we consider equal numbers of moles of two different gases under the same conditions, their properties are the same.

SAQ

1 The mass of one mole of carbon is 12 g. Determine:
   a the number of atoms in one mole of carbon
   b the number of moles and the number of atoms in 54 g of carbon
   c the number of atoms in 1.0 kg of carbon.

Answer

2 The molar mass of uranium is about $235\,\mathrm{g\,mol^{-1}}$.

   a Calculate the mass of a single atom of uranium.

   b A small pellet of uranium has a mass of 20 mg. For this pellet, calculate:

     i the number of moles

     ii the number of uranium atoms.

      Answer

3 'It can be useful to recall that 1.0 kg of matter contains of the order of 10^{26} atoms.' Making suitable estimates, test this statement.   Answer

Boyle's law

This law relates the pressure p and volume V of a gas. It was discovered in 1662 by Robert Boyle. If a gas is compressed, its pressure increases and its volume decreases. Pressure and volume are inversely related.

We can write **Boyle's law** as:

The pressure exerted by a fixed mass of gas is inversely proportional to its volume, provided the temperature of the gas remains constant.

Note that this law relates two variables, pressure and volume, and it requires that the other two, mass and temperature, remain constant.

Boyle's law can be written as:

$$p \propto \frac{1}{V}$$

or simply:

$$pV = \text{constant}$$

We can also represent Boyle's law as a graph, as shown in Figure 7.2. A graph of p against $1/V$ is a straight line passing through the origin, showing direct proportionality.

For solving problems, you may find it more useful to use the equation in this form:

$$p_1 V_1 = p_2 V_2$$

Here, p_1 and V_1 represent the pressure and volume of the gas before a change, and p_2 and V_2 represent

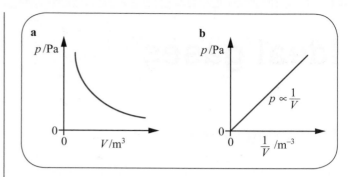

Figure 7.2 Graphical representations of the relationship between pressure and volume of a gas (Boyle's law).

the pressure and volume of the gas after the change. Worked example 1 shows how to use this equation.

Worked example 1

A cylinder contains 0.80 litres of nitrogen gas at a pressure of 1.2 atmosphere ($1\,\mathrm{atm} = 1.01 \times 10^5\,\mathrm{Pa}$). A piston slowly compresses the gas to a pressure of 6.0 atm. The temperature of the gas remains constant. Calculate the final volume of the gas.

Note from the question that the temperature of the gas is constant, and that its mass is fixed (because it is contained in a cylinder). This means that we can apply Boyle's law.

Step 1 We are going to use Boyle's law in the form $p_1 V_1 = p_2 V_2$. Write down the quantities that you know, and that you want to find out.

$p_1 = 1.2\,\mathrm{atm}$

$V_1 = 0.80\,\mathrm{litres}$

$p_2 = 6.0\,\mathrm{atm}$

$V_2 = ?$

Note that we don't need to worry about the particular units of pressure and volume being used here, so long as they are the same on both sides of the equation. The final value of V_2 will be in litres because V_1 is in litres.

continued

Step 2 Substitute the values in the equation, rearrange and find V_2.

$$p_1 V_1 = p_2 V_2$$

$$1.2 \times 0.8 = 6.0 \times V_2$$

$$V_2 = \frac{1.2 \times 0.8}{6.0} = 0.16 \text{ litres}$$

So the volume of the gas is reduced to 0.16 litres.

The pressure increases by a factor of 5, so the volume decreases by a factor of 5.

SAQ

4 A balloon contains 0.04 m^3 of air at a pressure of 120 kPa. Calculate the pressure required to reduce its volume to 0.025 m^3 at constant temperature.

Answer

Changing temperature

Boyle's law requires that the temperature of a gas is fixed. What happens if the temperature of the gas is allowed to change? Figure 7.3 shows the results of an experiment in which a fixed mass of gas is cooled at constant pressure. The gas contracts; its volume decreases.

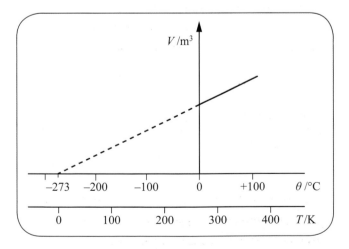

Figure 7.3 The volume of a gas decreases as its temperature decreases.

This graph does not show that the volume of a gas is proportional to its temperature on the Celsius scale. If a gas contracted to zero volume at 0 °C, the atmosphere would condense on a cold day and we would have a great deal of difficulty in breathing! However, the graph *does* show that there is a temperature at which the volume of a gas does, in principle, shrink to zero. Looking at the lower temperature scale on the graph, where temperatures are shown in kelvin (K), we can see that this temperature is 0 K, or absolute zero. (Historically, this is how the idea of absolute zero first arose.)

We can represent the relationship between volume V and thermodynamic temperature T as:

$$V \propto T$$

or simply:

$$\frac{V}{T} = \text{constant}$$

Note that this relationship only applies to a fixed mass of gas and where the pressure remains constant.

The relationship above is an expression of **Charles' law** after the French physicist Jacques Charles who in 1787 experimented with different gases kept at constant pressure.

Three variables, one equation

If we combine Boyle's law and Charles' law, we can arrive at a single equation for a fixed mass of gas:

$$\frac{pV}{T} = \text{constant}$$

or

$$\frac{p_1 V_1}{T_1} = \frac{p_2 V_2}{T_2}$$

This is useful because very often we have situations where all three variables, p, V and T, are changing at the same time. For example, if you increase the pressure on a gas, its volume will decrease and its temperature may also increase. Worked example 2 shows how to use this equation.

Worked example 2

A container of air, initial volume $2.4\,m^3$ and at a pressure of $100\,kPa$, is cooled from $57\,°C$ to $-23\,°C$. During cooling, its pressure drops to $90\,kPa$. Calculate the final volume of the air.

In this problem, you are given five pieces of data and are required to find a sixth; it will be simplest to use the equation

$$\frac{p_1V_1}{T_1} = \frac{p_2V_2}{T_2}$$

Step 1 Write down the quantities that you know and convert temperatures from °C to K.

Initially: $p_1 = 100\,kPa$
$V_1 = 2.4\,m^3$
$T_1 = 57\,°C = 330\,K$

Finally: $p_2 = 90\,kPa$
$V_2 = ?$
$T_2 = -23\,°C = 250\,K$

Step 2 Substitute values, rearrange and solve for V_2.

$$\frac{p_1V_1}{T_1} = \frac{p_2V_2}{T_2}$$

$$\frac{100\times2.4}{330} = \frac{90\times V_2}{250}$$

$$V_2 = \frac{100\times2.4\times250}{90\times330} = 2.02\,m^3$$

So the final volume of the air is about $2.0\,m^3$.

SAQ

5 A cylinder of oxygen contains 20 litres of oxygen compressed to a pressure of $2500\,kPa$ at $20\,°C$. The building in which the cylinder is stored catches fire and the temperature of the cylinder reaches $480\,°C$. Calculate its pressure at this temperature.

Hint

Answer

6 A cylinder contains nitrogen at $27\,°C$. A piston compresses the gas to half its original volume. The cylinder is then cooled so that its pressure returns to its original value. Calculate the temperature of the gas in K and in °C.

Answer

7 Use what you have learned about gases to explain the following observations:
   a The pressure in a car tyre increases on a hot day.
   b A toy balloon shrinks when placed in a fridge.

Answer

8 Figure 7.4 shows how the pressure of a fixed mass of gas depends on its thermodynamic temperature.
   a Apart from the mass of the gas, what other quantity must remain constant for this behaviour to be observed?
   b Write a sentence stating the mathematical relationship between the pressure p of the gas and its thermodynamic temperature T.

Answer

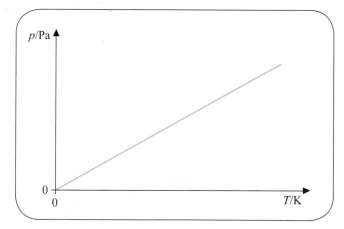

Figure 7.4 Graphical representation of the relationship between pressure and temperature for a gas.

Real and ideal gases

The relationships between p, V and T that we have considered above are based on experimental observations of gases such as air, helium, nitrogen, etc., at temperatures and pressures around room temperature and pressure. In practice, if we change to more extreme conditions, such as low temperatures or high pressures, gases start to deviate from these laws as the gas atoms exert significant electrical forces on each other. For example, Figure 7.5 shows what happens when nitrogen is cooled down towards absolute zero. At first, the graph of volume against temperature follows a good straight line. However, as it approaches the temperature at which it condenses, it deviates from ideal behaviour, and at 77 K it condenses to become liquid nitrogen.

Thus we have to attach a condition to the relationships discussed above. We say that they apply to an **ideal gas**. When we are dealing with real gases, we have to be aware that their behaviour may be significantly different from the ideal equation

$$\frac{pV}{T} = \text{constant}$$

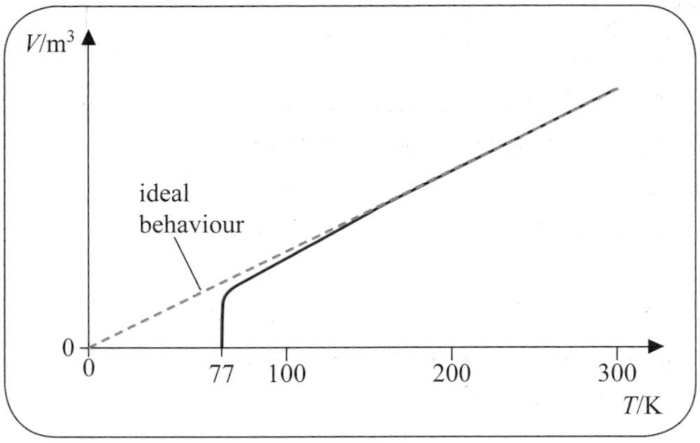

Figure 7.5 A real gas (in this case, nitrogen) deviates from the behaviour predicted by Charles' law at low temperatures.

An ideal gas is thus defined as one for which we can apply the equation:

$$\frac{pV}{T} = \text{constant}$$

for a fixed mass of gas.

Modelling gases

In this chapter, we are concentrating on the macroscopic properties of gases (pressure, volume, temperature). These can all be readily measured in the laboratory. The equation:

$$\frac{pV}{T} = \text{constant}$$

is an empirical relationship. In other words, it has been deduced from the results of experiments. It gives a good description of gases in many different situations. However, an empirical equation does not explain why gases behave in this way. An explanation requires us to think about the underlying nature of a gas and how this gives rise to our observations. We have considered this in Chapter 6.

A gas is made of particles (atoms or molecules). Its pressure arises from collisions of the particles with the walls of the container; more frequent, harder collisions give rise to greater pressure. Its temperature indicates the average kinetic energy of its particles;

the faster they move, the greater their average kinetic energy and the higher the temperature.

The **kinetic theory of gases** is a theory which links these microscopic properties of particles (atoms or molecules) to the macroscopic properties of a gas. Table 7.1 shows the assumptions on which the theory is based.

On the basis of these assumptions, it is possible to use Newtonian mechanics to show that pressure is inversely proportional to volume (Boyle's law), volume is directly proportional to thermodynamic (kelvin) temperature (Charles' law), and so on. The theory also shows that the particles of a gas have a range of speeds – some move faster than others.

Things are different when a gas is close to condensing. At temperatures a little above the boiling point, the molecules of a gas are moving more slowly and they tend to stick together – a liquid is forming. So we cannot consider them to be moving about freely, and the kinetic theory of

continued

95

Assumption	Explanation/comment
A gas contains a very large number of spherical particles (atoms or molecules).	A small 'cube' of air can have as many as 10^{20} molecules.
The forces between particles are negligible, except during collisions.	If the particles attracted each other strongly over long distances, they would all tend to clump together in the middle of the container. The particles travel in straight lines between collisions.
The volume of the particles is negligible compared to the volume occupied by the gas.	When a liquid boils to become a gas, its particles become much farther apart.
Most of the time, a particle moves in a straight line at a constant velocity. The time of collision with each other or with the container walls is negligible compared with the time between collisions.	The particles collide with the walls of the container and with each other, but for most of the time they are moving with constant velocity.
The collisions of particles with each other and with the container are perfectly elastic, so that no kinetic energy is lost.	Kinetic energy cannot be lost. The internal energy of the gas is the total kinetic energy of the particles.

Table 7.1 The basic assumptions of the kinetic theory of gases.

gases must be modified. This is often how Physics progresses. A theory is developed which explains a simple situation. Then the theory is modified to explain more complex situations.

The kinetic theory has proved to be a very powerful model. It convinced many physicists of the existence of particles long before it was ever possible to visualise them.

Ludwig Boltzmann (Figure 7.6) was one of those whose work extended the kinetic theory. He came under strong attack from some philosophers who believed it to be wrong to assume the existence of invisible particles without having direct observational evidence for them. These attacks contributed to Boltzmann's depression and, sadly, he committed suicide in 1906.

Figure 7.6 Ludwig Boltzmann, the Austrian physicist who did much to develop the kinetic theory of gases.

Ideal gas equation

So far, we have seen how p, V and T are related. It is possible to write a single equation relating these quantities which takes into account the amount of gas being considered. We can write the equation in two forms, depending on whether we think of the gas as consisting of N particles (atoms or molecules) or n moles.

For a gas consisting of N particles, we have:

$$pV = NkT$$

where k is the Boltzmann constant with an experimental value:

$$k = 1.38 \times 10^{-23}\,\text{J K}^{-1}$$

For n moles of an ideal gas, we have:

$$pV = nRT$$

Either of these equations can be called the **ideal gas equation** or the **equation of state** for an ideal gas. They are equations that relate all of the four variable quantities discussed at the beginning of this chapter. The constant of proportionality R is called the universal molar gas constant. Its experimental value is:

$$R = 8.31\,\text{J}\,\text{mol}^{-1}\,\text{K}^{-1}$$

Note that it doesn't matter what gas we are considering – it could be a very 'light' gas like hydrogen, or a much 'heavier' one like carbon dioxide. So long as it is behaving as an ideal gas, we can use the same equation of state with the same constant R.

The Boltzmann constant k and universal molar gas constant R are related to the Avogadro constant by:

$$k = \frac{R}{N_A}$$

Calculating the number n of moles

Sometimes we know the mass of gas we are concerned with, and then we have to be able to find how many moles this represents. To do this, we use this relationship:

$$\text{number of moles} = \frac{\text{mass (g)}}{\text{molar mass (g\,mol}^{-1})}$$

For example: How many moles are there in 1.6 kg of oxygen?

$$\text{molar mass of oxygen} = 32\,\text{g}\,\text{mol}^{-1}$$

$$\text{number of moles} = \frac{1600\,\text{g}}{32\,\text{g}\,\text{mol}^{-1}} = 50\,\text{mol}$$

(Note that this tells us that there are 50 moles of oxygen *molecules* in 1.6 kg of oxygen. An oxygen molecule consists of two oxygen atoms – its formula is O_2 – so 1.6 kg of oxygen contains 100 moles of oxygen *atoms*.)

Now look at Worked example 3 and Worked example 4.

Worked example 3

Calculate the volume occupied by 1.0 mol of an ideal gas at standard temperature (0 °C) and pressure (1.013×10^5 Pa).

Step 1 Write down the quantities given.

$p = 1.013 \times 10^5\,\text{Pa}$ $n = 1.0$

$T = 273\,\text{K}$

Step 2 Substituting in the equation of state gives:

$$V = \frac{nRT}{p} = \frac{1 \times 8.31 \times 273}{1.013 \times 10^5}$$

$$V = 0.0224\,\text{m}^3 = 2.24 \times 10^{-2}\,\text{m}^3$$

$$V = 22.4\,\text{dm}^3$$
$$(1\,\text{dm} = 0.1\,\text{m}; \text{ hence } 1\,\text{dm}^3 = 10^{-3}\,\text{m}^3)$$

This value, the volume of one mole of gas at standard temperature and pressure, is well worth remembering. It is certainly known by most chemists.

Worked example 4

A car tyre contains $0.020\,\text{m}^3$ of air at 27 °C and at a pressure of 3.0×10^5 Pa. Calculate the mass of the air in the tyre. (Molar mass of air = $28.8\,\text{g}\,\text{mol}^{-1}$.)

Step 1 Here, we need first to calculate the number of moles of air using the equation of state. We have:

$p = 3.0 \times 10^5\,\text{Pa}$ $V = 0.02\,\text{m}^3$

$T = 27\,°\text{C} = 300\,\text{K}$

So, from the equation of state:

$$n = \frac{pV}{RT} = \frac{3.0 \times 10^5 \times 0.02}{8.31 \times 300}$$

$$n = 2.41\,\text{mol}$$

Step 2 Now we can calculate the mass of air:

$$\text{mass} = \text{number of moles} \times \text{molar mass}$$

$$\text{mass} = 2.41 \times 28.8 = 69.4\,\text{g} \approx 69\,\text{g}$$

SAQ

For the questions which follow, you will need the following values:

$$k = 1.38 \times 10^{-23} \, J\,K^{-1}$$

$$R = 8.31 \, J\,mol^{-1}\,K^{-1}$$

9 At what temperature (in K) will 1.0 mol of a gas occupy 1.0 m³ at a pressure of 1.0×10⁴ Pa? [Answer]

10 Nitrogen consists of molecules N_2. The molar mass of nitrogen is 28 g mol⁻¹. For 100 g of nitrogen, calculate:
   a the number of moles
   b the volume occupied at standard temperature and pressure? (STP = 0 °C, 1.01×10⁵ Pa.) [Answer]

11 Calculate the volume of 5.0 mol of an ideal gas at a pressure of 1.0×10⁵ Pa and a temperature of 200 °C. [Hint] [Answer]

12 A sample of gas contains 3.0×10²⁴ atoms. Calculate the volume of the gas at a temperature of 300 K and a pressure of 120 kPa. [Answer]

13 At what temperature would 1.0 kg of oxygen occupy 1.0 m³ at a pressure of 1.0×10⁵ Pa? (Molar mass of O_2 = 32 g mol⁻¹.) [Answer]

14 A cylinder of hydrogen has a volume of 0.10 m³. Its pressure is found to be 20 atmospheres at 20 °C.
   a Calculate the mass of hydrogen in the cylinder.
   b If it was filled with oxygen instead to the same pressure, how much oxygen would it contain? (Molar mass of H_2 = 2.0 g mol⁻¹, molar mass of O_2 = 32 g mol⁻¹; 1 atmosphere = 1.01×10⁵ Pa.) [Answer]

Temperature and molecular kinetic energy

The equation of state for an ideal gas relates four macroscopic properties of a gas – pressure, volume, temperature and amount of gas. How does this relate to our microscopic picture of a gas? We picture a gas as being made up of a large number of fast-moving molecules (or atoms). They rush around in a rather haphazard way, colliding with one another and with the walls of their container. Collisions with the walls give rise to the pressure of the gas on the container; at higher temperatures, the molecules move faster.

Imagine taking the temperature of a hot gas using a mercury-in-glass thermometer. You place the bulb of the thermometer in the gas. The molecules of the gas collide with the bulb, sharing their energy with it. Eventually, the gas and the bulb are at the same temperature and you can read the temperature from the scale. At a higher temperature, the gas molecules have greater kinetic energy; they give more energy to the bulb and the mercury rises higher. Hence the reading on the thermometer is an indication of the kinetic energy of the gas molecules.

In fact, the following can be shown:

> The mean translational kinetic energy of an atom (or molecule) of an ideal gas is proportional to the thermodynamic temperature.

It is easier to recall this as:

mean translational kinetic energy of atom ∝ T

We need to consider two of the terms in this statement. Firstly, we talk about *translational* kinetic energy. This is the energy that the molecule has because it is moving along; a molecule made of two or more atoms may also spin or tumble around, and is then said to have rotational kinetic energy – see Figure 7.7.

Secondly, we talk about *mean* (or average) translational kinetic energy. There are two ways to find the average translational KE of a molecule of a gas: add up all the kinetic energies of the individual molecules of the gas and then calculate the average kinetic energy per molecule. Alternatively, watch an individual molecule over a period of time as it moves about, colliding with other molecules and the walls of the container and calculate its average kinetic energy over this time. Both should give the same answer.

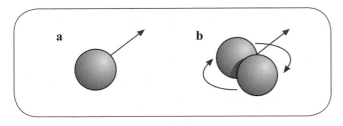

Figure 7.7 **a** A monatomic molecule has only translational kinetic energy. **b** A diatomic molecule can have both translational and rotational kinetic energy.

For a fixed amount of ideal gas in a container, we can also write:

total kinetic energy of gas $\propto T$

The total kinetic energy is the same as its internal energy for the ideal gas; there is no electrical potential energy because of the vast separation between the molecules. Therefore:

internal energy of gas $\propto T$

If we use the symbol E to represent the mean translational KE of an atom in a gas, we can write an equation linking E to the thermodynamic (kelvin) temperature:

$$E = \tfrac{3}{2}kT$$

Here k is the Boltzmann constant which we met before, in the ideal gas equation.

The equation shows that the mean KE of the atoms is directly proportional to the thermodynamic temperature, and the constant of proportionality is $\tfrac{3}{2}k$. This equation applies only to an ideal gas. If we double the thermodynamic temperature of an ideal gas, we double the mean translational kinetic energy of its atoms. (Look at the unit of k; it is 'joules per kelvin', showing that k links energy in joules to temperature in kelvin.)

Temperature and molecular speeds

You would not expect all the gas molecules in a container to have the same speed. The collisions between the molecules and the container walls give rise to a distribution of speeds. Some travel faster; some travel slower. In the mid-1800s, James Clerk Maxwell and Ludwig Boltzmann used Newtonian mechanics to deduce the distribution of the speed of the molecules of a gas in thermal equilibrium. Figure 7.8 shows the distribution of the speeds of gas molecules at different temperatures.

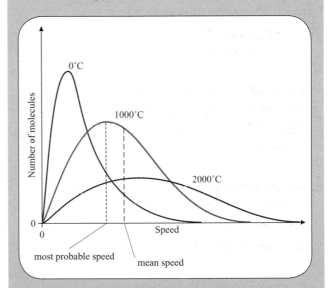

Figure 7.8 The Maxwell–Boltzmann speed distribution for molecules of a gas.

There are several interesting features of this Maxwell–Boltzmann distribution:
- The graph of number of molecules against speed is not symmetrical.
- The mean (average) speed increases with temperature of the gas.
- The mean speed of the molecules is greater than the most probable molecular speed. (The mean speed is a factor of 1.13 greater than the most probable speed.)
- A small fraction of the molecules have speeds more than three times the mean speed.

Mass, kinetic energy and temperature

Since mean KE $\propto T$, it follows that if we double the thermodynamic temperature of an ideal gas (e.g. from 300 K to 600 K), we double the mean KE of its molecules. It doesn't follow that we have doubled their speed; because KE $\propto v^2$, their mean speed has increased by a factor of $\sqrt{2}$.

Air is a mixture of several gases: nitrogen, oxygen, carbon dioxide, etc. In a sample of air, the mean KE of the nitrogen molecules is the same as that of the oxygen molecules and that of the carbon dioxide molecules. This comes about because they are all repeatedly colliding with one another, sharing their energy. Carbon dioxide molecules have greater mass than oxygen molecules; since their mean translational KE is the same, it follows that the carbon dioxide molecules move more slowly than the oxygen molecules.

SAQ

15 Calculate the mean translational KE of atoms in an ideal gas at 27 °C. [Answer]

16 The atoms in a gas have a mean translational KE equal to 5.0×10^{-21} J. Calculate the temperature of the gas in K and in °C. [Answer]

17 Show that, if the mean speed of the molecules in an ideal gas is doubled, the thermodynamic temperature of the gas increases by a factor of 4. [Answer]

18 A fixed mass of gas expands to twice its original volume at a constant temperature. How do the following change:
   a the pressure of the gas?
   b the mean translational kinetic energy of its molecules? [Answer]

19 Air consists of molecules of oxygen (molar mass = 32 g mol^{-1}) and nitrogen (molar mass = 28 g mol^{-1}). Calculate the mean translational KE of these molecules in air at 20 °C. Use your answer to estimate a typical speed for each type of molecule. [Hint] [Answer]

20 Show that the change in the internal energy of one mole of an ideal gas per unit change in temperature is always a constant. What is this constant? [Answer]

[Extension]

Summary

[Glossary]

- Boyle's law: The pressure exerted by a fixed mass of gas is inversely proportional to its volume, provided the temperature of the gas remains constant.

- For an ideal gas:

$$\frac{pV}{T} = \text{constant}$$

- One mole of any substance contains N_A particles (atoms or molecules). N_A = Avogadro constant = 6.02×10^{23} mol^{-1}.

- The equation of state for an ideal gas is:

  $pV = NkT$ for N atoms
  or $pV = nRT$ for n moles

- The mean translational kinetic energy E of a particle (atom or molecule) of an ideal gas is proportional to the thermodynamic temperature T.

- The mean translational kinetic energy E is related to temperature T by the equation:

  $E = \frac{3}{2}kT$ where k is the Boltzmann constant (1.38×10^{-23} J K^{-1}).

Questions

1 A bicycle tyre has a volume of $2.1 \times 10^{-3}\,m^3$. On a day when the temperature is $15\,°C$ the pressure of the air in the tyre is $280\,kPa$. Assume that air behaves as an ideal gas.

   a Calculate the number of moles n of air in the tyre. [3]

   b The bicycle is ridden vigorously so that the tyres warm up. The pressure in the tyres rises to $290\,kPa$. Calculate the new temperature of the air in the tyre in degrees Celsius. Assume that no air has leaked from the tyre and that the volume is constant. [3]

   c Calculate, for the air in the tyre, the ratio:

$$\frac{\text{internal energy at the higher temperature}}{\text{internal energy at } 15\,°C}$$

     Justify your reasoning. [2]

OCR Physics A2 (2824) January 2007   [Total 8]

Hint

Answer

2 a Very high temperatures, for example, the temperature of the solar corona at half a million degrees, are often stated without a complete unit, i.e. degrees Celsius or kelvin. Suggest why it is unnecessary to give degrees Celsius or kelvin in this case. [2]

   b Describe how the concept of absolute zero of temperature arises from:

    i the ideal gas laws [2]

    ii the kinetic theory of an ideal gas. [2]

   c Two students attempt the same experiment to find how air pressure varies with temperature. They heat identical sealed glass flasks of air, to be considered as an ideal gas, in an oil bath. The flasks are heated from $300\,K$ to $400\,K$. The pressure in flask A rises from atmospheric pressure p_0, as expected, but the pressure in flask B remains at p_0 because the rubber bung is defective and air leaks out of the flask.

    i Calculate the pressure in flask A at $400\,K$ in terms of p_0. [2]

    ii Calculate the fraction, f, of gas molecules in flask B compared to flask A at $400\,K$.

$$f = \frac{\text{number of gas molecules in B at } 400\,K}{\text{number of gas molecules in A at } 400\,K}$$ [2]

OCR Physics A2 (2824) January 2004   [Total 10]

Hint

Answer

continued

3 a The equation of state of an ideal gas is $pV = nRT$. Explain why the temperature must be measured in kelvin. [2]

A meteorological balloon rises through the atmosphere until it expands to a volume of $1.0 \times 10^6 \, m^3$, where the pressure is $1.0 \times 10^3 \, Pa$. The temperature also falls from $17\,°C$ to $-43\,°C$.

The pressure of the atmosphere at the Earth's surface $= 1.0 \times 10^5 \, Pa$.

Show that the volume of the balloon at take-off is about $1.3 \times 10^4 \, m^3$. [3]

c The balloon is filled with helium gas of molar mass $4.0 \times 10^{-3} \, kg \, mol^{-1}$ at $17\,°C$ at a pressure of $1.0 \times 10^5 \, Pa$. Calculate:

i the number of moles of gas in the balloon [2]

ii the mass of gas in the balloon. [1]

d The internal energy of the helium gas is equal to the random kinetic energy of all its molecules. When the balloon is filled at ground level at a temperature of $17\,°C$ the internal energy is $1900 \, MJ$. Estimate the internal energy of the helium when the balloon has risen to a height where the temperature is $-43\,°C$. [2]

e The upward force on the filled balloon at the Earth's surface is $1.3 \times 10^5 \, N$. The initial acceleration of the balloon as it is released is $27 \, m \, s^{-2}$. The total mass of the filled balloon and its load is M.

i Copy the diagram below and draw and label suitable arrows to represent the forces acting on the balloon immediately after lift off. [2]

ii Calculate the value of M. [3]

OCR Physics A2 (2824) June 2005 [Total 15]

Hint

Answer

Chapter 8

Electric fields

e-Learning

Objectives

Attraction and repulsion

You will already know a bit about electric (or electrostatic) fields, from your experience of static electricity in everyday life and from your studies in science (Figure 8.1). In this chapter, you will learn how we can make these ideas more formal.

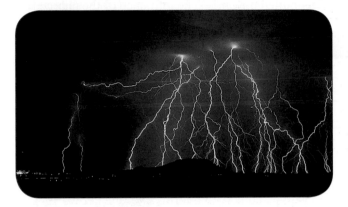

Figure 8.1 Lightning flashes – dramatic evidence of natural electric fields.

This chapter follows a parallel course to our exploration of ideas about gravity in Chapter 4. We will look at how electric forces are caused, and how we can represent their effects in terms of electric fields. Then we will find mathematical ways of calculating electric forces and field strengths.

Static electricity can be useful. It is important in the process of photocopying, in dust precipitation to clean up industrial emissions, and in crop-spraying, among many other applications. It can also be a nuisance. Who hasn't experienced a shock, perhaps when getting out of a car or when touching a door handle? Static electric charge has built up and gives us a shock when it discharges to the ground.

We explain these effects in terms of electric charge. Simple observations in the laboratory give us the following picture:

- Objects are usually electrically neutral (uncharged), but they may become electrically charged, for example when an insulator (e.g. plastic) is rubbed against another insulator.

- There are two types of charge, which we call positive and negative.
- Opposite charges attract one another; like charges repel (Figure 8.2).
- A charged object may also be able to attract an uncharged one; this is as a result of electrostatic induction.

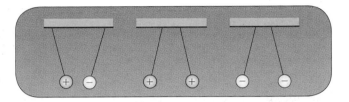

Figure 8.2 Attraction and repulsion between electric charges can be demonstrated by charging metal-coated polystyrene balls suspended from nylon threads.

These observations are macroscopic; that is, they are descriptions of phenomena that we can observe in the laboratory, without having to consider what is happening on the microscopic scale, at the level of particles such as atoms and electrons. However, we can give a more subtle explanation if we consider the microscopic picture of static electricity.

Matter may be modelled as consisting of three types of particles: negatively charged electrons, positively charged protons and electrically neutral neutrons. The magnitude of the charge of a proton is the same as that of an electron. An uncharged object must therefore have equal numbers of protons and electrons.

When one initially uncharged material is rubbed against another, there is friction between them, and electrons may be stripped off one material on to the other (Figure 8.3). The material that has gained electrons is now negatively charged, and the other material is positively charged.

If a positively charged object is brought close to an uncharged one, the electrons in the second object may be attracted. We observe this as a force of attraction between the two objects. This phenomenon is known as electrostatic induction.

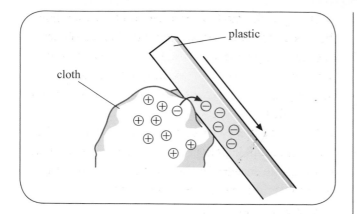

Figure 8.3 Friction can transfer electrons from one material to another.

It is important to appreciate that it is the electrons that are involved in moving within a material, or from one material to another. This is because electrons, which are on the outside of atoms, are less strongly held within a material than the protons. They may be free to move about within a material (like the conduction electrons in a metal), or they may be relatively weakly bound within atoms.

Investigating electric fields

If you rub a strip of plastic so that it becomes charged and then hold it close to your hair, you feel your hair being pulled upwards. The influence of the charged

The idea of positive and negative

If you lived in certain parts of Canada, the science curriculum would suggest that your teacher should allow you to play with plastic and glass rods so that you could discover for yourself the existence of positive and negative electric charges. This is a tall order, since it took some of the best scientific minds several decades to establish this idea!

By about 1730, physicists knew that, when rubbed, glass rods and pieces of amber appeared to have gained opposite types of 'electricity'. These were known as *vitreous electricity* (vitreous means glassy) and *resinous electricity* (amber is a type of resin). Nowadays we would say that vitreous electricity is positive charge while resinous is negative.

Two competing theories were developed to explain this:

- The *two fluids theory* proposed that there were two different electrical fluids at work, vitreous and resinous. An uncharged object had equal amounts of both, so their effects cancelled out. Adding vitreous fluid to an uncharged object made it positive, and so on.
- The alternative *single fluid theory* was proposed by Benjamin Franklin (Figure 8.4) in about 1750. He thought that all objects contained an electrical fluid. Uncharged objects contained a standard amount; adding excess fluid made them positively charged.

Franklin's idea wasn't accepted immediately. It was only in 1839 that Michael Faraday managed to show that static electricity and current electricity were aspects of the same phenomenon, together with 'bioelectricity' – electrical phenomena associated with living creatures.

Today, we accept Franklin's idea that there is only one type of electric 'fluid', and that it comes in positive and negative forms. No-one knows why Franklin chose to label 'vitreous electricity' as positive. His arbitrary choice has proved something of an inconvenience, since it means that the direction of an electric current in a metal wire is from positive to negative, but in fact consists of electrons flowing from negative to positive.

Figure 8.4 Benjamin Franklin. In this illustration, published long after his death, he is shown experimenting with static electricity. This work led him to invent the lightning conductor.

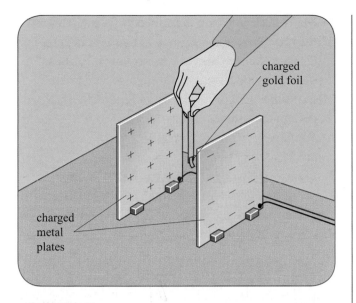

Figure 8.5 Investigating the electric field between two charged metal plates using a charged strip of gold foil.

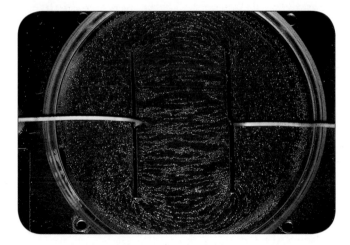

Figure 8.6 Apparatus for showing the uniform electric field between two parallel charged plates using semolina.

plastic spreads into the space around it; we say that there is an electric field around this charged object. In order to detect the electric field, we need to put something in it that will respond to the field (as your hair responded). There are two simple ways in which you can do this in the laboratory.

The first uses a charged strip of gold foil, attached to an insulating handle (Figure 8.5). The second uses grains of a material such as semolina (Figure 8.6); these line up in the electric field, just as iron filings line up in a magnetic field.

Representing electric fields

Electric field patterns can be mapped out using **electric field lines** in much the same way that we represent gravitational and magnetic fields. Figure 8.7 shows the electric field patterns for two charged parallel plates, a charged sphere and a positively charged sphere placed close to a negatively charged (earth) plate.

As with gravitational fields, the field lines indicate two things about the field: its direction (from the direction of the lines) and how strong it is (from their separation). The direction of the electric field is from positive to negative; it shows the direction of the electric force on a small positive charge placed at a point in the field. Closely bunched field lines indicate a stronger electric field.

- A uniform field has the same strength at all points. Example: the electric field between oppositely charged parallel plates.
- A radial field spreads outwards in all directions. Example: the electric field around a point charge or a charged sphere.

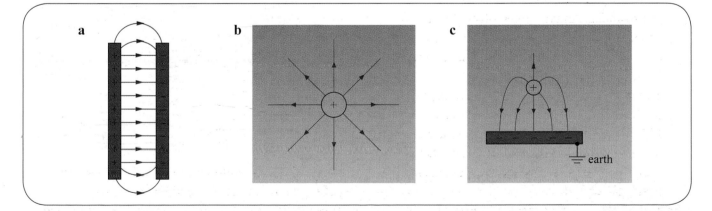

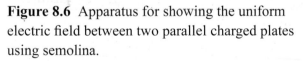

Figure 8.7 a A uniform electric field is produced between two oppositely charged plates. **b** A radial electric field surrounds a charged sphere. **c** The electric field between a charged sphere and an earthed plate.

SAQ

1 State which of the three field patterns in Figure 8.8 represents:

Hint

Answer

a two positive charges
b two negative charges
c two opposite charges.

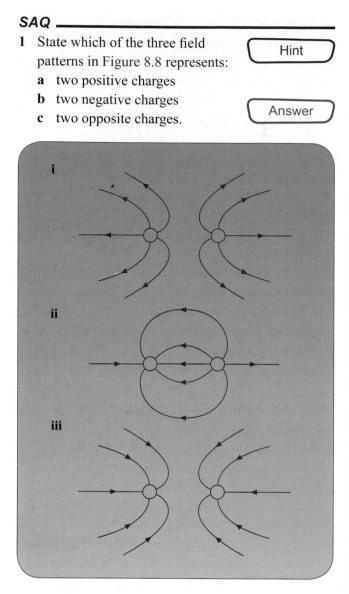

Figure 8.8 Electric fields between charges – see SAQ 1.

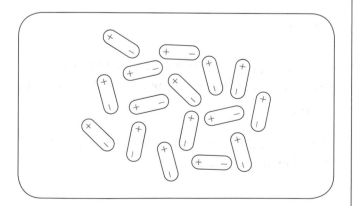

Figure 8.9 Polar molecules – see SAQ 2.

2 Many molecules are described as 'polar'; that is, they have regions that are positively or negatively charged, though they are neutral overall. Draw a diagram to show how sausage-shaped polar molecules like those shown in Figure 8.9 might realign themselves in a liquid.

Answer

3 Figure 8.10 shows the electric field pattern between a thundercloud and a building. State and explain where the electric field strength is greatest.

Answer

Figure 8.10 Predict where the electric field will be strongest – that's where lightning may strike – see SAQ 3.

Electric field strength

For a gravitational field, we defined its strength at a point as being the gravitational force per unit mass exerted on a mass placed at that point. Similarly, for electric fields, we can define **electric field strength** E at a point as follows:

The electric field strength at a point is the force per unit charge exerted on a positive charge placed at that point.

So to determine the electric field strength, we imagine putting a small positive test charge $+Q$ in the field and measuring the electric force F that acts on it (Figure 8.11). (If you have used a charged gold leaf to investigate a field, this illustrates the principle of testing the field with a charge.)

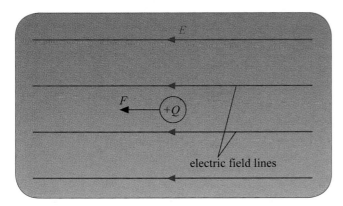

Figure 8.11 A field of strength E exerts force F on charge $+Q$.

From this definition, we can write an equation for the electric field strength E as:

$$E = \frac{F}{Q}$$

The equation above shows that the unit of electric field strength is the newton per coulomb ($N\,C^{-1}$). You can determine the force F acting on a charge Q placed in an electric field of strength E using the equation:

$$F = EQ$$

The strength of a uniform field

You can set up a uniform field between two parallel metal plates by connecting them to the terminals of a high-voltage power supply (Figure 8.12). You can see that the field is uniform because the field lines are straight, parallel and evenly spaced.

The strength E of the electric field between the plates depends on two factors:
- the potential difference V between the plates
- the separation d of the plates.

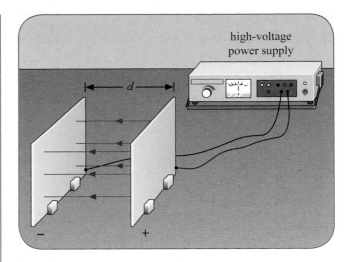

Figure 8.12 There is a uniform field between two parallel, charged plates.

Experiments show that the electric field strength is:
- directly proportional to the voltage, $E \propto V$
- inversely proportional to the separation, $E \propto \dfrac{1}{d}$.

These relationships can be combined to give an equation for E:

$$E = -\frac{V}{d}$$

See Worked example 1 for a derivation of this. Note that the minus sign is necessary because, in Figure 8.12, the voltage V increases towards the right while the force F acts in the opposite direction towards the left. E is a vector quantity. In calculations, we are often interested in the *magnitude* of the electric field strength, hence we can write:

$$E = \frac{V}{d}$$

From this equation, we can see that the unit of electric field strength is volts per metre ($V\,m^{-1}$). Note:

$$1\,V\,m^{-1} = 1\,N\,C^{-1}$$

Worked example 2 shows how to solve problems involving uniform fields.

Worked example 1

Two metal plates are separated by a distance d. The potential difference between the plates is V. A positive charge Q is pulled at a constant speed with a constant force F from the negative plate all the way to the positive plate. Using the definition for electric field strength and the concept of work done, show that the magnitude of the electric field strength E is given by the equation:

$$E = \frac{V}{d}$$

Step 1 We have

work done on charge = energy transformed

From their definitions, we can write:

work done = force × distance   or $W = Fd$

energy transformed = VQ

Step 2 Substituting gives:

$$Fd = VQ$$

and rearranging gives:

$$\frac{F}{Q} = \frac{V}{d}$$

Step 3 The left hand side of the equation is the electric field strength E. Hence:

$$E = \frac{V}{d}$$

Worked example 2

Two parallel metal plates separated by 2.0 cm have a potential difference of 5.0 kV. Calculate the electric force acting on a dust particle between the plates that has a charge of 8.0×10^{-19} C.

Step 1 Write down the quantities given (convert the prefixes to powers of 10).

$d = 2.0 \times 10^{-2}$ m $V = 5.0 \times 10^3$ V
$Q = 8.0 \times 10^{-19}$ C

continued

Step 2 In order to calculate the force F, you need to first determine the strength of the electric field.

$$E = \frac{V}{d}$$

$$E = \frac{50 \times 10^3}{2.0 \times 10^{-2}} = 2.5 \times 10^5 \, \text{V m}^{-1}$$

Step 3 Now calculate the force on the dust particle.

$$F = EQ$$

$$F = 2.5 \times 10^5 \times 8.0 \times 10^{-19} = 2.0 \times 10^{-13} \, \text{N}$$

SAQ

4 Figure 8.13 shows an arrangement of parallel plates, each at a different voltage. The electric field lines are shown in the space between the first two. Copy and complete the diagram to show the electric field lines in the other two spaces.

Answer

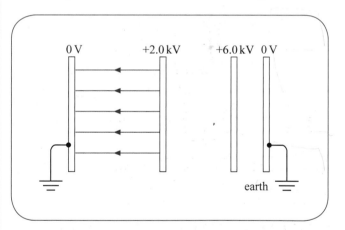

Figure 8.13 An arrangement of parallel plates.

5 An electron is situated in the uniform electric field between two charged electrodes. The electric force that acts on it is 8.0×10^{-16} N. Calculate the electric field strength.

Answer

6 Air is usually a good electrical insulator. However, a spark can jump through dry air when the electric field strength is greater than about 4.0×10^6 V m^{-1} (40 000 V cm^{-1}). This is called electrical

Hint

breakdown. The spark shows that electrical charge is passing through the air, giving rise to a current. (Do not confuse this with a chemical spark such as you might see when watching fireworks; in that case, small particles of a chemical substance are burning quickly.)

a   A Van de Graaff generator (Figure 8.14) is found to be able to make sparks jump across a 4.0 cm gap. Estimate the voltage between its dome and the other electrode.

b   The maximum voltage reached by the live wire of a conventional mains supply is 325 V. Estimate (but DO NOT try this) how close you would have to get to a live wire to get an electrical shock from it.

c   Estimate the voltage of a thundercloud from which lightning strikes the ground 100 m below. (Assume the ground is at 0 V.)

Answer

Figure 8.14 A Van de Graaff generator produces voltages sufficient to cause sparks in air.

Force on a charge

Now we can calculate the force F on a charge Q in the uniform field between two parallel plates. We have to combine the general equation for field strength $E = \dfrac{F}{Q}$ with the equation for the magnitude of the electric field $E = \dfrac{V}{d}$. This gives:

$$F = QE = \frac{QV}{d}$$

The magnitude of the charge on an electron is e. Hence the force experienced by an electron between charged parallel plates is given by the equation:

$$F = \frac{eV}{d}$$

Figure 8.15 shows a situation where this force is important. A beam of electrons is entering the space between two charged parallel plates. How will the electrons move?

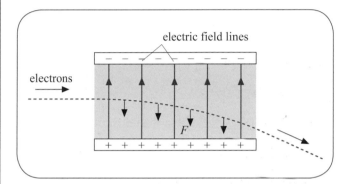

Figure 8.15 The parabolic path of a moving electron in a uniform electric field.

We have to think about the force on a single electron. In the diagram, the upper plate is negative relative to the lower plate, and so the electron experiences a downward force. You can think of this simply as the negatively charged electron being attracted by the positive plate, and repelled by the negative plate.

Note that the force F on the electron is the same at all points between the plates, and in this case it is always in the same direction (downwards).

If the electron was stationary, it would accelerate directly downwards. However, in this situation, the electron is moving to the right. Its horizontal velocity will be unaffected by the force because it acts at right angles to the horizontal direction ($F\cos 90°$). However, as it moves sideways, it will also accelerate downwards. It will follow a curved path, as shown. This curve is a parabola.

The motion of the electron in a uniform electric field is equivalent to a ball being thrown horizontally in the Earth's uniform gravitational field (Figure 8.16). It continues to move at a steady speed horizontally, but at the same time it accelerates downwards. The result is the familiar curved trajectory shown. For the electron described above, the force of gravity is negligible compared to the electric force on it. (The ratio of the weight mg of an electron to the electric force $F = \dfrac{eV}{d}$ on an electron is typically 10^{-18}.)

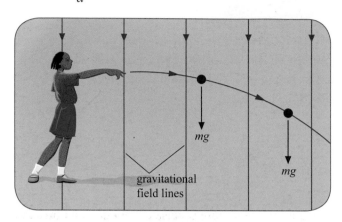

Figure 8.16 A ball thrown in the uniform gravitational field of the Earth follows a parabolic path.

SAQ

7 In Figure 8.17, two parallel plates are shown, separated by 25 cm.

   a Copy the diagram and draw field lines to represent the field between the plates.

   b Determine the potential difference between points A and B.

   c Calculate the electric field strength at C and at D.

   d Calculate the electric force on a charge of $+5.0\,\mu C$ placed at C. In which direction does the force act?   [Answer]

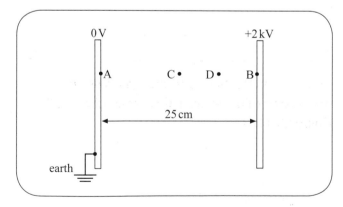

Figure 8.17 Two parallel, charged plates.

8 A particle of charge $+2.0\,\mu C$ is placed between two parallel plates, 10 cm apart, and with a potential difference of 5.0 kV between them. Calculate: [Hint]

   a the field strength between the plates

   b the force exerted on the charge.   [Answer]

9 We are used to experiencing accelerations that are usually less than $10\,\mathrm{m\,s^{-2}}$. For example, when we fall, our acceleration is about $9.8\,\mathrm{m\,s^{-2}}$. When a fast car turns a corner sharply, its acceleration is unlikely to be more than $5.0\,\mathrm{m\,s^{-2}}$. However, if you were an electron, you would be used to experiencing much greater accelerations than this.

   Calculate the acceleration of an electron (charge $-e = -1.6\times10^{-19}\,\mathrm{C}$, mass $m_e = 9.11\times10^{-31}\,\mathrm{kg}$) in a television tube where the electric field strength is $5.0\times10^4\,\mathrm{V\,cm^{-1}}$.   [Hint] [Answer]

10 a Use a diagram to explain how the electric force on a charged particle could be used to separate a beam of electrons (e^-) and positrons (e^+) into two separate beams. (A positron is a positively charged particle that has the same mass as an electron but opposite charge. Positron–electron pairs are often produced in collisions in a particle accelerator.)

   b Explain how this effect could be used to identify different ions that have different masses and charges.   [Answer]

[Extension]

Coulomb's law

Charles Coulomb was a French physicist. In 1785 he proposed a law that describes the force that one charged particle exerts on another. This law is remarkably similar in form to Newton's law of gravitation.

A statement of **Coulomb's law** is as follows:

> Any two point charges exert an electrical force on each other that is proportional to the product of their charges and inversely proportional to the square of the distance between them.

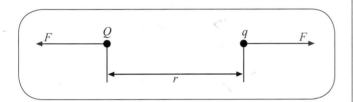

Figure 8.18 The variables involved in Coulomb's law.

We consider two point charges Q and q separated by a distance r (Figure 8.18). The force each charge exerts on the other is F. According to Newton's third law of motion, the point charges interact with each other and therefore exert equal but opposite forces on each other.

According to Coulomb's law, we have:

force ∝ product of the charges $F \propto Qq$

force ∝ $\dfrac{1}{\text{distance}^2}$ $F \propto \dfrac{1}{r^2}$

Therefore:

$$F \propto \frac{Qq}{r^2}$$

We can write this in a mathematical form:

$$F = k\frac{Qq}{r^2}$$

The constant of proportionality is:

$$k = \frac{1}{4\pi\varepsilon_0}$$

where ε_0 is known as the *permittivity of free space* (ε is the Greek letter epsilon). The value of ε_0 is approximately $8.85 \times 10^{-12}\,\mathrm{F\,m^{-1}}$. An equation for Coulomb's law is thus:

$$F = \frac{Qq}{4\pi\varepsilon_0 r^2}$$

By substituting for π and ε_0, we can show that the force F can also be given by the equation:

$$F \approx 9.0 \times 10^9 \frac{Qq}{r^2}$$

i.e. k has the approximate numerical value of $9.0 \times 10^9\,\mathrm{N\,m^2\,C^{-1}}$.

This approximation can be useful for making rough calculations, but more precise calculations require the value of ε_0 given above to be used.

Following your earlier study of Newton's law of gravitation, you should not be surprised by this relationship. The force depends on each of the properties producing it (in this case, the charges), and it is an inverse square law with distance – if the particles are twice as far apart, the electrical force is a quarter of its previous value (Figure 8.19).

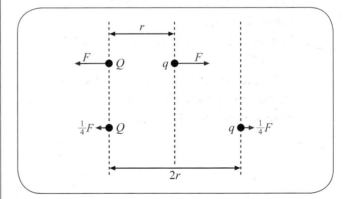

Figure 8.19 Double the separation results in one-quarter of the force, a direct consequence of Coulomb's law.

Note also that, if we have a positive and a negative charge, then the force F is negative. We interpret this as an attraction. Positive forces, as between two like charges, are repulsive. In gravity, we only have attraction.

So far we have considered point charges. If we are considering uniformly charged spheres we measure the distance from the centre of one to the centre of the other – they behave as if their charge was all concentrated at the centre. Hence we can apply the equation for Coulomb's law for both point charges (e.g. protons, electrons, etc.) and uniform charged spheres as long as we use the *centre-to-centre* distance between the objects.

Investigating Coulomb's law

It is quite tricky to investigate the force between charged objects, because charge tends to leak away into the air or to the Earth during the course of any experiment. The amount of charge we can investigate is difficult to measure, and usually small, giving rise to tiny forces.

Figure 8.20 shows one method for investigating the inverse square law for two charged metal balls (polystyrene balls coated with conducting silver paint). As one charged ball is lowered down towards the other, their separation decreases and so the force increases, giving an increased reading on the balance.

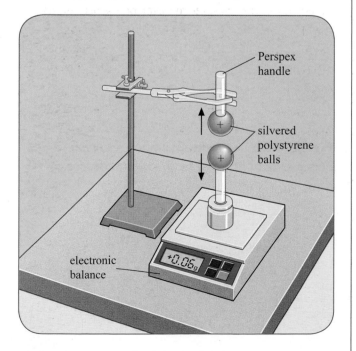

Figure 8.20 Investigating Coulomb's law.

Electric field strength for a radial field

We have already seen that the electric field strength at a point is defined as the force per unit charge exerted on a positive charge placed at that point, $E = F/Q$.

So to find the field strength near a point charge (or outside a uniformly charged sphere), we have to imagine a small positive test charge placed in the field, and determine the force per unit charge on it. We can use the definition above to determine the electric field strength for a point (or spherical) charge.

The force between two point charges is given by:

$$F = \frac{Qq}{4\pi\varepsilon_0 r^2}$$

The electric field strength E due to the charge Q at a distance of r from its centre is thus:

$$E = \frac{\text{force}}{\text{test charge}} = \frac{Qq}{4\pi\varepsilon_0 r^2 q}$$

or

$$E = \frac{Q}{4\pi\varepsilon_0 r^2}$$

The field strength E is not a constant; it decreases as the distance r increases. The field strength obeys the inverse square law with distance – just as gravitational field strength for a point mass. The field strength will decrease by a factor of four when the distance from the centre is doubled.

Note also that, since force is a vector quantity, it follows that electric field strength is also a vector. We need to give its direction as well as its magnitude in order to specify it completely.

Now look at Worked example 3.

Worked example 3

A spherical metal dome of diameter 12 cm is positively charged. The electric field strength at the surface of the dome is $4.0 \times 10^5 \, \text{V m}^{-1}$. Draw the electric field pattern for the dome and determine the total surface charge.

Step 1 Draw the electric field pattern (Figure 8.21). The electric field lines must be normal to the surface and radial.

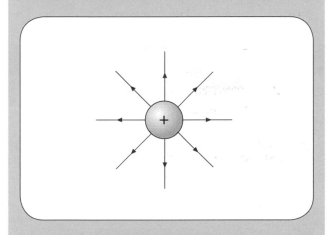

Figure 8.21 The electric field around a charged sphere.

Step 2 Write down the quantities given.

electric field strength $E = 4.0 \times 10^5 \, \text{V m}^{-1}$

$$\text{radius } r = \frac{0.12}{2} = 0.06 \, \text{m}$$

Step 3 Use the equation for the electric field strength to determine the surface charge.

$$E = \frac{Q}{4\pi\varepsilon_0 r^2}$$

$$Q = 4\pi\varepsilon_0 r^2 \times E$$

$$Q = 4\pi \times 8.85 \times 10^{-12} \times (0.06)^2 \times 4.0 \times 10^5$$

$$Q = 1.6 \times 10^{-7} \, \text{C} \qquad (0.16 \, \mu\text{C})$$

SAQ

You will need the data below to answer the following SAQs.

$\varepsilon_0 = 8.85 \times 10^{-12} \, \text{F m}^{-1}$

11 A metal sphere of radius 20 cm carries a positive charge of 2.0 μC.
   a What is the electric field strength at a distance of 25 cm from the centre of the sphere?
   b An identical metal sphere carrying a negative charge of 1.0 μC is placed next to the first sphere. There is a gap of 10 cm between them. Calculate the electric force that each sphere exerts on the other.

   > Hint

   c Determine the electric field strength midway along a line joining the centres of the spheres.

   > Answer

12 A Van de Graaff generator produces sparks when the field strength at its surface is $4.0 \times 10^4 \, \text{V cm}^{-1}$. If the diameter of the sphere is 40 cm, what is the charge on it?

   > Answer

Comparing gravitational and electric fields

There are obvious similarities between the ideas we have used in this chapter to describe electric fields and those we used in Chapter 4 for gravitational fields. This can be helpful, or it can be confusing! The summary given in Table 8.1 is intended to help you to sort them out.

An important difference is this: electric charges can be positive or negative, so they can attract and repel. There are no negative masses so there is only attraction in a gravitational field.

Gravitational fields	Electric fields
Origin arise from masses	*Origin* arise from electric charges
Vector forces only gravitational attraction, no repulsion	*Vector forces* both electrical attraction and repulsion are possible (because of positive and negative charges)

All gravitational fields
 	
   field strength $g = \dfrac{F}{m}$
 	
i.e. field strength is force per unit mass
	All electric fields
	
	   field strength $E = \dfrac{F}{Q}$
	
	i.e. field strength is force per unit positive charge

Units F in N, g in $N\,kg^{-1}$ or $m\,s^{-2}$	*Units* F in N, E in $N\,C^{-1}$ or $V\,m^{-1}$
Uniform gravitational fields parallel gravitational field lines g = constant	*Uniform electric fields* parallel electric field lines $E = V/d$ = constant

Spherical gravitational fields
radial field lines
force given by Newton's law:
 	
   $F = -\dfrac{GMm}{r^2}$
 	
field strength is therefore:
 	
   $g = -\dfrac{GM}{r^2}$
 	
force and field strength obey an inverse square law with distance
	Spherical electric fields
	radial field lines
	force given by Coulomb's law:
	
	   $F = \dfrac{Qq}{4\pi\varepsilon_0 r^2}$
	
	field strength is therefore:
	
	   $E = \dfrac{Q}{4\pi\varepsilon_0 r^2}$
	
	force and field strength obey an inverse square law with distance

Table 8.1 Gravitational and electric fields compared.

SAQ

You will need the data below to answer the question.

proton: mass = 1.67×10^{-27} kg

   charge = $+1.6 \times 10^{-19}$ C

$\varepsilon_0 = 8.85 \times 10^{-12}\,F\,m^{-1}$

$G = 6.67 \times 10^{-11}\,N\,m^2\,kg^{-2}$

13 Two protons in the nucleus of an atom are separated by a distance of 10^{-15} m. Calculate the electrostatic force of repulsion between them, and the force of gravitational attraction between them. (Assume the protons behave as point charges and point masses.) Is the attractive gravitational force enough to balance the repulsive electrical force? What does this suggest to you about the forces between protons within a nucleus?

Answer

Summary

- An electric field is created by electric charges, and can be represented by electric field lines.

- The strength of the field is the force acting per unit positive charge at a point in the field; that is $E = \dfrac{F}{Q}$.
  Unit: NC^{-1} or Vm^{-1}.

- In a uniform field (e.g. between two charged parallel plates), the force on a charge is the same at all points. The magnitude of the electric field strength is given by:

  $$E = \frac{V}{d}$$

- Coulomb's law states that two point charges exert an electrical force on each other that is proportional to the product of their charges and inversely proportional to the square of the distance between them.

- Coulomb's law gives the force between two point charges or two spherical charges. The distance must be from centre to centre.

- The equation for Coulomb's law is:

  $$F = \frac{Qq}{4\pi\varepsilon_0 r^2}$$

- A point charge Q gives rise to a radial field. The electric field strength is given by the equation:

  $$E = \frac{Q}{4\pi\varepsilon_0 r^2}$$

- The force between point charges and the electric field strength due to a point charge both obey the inverse square law with distance.

Questions

1 This question is about electric forces.
   A very small negatively charged conducting sphere is suspended by an insulating thread from support S.
   It is placed close to a vertical metal plate carrying a positive charge. The sphere is attracted towards the
   plate and hangs with the thread at an angle of 20° to the vertical as shown in Figure 1.

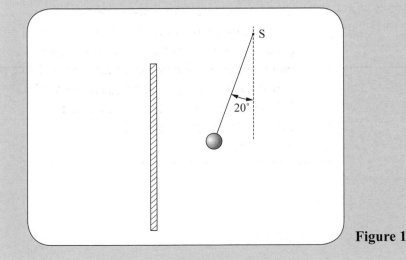

Figure 1

continued

a Copy Figure 1 and draw at least <u>five</u> electric field lines on the diagram to show
   the pattern of the field between the plate and the sphere. [3]

b The sphere of weight 1.0×10^{-5} N carries a charge of -1.2×10^{-9} C.
   i Show that the magnitude of the attractive force between the sphere and the
      plate is about 3.6×10^{-6} N. [3]
   ii Hence show that the value of the electric field strength at the sphere, treated
      as a point charge, is 3.0×10^3 in SI units. State the unit. [3]

c The plate is removed. Figure 2 shows an identical sphere carrying a
   charge of $+1.2 \times 10^{-9}$ C, mounted on an insulating stand. It is placed so that the
   hanging sphere remains at $20°$ to the vertical.

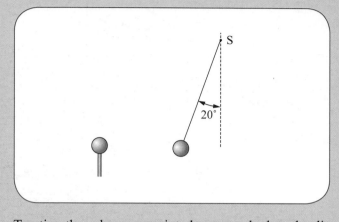

S

20°

Figure 2

   Treating the spheres as point charges, calculate the distance r between their centres. [3]

d Sketch a copy of Figure 2 and then draw the electric field pattern between the
   two charges. By comparing this sketch with your answer to **a**, suggest why the
   distance between the plate and the sphere in Figure 1 is half of the distance
   between the two spheres in Figure 2. [2]

OCR Physics A2 (2824) January 2006 [Total 14]

2 This question is about changing the motion of electrons using electric fields. The diagram below shows
   a horizontal beam of electrons moving in a vacuum. The electrons pass through a hole in the centre of a
   metal plate A. At B is a metal grid through which the electrons can pass. At C is a further metal sheet.
   The three vertical conductors are maintained at voltages of $+600$ V at A, 0 V at B and $+1200$ V at C.
   The distance from plate A to grid B is 40 mm.

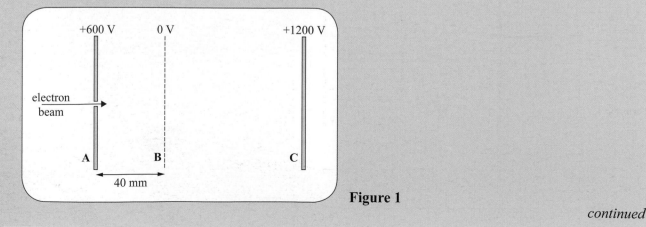

+600 V   0 V   +1200 V

electron
beam

A   B   C

40 mm

Figure 1

continued

a Make a sketch of the diagram and draw on the electric field lines to represent the fields in the regions between the three plates. [3]

b Show that the magnitude of the electric field strength between plate A and grid B is $1.5 \times 10^4 \, \text{V m}^{-1}$. [2]

c Calculate the horizontal force on an electron after passing through the hole in A. [2]

d Show that the minimum speed that an electron in the beam must have at the hole in A to reach the grid at B is about $1.5 \times 10^7 \, \text{m s}^{-1}$. [2]

e Calculate the speed of these electrons when they collide with sheet C. [1]

f Describe and explain the effect on the current detected at C when the voltage of the grid B is increased negatively. [2]

OCR Physics A2 (2824) January 2005   [Total 12]

Hint

Answer

3 a Define *electric field strength* at a point in space. [2]

b Figure 1 shows two point charges of equal magnitude, $1.6 \times 10^{-19} \, \text{C}$, and opposite sign, held a distance $8.0 \times 10^{-10} \, \text{m}$ apart at points A and B. The charge at A is positive.

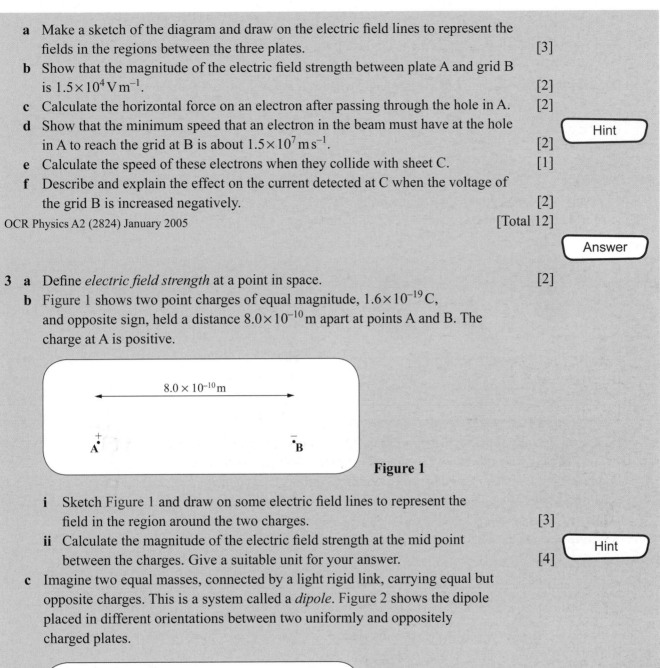

Figure 1

i Sketch Figure 1 and draw on some electric field lines to represent the field in the region around the two charges. [3]

ii Calculate the magnitude of the electric field strength at the mid point between the charges. Give a suitable unit for your answer. [4]

Hint

c Imagine two equal masses, connected by a light rigid link, carrying equal but opposite charges. This is a system called a *dipole*. Figure 2 shows the dipole placed in different orientations between two uniformly and oppositely charged plates.

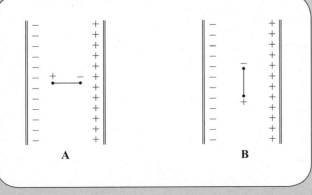

Figure 2

continued

Any effects of gravity are negligible.

  i Describe the electric forces acting on the charges by drawing suitable arrows on a copy of the diagrams. [2]

  ii Explain the motion, if any, of the dipole when it is released from rest in the diagram on the left and on the right. [3]

OCR Physics A2 (2824) January 2004   [Total 14]

            (Answer)

4 This question is about a simple model of a hydrogen iodide molecule. Figure 1 shows a simple representation of the hydrogen iodide molecule. It consists of two ions, $^1_1H^+$ and $^{127}_{53}I^-$, held together by electric forces.

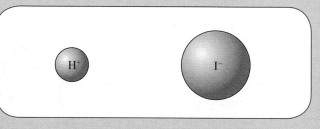

Figure 1

a **i** Copy Figure 1 and draw on it lines to represent the resultant electric field between the two ions. [2]

  ii Calculate the electrical force F of attraction between the ions.
Treat the ions as point charges a distance 5.0×10^{-10} m apart. Each ion has a charge of magnitude 1.6×10^{-19} C. [4]

b The electrical attraction is balanced by repulsive forces so that the two ions are in equilibrium. When disturbed the ions oscillate in simple harmonic motion. Figure 2 shows a simple mechanical model of the molecule consisting of two unequal masses connected by a spring of negligible mass.

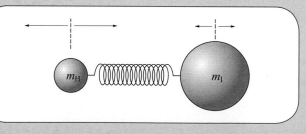

Figure 2

Use Newton's laws of motion and the definition of simple harmonic motion to explain why the amplitude of oscillation of the hydrogen ion is 127 times the amplitude of oscillation of the iodine ion. [4]

continued

c   The natural frequency of oscillation of the hydrogen ion is 6.7×10^{13} Hz. Take
the amplitude of oscillation to be 8.0×10^{-12} m.

i   Copy the axes in Figure 3 and sketch a displacement against time graph for
the hydrogen ion. [3]

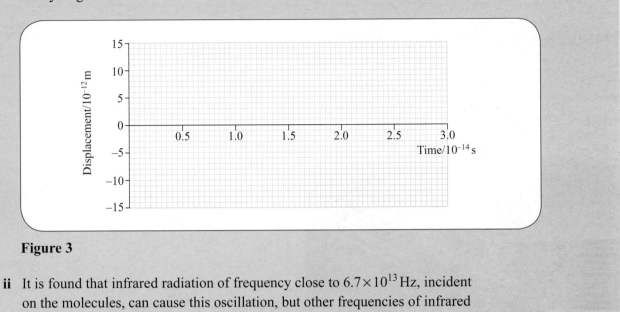

Figure 3

ii It is found that infrared radiation of frequency close to 6.7×10^{13} Hz, incident
on the molecules, can cause this oscillation, but other frequencies of infrared
do not. Suggest how this result can be explained. [2]

OCR Physics A2 (2824) June 2007 [Total 15]

Answer

119

Chapter 9

Magnetic fields

Objectives

Magnets and currents

The train shown in Figure 9.1 is supported at a precise distance above the track by computer-controlled electromagnets. In this chapter, we will look at magnetic forces and fields, how they arise, and how they interact.

Figure 9.1 This high-speed train is magnetically levitated so that it avoids friction with the track.

You can make a magnetic field in two ways: using a permanent magnet, or using an electric current. You should be familiar with the magnetic field patterns of bar magnets (Figure 9.2). These can be shown up using iron filings or plotting compasses.

We represent magnetic field patterns by drawing magnetic field lines.

- The magnetic field lines come out of north poles and go into south poles.
- The direction of a field line at any point in the field shows the direction of the force that a 'free' magnetic north pole would experience at that point.
- The field is strongest where the field lines are closest together.

An electromagnet makes use of the magnetic field created by an electric current (Figure 9.3). A coil is used because this concentrates the magnetic field. One end becomes a north pole (field lines emerging), while the other end is the south pole. Another name

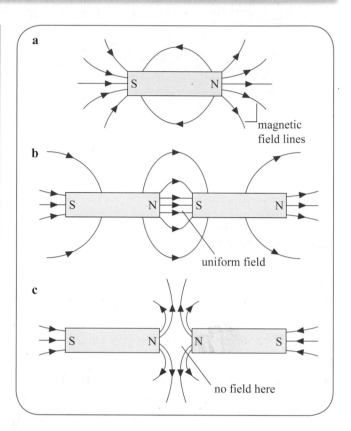

Figure 9.2 Magnetic field patterns **a** for a bar magnet; **b** for two attracting bar magnets; **c** for two repelling bar magnets.

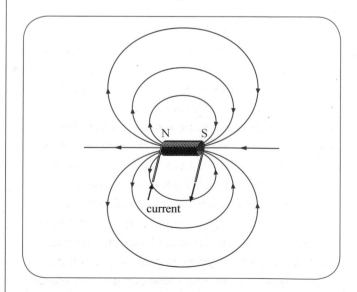

Figure 9.3 The magnetic field pattern of a current-carrying coil (a solenoid).

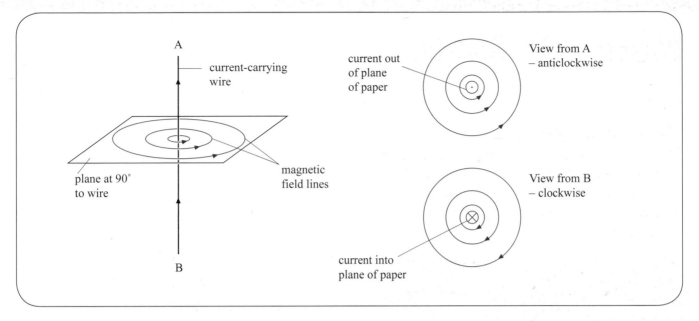

Figure 9.4 The magnetic field pattern around a current-carrying wire. The diagram also shows the convention used to indicate the direction of current.

for a coil like this is a **solenoid**. The field pattern for the solenoid looks very similar to that of a bar magnet (see Figure 9.2a), with field lines emerging from a north pole at one end and returning to a south pole at the other.

If we unravel an electromagnet, we get a weaker field. This too can be investigated using iron filings or compasses. The magnetic field pattern for a long current-carrying wire is very different from that of a solenoid. The magnetic field lines shown in Figure 9.4 are circular, centred on the long current-carrying wire. Further away from the wire, the field lines are drawn further apart, representing the weaker field at this distance. Reversing the current reverses the direction of the field.

All magnetic fields are created by *moving* charges. (In the case of a wire, the moving charges are free electrons.) This is even true for a permanent bar magnet. In a permanent magnet, the magnetic field is produced by the movement of electrons within the atoms of the magnet. Each electron represents a tiny current as it circulates around within its atom, and this current sets up a magnetic field. In a ferrous material such as iron, the weak fields due to all the electrons combine together to make a strong field, which spreads out into the space beyond the magnet. In non-magnetic materials, the fields produced by the electrons cancel each other out.

Field direction

The idea that magnetic field lines emerge from north poles and go into south poles is simply a convention.

Figure 9.5 shows some useful rules for remembering the direction of the magnetic field produced by a current:

- The right-hand grip rule gives the direction of magnetic field lines in an electromagnet. Imagine gripping the coil, so that your fingers go around it following the direction of the current. Your thumb now points in the direction of the field lines inside the coil, i.e. it points towards the electromagnet's north pole.
- Another way to identify the poles of an electromagnet is to look at it end on, and decide which way round the current is flowing. The diagrams show how you can remember that clockwise is a south pole, anticlockwise is a north pole.
- The right-hand corkscrew rule is a way of remembering the direction of the field lines around a long current-carrying wire. Imagine pushing a corkscrew into a cork, turning it as you do so. The direction in which you push is the direction of the conventional current, and the field lines go round in the direction in which you are turning the corkscrew.

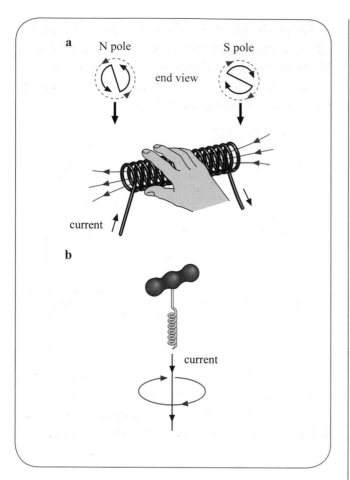

Figure 9.5 Two rules for determining the direction of a magnetic field, **a** inside a solenoid and **b** around a current-carrying wire.

SAQ

1 Sketch the magnetic field pattern around a long straight wire carrying an electric current. Now, alongside this first sketch, draw a second to show the field pattern if the current flowing was doubled and its direction reversed.

Answer

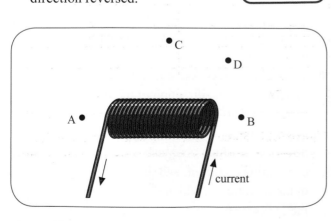

Figure 9.6 A current-carrying solenoid – see SAQ 2.

2 Sketch the diagram in Figure 9.6, and label the N and S poles of the electromagnet. Show on your sketch the direction of the magnetic field (as shown by the needle of a plotting compass) at each of the positions A, B, C and D.

Answer

3 State which of the pairs of electromagnets shown in Figure 9.7 will attract one another, and which will repel.

Answer

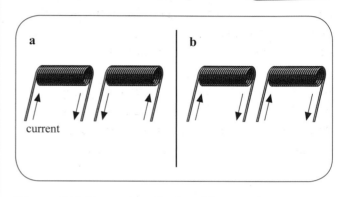

Figure 9.7 Two pairs of solenoids – see SAQ 3.

Magnetic force

A current-carrying wire is surrounded by a magnetic field. This magnetic field can interact with an external magnetic field, giving rise to a force on the conductor, just like the fields of two interacting magnets. The simplest situation is shown in Figure 9.8.

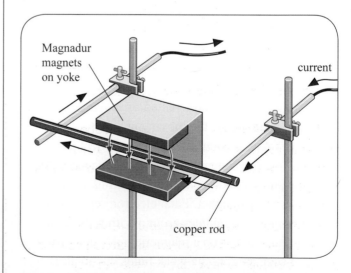

Figure 9.8 The copper rod is free to roll along the two horizontal aluminium 'rails'.

The magnets create a fairly uniform magnetic field. As soon as the current in the copper rod is switched on, the rod starts to roll, showing that a force is acting on it.

We use **Fleming's left-hand (motor) rule** to predict the direction of the force on the current-carrying conductor. There are three things here, all of which are mutually at right angles to each other – the magnetic field, the current in the rod, and the force on the rod. These can be represented by holding the thumb and the first two fingers of your left hand so that they are mutually at right angles (Figure 9.9). Your thumb and fingers then represent:

- thuMb – direction of Motion
- First finger – direction of external magnetic Field
- seCond finger – direction of conventional Current

You should practise using your left hand to check that the rule correctly predicts these directions.

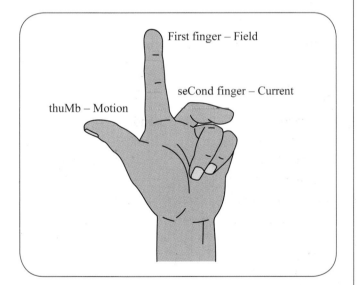

Figure 9.9 Fleming's left-hand (motor) rule.

We can explain this force by thinking about the magnetic fields of the magnets and the current-carrying conductor. These fields combine or interact to produce the force on the rod.

Figure 9.10 shows:

- the external magnetic field of the magnets
- the magnetic field of the current-carrying conductor
- the combined fields of the current-carrying conductor and the magnets.

The production of this force is known as the *motor effect*, because this force is used in electric motors. In a simple motor, a current in a coil produces a magnetic field; this field interacts with a second field produced by a permanent magnet.

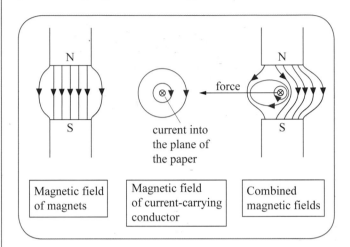

Figure 9.10 In the field of a permanent magnet, a current-carrying conductor experiences a force in accordance with Fleming's left-hand rule. The fields due to the permanent magnet and the current (left and centre) combine as shown on the right.

SAQ

4 Figure 9.11 shows three examples of current-carrying conductors in magnetic fields. For each example, decide whether there will be a magnetic force on the conductor. If there is a force, in what direction will it act?

Answer

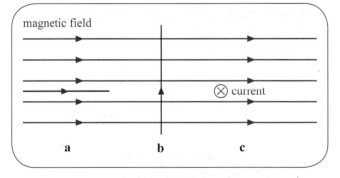

Figure 9.11 Three conductors in a magnetic field.

Magnetic flux density

In electric or gravitational field diagrams, the strength of the field is indicated by the separation between the field lines. The field is strongest where the field lines are close together. The same is also true for magnetic fields. The *strength* of a magnetic field is known as its **magnetic flux density**. (You can imagine this quantity to represent the number of magnetic field lines passing through a region per unit area.) The magnetic flux density is greater close to the pole of a bar magnet, and gets smaller as you move away from it.

The symbol used for magnetic flux density is B and its unit is the **tesla** (T).

We define gravitational field strength g at a point as the force per unit mass:

$$g = \frac{F}{m}$$

Electric field strength E is defined as the force per unit positive charge:

$$E = \frac{F}{Q}$$

In a similar way, magnetic flux density is defined in terms of the magnetic force experienced by a current-carrying conductor placed at *right angles* to a magnetic field. For a uniform magnetic field, the flux density B is defined by the equation:

$$B = \frac{F}{IL}$$

where F is the force experienced by a current-carrying conductor, I is the current in the conductor and L is the length of the conductor in the uniform magnetic field of flux density B. The direction of the force F is given by Fleming's left-hand rule.

The unit for magnetic flux density is $NA^{-1}m^{-1}$ or simply tesla (T). Note that $1\,T = 1\,NA^{-1}m^{-1}$.

The tesla is defined as follows:

> The magnetic flux density is 1 T when a wire carrying a current of 1 A placed at right angles to the magnetic field experiences a force of 1 N per metre of its length.

The force on the conductor is given by the equation:

$$F = BIL$$

Note that you can only use this equation when the field is at right angles to the current.

(Extension)

Determining magnetic flux density

Figure 9.12 shows a simple arrangement that can be used to determine the flux density between two magnets. The magnetic field between these magnets is (roughly) uniform. The length L of the current-carrying wire in the uniform magnetic field can be measured using a ruler.

When there is no current in the wire, the magnet arrangement is placed on the top pan and the balance is zeroed. Now, when a current I flows in the wire, its value is shown by the ammeter. The wire experiences an upward force and, according to Newton's third law of motion, there is an equal and opposite force on the magnets. The magnets are pushed downwards and a reading appears on the scale of the balance. The force F is given by mg, where m is the mass indicated on the balance in kilograms and g is the acceleration of free fall ($9.81\,m\,s^{-2}$).

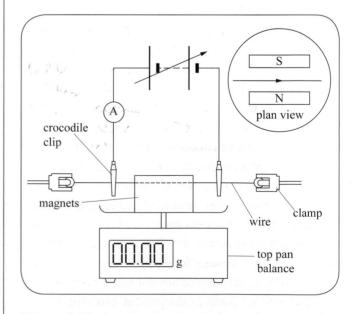

Figure 9.12 An arrangement to determine magnetic flux density in the laboratory.

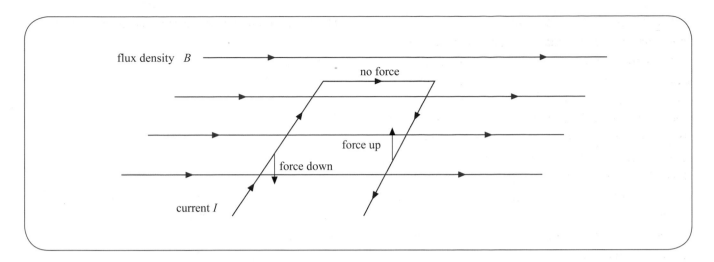

Figure 9.13 The force on a current-carrying conductor crossing a magnetic field.

Knowing F, I and L, the magnetic flux density B between the magnets can be determined using the equation:

$$B = \frac{F}{IL}$$

You can also use the arrangement in Figure 9.12 to show that force is directly proportional to the current.

Currents crossing fields

At right angles
We explained the force on a current-carrying conductor in a field in terms of the interaction of the two magnetic fields: the field due to the current and the external field. Here is another, more abstract, way of thinking of this.

Whenever an electric current cuts across magnetic field lines (Figure 9.13), a force is exerted on the current-carrying conductor. This helps us to remember that a conductor experiences no force when the current is parallel to the field.

This is a useful idea, because it saves us thinking about the field due to the current. In Figure 9.13, we can see that there is only a force when the current cuts across the magnetic field lines.

This force is very important – it is the basis of electric motors. Worked example 1 shows why a current-carrying coil placed in a magnetic field rotates.

Worked example 1

An electric motor has a rectangular loop of wire with the dimensions shown in Figure 9.14. The loop is in a magnetic field of flux density 0.10 T. The current in the loop is 2.0 A. Calculate the torque that acts on the loop in the position shown.

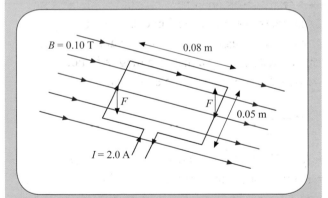

Figure 9.14 A simple electric motor – a current-carrying loop in a magnetic field.

Step 1 The quantities we know are:

$B = 0.10\,\text{T}$, $I = 2.0\,\text{A}$ and $L = 0.05\,\text{m}$

Step 2 Now we can calculate the force on one side of the loop using the equation $F = BIL$:

$F = 0.10 \times 2.0 \times 0.05$

$F = 0.01\,\text{N}$

continued

Step 3 The two forces on opposite sides of the loop are equal and anti-parallel. In other words, they form a couple. From *Physics 1*, you should recall that the torque (moment) of a couple is equal to the magnitude of one of the forces times the perpendicular distance between them. The two forces are separated by 0.08 m, so:

torque = force × separation

torque = $0.01 \times 0.08 = 8.0 \times 10^{-4}$ N m

SAQ

5   A wire of length 50 cm carrying a current of 2.4 A lies at right angles to a magnetic field of flux density 5.0 mT. Calculate the force on the wire.

   Hint

   Answer

6   A current balance is a rectangular frame made of copper wire that can be adapted to determine the magnetic flux density, see Figure 9.15. The current in the frame is 0.50 A. A counterweight of mass 0.020 g is needed to restore equilibrium of the frame. The length of the frame in the magnetic field is 5.0 cm. Use the information provided to determine the magnetic flux density between the magnets.

   Hint

   Answer

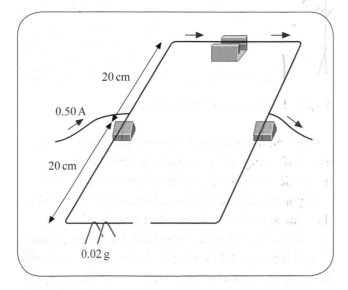
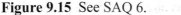

Figure 9.15 See SAQ 6.

7   The coil of an electric motor is made up of 200 turns of wire carrying a current of 1.0 A. The coil is square, with sides of length 20 cm, and it is placed in a magnetic field of flux density 0.05 T.
   a   Determine the maximum force exerted on the side of the coil.
   b   In what position must the coil be for this force to have its greatest turning effect?
   c   List four ways in which the motor could be made more 'powerful' – that is, have greater torque.

   Answer

At an angle other than 90°

Now we must consider the situation where the current-carrying conductor cuts across a magnetic field at an angle other than a right angle. In Figure 9.16, the force gets weaker as the conductor is moved round from OA to OB, to OC and finally to OD. In the position OD, there is no force on the conductor. To calculate the force, we need to find the component of the magnetic flux density B at right angles to the current. This component is $B \sin \theta$, where θ is the angle between the magnetic field and the current or the conductor. Substituting this into the equation $F = BIL$ gives:

$$F = (B \sin \theta)IL$$

or simply:

$$F = BIL \sin \theta$$

Now look at Worked example 2.

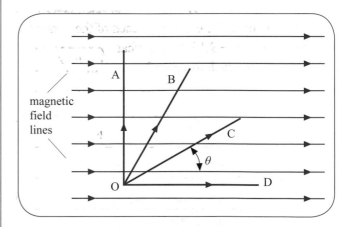

Figure 9.16 The force on a current-carrying conductor depends on the angle it makes with the magnetic field lines.

Worked example 2

A conductor OC (see Figure 9.16) of length 0.20 m lies at an angle θ of 25° to a magnetic field of flux density 0.050 T. Calculate the force on the conductor when it carries a current of 400 mA.

Step 1 Write down what you know, and what you want to know:

$B = 0.050 \, T$ $L = 0.20 \, m$

$I = 400 \, mA = 0.40 \, A$ $\theta = 25°$

$F = ?$

Step 2 Write down the equation, substitute values and solve:

$F = BIL \sin\theta$

$F = 0.050 \times 0.40 \times 0.20 \times \sin 25° \approx 1.7 \times 10^{-3} \, N$

Step 3 Give the direction of the force. The force acts at 90° to the field and the current, i.e. perpendicular to the page. The left-hand rule shows that it acts downwards into the plane of the paper.

Note that the component of B parallel to the field is $B\cos\theta$, but this does not contribute to the force; there is no force when the field and current are parallel. The force F is at right angles to both the current and the field.

SAQ

8 What force will be exerted on each of the currents shown in Figure 9.17, and in what direction will each force act?

Answer

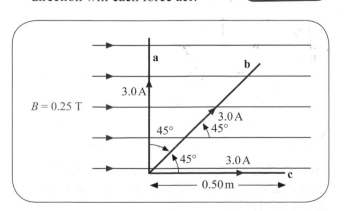

Figure 9.17 Three currents crossing a magnetic field.

Moving particles

The world of atomic physics is populated by a great variety of particles – electrons, protons, neutrons, positrons and many more. Many of these particles are electrically charged, and so their motion is influenced by electric and magnetic fields. Indeed, we use this fact to help us to distinguish one particle from another.

You can use your knowledge of how charged particles and electric currents are affected by fields to interpret diagrams of moving particles. You must bear in mind that, by convention, the direction of conventional electric current is the direction of flow of positive charge. When electrons are moving, the conventional current is regarded as flowing in the opposite direction.

Observing the force

Electron beam tubes (Figure 9.18) can be used to demonstrate the magnetic force on a moving charge. A beam of electrons is produced by an 'electron gun', and magnets or electromagnets can be used to apply a magnetic field.

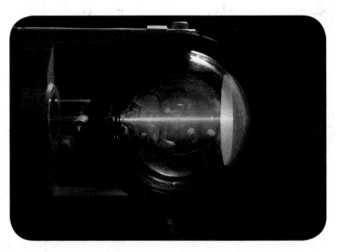

Figure 9.18 An electron beam tube.

You can use such an arrangement to observe the effect of changing the strength and direction of the magnetic field, and the effect of reversing the field.

If you are able to observe a beam of electrons like this, you should find that the force on the electrons moving through the magnetic field can be predicted using Fleming's left-hand rule. In Figure 9.19, a beam of electrons is moving from right to left, into a region where a magnetic field is directed into the plane of the paper. Since electrons are negatively charged, they

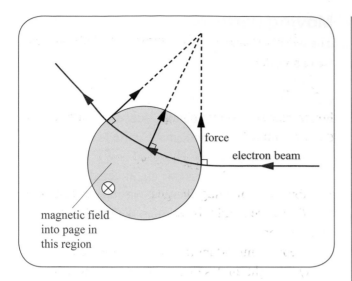

Figure 9.19 A beam of electrons is deflected as it crosses a magnetic field. The magnetic field into the plane of the paper is represented by the cross in the circle.

represent a conventional current from left to right. Fleming's left-hand rule predicts that, as the electrons enter the field, the force on them will be upwards and so the beam will be deflected up the page. As the direction of the beam changes, so does the direction of the force. The force due to the magnetic field is always at 90° to the velocity of the electrons.

It is this force that gives rise to the motor effect. The electrons in a wire experience a force when they flow across a magnetic field, and they transfer the force to the wire itself.

Using electron beams

Oscilloscopes, as well as some computer monitors and television sets, make use of beams of electrons. Electrons are moved about using magnetic and electric fields, and the result can be a rapidly changing image on the screen.

Figure 9.20 shows the construction of a typical tube. The electron gun has a heated cathode. The positively charged anode attracts electrons from the negative cathode, and they pass through the anode to form a narrow beam in the space beyond. The direction of the beam can be changed using an electric field between two plates (as shown in Figure 9.20), or a magnetic field created by electromagnetic coils.

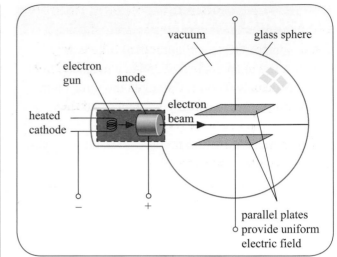

Figure 9.20 The construction of an electron beam tube.

SAQ

9 In the diagram in Figure 9.21, radiation from a radioactive material passes through a region of uniform magnetic field. Identify which tracks are those of α-particles (alpha particles, positive charge), β-particles (beta particles, negative charge) and γ-rays (gamma-rays, no charge).

Hint

Answer

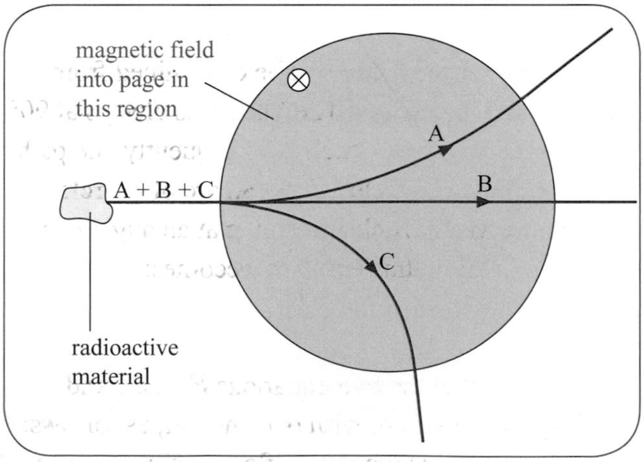

Figure 9.21 Three types of radiation passing through a magnetic field.

The magnetic force on a moving charge

We can make an intelligent guess about the factors that determine the size of the force on a moving charge in a uniform magnetic field (Figure 9.22). It will depend on:

- the magnetic flux density B (strength of the magnetic field)
- the charge Q on the particle
- the speed v of the particle.

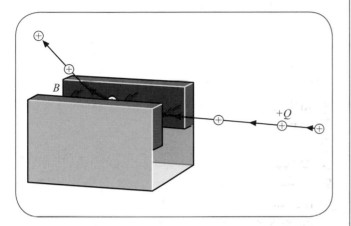

Figure 9.22 The path of a charged particle is curved in a magnetic field.

The magnetic force F on a moving particle at right angles to a magnetic field is given by the equation:

$$F = BQv$$

The direction of the force can be determined from Fleming's left-hand rule. The force F is always at 90° to the velocity of the particle. Consequently, the path described by the particle will be an arc of a circle.

If the charged particle is moving at an angle θ to the magnetic field, this equation becomes:

$$F = BQv \sin \theta$$

We can show that the two equations $F = BIL$ and $F = BQv$ are consistent with one another, as follows:

Since current I is the rate of flow of charge, we can write $I = \dfrac{Q}{t}$. Substituting in $F = BIL$ gives:

$$F = \frac{BQL}{t}$$

Now, $\dfrac{L}{t}$ is the speed v of the moving particle, and so we can write:

$$F = BQv$$

For an electron, whose charge is $-e$, the magnitude of the force on it is:

$$F = Bev \qquad (e = 1.6 \times 10^{-19}\,\text{C})$$

The force on a moving charge is sometimes called 'the Bev force', and it is really no different from 'the BIL force'.

Here is an important reminder: The force F is always at right-angles to the particle's velocity v, and its direction can be found using the left-hand rule (Figure 9.23).

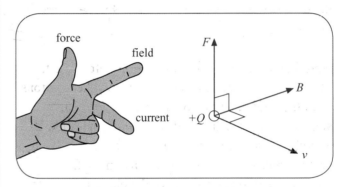

Figure 9.23 Fleming's left-hand rule, applied to a moving positive charge.

SAQ

10 A beam of electrons, moving at $1.0 \times 10^6\,\text{m s}^{-1}$, is directed through a magnetic field of flux density $0.50\,\text{T}$. Calculate the force on each electron when **a** the beam is at right angles to the magnetic field, and **b** the beam is at an angle of 45° to the field.

Answer

11 Positrons are particles identical to electrons, except that their charge is positive $(+e)$. Use a diagram to explain how a magnetic field could be used to separate a mixed beam of positrons and electrons.

Answer

Orbiting charges

Consider a charged particle moving at right angles to a uniform magnetic field. It will describe a circular path because the magnetic force F is always perpendicular to its velocity. We can describe F as a *centripetal force*, because it is always directed towards the centre of the circle.

Figure 9.24 shows a fine-beam tube. In this tube, a beam of fast-moving electrons is produced by an electron gun. This is similar to the cathode and anode shown in Figure 9.20, but in this case the beam is directed vertically downwards as it emerges from the gun. It enters the spherical tube, which has a uniform horizontal magnetic field. The beam is at right angles to the field and the Bev force pushes it round in a circle.

The fact that the Bev force acts as a centripetal force gives us a clue as to how we can calculate the radius of the orbit of a charged particle in a uniform magnetic field. The centripetal force on the charged particle is given by:

$$\text{centripetal force} = \frac{mv^2}{r}$$

The centripetal force is provided by the magnetic force Bev. Therefore:

$$Bev = \frac{mv^2}{r}$$

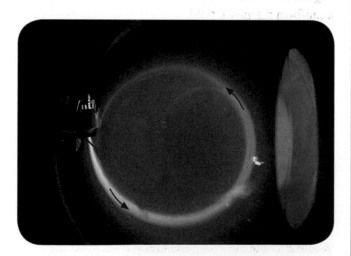

Figure 9.24 In this fine-beam tube, a beam of electrons is bent around into a circular orbit by an external magnetic field. The beam is shown up by the presence of a small amount of gas in the tube. (The electrons travel in an anticlockwise direction.)

Cancelling and rearranging to find r gives:

$$r = \frac{mv}{Be}$$

You can also write this equation in terms of the momentum p of the particle, that is:

$$p = Ber$$

The equation $r = \dfrac{mv}{Be}$ shows that:

- faster-moving particles move in bigger circles ($r \propto v$)
- particles with greater masses also move in bigger circles (they have more inertia; $r \propto m$)
- a stronger field makes the particles move in tighter circles ($r \propto 1/B$).

This is made use of in a variety of scientific applications, such as particle accelerators and mass spectrometers – see Worked example 3.

Worked example 3

An electron is travelling at right angles to a uniform magnetic field of flux density 1.2 mT. The speed of the electron is $8.0 \times 10^6 \, \text{m s}^{-1}$. Calculate the radius of circle described by this electron. (For an electron, charge $e = 1.6 \times 10^{-19} \, \text{C}$ and mass $= 9.11 \times 10^{-31} \, \text{kg}$.)

Step 1 Calculate the magnetic force on the electron.

$$F = Bev = 1.2 \times 10^{-3} \times 1.6 \times 10^{-19} \times 8.0 \times 10^6$$

$$F = 1.536 \times 10^{-15} \, \text{N} \approx 1.5 \times 10^{-15} \, \text{N}$$

Step 2 Use your knowledge of motion in a circle to determine the radius r:

$$F = \frac{mv^2}{r}$$

Therefore:

$$r = \frac{mv^2}{F} = \frac{9.11 \times 10^{-31} \times (8.0 \times 10^6)^2}{1.536 \times 10^{-15}}$$

$$r \approx 3.8 \times 10^{-2} \, \text{m} \qquad (3.8 \, \text{cm})$$

continued

Note: The same result could have been obtained simply by using the equation:

$$r = \frac{mv}{Be}$$

SAQ

12 Look at the photograph of the electron beam in the fine-beam tube (Figure 9.24). In which direction is the magnetic field (into or out of the plane of the photograph)?

Answer

13 The particles in the circular beam shown in Figure 9.24 all travel round in the same orbit. What can you deduce about their mass, charge and speed?

Answer

14 An electron beam in a vacuum tube is directed at right angles to a magnetic field, so that it travels along a circular path. Predict the effect on the size and shape of the path that would be produced (separately) by each of the following changes:

a increasing the magnetic flux density
b reversing the direction of the magnetic field
c slowing down the electrons
d tilting the beam, so that the electrons have a component of velocity along the magnetic field.

Answer

Electric and magnetic fields

A deflection tube (Figure 9.25) is designed to show a beam of electrons passing through a combination of electric and magnetic fields. By adjusting the strengths of the electric and magnetic fields, you can balance the two forces on the electrons, and the beam will remain horizontal. The magnetic field is provided by two coils, called Helmholtz coils (Figure 9.26), which give a very uniform field in the space between them.

To find the speed of the electrons emerging from the anode, you need to know the cathode–anode voltage, V_{ca}. An individual electron has charge $-e$, and an amount of work $e \times V_{ca}$ is done on it in accelerating it from the cathode to the anode. This is its kinetic energy:

$$eV_{ca} = \tfrac{1}{2}mv^2$$

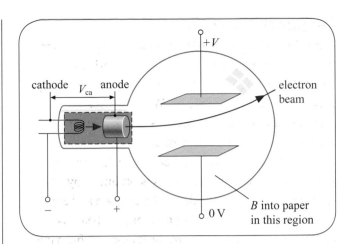

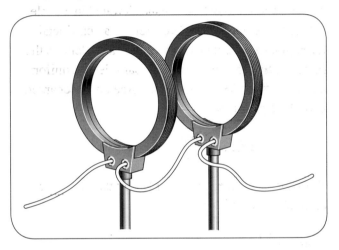

Figure 9.25 The path of an electron beam in a deflection tube.

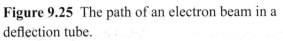

Figure 9.26 A pair of Helmholtz coils is used to give a uniform magnetic field.

where m is electron mass and v is electron speed. If the electron beam remains straight, it follows that the electric and magnetic forces on each electron must have the same magnitude and act in opposite directions. Therefore:

electric force = magnetic force
(upward)   (downward)

$$eE = Bev$$

where E is the electric field strength between the parallel plates with a p.d of V. The speed v of the electrons is simply related to the strengths of the two fields. That is:

$$v = \frac{E}{B}$$

The electric field strength is given by:

$$E = \frac{V}{d}$$

therefore:

$$v = \frac{V}{Bd}$$

Substituting v into the kinetic energy equation on page 131 gives the following expression for the ratio of the charge on the electron to its mass:

$$\frac{e}{m} = \frac{V^2}{2V_{ca}B^2d^2}$$

The voltages V and V_{ca}, the flux density B and the plate separation d can all be measured, and the charge/mass ratio of an individual electron can then be calculated. Since we know the electron charge $-e = -1.6 \times 10^{-19}$ C, this experiment can also be used to find the electron mass m.

SAQ

15 Use your knowledge of the forces on charged particles to work out where the electron beam will strike the screen in the tube shown in Figure 9.27. Break the problem into small steps as follows. (Electron charge $-e = -1.6 \times 10^{-19}$ C; electron mass $m = 9.11 \times 10^{-31}$ kg.)

   a Electrons are attracted from the cathode to the anode by the potential difference between them. Calculate the kinetic energy gained by an electron as it accelerates from the cathode to the anode, and use this value to calculate the speed of the electron.

   b In this tube, the electron beam is deflected by the electric field between two parallel plates. Calculate the strength of the field, and the force on a single electron.

   c The horizontal component of the electron's velocity is not affected by the electric field. Why is this? Calculate the time the electron takes to travel through the space between the plates.

   d The electrons are accelerated upwards by the electric force on them. Calculate their acceleration, and use your answer to deduce the upward component of the electron's velocity as it emerges from the space between the plates.

   e From your knowledge of the components of the electron's velocity, calculate the angle ϕ.

   f Calculate how far up the screen the beam will strike.

   g Explain how your answer would differ if the anode–cathode voltage was increased, and if the voltage between the deflecting plates was increased.

   h The beam can be restored to its horizontal path if a magnetic field is applied in the region between the two parallel plates. Calculate the flux density B needed to do this. In what direction must the magnetic field act?

Answer

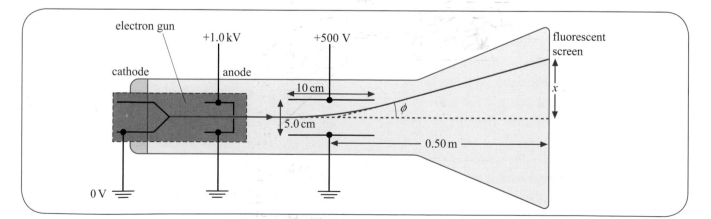

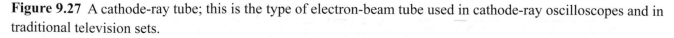

Figure 9.27 A cathode-ray tube; this is the type of electron-beam tube used in cathode-ray oscilloscopes and in traditional television sets.

Mass spectrometer

In a mass spectrometer (Figure 9.28), chemists separate ions of different masses and charges by passing them through a uniform magnetic field. We have already seen that the radius r of the circle described by a charged particle is given by:

$$r = \frac{mv}{BQ}$$

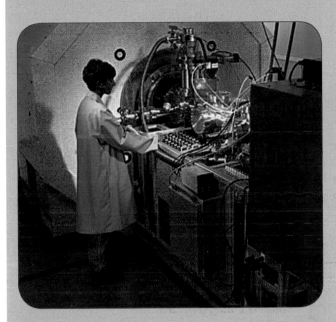

Figure 9.28 A mass spectrometer. On the left you can see the large cylindrical electromagnet used to separate ions of different masses.

The charge e has been replaced by the charge Q. The greater the mass and the smaller the charge, the less the ions are deflected by the magnetic field.

Figure 9.29 shows the principle of the mass spectrometer. In this case, it is being used to separate ionised carbon dioxide molecules of different masses. (Most CO_2 molecules have a relative molecular mass of 44, because C = 12 and O = 16. However, a few are heavier because they contain heavier isotopes of carbon, C-13 and C-14, giving relative masses of 45 and 46.)

The molecules are given a single positive charge $+e$ in the ion source, where they are also accelerated through a voltage V_{ca}. Then they pass through a strong magnetic field. (Notice that the paths of the ion beams are curved only in the region of the field; elsewhere they are straight.)

Ions of relative molecular mass 44 are deflected more than the heavier ones. The radius r of the path is directly proportional to the mass m of the ion; $r \propto m$ (see page 130). The ion detectors are positioned to catch and count the different molecules. Because the heavier carbon isotopes C-13 and C-14 are rare, few of these are detected – roughly 1% of molecules have relative molecular mass 45, and perhaps only one in 10^{12} molecules

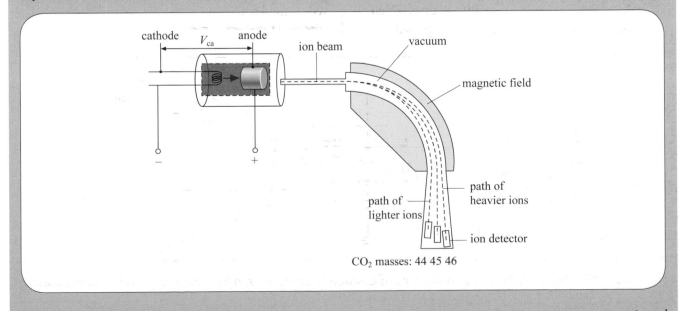

Figure 9.29 How a mass spectrometer works.

continued

has relative molecular mass 46. It is remarkable to be able to measure such a tiny proportion.

Figure 9.28 shows the typical size of a laboratory mass spectrometer – they are big machines. When the Beagle 2 lander was sent to Mars in 2003, it was equipped with many instruments to analyse the Martian environment (Figure 9.30). One was a tiny mass spectrometer, less than 50 cm across, designed by scientists and technicians at the UK's Open University. Sad to say, Beagle 2 crashed on landing and was never heard from.

However, the technology will be put to use in future space missions and in other applications here on Earth.

Figure 9.30 The Beagle 2 lander; an artist's impression of the spacecraft on the surface of Mars. It carried a complete, miniaturised, automated laboratory, including a mass spectrometer to analyse carbon in the Martian rocks.

SAQ

16 All charged ions entering a mass spectrometer tend to have the same speed. This is achieved by an arrangement known as a velocity selector, see Figure 9.31.

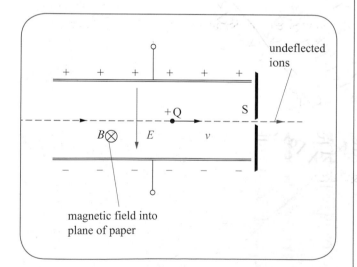

Figure 9.31 A velocity selector – only particles with the correct combination of charge, mass and velocity will emerge through the slit S.

The arrangement in Figure 9.31 is situated in an evacuated chamber. The parallel plates provide a uniform electric field of strength E. The region between the plates is also occupied by a uniform magnetic field of flux density B which is at right angles to the electric field. Positively charged ions travelling at a speed v emerge undeflected from the slit S. The charge on a single ion is $+Q$.

a State the directions of the magnetic and electric forces on an ion travelling towards the slit S.

b Show that the speed of the ion is independent of the charge of the ion and is given by the equation: [Hint]

$$v = \frac{E}{B}$$

c Calculate the speed of the ions emerging from the slit S when the magnetic flux density is 0.30 T and the electric field strength is $1.5 \times 10^3 \, V \, m^{-1}$.

d Explain why ions travelling at a speed greater than your answer to c will not emerge from the slit. [Answer]

Summary

Glossary

- Moving charges produce a magnetic field; this is electromagnetism.

- A current-carrying conductor has concentric magnetic field lines. The magnetic field pattern for a solenoid resembles that of a bar magnet.

- The separation between magnetic field lines is an indication of the field's strength.

- Magnetic flux density B is defined by the following equation:

$$B = \frac{F}{IL}$$

where F is the force experienced by a current-carrying conductor, I is the current in the conductor and L is the length of the conductor in the uniform magnetic field.

- The unit of magnetic flux density is the tesla (T). $1\,T = 1\,NA^{-1}m^{-1}$.

- The magnetic flux density is 1 T when a wire carrying a current of 1 A placed at right angles to the magnetic field experiences a force of 1 N per metre of its length.

- The magnetic force on a current-carrying conductor is given by $F = BIL$ or $F = BIL\sin\theta$.

- The magnetic force on a moving charged particle is given by the equation $F = BQv$. For an electron the equation is $F = Bev$.

- A charged particle entering at right angles to a uniform magnetic field describes a circular path because the magnetic force is perpendicular to the velocity.

- The equation for an electron travelling in a uniform magnetic field is:

$$\frac{mv^2}{r} = Bev$$

- The velocity of an undeflected charged particle in a region where electric and magnetic fields are at right angles is given by the equation:

$$v = \frac{E}{B}$$

Questions

1   The diagram below shows a section through a loudspeaker.

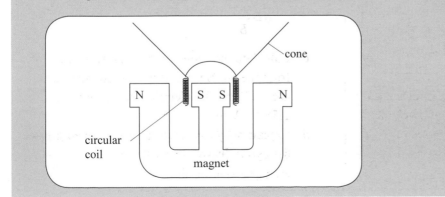

continued

The circular coil is free to move up and down in the space between the north and south poles of the magnet. The coil is connected to a d.c. supply of e.m.f. 1.5 V and of negligible internal resistance.

a Copy the diagram and draw arrows to show the directions of the magnetic field between the poles of the magnet. [1]

b The length of the wire in the coil is 24 m and its resistance is 8.0 Ω. The magnetic flux density of the magnetic field at the position of the coil is 1.2×10^{-2} T. Calculate the force experienced by the wire in the coil due to the magnetic field. [4]

c Wire of the same length and material but half the diameter of the original wire is used to make a similar coil. State and explain the change to your answer to **b** when this coil is used in place of the original one. [2]

OCR Physics AS (2822) January 2008 [Total 7]

Answer

2 This question is about the electron beam inside a television tube.

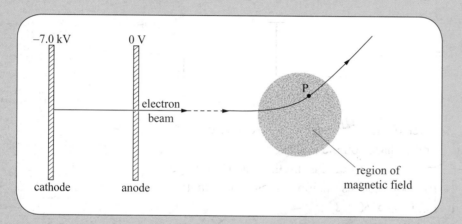

-7.0 kV   0 V

electron beam

P

region of magnetic field

cathode   anode

a The diagram above shows a section through a simplified model of an electron gun in an evacuated TV tube.

i Copy the diagram and draw some electric field lines to represent the field between the cathode and the anode. [2]

ii The electrons, emitted at negligible speed from the cathode, are accelerated through a p.d. of 7.0 kV. Show that the speed of the electrons at the anode is about 5.0×10^7 m s^{-1}. [2]

b Some electrons pass through a small hole in the anode. They enter a region of uniform magnetic field strength shown by the shaded area on the diagram. They follow a circular arc in this region before continuing to the TV screen.

i Draw an arrow through the point labelled P to show the direction of the force on the electrons at this point. [1]

ii State the direction of the magnetic field in the shaded area. Explain how you arrived at your answer. [2]

iii Calculate the radius of the arc of the path of the electron beam when the value of the magnetic flux density is 3.0×10^{-3} T. [4]

continued

c The region of uniform magnetic field is created by the electric current in an arrangement of coils. Suggest how the end of the electron beam is swept up and down the TV screen. [2]

OCR Physics A2 (2824) January 2007 [Total 13]

Answer

3 A nitrogen atom is initially stationary at point P in Figure 1, midway between two large horizontal parallel plates in an evacuated chamber. The nitrogen atom becomes charged. There is an electric field between the plates. Ignore any effects of gravity.

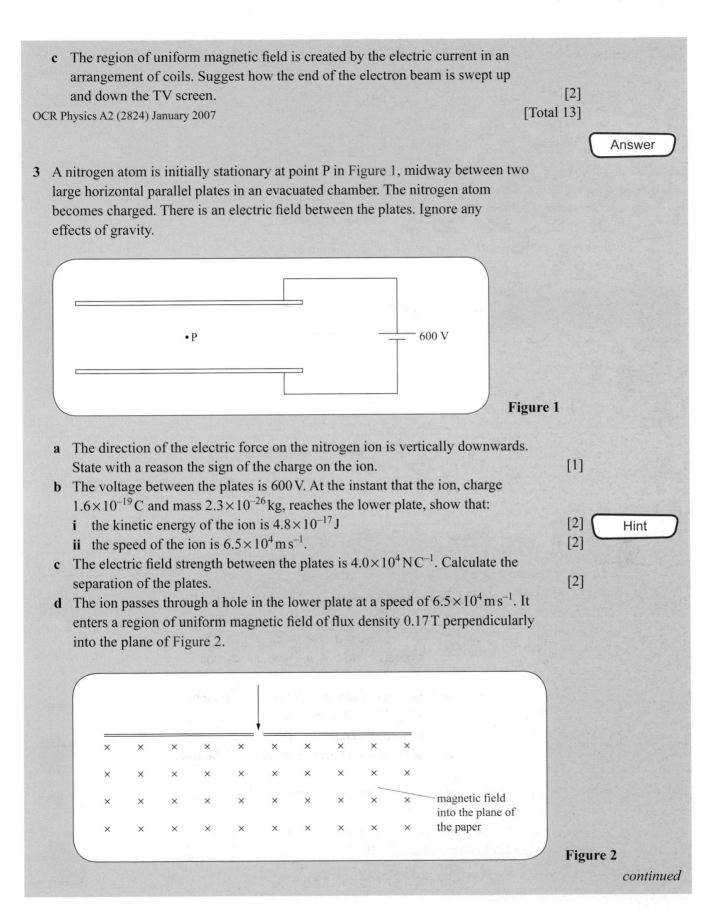

Figure 1

a The direction of the electric force on the nitrogen ion is vertically downwards. State with a reason the sign of the charge on the ion. [1]

b The voltage between the plates is 600 V. At the instant that the ion, charge 1.6×10^{-19} C and mass 2.3×10^{-26} kg, reaches the lower plate, show that:

  i the kinetic energy of the ion is 4.8×10^{-17} J [2]

  ii the speed of the ion is 6.5×10^4 m s^{-1}. [2]

Hint

c The electric field strength between the plates is 4.0×10^4 N C^{-1}. Calculate the separation of the plates. [2]

d The ion passes through a hole in the lower plate at a speed of 6.5×10^4 m s^{-1}. It enters a region of uniform magnetic field of flux density 0.17 T perpendicularly into the plane of Figure 2.

magnetic field into the plane of the paper

Figure 2

continued

137

    i Sketch Figure 2 and mark the semicircular path taken by the ion.   [1]

    ii Calculate how far from the hole the ion will collide with the plate. Use data from **b**.   [5]

OCR Physics A2 (2824) June 2006   [Total 13]

Hint

Answer

4 **a** Define *magnetic flux density*.   [2]

    b The diagram below shows an evacuated circular tube in which charged particles can be accelerated. A uniform magnetic field of flux density B acts in a direction perpendicular to the plane of the tube.

        Protons move with a speed v along a circular path within the tube.

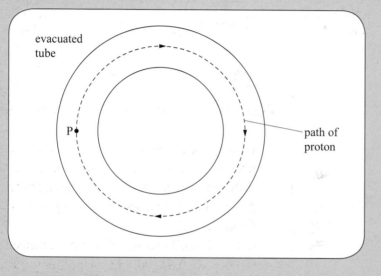

    i Sketch the diagram and draw on an arrow at P to indicate the direction of the force on the protons for them to move in a circle within the tube.   [1]

    ii State the direction of the magnetic field. Explain how you arrived at your answer.   [2]

    iii Write down an algebraic expression for the force F on a proton in terms of the magnetic field at point P.   [1]

    iv Calculate the value of the flux density B needed to contain protons of speed $1.5 \times 10^7 \, \mathrm{m \, s^{-1}}$ within a tube a radius 60 m. Give a suitable unit for your answer.   [5]

    v State and explain what action must be taken to contain protons, injected at twice the speed ($2v$), within the tube.   [2]

OCR Physics A2 (2824) June 2005   [Total 13]

Hint

Answer

Chapter 10

Electromagnetic induction

e-Learning

Objectives

Generating electricity

Most of the electricity we use is generated by electromagnetic induction. This process goes on in the generators at work in power stations and in wind turbines (Figure 10.1) and, on a much smaller scale, in bicycle dynamos. It is the process whereby a conductor and a magnetic field are moved relative to each other to induce, or generate, a current or electromotive force (e.m.f.).

Figure 10.1 This giant wind turbine uses electromagnetic induction to produce electricity. Look for the two engineers at work. (You can identify them by their white helmets.) This gives you an idea of the size of the generator.

Here are some simple experiments in which you can observe some of the features of electromagnetic induction. In each case, try to predict what you will observe before you try the experiment.

- *Experiment 1*
  Connect a small electric motor to a moving-coil voltmeter (Figure 10.2). Spin the shaft of the motor and observe the deflection of the voltmeter. What happens when you spin the motor more slowly? What happens when you stop?

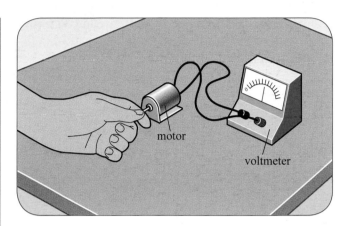

Figure 10.2 A motor works in reverse as a generator.

Usually, we connect a motor to a power supply and it turns. In this experiment, you have turned the motor and it generates a voltage across its terminals. A generator is like a motor working in reverse.

- *Experiment 2*
  Connect a coil to a sensitive microammeter (Figure 10.3). Move a bar magnet in towards the coil. Hold it still, and then remove it. How does the deflection on the meter change? Try different speeds, and the opposite pole of the magnet. Try weak and strong magnets.
  With the same equipment, move the coil towards the magnet and observe the deflection of the meter.

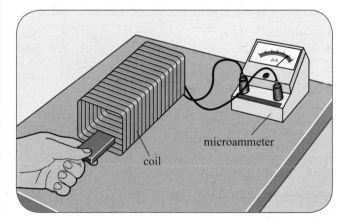

Figure 10.3 A magnet moving near a coil generates a small current.

● *Experiment 3*

Connect a long wire to a sensitive microammeter. Move the middle section of the wire up and down through the magnetic field between the magnets (Figure 10.4). Double up the wire so that twice as much passes through the magnetic field. What happens to the meter reading? How can you form the wire into a loop to give twice the deflection on the meter?

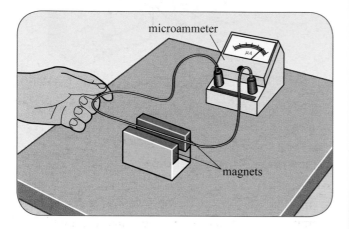

Figure 10.4 Investigating the current induced when a wire moves through a magnetic field.

In all these experiments, you have seen an electric current or an e.m.f. induced. In each case, there is a magnetic field and a conductor. When you move the magnet or the conductor, there is an induced current. When you stop, the current stops.

From the three experiments, you should see that the size of the induced current or e.m.f. depends on several factors.

For a straight wire, the induced current or e.m.f. depends on:
● the magnitude of the magnetic flux density
● the length of the wire in the field
● the speed of movement of the wire.

For a coil of wire, the induced current or e.m.f. depends on:
● the magnitude of the magnetic flux density
● the cross-sectional area of the coil
● the number of turns of wire
● the rate at which the coil turns in the field.

Explaining electromagnetic induction

You have seen that relative movement of a conductor and a magnetic field induces a current in the conductor when it is part of a complete circuit. (In the experiments above, the meter was used to complete the circuit.) Now we need to think about how to explain these observations, using what we know about magnetic fields.

Cutting magnetic field lines

Start by thinking about a simple bar magnet. It has a magnetic field in the space around it. We represent this field by magnetic field lines. Now think about what happens when a wire is moved into the magnetic field (Figure 10.5). As it moves, it *cuts across* the magnetic field. Remove the wire from the field, and again it must cut across the field lines, but in the opposite direction.

We think of this cutting of magnetic field by a conductor as the effect that gives rise to an induced current in the conductor. It doesn't matter whether the conductor is moved through the field, or the magnet is moved past the conductor, the result is the same – there will be an induced current.

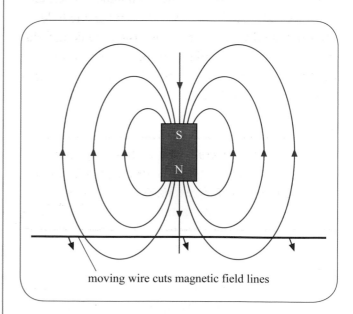

moving wire cuts magnetic field lines

Figure 10.5 Inducing a current by moving a wire through a magnetic field.

The effect is magnified if we use a coil of wire. For a coil of N turns, the effect is N times greater than for a single turn of wire. With a coil, it is helpful to imagine the number of field lines *linking* the coil. If there is a change in the number of field lines which pass through the coil, an e.m.f. will be induced across the ends of the coil (or there will be an induced current if the coil forms part of a complete circuit).

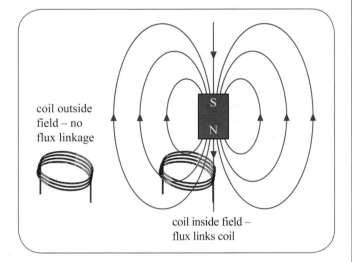

Figure 10.6 The flux passing through a coil changes as it is moved into and out of a magnetic field.

Figure 10.6 shows a coil near a magnet. When the coil is outside the field, there are no magnetic field lines linking the coil. When it is inside the field, field lines link the coil. Moving the coil into or out of the field changes this linkage, and this induces an e.m.f. across the ends of the coil.

SAQ

1   Use the idea of a conductor cutting magnetic field lines to explain how a current is induced in a bicycle dynamo (Figure 10.7).

> Answer

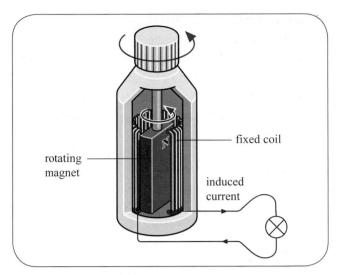

Figure 10.7 In a bicycle dynamo, a permanent magnet rotates inside a fixed coil of wire – see SAQ 1.

Current direction

How can we predict the direction of the induced current? For the motor effect in Chapter 9, we used Fleming's left-hand (motor) rule. Electromagnetic induction is like the mirror image of the motor effect. Instead of a current producing a force on a current-carrying conductor in a magnetic field, we provide an external force on a conductor by moving it through a magnetic field and this induces a current in the conductor. So you should not be too surprised to find that we use the mirror image of the left-hand rule: **Fleming's right-hand (dynamo) rule**.

The three fingers represent the same things again (Figure 10.8):

- thu<u>M</u>b – direction of <u>M</u>otion
- <u>F</u>irst finger – direction of external magnetic <u>F</u>ield
- se<u>C</u>ond finger – direction of (conventional) induced <u>C</u>urrent

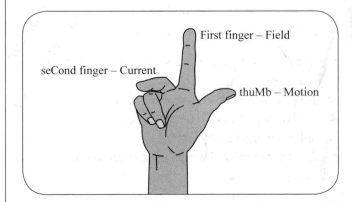

Figure 10.8 Fleming's right-hand (dynamo) rule.

In the example shown in Figure 10.9, the conductor is being moved downwards across the magnetic field. There is an induced current in the conductor as shown. Check this with your own right hand. You should also check that reversing the movement or the field will result in the current flowing in the opposite direction.

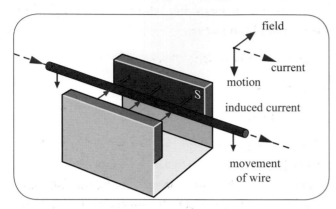

Figure 10.9 Deducing the direction of the induced current using Fleming's right-hand rule.

Induced e.m.f.

When a conductor is not part of a complete circuit, there cannot be an induced current. Instead, negative charge will accumulate at one end of the conductor, leaving the other end positively charged. We have induced an e.m.f. across the ends of the conductor.

Is e.m.f. the right term? Should it be voltage? In *Physics 1*, you saw the distinction between voltage and e.m.f. The latter is the correct term here because, by pushing the wire through the magnetic field, work is done and this is transformed into electrical energy. Think of this in another way. Since we could connect the ends of the conductor so that there is a current in some other component, such as a lamp, which would light up, it must be an e.m.f. – a source of electrical energy.

Figure 10.10 shows how the induced current gives rise to an induced e.m.f. Notice that, within the conductor, conventional current is from negative to positive, in the same way as inside a battery or any other source of e.m.f. In reality, the free electrons within the conductor travel from right to left, making the left-hand side of the conductor negative. What causes these electrons to move? Moving the conductor is equivalent to giving as electron within the conductor a velocity in the direction of this motion.

This electron is in an external magnetic field and hence experiences a magnetic force Bev from right to left. Check this out for yourself.

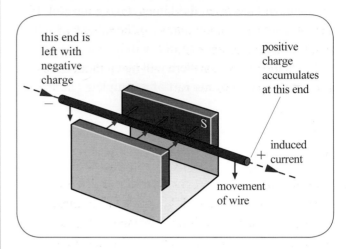

Figure 10.10 An e.m.f. is induced across the ends of the conductor.

SAQ

2 The coil in Figure 10.11 is rotating in a uniform magnetic field. Deduce the direction of the induced current in sections AB and CD. State which terminal, X or Y, will become positive.

Answer

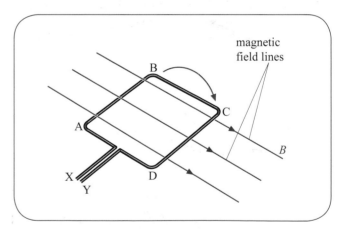

Figure 10.11 A coil rotated in a magnetic field.

3 When an aircraft flies from east to west, its wings are an electrical conductor cutting across the Earth's magnetic flux. In the Northern Hemisphere, which wingtip will become positively charged? Why will this wingtip be negative in the Southern Hemisphere?

Answer

Magnetic flux and magnetic flux linkage

So far in this chapter we have looked at the ideas of electromagnetic induction in a descriptive way. Now we will see how to calculate the value of the induced e.m.f. and look at a general way of determining its direction.

In Chapter 9, we saw how magnetic flux density B is defined by the equation

$$B = \frac{F}{IL}$$

Now we can go on to define **magnetic flux** as a quantity. We picture **magnetic flux density** B as the number of magnetic field lines passing through a region *per unit area*. Similarly, we can picture magnetic flux as the total number of magnetic field lines passing through an area A. For a magnetic field normal to A, the magnetic flux ϕ (Greek letter phi) must therefore be equal to the product of magnetic flux density and the area A (Figure 10.12a).

> The magnetic flux ϕ through area A is defined as:
>
> $$\phi = BA$$
>
> where B is the component of the magnetic flux density perpendicular to the area.

How can we calculate the magnetic flux when B is not perpendicular to A? You can easily see that when the field is parallel to the plane of the area, the magnetic flux through A is zero. To find the magnetic flux in general, we need to find the component of the magnetic flux density perpendicular to the area. Figure 10.12b shows a magnetic field at an angle θ to the normal. In this case:

$$\text{magnetic flux} = (B\cos\theta) \times A$$

or simply

$$\text{magnetic flux} = BA\cos\theta$$

(Note that, when $\theta = 90°$, flux $= 0$ and when $\theta = 0°$, flux $= BA$.)

For a coil with N turns, the **magnetic flux linkage** is defined as the product of the magnetic flux and the number of turns; that is:

$$\text{magnetic flux linkage} = N\phi$$

or

$$\text{magnetic flux linkage} = BAN\cos\theta$$

The unit for magnetic flux or flux linkage is the weber (Wb).

> One weber is equal to one tesla metre-squared;
> $1\,\text{Wb} = 1\,\text{T}\,\text{m}^2$.

An e.m.f. is induced in a circuit whenever there is a *change* in the magnetic flux linking the circuit. Since magnetic flux is equal to $BA\cos\theta$, there are three ways an e.m.f. can be induced:

- changing the magnetic flux density B
- changing the area A of the circuit
- changing the angle θ.

Now look at Worked example 1.

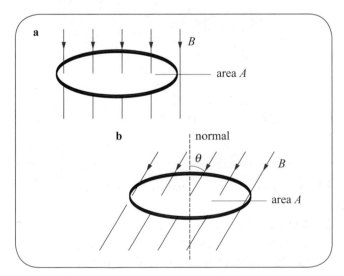

Figure 10.12 a The magnetic flux is equal to BA when the field is normal to the area. **b** The magnetic flux becomes $BA\cos\theta$ when the field is at an angle θ to the normal of the area.

Worked example 1

Figure 10.13 shows a solenoid with a cross-sectional area $0.10\,m^2$. It is linked by a magnetic field of flux density $2.0 \times 10^{-3}\,T$ and has 250 turns. Calculate the magnetic flux and flux linkage for this solenoid.

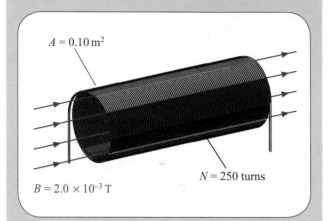

$A = 0.10\,m^2$

$N = 250$ turns

$B = 2.0 \times 10^{-3}\,T$

Figure 10.13 A solenoid in a magnetic field.

Step 1 We have $B = 2.0 \times 10^{-3}\,T$, $A = 0.10\,m^2$, $\theta = 0°$ and $N = 250$ turns. Hence we can calculate the flux ϕ.

$$\phi = BA$$

$$\phi = 2.0 \times 10^{-3} \times 0.10 = 2.0 \times 10^{-4}\,Wb$$

Step 2 Now calculate the flux linkage.

magnetic flux linkage $= N\phi$

magnetic flux linkage $= 2.0 \times 10^{-4} \times 250$
$$= 5.0 \times 10^{-2}\,Wb$$

SAQ

4 Use the idea of magnetic flux linkage to explain why, when a magnet is moved into a coil, the e.m.f. induced depends on the strength of the magnet and the speed at which it is moved.

Answer

5 In an experiment to investigate the factors that affect the magnitude of an induced e.m.f., a student moves a wire back and forth between two magnets, as shown in Figure 10.14. Explain why the e.m.f. generated in this way is much smaller than if the wire is moved up and down in the field.

Answer

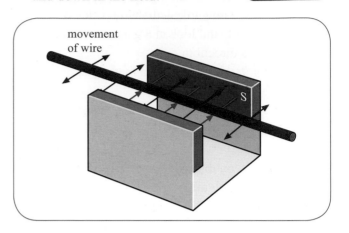

movement of wire

S

Figure 10.14 A wire is moved horizontally in a horizontal magnetic field – see SAQ 5.

6 In the type of generator found in a power station (Figure 10.15), a large electromagnet is made to rotate inside a fixed coil. An e.m.f. of 25 kV is generated; this is an alternating voltage of frequency 50 Hz. What factor determines the frequency? What factors do you think would affect the magnitude of the e.m.f.?

Answer

Figure 10.15 The generators of this power station produce electricity at an induced e.m.f. of 25 kV – see SAQ 6.

7 A bar magnet produces a uniform flux density of 0.15 T at the surface of its north pole. The pole measures $1.0\,cm \times 1.5\,cm$. Calculate the magnetic flux at this pole.

Hint

Answer

8 In the British Isles, the Earth's magnetic field has a flux density of 5.3×10^{-5} T, and it makes an angle of 70° with the horizontal. The area of the British Isles is about 2.9×10^{11} m². Estimate the magnetic flux which passes through this area.

Hint

Answer

9 A solenoid has diameter 5.0 cm and length 25 cm (Figure 10.16). There are 200 turns of wire. A current of 2.0 A creates a magnetic field of flux density 2.0×10^{-5} T through the core of this solenoid. Calculate the magnetic flux linkage for this solenoid.

Answer

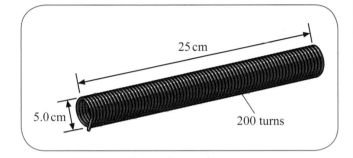

25 cm

5.0 cm

200 turns

Figure 10.16 A solenoid – see SAQ 9.

10 A rectangular coil, 5.0 cm × 7.5 cm, and having 120 turns, is at right angles to a magnetic field of flux density 1.2 T. Calculate the magnetic flux linkage for this coil.

Hint

Answer

Faraday's law of electromagnetic induction

Earlier in this chapter, we saw that electromagnetic induction occurs whenever a conductor cuts across lines of magnetic flux – for example, when a coil is rotated in a magnetic field so that the magnetic flux linking the coil changes. We can use Faraday's law of electromagnetic induction to determine the magnitude of the induced e.m.f. in a circuit.

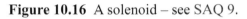

> The magnitude of the induced e.m.f. is proportional to the rate of change of magnetic flux linkage.

We can write this mathematically as:

$$E \propto \frac{\Delta(N\phi)}{\Delta t}$$

where $\Delta(N\phi)$ is the change in the flux linkage in a time Δt. The constant of proportionality is equal to −1. (The reason for the minus sign, which represents Lenz's law, will be dealt with in the next section, on page 147.) Therefore:

$$E = -\frac{\Delta(N\phi)}{\Delta t}$$

The equation above is a mathematical statement of Faraday's law. You can also state Faraday's law as:

> The magnitude of the induced e.m.f. is equal to the rate of change of magnetic flux linkage.

Now look at Worked example 2 and Worked example 3.

Worked example 2

A straight wire of length 0.20 m moves at a steady speed of 3.0 m s^{-1} at right angles to a magnetic field of flux density 0.10 T. Use Faraday's law to determine the e.m.f. induced across the ends of the wire.

Step 1 With a single conductor $N = 1$. To determine the e.m.f. E, we need to find the rate of change of magnetic flux; in other words, the change in magnetic flux per second.

Figure 10.17 shows that, in 1.0 s, the wire travels 3.0 m. Therefore:

change in magnetic flux = $B \times$ change in area

change in magnetic flux = $0.10 \times (3.0 \times 0.20)$
$= 6.0 \times 10^{-2}$ Wb

continued

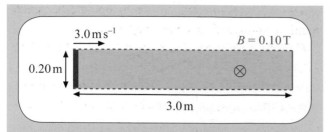

Figure 10.17 A moving wire cuts across the magnetic field.

Step 2 Use Faraday's law to determine the e.m.f.

$$E = \frac{\Delta(N\phi)}{\Delta t} \qquad (N = 1)$$

$$\Delta\phi = 6.0 \times 10^{-2}\,\text{Wb} \quad \text{and} \quad \Delta t = 1.0\,\text{s}$$

$$E = \frac{6.0 \times 10^{-2}}{1.0} = 0.06\,\text{V}$$

The induced e.m.f. across the ends of the wire is about 60 mV.

Worked example 3

This example shows one way in which the flux density of a magnetic field can be measured – Figure 10.18.

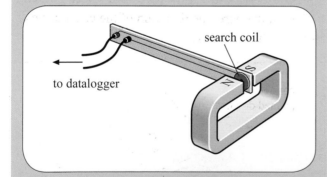

Figure 10.18 A search coil can be moved into and out of a magnetic field to detect magnetic flux.

A search coil of wire having 2500 turns and of area 1.2 cm² is placed between the poles of a magnet so that the magnetic flux passes perpendicularly through the coil. The flux density of the field is 0.50 T. The coil is pulled rapidly

continued

out of the field in a time of 0.10 s. What average e.m.f. is induced across the ends of the coil?

Step 1 When the coil is pulled from the field, the flux linking it falls to zero. We have to calculate the magnetic flux linking the coil when it is in the field.

To convert cm² into m², multiply by a factor of 10^{-4}. Hence $A = 1.2 \times 10^{-4}\,\text{m}^2$.

$$\text{magnetic flux linkage} = N\phi = BAN$$
$$= 0.50 \times 1.2 \times 10^{-4} \times 2500$$

$$\text{magnetic flux linkage} = 0.15\,\text{Wb}$$

Step 2 Now calculate the induced e.m.f. using Faraday's law of electromagnetic induction. $\Delta(N\phi) = 0.15\,\text{Wb}$ and $\Delta t = 0.10\,\text{s}$

magnitude of induced e.m.f.
$$= \text{rate of change of flux linkage}$$

$$E = \frac{\Delta(N\phi)}{\Delta t} = \frac{0.15}{0.10} = 1.5\,\text{V}$$

Note that, in this example, we have assumed that the flux linking the coil falls steadily to zero during the time interval of 0.10 s. Our answer is thus the average value of the e.m.f.

SAQ

11 A conductor of length L moves at a steady speed v at right angles to a uniform magnetic field of flux density B. Show that the e.m.f. E across the ends of the conductor is given by the equation: $E = BLv$.

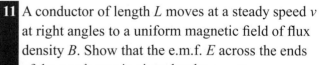

Answer

(You can use Worked example 2 to guide you through SAQ 12.)

12 A wire of length 10 cm is moved through a distance of 2.0 cm in a direction at right angles to its length in the space between the poles of a magnet, and perpendicular to the magnetic field. The flux density is 1.5 T. If this takes 0.50 s, calculate the average e.m.f. induced across the ends of the wire.

Answer

13 An aircraft of wingspan 40 m flies horizontally at a speed of 300 m s^{-1} in an area where the vertical component of the Earth's magnetic field is 5.0×10^{-5} T. Calculate the e.m.f. generated between the aircraft's wingtips.

[Answer]

14 Figure 10.19 shows a search coil,
[Hint]
having 2000 turns and of area 1.2 cm^2, placed between the poles of a strong magnet. The ends of the coil are connected to a voltmeter. The coil is then pulled out of the magnetic field, and the voltmeter records an average e.m.f. of 0.40 V over a time interval of 0.20 s. Calculate the magnetic flux density between the poles of the magnet.

[Answer]

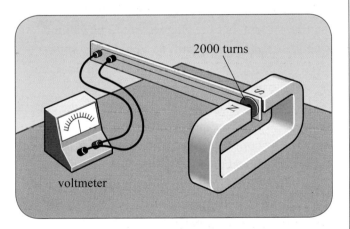

Figure 10.19 Using a search coil to measure flux.

15 A square coil of 100 turns of wire has sides of length 5.0 cm. It is placed in a magnetic field of flux density 20 mT, so that the flux is perpendicular to the plane of the coil.
a Calculate the flux linking the coil.
b The coil is now pulled from the magnetic field in a time of 0.10 s. Calculate the average e.m.f. induced in it.

[Answer]

Lenz's law

We use Faraday's law to calculate the magnitude of an induced e.m.f. Now we can go on to think about the direction of the e.m.f. – in other words, which end

of a wire or coil moving in a magnetic field becomes positive, and which becomes negative.

Fleming's right-hand rule gives the direction of an induced current. This is a particular case of a more general law, Lenz's law, which will be explained in this section. First, we will see how the motor effect and the dynamo effect are related to each other.

The origin of electromagnetic induction

So far, we have not given an explanation of electromagnetic induction. You have seen, from the experiments at the beginning of this chapter, that it does occur, and you know the factors that affect it. But what is the origin of the induced current?

Figure 10.20 gives an explanation. A straight wire XY is being pushed downwards through a horizontal magnetic field of flux density B. Now, think about the free electrons in the wire. They are moving downwards, so they are in effect an electric current. Of course, because electrons are negatively charged, the conventional current is flowing upwards.

We now have a current flowing across a magnetic field, and the motor effect will therefore come into play. Each electron experiences a force of magnitude Bev. Using Fleming's left-hand rule, we can find the direction of the force on the electrons. The diagram shows that the electrons will be pushed in the direction from X to Y. So a current has been induced to flow in the wire; the direction of the conventional current is from Y to X.

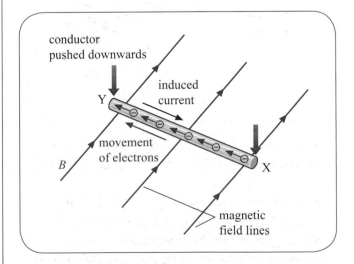

Figure 10.20 Showing the direction of the induced current.

Now we can check that Fleming's right-hand rule gives the correct directions for motion, field and current, which indeed it does.

So, to summarise, there is an induced current because the electrons are pushed by the motor effect. Electromagnetic induction is simply a consequence of the motor effect.

In Figure 10.20, electrons are found to accumulate at Y. This end of the wire is thus the negative end of the e.m.f. and X is positive. If the wire was connected to an external circuit, electrons would flow out of Y, round the circuit, and back into X. Figure 10.21 shows how the moving wire is equivalent to a cell (or any other source of e.m.f.).

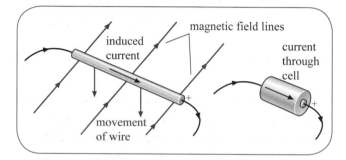

Figure 10.21 A moving conductor in a magnetic field is a source of e.m.f., equivalent to a cell.

Forces and movement

Electromagnetic induction is how we generate most of our electricity. We turn a coil in a magnetic field, and the mechanical energy we put in is transferred to electrical energy. By thinking about these energy transfers, we can deduce the direction of the induced current.

Figure 10.22 shows one of the experiments from earlier in this chapter. The north pole of a magnet is being pushed towards a coil of wire. There is an induced current in the coil, but what is its direction? The diagram shows the two possibilities.

The current in the coil turns it into an electromagnet. One end becomes the north pole, the other the south pole. In Figure 10.22a, if the induced current is in this direction, the coil end nearest the approaching north pole of the magnet would be a south pole. These poles will attract one another, and you could let go of the magnet and it would be dragged into the coil. The magnet would accelerate into the coil, the induced current would increase

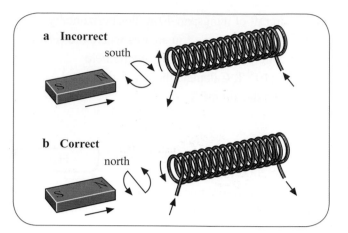

Figure 10.22 Moving a magnet towards a coil: the direction of the induced current is as shown in **b**, not **a**.

further, and the force of attraction between the two would also escalate.

In this situation, we would be putting no energy into the system, but the magnet would be gaining kinetic energy, and the current would be gaining electrical energy. A nice trick if you could do it, but against the principle of conservation of energy!

It follows that Figure 10.22b must show the correct situation. As the north pole of the magnet is pushed towards the coil, the induced current makes the end of the coil nearest the magnet become a north pole. The two poles repel one another, and you have to do work to push the magnet into the coil. The energy transferred by your work is transferred to electrical energy of the current. The principle of energy conservation is not violated.

SAQ

16 Use these ideas to explain what happens if **a** you stop pushing the magnet towards the coil, and **b** you pull the magnet away from the coil.

Answer

Figure 10.23 shows how we can apply the same reasoning to a straight wire being moved in a downward direction through a magnetic field. There will be an induced current in the wire, but in which direction? Since this is a case of a current across a magnetic field, a force will act on it (the motor effect), and we can use Fleming's left-hand rule to deduce its direction.

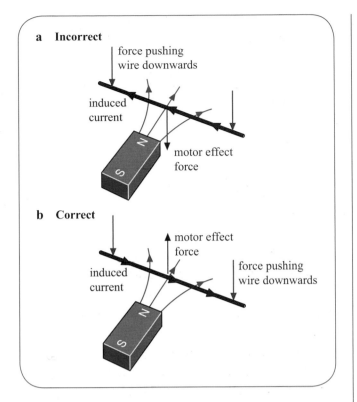

Figure 10.23 Moving a conductor through a magnetic field: the direction of the induced current is as shown in **b**, not **a**.

First we will consider what happens if the induced current is in the wrong direction. This is shown in Figure 10.23a. The left-hand rule shows that the force that results would be downward – in the direction in which we are trying to move the wire. The wire would thus be accelerated, the current would increase, and again we would be getting both kinetic and electrical energy for no energy input.

The induced current must be as shown in Figure 10.23b. The force that acts on it due to the motor effect pushes against you as you try to move the wire through the field. You have to do work to move the wire, and hence to generate electrical energy. Once again, the principle of energy conservation is not violated.

SAQ

17 Draw a diagram to show the directions of the induced current and of the opposing force if you now try to move the wire shown in Figure 10.23 upwards through the magnetic field.

Answer

A general law for induced e.m.f.

Lenz's law summarises this general principle of energy conservation. The direction of an induced current is such that it always produces a force that opposes the motion that is being used to produce it. If the direction of the current were opposite to this, we would be getting energy for nothing. Here is a statement of **Lenz's law**:

> Any induced current or induced e.m.f. will be established in a direction so as to produce effects which oppose the change that is producing it.

The idea of this opposition to change is encapsulated in the *minus* sign in the equation for Faraday's law:

$$E = -\frac{\Delta(N\phi)}{\Delta t}$$

SAQ

18 A bar magnet is dropped vertically downwards through a long solenoid, which is connected to an oscilloscope (Figure 10.24). The oscilloscope trace shows how the e.m.f. induced in the coil varies as the magnet accelerates downwards.

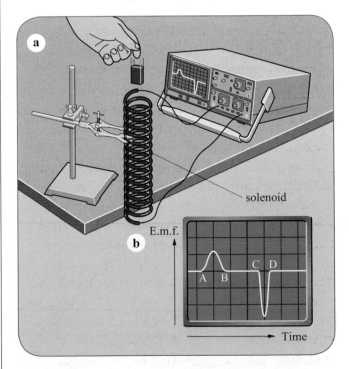

Figure 10.24 a A bar magnet falls through a long coil. **b** The oscilloscope trace shows how the induced e.m.f. varies with time.

a Explain why an e.m.f. is induced in the coil as the magnet enters it (section AB of the trace).

b Explain why no e.m.f. is induced while the magnet is entirely inside the coil (section BC).

c Explain why section CD shows a negative trace, why the peak e.m.f. is greater over this section, and why CD represents a shorter time interval than AB. 〔Answer〕

19 You can turn a bicycle dynamo by hand and cause the lamps to light up. Use the idea of Lenz's law to explain why it is easier to turn the dynamo when the lamps are switched off than when they are on. 〔Answer〕

〔Extension〕 ━━━━━━━━━━━━━━━

Using induction: a.c. generator

An induced e.m.f. can be generated in a variety of ways. What they all have in common is that a conductor is cutting across magnetic field lines. (In some cases, the conductor moves; in others, the field lines move.)

We can generate electricity by spinning a coil in a magnetic field. This is equivalent to using an electric motor backwards. Figure 10.25 shows such a coil in three different orientations as it spins. Notice that the rate of change of flux linkage is maximum when the coil is moving through the horizontal position – one side is cutting rapidly downwards through the field lines, the other is cutting rapidly upwards. In this position, we get a large induced e.m.f. As the coil moves through the vertical position, the rate of change of flux is zero – the sides of the coil are moving parallel to the field lines, not cutting them, so that there is hardly any change in the flux linkage.

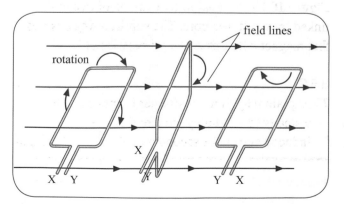

Figure 10.25 A coil rotating in a magnetic field.

The flux linkage is $BAN \cos \theta$. Hence, by Faraday's law of electromagnetic induction, the induced e.m.f. is:

$$E = -\frac{\Delta(BAN \cos \theta)}{\Delta t}$$

Note that there is an induced e.m.f. because angle θ changes, hence

$$E \propto \frac{\Delta(\cos \theta)}{\Delta t}$$

Figure 10.26 shows how the flux linkage varies with time for a rotating coil. According to Faraday's law, the induced e.m.f. is equal to minus the gradient of the flux linkage against time graph.

- When the flux linking the coil is maximum, the rate of change of flux is zero and hence the induced e.m.f. is zero.
- When the flux linking the coil is zero, the rate of change of flux is maximum (the graph is steepest) and hence the induced e.m.f. is also maximum.

Hence, for a coil like this we get a varying e.m.f. – this is how alternating current is generated. In practice, it is simpler to keep the large coil fixed and spin an electromagnet inside it (Figure 10.27). A bicycle dynamo (see Figure 10.7) is similar, but in this case a permanent magnet is made to spin inside a fixed coil. This makes for a very robust device.

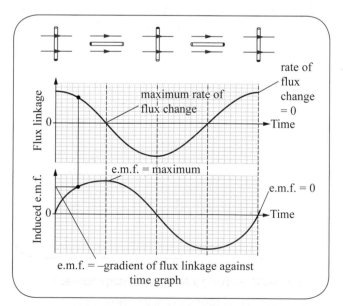

Figure 10.26 The magnetic flux linking a rotating coil changes as it rotates. This gives rise to an alternating induced e.m.f. The orientation of the coil is shown above the graphs.

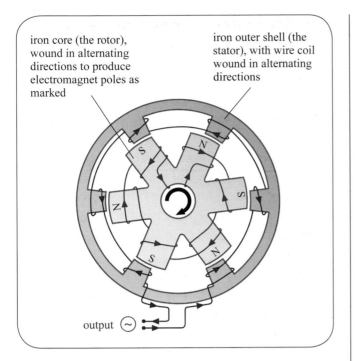

iron core (the rotor), wound in alternating directions to produce electromagnet poles as marked

iron outer shell (the stator), with wire coil wound in alternating directions

output $\sim$

Figure 10.27 In a generator, an electromagnet rotates inside a coil.

SAQ

20 Figure 10.28 represents a coil of wire ABCD being rotated in a uniform horizontal magnetic field. Copy and complete the diagram to show the direction of the induced current in the coil, and the directions of the forces on sides AB and CD that oppose the rotation of the coil.

Hint

Answer

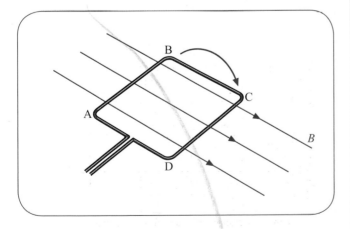

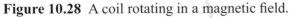

Figure 10.28 A coil rotating in a magnetic field.

21 Does a bicycle dynamo (Figure 10.7) generate alternating or direct current? Justify your answer.

Answer

22 The peak e.m.f. induced in a rotating coil in a magnetic field depends on four factors: magnetic flux density B, area of the coil A, number of turns N, and frequency f of rotation. Use the ideas of Faraday's and Lenz's laws to explain why the e.m.f. must be proportional to each of these quantities.

Answer

Using induction: transformers

Another use of electromagnetic induction is in transformers. An alternating current in the primary coil produces a varying magnetic field in the soft iron core (Figure 10.29). The secondary coil is also wound round this core, so the magnetic flux linking the secondary coil is constantly changing. Hence, according to Faraday's law, a varying e.m.f. is induced across the secondary coil.

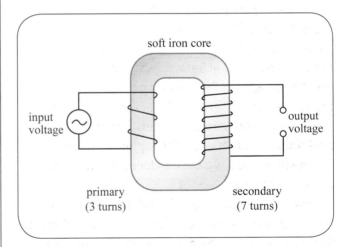

soft iron core

input voltage

output voltage

primary (3 turns)

secondary (7 turns)

Figure 10.29 A transformer consists of two coils linked by a soft iron core. The soft iron ring ensures that magnetic flux from the primary is not 'lost'.

SAQ

23 Explain why, if a transformer is connected to a steady (d.c.) supply, no e.m.f. is induced across the secondary coil.

Answer

Step-up, step-down

The transformer represented in Figure 10.29 on page 151 has 3 turns on its primary coil and 7 on its secondary coil. It is described as a *step-up transformer* because the output voltage is greater than the input voltage (the voltage has been 'stepped up').

How does this happen? We have 3 turns producing magnetic flux. This flux links the 7 turns of the secondary coil. Because flux linkage $N\phi$ is proportional to the number of turns, it follows that there is more magnetic flux linking the secondary coil than the primary. As the magnetic flux changes (because we are using alternating voltages), the e.m.f. induced in the secondary coil is greater than the voltage across the primary coil.

We can write an equation relating the voltages across the coils to the number of turns in each coil:

$$\frac{V_s}{V_p} = \frac{n_s}{n_p}$$

The equation above is known as the **turns-ratio equation** for a transformer.

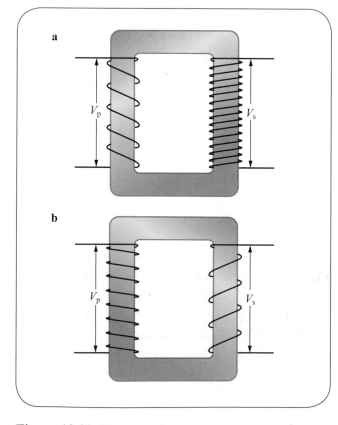

Figure 10.30 Two transformers: **a** step-up, and **b** step-down.

Here, the subscripts relate to the primary (p) and secondary (s) coils. In words, the ratio of the voltages is equal to the ratio of the turns of the transformer. For the transformer in Figure 10.29, a voltage of 3.0 V applied to the primary coil will result in an output of 7.0 V across the secondary coil; 6.0 V will give 14 V, and so on.

A transformer with fewer turns on the secondary coil than on the primary coil is described as a *step-down transformer*. It lowers the voltage at the primary coil. Figure 10.30 shows both types of transformer.

Now look at Worked example 4.

Worked example 4

A radio requires a 6.0 V supply but has to be operated from a 230 V mains supply. It is fitted with a transformer to reduce the mains voltage. Calculate the turns ratio for this transformer. If the primary coil has 5000 turns, how many turns must the secondary have?

Step 1 The turns ratio $\dfrac{n_s}{n_p}$ is given by

$$\frac{V_s}{V_p} = \frac{n_s}{n_p}$$

Hence:

$$\frac{n_s}{n_p} = \frac{V_s}{V_p} = \frac{6.0}{230} = 0.026$$

This ratio is less than one because we are reducing the voltage.

Step 2 We know that $n_p = 5000$, so we can calculate n_s.

$$n_s = n_p \times 0.026 = 5000 \times 0.026 = 130$$

So the secondary coil must have 130 turns. Check that this seems reasonable: the voltage has to be reduced by a factor of about 40, so the number of turns must be *reduced* by the same factor.

SAQ

24 a What is the turns ratio of the transformer shown in Figure 10.30a?

b What is the turns ratio of the transformer shown in Figure 10.30b?

c If an alternating p.d. of value 10.0 V is connected across the primary coil of each, what will be the induced e.m.f. across each secondary?

Answer

25 A power station generates electricity at a voltage of 25 kV. This must be transformed for onward transmission at 400 kV. If the primary coil of the transformer used has 2000 turns, how many turns must the secondary coil have?

Answer

Greener power transmission

It may seem that, if we can transform an alternating voltage to a higher value, we are getting something for nothing. However, we are not. A step-up transformer has a higher voltage across its secondary coil, but the current flowing from it is smaller than the current in the primary coil.

Think about the equation for electrical power: $P = VI$. The power in the secondary coil is roughly equal to the power in the primary (because energy cannot appear from nowhere), so if the voltage V increases, the current I must decrease. In practice, some power is lost through the electrical resistance of the coils and through magnetic losses in the soft iron core.

For a 100% efficient transformer, the input power into the primary coil must be equal to the output power from the secondary coil. That is:

$$V_p I_p = V_s I_s$$

where I_p and I_s are the currents in the primary and secondary coils, respectively.

The transformers used in the electricity supply industry are large (Figure 10.31). They must be designed with great care to minimise energy losses. The electricity supply may pass through as many as ten transformers between the generator and the consumer. If each transformer wasted just 1% of the power, that would give an overall loss of 10%. Since there are roughly 100 big power stations in the UK, that would require ten power stations just to cope with the losses in transformers.

Today's well-designed transformers have losses of under 0.1%. This contributes greatly to energy savings in the power transmission industry.

Figure 10.31 Transformers at a power station; you can see the thick cables bringing the power to the transformers, which are the white, rectangular boxes beyond. The dark cylinders are insulators.

Summary

- In a magnetic field of magnetic flux density B, the magnetic flux passing through an area A is given by $\phi = BA\cos\theta$.

- The magnetic flux linking a coil of N turns is the magnetic flux linkage, $N\phi$.

- Flux and flux linkage are measured in webers (Wb).

- One weber is equal to one tesla metre-squared. $1\,\text{Wb} = 1\,\text{T}\,\text{m}^2$.

- When a conductor moves so that it cuts across a magnetic field, an e.m.f. is induced across its ends. When the magnetic flux linking a coil changes, an e.m.f. is induced in the coil.

- Faraday's law states that the magnitude of the induced e.m.f. is equal to the rate of change of magnetic flux linkage:

$$E = \frac{\Delta(N\phi)}{\Delta t}$$

- Lenz's law states that the induced current or e.m.f. is in a direction so as to produce effects which oppose the change that is producing it.

- In an a.c. generator, an e.m.f. is induced because the rotating coil changes the magnetic flux linking the coil.

- For a transformer, $\dfrac{V_s}{V_p} = \dfrac{n_s}{n_p}$. If it is 100% efficient, then $V_p I_p = V_s I_s$.

Questions

1 This question is about forcing a liquid metal, such as molten sodium, through a tube.

a The liquid metal is in a tube of square cross-section, side w, made of electrically insulating material. See Figure 1. Two electrodes are mounted on opposite sides of the tube and a magnetic field of flux density B fills the region between the electrodes. An electric current I passes across the tube between the electrodes, perpendicular to the magnetic field. The interaction between the current and the field provides the force to move the liquid.

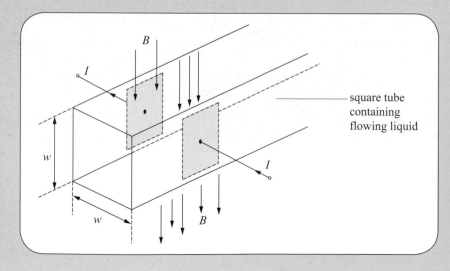

square tube containing flowing liquid

Figure 1   *continued*

   i Make a sketch of Figure 1 and draw on an arrow labelled *F* to indicate the direction of the force on the liquid metal. Explain how you determined the direction. [2]

   ii State the relationship for the force *F* in terms of the current *I*, the magnetic field *B* and the width *w* of the tube. [1]

   iii Data for this device are shown below:

   $B = 0.15\,\text{T}$

   $I = 800\,\text{A}$

   $w = 25\,\text{mm}$

   Calculate the force on the liquid metal in the tube. [2]

b To monitor the speed of flow of the liquid metal, a similar arrangement of electrodes and magnetic field is set up further down the tube, as shown in Figure 2. A voltmeter is connected across the electrodes instead of a power supply.

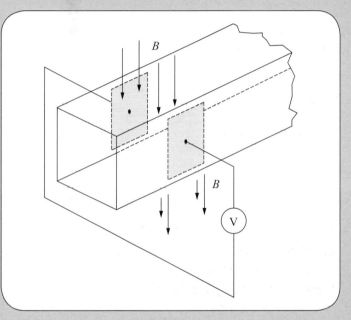

Figure 2

   i Explain, using the law of electromagnetic induction, why the voltmeter will register a reading which is proportional to the speed of flow of the metal. [3]

   ii State how and explain why the voltmeter reading changes when the magnetic flux density across the tube is doubled. [2]

OCR Physics A2 (2824) January 2006 [Total 10]

Answer

continued

2 This question is about electromagnetic induction.

a State Faraday's law of electromagnetic induction. Explain the terms *magnetic flux* and *magnetic flux linkage* which you may have used in your statement of the law. [5]

b The diagram below shows a simple a.c. generator used for demonstrations in the laboratory. It consists of a magnet being rotated inside a cavity in a soft iron core. The output from the coil, wound on the iron core, is connected to an oscilloscope.

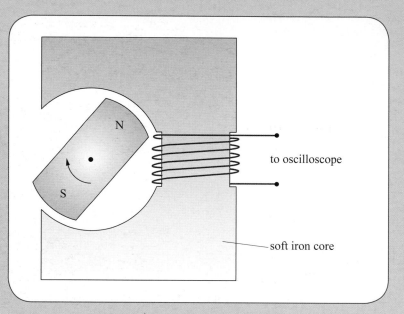

On a grid, sketch a typical output voltage which would be seen on the oscilloscope screen. State and explain, using Faraday's law and/or the terms given in **a**, how doubling each of the following factors will alter this output voltage:

- the speed of rotation of the magnet
- the number of turns on the coil.

Finally, explain how the output voltage would be different if the soft iron core were removed, leaving the magnet and coil in the same positions. [7]

OCR Physics A2 (2824) June 2006 [Total 12]

Answer

continued

3   Figure 1 shows a square flat coil of insulated wire placed in a region of
    uniform magnetic field of flux density B. The direction of the field is vertically out
    of the paper. The coil of side x has N turns.

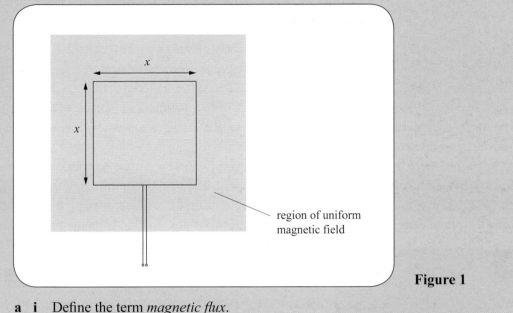

Figure 1

a i Define the term *magnetic flux*.   [1]
    ii Show that the magnetic flux linkage of the coil in Figure 1 is NBx^2.   [2]
b The coil of side $x = 0.020\,\text{m}$ is placed at position Y in Figure 2. The ends of the
    1250 turn coil are connected to a voltmeter. The coil moves sideways steadily
    through the region of magnetic field of flux density 0.032 T at a speed of
    $0.10\,\text{m s}^{-1}$ until it reaches position Z. The total motion takes 1.0 s.

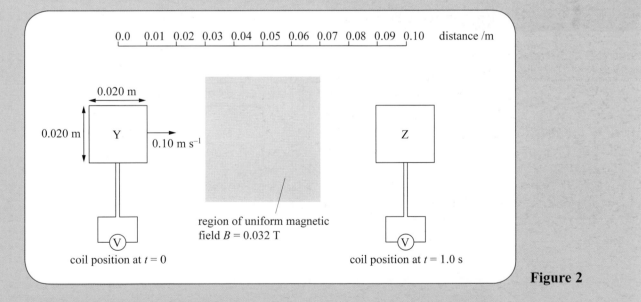

Figure 2

Show that the voltmeter reading as the coil enters the field region, after $t = 0.2\,\text{s}$, is
80 mV. Explain your reasoning fully.   [3]

OCR Physics A2 (2824) June 2004   [Total 6]

Answer

Chapter 11

Capacitors

Objectives

Using capacitors

Capacitors are components used in many electrical and electronic circuits. They store electrical charge (and energy), and this means that they have many valuable applications. For example, capacitors are used in computers; they are charged up in normal use, and then they gradually discharge if there is a power failure, so that the computer will operate long enough to save valuable data. The photograph (Figure 11.1) shows a variety of shapes and sizes of capacitors.

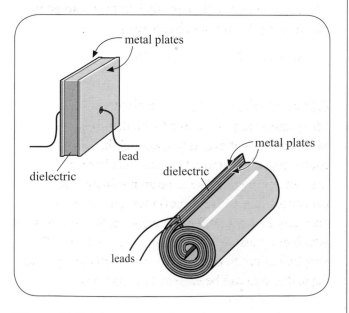

Figure 11.1 A variety of capacitors.

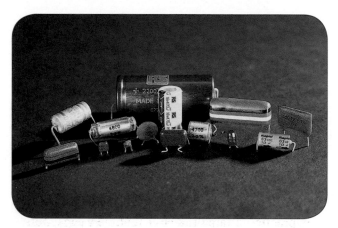
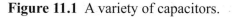

Figure 11.2 The construction of some capacitors.

All capacitors have two leads, connected to two metal plates where the charge is stored. Between the plates is an insulating material called the *dielectric*. Figure 11.2 shows a simplified version of the construction of a capacitor; in practice, many have a spiral 'Swiss-roll' form.

To charge a capacitor, it must be connected to a voltage supply. The negative terminal of the supply pushes electrons onto one plate, making it negatively charged. Electrons are repelled from the other plate, making it positively charged. Figure 11.3 shows that there is a flow of electrons all the way round the circuit. The ammeters show the current in the circuit. The current eventually stops when the capacitor is fully charged. When this happens, the potential difference (p.d.) across the capacitor is equal to the electromotive force (e.m.f.) of the supply.

Note: The convention is that current is the flow of positive charge. Here, it is free electrons that flow. Electrons are negatively charged; the current flows in the opposite direction to the electrons (Figure 11.4).

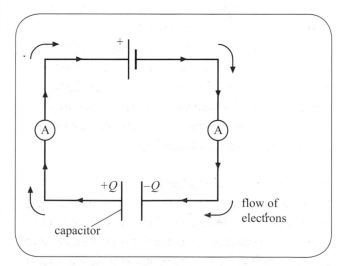

Figure 11.3 The flow of charge when a capacitor is charged up.

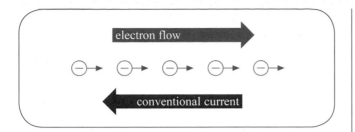

Figure 11.4 A flow of electrons to the right constitutes a conventional current to the left.

Stored charge

If one plate of the capacitor stores charge $+Q$, then the other stores an equal and opposite charge $-Q$. We say that the charge stored by the capacitor is Q. (In fact, the total charge on the capacitor is zero. We focus our attention on one of the capacitor plates where there is an excess or deficiency of electrons. Connecting the capacitor to a supply *separates* the charges into $+Q$ and $-Q$.)

To make the capacitor store more charge, we would have to use a supply of higher e.m.f. If we connect the leads of the charged capacitor together, electrons flow back around the circuit and the capacitor is discharged.

You can observe a capacitor discharging as follows: Connect the two leads of a capacitor to the terminals of a battery. Disconnect, and then reconnect the leads to a light-emitting diode (LED). It is best to have a protective resistor in series with the LED. The LED will glow briefly as the capacitor discharges.

In any circuit, the charge that flows past a point in a given time is equal to the area under a current against time graph (just as distance is equal to the area under a graph of speed against time). So the charge stored by a capacitor is given by the area under the current against time graph recorded while the capacitor is being charged up.

The meaning of capacitance

If you look at some capacitors, you will see that they are marked with the value of their **capacitance**. The greater the capacitance, the greater is the charge stored by the capacitor for a given potential difference across it. The capacitance C of a capacitor is defined by:

$$\left(\text{capacitance} = \frac{\text{charge}}{\text{potential difference}} \right)$$

or
$$\left(C = \frac{Q}{V} \right)$$

where Q is the charge stored by the capacitor and V is the potential difference across it.

> The capacitance of a capacitor is the charge stored per unit of potential difference across it.

The charge on the capacitor may be calculated using the equation:

$$Q = VC$$

This equation shows that the charge stored depends on two things: the capacitance C and the voltage V (double the voltage stores double the charge).

Units of capacitance

The unit of capacitance is the **farad**, F. From the equation that defines capacitance, you can see that this must be the same as the units of charge (coulombs, C) divided by volts (V):

$$1\,F = 1\,C\,V^{-1}$$

(It is unfortunate that the letter 'C' is used for both capacitance and coulomb. There is room for confusion here!)

In practice, a farad is a large unit. Few capacitors are big enough to store 1 C when charged up to 1 V. Capacitors usually have their values marked in picofarads (pF) or microfarads (μF):

$$1\,pF = 10^{-12}\,F \qquad 1\,\mu F = 10^{-6}\,F$$

Other markings on capacitors

Many capacitors are marked with their highest safe working voltage. If you exceed this value, charge may leak across between the plates, and the dielectric will cease to be an insulator. Some capacitors (electrolytic ones) must be connected correctly in a circuit. They have an indication to show which end must be connected to the positive of the supply. Failure to connect correctly will damage the capacitor, and can be extremely dangerous.

Extension

159

SAQ

1   Calculate the charge stored by a 220 μF capacitor charged up to 15 V. Give your answer in microcoulombs (μC) and in coulombs (C).

Answer

2   A capacitor stores 1.0×10^{-3} C of charge when charged to 500 V. Calculate its capacitance in farads (F), microfarads (μF) and picofarads (pF).

Answer

3   Calculate the average current required to charge a 50 μF capacitor to a p.d. of 10 V in a time interval of 0.01 s.

Answer

4   A student connects an uncharged capacitor of capacitance C in series with a resistor, a cell and a switch. The student closes the switch and records the current I at intervals of 10 s. The results are shown in Table 11.1. The potential difference across the capacitor after 60 s was 8.5 V. Plot a current against time graph, and use it to estimate the value of C.

Answer

t/s	0	10	20	30	40	50	60
I/μA	200	142	102	75	51	37	27

Table 11.1

Energy stored in a capacitor

When you charge a capacitor, you use a power supply to push electrons onto one plate and off the other. The power supply does work on the electrons, so their potential energy increases. You recover this energy when you discharge the capacitor.

If you charge a large capacitor (1000 μF or more) to a potential difference of 6.0 V, disconnect it from the supply, and then connect it across a 6.0 V lamp, you can see the energy as it is released from the capacitor. The lamp will flash briefly. Clearly, such a capacitor does not store much energy when it is charged.

The energy W that a capacitor stores depends on its capacitance C and the potential difference V to which it is charged:

$$W = \tfrac{1}{2}CV^2$$

Suppose we charge a 2000 μF capacitor to a p.d. of 10 V. How much energy is stored by the capacitor? Using $W = \tfrac{1}{2}CV^2$ we have

$$W = \tfrac{1}{2} \times 2000 \times 10^{-6} \times 10^2 = 0.10 \text{ J}$$

This is a small amount of energy – compare it with the energy stored by a rechargeable battery, typically of the order of 10 000 J. A charged capacitor will not keep an MP3 player running for any length of time.

The energy W stored is proportional to the square of the potential difference V ($W \propto V^2$). It follows that doubling the charging voltage means that four times as much energy is stored. This comes about because, when you double the voltage, not only is twice as much charge stored, but it is stored at twice the voltage.

Investigating energy stored

If you have a sensitive joulemeter (capable of measuring millijoules, mJ), you can investigate the equation for energy stored. A suitable circuit is shown in Figure 11.5.

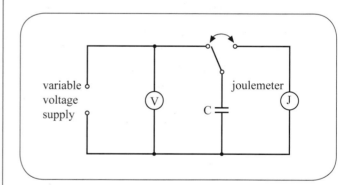

Figure 11.5 With the switch to the left, the capacitor charges up; to the right, it discharges through the joulemeter.

The capacitor is charged up when the switch connects it to the power supply. When the switch is altered, the capacitor discharges through the joulemeter. (It is important to wait for the capacitor to discharge completely.) The joulemeter will measure the amount of energy released by the capacitor.

By using capacitors with different values of C, and by changing the charging voltage V, you can investigate how the energy W stored depends on C and V.

SAQ

5 Calculate the energy stored for the following capacitors: Hint
   a a 5000 μF capacitor charged to 5.0 V
   b a 5000 pF capacitor charged to 5.0 V
   c a 200 μF capacitor charged to 230 V. Answer

6 Which stores more charge, a 100 μF capacitor charged to 200 V or a 200 μF capacitor charged to 100 V? Which stores more energy? Hint Answer

7 A 10 000 μF capacitor is charged to 12 V, and then connected across a lamp rated at '12 V, 36 W'.
   a Calculate the energy stored by the capacitor.
   b Estimate the time the lamp stays fully lit. Assume that energy is dissipated in the lamp at a steady rate. Answer

8 In a simple photographic flashgun, a 0.20 F capacitor is charged by a 9.0 V battery. It is then discharged in a flash of duration 0.01 s. Calculate:
   a the charge and energy stored by the capacitor
   b the average power dissipated during the flash
   c the average current in the flash bulb
   d the approximate resistance of the bulb. Answer

Deriving $W = \frac{1}{2}QV$

In order to charge a capacitor, work must be done to push electrons onto one plate and off the other (Figure 11.6). At first, there is only a small amount of negative charge on the left-hand plate. Adding more electrons is relatively easy, because there is not much repulsion. As the charge stored increases, the repulsion between the electrons on the plate and the new electrons increases, and a greater amount of work must be done to increase the charge stored.

This can be seen qualitatively in Figure 11.7a. This graph shows how the p.d. V increases as the amount of charge stored Q increases. It is a straight line because Q and V are related by:

$$V = \frac{Q}{C}$$

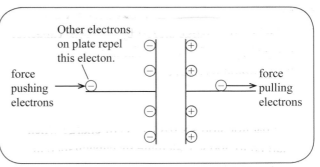

Figure 11.6 When a capacitor is charged, work must be done to push additional electrons against the repulsion of the electrons that are already present.

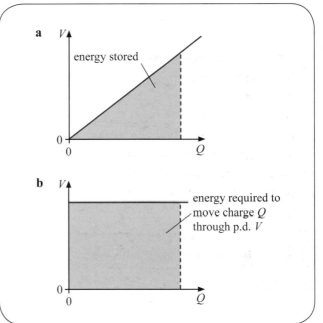

Figure 11.7 The area under a voltage against charge graph gives a quantity of energy. The area in **a** shows the energy stored in a capacitor; the area in **b** shows the energy required to drive a charge through a p.d.

We can use Figure 11.7a to calculate the work done in charging up the capacitor.

First, consider the work done W in moving charge Q through a constant p.d. V. This is given by:

$$W = QV$$

(You studied this equation in Chapter 11 of *Physics 1*.) From the graph of Q against V (Figure 11.7b), we can see that the quantity $Q \times V$ is given by the area under the graph.

The area under a p.d. against charge graph is equal to work done.

If we apply the same idea to the capacitor graph (Figure 11.7a), then the area under the graph is the shaded triangle, with an area of $\frac{1}{2}$ base×height. Hence the work done in charging a capacitor to a particular p.d. is given by:

$$W = \frac{1}{2}QV$$

Substituting $Q = CV$ into this equation gives two further equations:

$$W = \frac{1}{2}CV^2$$

and

$$W = \frac{1}{2}\frac{Q^2}{C}$$

These three equations show the work done in charging up the capacitor. This is equal to the energy stored by the capacitor, since this is the amount of energy released when the capacitor is discharged.

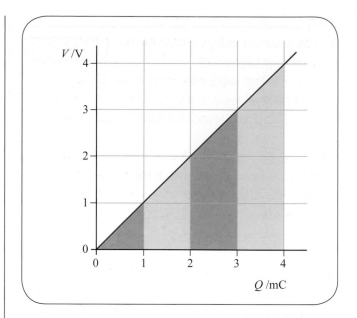

Figure 11.8 The energy stored by a capacitor is equal to the area under the voltage against charge graph.

SAQ

9 State the quantity represented by the gradient of the straight line shown in Figure 11.7a.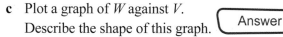

10 The graph of Figure 11.8 shows how V depends on Q for a particular capacitor. The area under the graph has been divided into strips to make it easy to calculate the energy stored. The first strip (which is simply a triangle) shows the energy stored when the capacitor is charged up to 1.0 V. The energy stored is

$$\frac{1}{2}QV = \frac{1}{2} \times 1.0\,\text{mC} \times 1.0\,\text{V} = 0.5\,\text{mJ}.$$

a Calculate the capacitance C of the capacitor.
b Copy Table 11.2 and complete it by calculating the areas of successive strips, to show how W depends on V.
c Plot a graph of W against V. Describe the shape of this graph. _Answer_

Q/mC	V/V	Area of strip ΔW/mJ	Sum of areas W/mJ
1.0	1.0	0.5	0.5
2.0	2.0	1.5	2.0
3.0			
4.0			

Table 11.2

Capacitors in parallel

Capacitors are used in electric circuits to store charge and energy. Situations often arise where two or more capacitors are connected together in a circuit. In this section, we will look at capacitors connected in parallel. The next section deals with capacitors in series.

When two capacitors are connected in parallel (Figure 11.9), their combined or total capacitance C_{total} is simply the sum of their individual capacitances C_1 and C_2:

$$C_{total} = C_1 + C_2$$

This is because, when two capacitors are connected together, they are equivalent to a single capacitor with larger plates. The bigger the plates, the more charge that can be stored for a given voltage, and hence the greater the capacitance.

The total charge Q stored by two capacitors connected in parallel and charged to a potential difference V is simply given by:

$$Q = C_{total} \times V$$

For three or more capacitors connected in parallel, the equation for their total capacitance becomes:

$$C_{total} = C_1 + C_2 + C_3 + \ldots$$

For capacitors in parallel, the following rules apply:
● The p.d. across each capacitor is the same.
● The total charge stored by the capacitors is equal to the sum of the charges:

$$Q_{total} = Q_1 + Q_2 + Q_3 + \ldots$$

● The total capacitance C_{total} is given by:

$$C_{total} = C_1 + C_2 + C_3 + \ldots$$

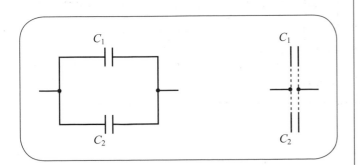

Figure 11.9 Two capacitors connected in parallel are equivalent to a single, larger capacitor.

SAQ

11 a Calculate the total capacitance of two $100\,\mu F$ capacitors connected in parallel.

   b Calculate the total charge they store when charged to a p.d. of $20\,V$.

> Hint

> Answer

12 A capacitor of capacitance $50\,\mu F$ is required, but the only values available to you are $10\,\mu F$, $20\,\mu F$ and $100\,\mu F$ (you may use more than one of each value). How would you achieve the required value by connecting capacitors in parallel? Give at least two answers.

> Answer

> Extension

Capacitors in series

In a similar way to the case of capacitors connected in parallel, we can consider two or more capacitors connected in series (Figure 11.10). The total capacitance C_{total} of two capacitors of capacitances C_1 and C_2 is given by:

$$\frac{1}{C_{total}} = \frac{1}{C_1} + \frac{1}{C_2}$$

Here, it is the reciprocals of the capacitances that must be added to give the reciprocal of the total capacitance. For three or more capacitors connected in series, the equation for their total capacitance is:

$$\frac{1}{C_{total}} = \frac{1}{C_1} + \frac{1}{C_2} + \frac{1}{C_3} + \ldots$$

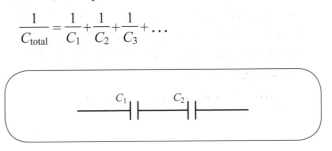

Figure 11.10 Two capacitors connected in series.

For capacitors in series, the following rules apply:
- The charge stored by each capacitor is the same.
- The total p.d. V_{total} across the capacitors is equal to the sum of the p.d.s:

$$V_{\text{total}} = V_1 + V_2 + V_3 + \ldots$$

- The total capacitance C_{total} is given by:

$$\frac{1}{C_{\text{total}}} = \frac{1}{C_1} + \frac{1}{C_2} + \frac{1}{C_3} + \ldots$$

Now look at Worked example 1.

Worked example 1

Calculate the total capacitance of a 300 μF capacitor and a 600 μF capacitor connected in series.

Step 1 The calculation should be done in two steps; this is relatively simple using a calculator with a '1/x' or x^{-1} key.

Substituting the values into

$$\frac{1}{C_{\text{total}}} = \frac{1}{C_1} + \frac{1}{C_2}$$

gives:

$$\frac{1}{C_{\text{total}}} = \frac{1}{300} + \frac{1}{600}$$

$$\frac{1}{C_{\text{total}}} = 0.005 \ \mu\text{F}^{-1}$$

Step 2 Now take the reciprocal of this value to determine the capacitance in μF:

$$C_{\text{total}} = \frac{1}{0.005} = 200 \ \mu\text{F}$$

Notice that the total capacitance of two capacitors in series is less than either of the individual capacitances.

Using the x^{-1} key on your calculator, you can also do this calculation in one step:

$$C_{\text{total}} = (300^{-1} + 600^{-1})^{-1} = 200 \ \mu\text{F}$$

Comparing capacitors and resistors

It is helpful to compare the formulae for capacitors in series and parallel with the corresponding formulae for resistors (Table 11.3).

Notice that the reciprocal formula applies to capacitors in series but to resistors in parallel. This comes from the definitions of capacitance and resistance. Capacitance indicates how good a capacitor is at storing charge for a given voltage, and resistance indicates how *bad* a resistor is at letting current through for a given voltage.

	Capacitors	Resistors
In series	C_1 C_2 C_3 ...	R_1 R_2 R_3 ...
	store same charge	have same current
	$\dfrac{1}{C_{total}} = \dfrac{1}{C_1} + \dfrac{1}{C_2} + \dfrac{1}{C_3} + \ldots$	$R_{total} = R_1 + R_2 + R_3 + \ldots.$
In parallel	C_1 C_2 C_3	R_1 R_2 R_3
	have same p.d.	have same p.d.
	$C_{total} = C_1 + C_2 + C_3 + \ldots$	$\dfrac{1}{R_{total}} = \dfrac{1}{R_1} + \dfrac{1}{R_2} + \dfrac{1}{R_3} + \ldots$

Table 11.3 Capacitors and resistors compared.

Capacitor networks

There are four ways in which three capacitors may be connected together. These are shown in Figure 11.11. The combined capacitance of the first two arrangements (three capacitors in series, three in parallel) can be calculated using the formulae above. The other combinations must be dealt with in a different way:

- Figure 11.11a
  All in series. Calculate C_{total} as in Table 11.3.
- Figure 11.11b
  All in parallel. Calculate C_{total} as in Table 11.3.
- Figure 11.11c
  Calculate C_{total} for the two capacitors of capacitances C_1 and C_2, which are connected in parallel, and then take account of the third capacitor of capacitance C_3, which is connected in series.
- Figure 11.11d
  Calculate C_{total} for the two capacitors of capacitances C_1 and C_2, which are connected in series, and then take account of the third capacitor of capacitance C_3, which is connected in parallel.

These are the same approaches as would be used for networks of resistors.

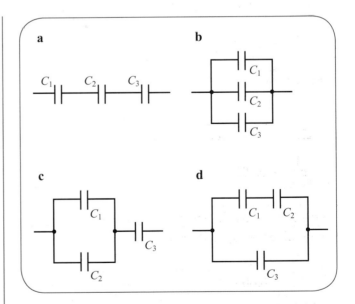

Figure 11.11 Four ways to connect three capacitors.

SAQ

16 For each of the four circuits shown in Figure 11.11, calculate the total capacitance in μF if each capacitor has capacitance 100 μF.

Answer

17 Given a number of 100 μF capacitors, how might you connect networks to give the following values of capacitance:

a 400 μF?

b 25 μF?

c 250 μF?

Answer

18 You have three capacitors of capacitances 100 pF, 200 pF and 600 pF. Determine the maximum and minimum values of capacitance that you can make by connecting them together to form a network. State how they should be connected in each case.

Answer

19 Calculate the capacitance in μF of the network of capacitors shown in Figure 11.12.

Answer

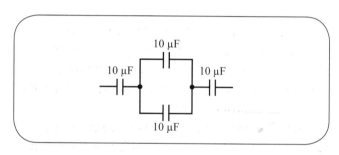

Figure 11.12 A capacitor network – see SAQ 19.

Sharing charge, sharing energy

If a capacitor is charged and then connected to a second capacitor (Figure 11.13), what happens to the charge and the energy that it stores? Note that, when the capacitors are connected together, they are in parallel, because they have the same p.d. across them. Their combined capacitance C_{total} is equal to the sum of their individual capacitances. Now we can think about the charge stored, Q. This is shared between the two capacitors; the total amount of charge stored must remain the same, since charge is conserved. The charge is shared between the two capacitors in proportion to their capacitances. Now the p.d. can be calculated from $V = \dfrac{Q}{C}$, and the energy from $W = \frac{1}{2}CV^2$.

If we look at a numerical example, we find an interesting result (Worked example 2).

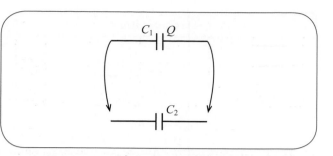

Figure 11.13 Capacitor of capacitance C_1 is charged and then connected across C_2.

Worked example 2

Consider two 100 mF capacitors. One is charged to 10 V, disconnected from the power supply, and then connected across the other. Calculate the energy stored by the combination.

Step 1 Calculate the charge and energy stored for the single capacitor.

initial charge $Q = VC = 10 \times 100 \times 10^{-3} = 1.0\,\text{C}$

initial stored energy
$$= \tfrac{1}{2}CV^2 = \tfrac{1}{2} \times 100 \times 10^{-3} \times 10^2 = 5.0\,\text{J}$$

Step 2 Calculate the final p.d. across the capacitors. The capacitors are in parallel and have a total charge stored of 1.0 C.

$$C_{total} = C_1 + C_2 = 100 + 100 = 200\,\text{mF}$$

The p.d. V can be determined using $Q = VC$.

$$V = \frac{Q}{C} = \frac{1.0}{200 \times 10^{-3}} = 5.0\,\text{V}$$

This is not surprising because the charge is shared equally, with the original capacitor losing half of its charge.

Step 3 Now calculate the total energy stored by the capacitors.

$$\text{total energy} = \tfrac{1}{2}CV^2 = \tfrac{1}{2} \times 200 \times 10^{-3} \times 5.0^2 = 2.5\,\text{J}$$

The charge stored remains the same, but half of the stored energy is lost. This energy is lost in the connecting wires as heat as electrons migrate between the capacitors.

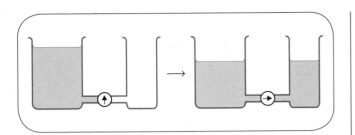

Figure 11.14 An analogy for the sharing of charge between capacitors.

Figure 11.14 shows an analogy to the situation described in Worked example 2. Capacitors are represented by containers of water. A wide (high capacitance) container is filled to a certain level (p.d.). It is then connected to a container with a smaller capacitance, and the levels equalise. (The p.d. is the same for each.) Notice that the potential energy of the water has decreased, because the height of its centre of gravity above the base level has decreased. Energy is dissipated as heat, as there is friction both within the moving water and between the water and the container.

SAQ

20 Three capacitors, each of capacitance 120 μF, are connected together in series. This network is then connected to a 10 kV supply. Calculate:
   a their combined capacitance in μF
   b the charge stored
   c the total energy stored.

    Answer

21 A 20 μF capacitor is charged up to 200 V and then disconnected from the supply. It is then connected across a 5.0 μF capacitor. Calculate:
   a their combined capacitance in μF
   b the charge they store
   c the p.d. across the combination   Hint
   d the energy dissipated when they are connected together.   Answer

Capacitor discharge

When a capacitor is discharged through a resistor there is a current in the wires and the resistor. A suitable circuit for investigating this is shown in Figure 11.15.

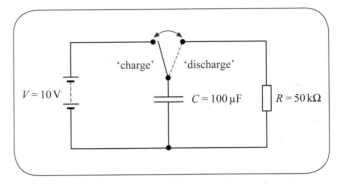

Figure 11.15 A circuit for investigating the discharge of a capacitor through a resistor.

With the switch to the left, the capacitor of capacitance C is connected directly to the battery. There is no resistance in the circuit (other than the internal resistance of the battery) and so the capacitor charges up almost instantly.

Moving the switch to the right disconnects the capacitor from the battery. Now it is in a circuit with the resistor, of resistance $R = 50\,\text{k}\Omega$, and current can flow. Since the capacitor and the resistor are in parallel, the p.d. across each is the same. The capacitor gradually discharges. It does not discharge instantly because the resistance in the circuit limits the current that flows.

There are three important quantities that change as charge flows from the capacitor:
● the charge Q stored by the capacitor
● the current I in the circuit
● the p.d. V across the capacitor or the resistor.
Each of these decreases during the discharge. As you can see from the graphs of Figure 11.16, all three follow the same pattern of decrease. Each starts from a high initial value at time zero and decreases rapidly at first, and then more and more slowly. This pattern of decrease is described as **exponential decay**.

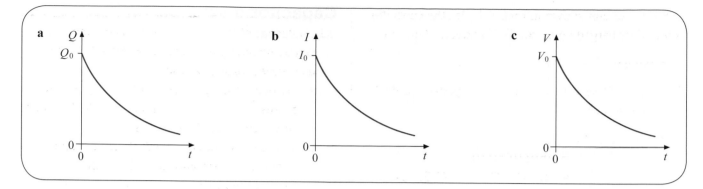

Figure 11.16 Graphs to show how three quantities vary during the discharge of a capacitor through a resistor: **a** charge stored by the capacitor, **b** current in the circuit, and **c** p.d. across the capacitor or resistor.

You may recognise this as the same pattern seen in radioactive decay (which we will look at in detail in Chapter 14). In radioactive decay, a substance decays by half in a certain amount of time, called the half-life. In a further half-life, it decays again by half so that one-quarter remains, and so on.

The discharge graphs for a capacitor are the same. In fact, the fraction we consider does not have to be a half. If the graph drops by, say, one-tenth in 30 s, it will drop by a further one-tenth in the next 30 s. If it drops by 90% in 1.0 minute, it will drop by a further 90% in the next 1.0 minute. An **exponential decay graph** has a *constant-ratio property*. Figure 11.17 illustrates this idea for a charge Q against time t graph, where the charge is measured at equal intervals of time Δt. For an exponential decay we have:

$$\frac{Q_1}{Q_0} = \frac{Q_2}{Q_1} = \frac{Q_3}{Q_2} = \ldots = \text{constant}$$

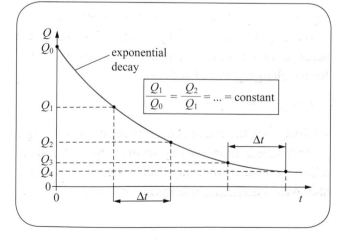

Figure 11.17 An exponential decay graph has a constant-ratio property.

Analysing the discharge graphs

It is useful to gain an understanding of the reasons for the shape of the three graphs in Figure 11.6. Why do they all follow the same pattern?

Initially, the capacitor is charged up. The electrons on one plate all repel one another. Connecting up via the resistor gives them the chance to start flowing round the circuit.

With a lot of charge stored by the capacitor, the p.d. is high, and so the initial current is high. As the charge on the capacitor decreases, the p.d. decreases and so the current decreases. This means that the charge decreases more slowly, the p.d. decreases more slowly, and the current decreases more slowly too. The consequence is that the slope of each graph gets progressively less and less, although it never quite reaches zero.

We can explain the relationship between the two graphs in a more mathematical way using just two familiar equations:

capacitor $Q = VC$

resistor $V = IR$

For a discharging capacitor connected across a resistor, the p.d. V across both the resistor and the capacitor is always the same, as they are connected in parallel.

How can we know the initial values shown on the graphs of Figure 11.16? (Initial values, when $t = 0$, are shown with a subscript zero.)

For the circuit shown in Figure 11.15, the capacitor is initially charged up by the 10 V battery. Therefore:

initial p.d. $V_0 = 10\,\text{V}$

From $Q = VC$ we can find the initial charge Q_0 stored by the capacitor:

initial charge $Q_0 = V_0 C$
$$= 100 \times 10^{-6} \times 10$$
$$= 1.0 \times 10^{-3}\,\text{C} \qquad (1.0\,\text{mC})$$

Finally, from $V = IR$ we can find the initial current in the resistor:

initial current $I_0 = \dfrac{V_0}{R}$

$$= \dfrac{10}{50 \times 10^3} = 2.0 \times 10^{-4}\,\text{A} \quad (200\,\mu\text{A})$$

Later, when the current has halved to $100\,\mu\text{A}$, the p.d. and charge stored will both also have halved.

SAQ

22 For the circuit we have been discussing (Figure 11.15), what will be the values of the current and the charge stored when the p.d. across the capacitor has dropped to 4.0 V?

> Hint

> Answer

Looking at gradients and areas

There are two more relationships that you should be aware of between the graphs of charge and current shown in Figure 11.16.

1 The gradient of the charge against time graph is the current. At first, the gradient is steep, which means that the current is high. Later, the gradient of the Q against t graph has decreased, so the current must be less.

2 The area under the current against time graph represents the charge that has flowed from the capacitor. At first, the current is high, so the area under the graph is high: charge is leaving the capacitor quickly. Later, the current has decreased, so the area under the graph is increasing only slowly – the charge must be changing only slowly.

SAQ

23 The graph of Figure 11.18 shows how the charge stored by a capacitor decreased as it was discharged through a resistor.

   a By determining the gradient of the graph at points A–E along its length, estimate the values of the current at these times.

   b Using the values obtained, sketch a graph to show how the current varies with time as the capacitor discharges.

> Answer

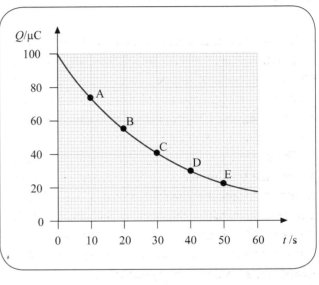

Figure 11.18 For SAQ 23.

Discharge equations

The graphs of Figure 11.16 can be represented by equations. These involve a special number represented by the letter 'e' (base of natural logs).

A charged capacitor of capacitance C is connected across a resistor of resistance R. Here is the equation for the charge Q stored at time t:

$$Q = Q_0 e^{-\frac{t}{CR}}$$

At time $t = 0$, the initial charge on the capacitor is Q_0.

At first, this equation may seem complex, but with a little practice its meaning becomes clear. It is best to start with a numerical example (Worked example 3).

Worked example 3

A 1000 µF capacitor initially stores 20 mC of charge. It is discharged through a resistor of resistance 500 kΩ. Calculate the charge left on the capacitor after 100 s.

Step 1 Write down the quantities that you know, converting the prefixes (m, k and µ) to powers of 10:

$$Q_0 = 20\,mC = 20 \times 10^{-3}\,C$$

$$t = 100\,s$$

$$C = 1000\,\mu F = 1000 \times 10^{-6}\,F$$

$$R = 500\,k\Omega = 500 \times 10^{3}\,\Omega$$

Step 2 We are going to calculate Q using the equation

$$Q = Q_0 e^{-\frac{t}{CR}}$$

First, calculate the power to which 'e' is raised:

$$-\frac{t}{CR} = -\frac{100}{1000 \times 10^{-6} \times 500 \times 10^{3}} = -0.2$$

Step 3 Use the e^x key of your calculator to calculate $e^{-0.2}$, and multiply by the value of Q_0.

$$Q = Q_0 e^{-0.2} = 20 \times 10^{-3} \times e^{-0.2}$$

$$= 20 \times 10^{-3} \times 0.8187 \approx 1.64 \times 10^{-2}\,C\ (16.4\,mC)$$

With practice, you will be able to combine Steps 2 and 3 in a single calculation on your calculator.

SAQ

24 For the situation described in Worked example 3, calculate the charge stored by the capacitor after 1000 s.

Answer

A general equation

As we have seen, the graphs for the decrease of current and p.d. have the same shape as the graph for charge. As you might expect, it follows that the equations for current I in the resistor and p.d. V across

the capacitor have the same form as the equation for charge. Here are all three:

charge	$Q = Q_0 e^{-\frac{t}{CR}}$
current	$I = I_0 e^{-\frac{t}{CR}}$
p.d.	$V = V_0 e^{-\frac{t}{CR}}$

Most people remember one of these equations, and know how to change between Q, I and V. The three equations are examples of a general equation of the form:

$$x = x_0 e^{-\frac{t}{CR}}$$

SAQ

25 The capacitor shown in Figure 11.19 is initially charged to 10 V. Calculate the p.d. across the capacitor 1.0 minute after the switch is closed.

Answer

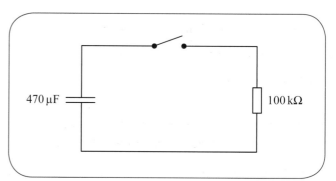

Figure 11.19 For SAQ 25.

26 A 500 µF capacitor is charged to 200 V. It is connected across of resistor of resistance 400 kΩ.

  a Calculate the initial current in the resistor.

  b Write an equation of the form $x = x_0 e^{-\frac{t}{CR}}$ to show how the current I decreases as the capacitor discharges.

  c Use your equation to calculate values of I at intervals of 100 s. Copy and complete the table below to show your results.

  d Plot a graph of your results.

Answer

t/s	0	100	200	300	400	500
$I/10^{-6}\,A$						

Time constant τ

The quantity CR appears in the equations for the exponential decrease of charge, current and p.d. It should not be surprising that the values of capacitance C and resistance R affect the rate at which a capacitor discharges through a resistor.

- With a large value of C, a lot of charge is stored. It takes longer for the charge to drain from the capacitor.
- With a large value of R, the current will be small. Again, it takes longer for the capacitor to discharge.

The quantity CR is called the **time constant** of the circuit. It is given the symbol τ (*tau*, Greek letter t):

time constant $\tau = CR$

The name 'time constant' suggests the unit of τ is seconds. The time constant of a capacitor–resistor circuit is defined as follows:

> The time constant is the time taken for the current, charge stored or p.d. to fall to $\dfrac{1}{e}$ (about 37%) of its initial value.

(Note, when $t = CR$, $x = x_0 e^{-\frac{t}{CR}} = x_0 e^{-1} \approx 0.37 x_0$.)

After twice the time constant, the value will have fallen to $\dfrac{1}{e^2}$ of its initial value, and so on. Figure 11.20 shows this. The graph shows the 'constant-ratio' property of capacitor discharge, and will remind you of similar graphs to show the half-life of a radioactive substance. Theoretically, a capacitor is never fully discharged. However, for practical purposes, a capacitor is considered to be discharged after a time equal to five time constants. At $t = 5\tau$, the capacitor has lost about 99.3% of its charge.

Circuits in which a capacitor discharges through a resistor ('R–C circuits') are often used in electronic timers. At the start of a time interval, the capacitor is charged up. It gradually discharges, and eventually falls below a set value. This triggers a switching circuit to make an alarm sound, or to have some other effect.

Increasing the time constant of the R–C circuit makes the time interval longer. There are two ways to do this: by increasing C, or by increasing R.

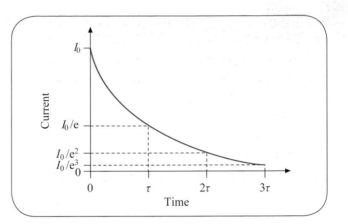

Figure 11.20 After time τ, the current has fallen to $1/e$ of its initial value; after 2τ, to $1/e^2$; and so on … .

SAQ

27 A 220 μF capacitor is discharged through a resistor of resistance 100 Ω. Calculate the time constant for this circuit. Give your answer in milliseconds (ms).

> Answer

28 Understanding the idea of the time constant of an R–C circuit can form the basis for the measurement of an unknown capacitance. Figure 11.21 shows the results of an experiment in which a capacitor C was discharged through a fixed resistor of resistance 1000 Ω.

  a Use the graph to find the initial value of the current I_0.

  b Calculate $\dfrac{1}{e}$ of this (i.e. $0.37 I_0$).

  c From the graph, find the time when the current has fallen to this value. This time is the time constant τ.

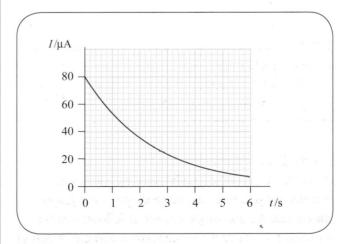

Figure 11.21 For SAQ 28.

d Use the equation $\tau = CR$ to determine the value of the capacitance C of the capacitor.

e Now use the graph to find the value of 2τ, and deduce another value for C.

Answer

29 A capacitor is discharged through a resistor. The current in the resistor in milliamperes (mA) varies with time t in seconds (s) according to the following equation:

$$I = 0.50\,e^{-0.02t}$$

a State the initial current in the resistor.

b Calculate the current after 30 s.

c Determine the time constant for this circuit.

Answer

30 A 100 µF capacitor is charged to 6.0 V. It is then discharged through a resistor of resistance 500 kΩ.

a Calculate the time constant for this circuit.

b Write down equations of the form $x = x_0\,e^{-\frac{t}{CR}}$ to show how the charge stored by the capacitor, the current in the resistor and the p.d. across it vary with time.

c Calculate the current after 1.0 minute.

Hint

Answer

Capacitors at work

Because charged capacitors store energy, they have many uses. For example, a camera's flashgun is powered by a capacitor, which is charged from the camera's battery via a system that increases the voltage. When you take a picture, the charge is released and flows very rapidly through the lamp, producing a flash. (It may take a few seconds to recharge the capacitor, so you will not be able to take another photo right away.)

A similar system on a much larger scale is used to power lasers in nuclear fusion experiments. The capacitors are charged to thousands of volts. Their energy is released to power lasers whose brilliant flash forces atomic nuclei of hydrogen together, causing them to fuse (join) to form helium nuclei. The fusion of the nuclei releases energy.

A more everyday application is in computers, where capacitors with high capacitance but relatively small volume are used as back-up power supplies. They are charged up when the computer is in use; if the battery or mains supply fails, they provide the electrical power needed to save data and shut down the computer safely.

Capacitors are used in applications like this rather than batteries because they can release their stored energy very quickly, provided they are in a circuit with low resistance. Batteries have internal resistance (see Chapter 13 of *Physics 1*).

'Supercapacitors' are currently under development which might have a number of uses, such as replacing batteries in electric vehicles and acting as energy stores in homes fitted with photovoltaic cells. It seems unlikely that there will be a single breakthrough which will bring these on to the market; rather, there will be a number of small developments, each of which will push the technology a bit further towards the goal of a compact device capable of storing large amounts of energy.

Figure 11.22 A giant capacitor. This is part of the energy supply system for a high-power particle accelerator at Fermilab in the USA.

Summary

- Capacitors are constructed from two metal sheets ('plates'), separated by an insulating material. They store charge.

- For a capacitor, the charge stored is directly proportional to the p.d. between the plates: $Q = VC$.

- Capacitance is the charge stored per unit of p.d.

- A farad is a coulomb per volt: $1\,F = 1\,C\,V^{-1}$.

- Capacitors store energy. The energy W stored at p.d. V is:

$$W = \tfrac{1}{2}QV = \tfrac{1}{2}CV^2 = \tfrac{1}{2}\frac{Q^2}{C}$$

- For capacitors connected in parallel and in series, the combined capacitances are as follows:

  parallel: $C_{total} = C_1 + C_2 + C_3 + \ldots$

  series: $\dfrac{1}{C_{total}} = \dfrac{1}{C_1} + \dfrac{1}{C_2} + \dfrac{1}{C_3} + \ldots$

- When a capacitor is discharged through a resistor, the charge, current and p.d. show an exponential decrease with time, which can be represented by equations of the form:

$$x = x_0\, e^{-\frac{t}{CR}}$$

- An exponential decay graph has a constant-ratio property.

- The time constant is defined as the time it takes for the current, charge or p.d. to fall to $\dfrac{1}{e}$ of its initial value; that is, to about 37% of its initial value.

- Time constant $\tau = CR$ and is measured in seconds (s).

Questions

1 This question is about the energy stored in a capacitor.

a i One expression for the energy W stored on a capacitor is

$$W = \tfrac{1}{2}QV$$

where Q is the charge stored and V is the potential difference across the capacitor. Show that another suitable expression for the energy stored is:

$$W = \tfrac{1}{2}CV^2$$

where C is the capacitance of the capacitor. [2]

ii Draw a graph to show how the energy W stored on a 2.2 F capacitor varies with the potential difference V across the capacitor. [2]

b The 2.2 F capacitor is connected in parallel with the power supply to a digital display for a video/DVD recorder. The purpose of the capacitor is to keep the display working during any disruptions to the electrical power supply. The diagram below shows the 5.0 V power supply, the capacitor and the display. The input to the display behaves as a 6.8 kΩ resistor. The display will light up as long as the voltage across it is at or above 4.0 V.

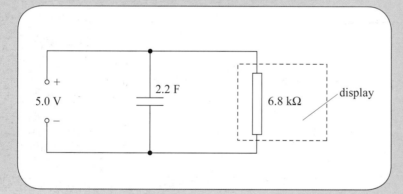

Suppose the power supply is disrupted.

i Show that the time constant of the circuit in the figure above is more than 4 hours. [2]

ii Find the energy lost by the capacitor as it discharges from 5.0 V to 4.0 V. [2]

iii The voltage V across the capacitor varies with time t according to the equation:

$$V = V_0 e^{-\frac{t}{CR}}$$

Calculate the time that it takes for the voltage to fall to 4.0 V. [2]

iv Calculate the mean power consumption of the display during this time. [1]

OCR Physics A2 (2824) June 2007 [Total 11]

Hint

Hint

Answer

continued

2 The diagram below shows a football balanced above a metal bench on a length of plastic drain pipe. The surface of the ball is coated with a smooth layer of electrically conducting paint. The pipe insulates the ball from the bench.

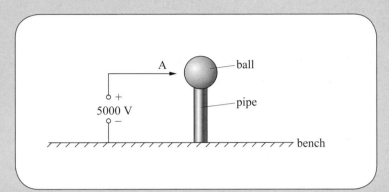

a The ball is charged by touching it momentarily with a wire A connected to the positive terminal of a 5000 V power supply. The capacitance C of the ball is 1.2×10^{-11} F. Calculate the charge Q_0 on the ball. Give a suitable unit for your answer. [3]

b The charge on the ball leaks slowly to the bench through the plastic pipe, which has a resistance R of $1.2 \times 10^{15} \, \Omega$.

   i Show that the time constant for the ball to discharge through the pipe is about 1.5×10^4 s. [1]

   ii Show that the initial value of the leakage current is about 4×10^{-12} A. [1]

   iii Suppose that the ball continues to discharge at the constant rate calculated in ii. Show that the charge Q_0 would leak away in a time equal to the time constant. [2]

   iv Using the equation for the charge Q at time t:

   $$Q = Q_0 e^{-\frac{t}{CR}}$$

   show that, in practice, the ball only loses about $\frac{2}{3}$ of its charge in a time equal to one time constant. [2]

OCR Physics A2 (2824) January 2007 [Total 9]

Answer

continued

3 In a thundercloud, thermally induced vertical winds separate out electrical charges. The base of the cloud acquires a negative charge while the centre of the cloud, 1.5 km above it, becomes positively charged (Figure 1). Lightning flashes occur inside the cloud on average every 25 s, discharging the cloud, which is then recharged by the wind. The typical charge at breakdown is 20 C when the electric field strength in the cloud is $3.0 \times 10^5 \, \text{V m}^{-1}$.

Figure 2 shows two cloud-sized uniformly charged parallel plates 1.5 km apart which can be imagined as a very simple model to simulate the electrical mechanism within a thundercloud.

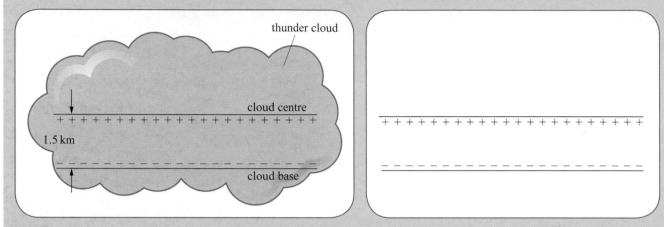

Figure 1   **Figure 2**

a **i** Make a copy of Figure 2. On your copy, draw arrows to represent the
electric field between the plates. [2]

ii Show that the voltage between the plates at discharge is 450 MV. [1]

b The theoretical circuit shown in Figure 3 can be used to model the charging
process in the thundercloud.

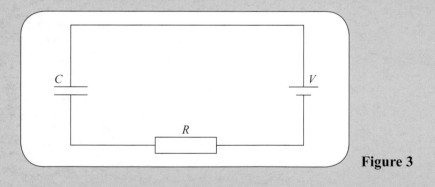

Figure 3

Explain what part each component plays so that the circuit models the charging
of the cloud. [3]

c Use the data above to calculate for the theoretical circuit:

i the mean current through the resistor R during charging [2]

ii the value of R, taking the initial current to be 5 times the mean current [2]

iii the value of C [2]

iv the time constant of the circuit. [2]

OCR Physics A2 (2824) June 2003   [Total 14]

Answer

continued

4 **a** Define the term *capacitance* of a capacitor. [1]

b Figure 1 shows a circuit where a 0.47 μF capacitor may be connected by a two-way switch S either to an 11.0 V d.c. supply or to a 2200 Ω resistor.

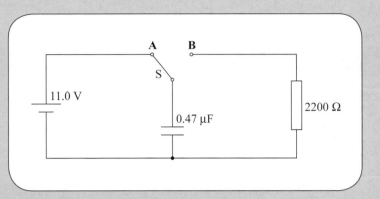

Figure 1

  i The capacitor is charged with switch S in position A. Calculate:

    1 the charge stored in the capacitor [2]

    2 the energy stored in the capacitor. [2]

  ii The switch is moved to position B at time $t = 0$ to discharge the capacitor. Calculate:

    1 the initial current in the resistor [2]

    2 the time constant of the circuit. [2]

c Figure 2 shows the variation in current in the resistor with time for part of the discharge.

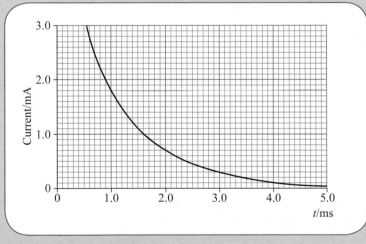

Figure 2

  i Show that the shape of the graph is exponential. [2]

  ii Estimate the charge which flows from the capacitor during the time $t = 1.0$ ms to $t = 2.0$ ms. [3]

OCR Physics A2 (2824) June 2004 [Total 14]

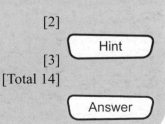

Chapter 12

Atomic structure

e-Learning

Objectives

Looking inside the atom

The idea that matter is composed of very small particles called atoms was first suggested by the Greeks some two thousand years ago. However, it was not until the middle of the nineteenth century that any ideas about the *inside* of the atom were proposed.

It was the English scientist J. J. Thomson (Figure 12.1) who suggested that the atom is a neutral particle made of a positive charge with lumps of negative charge (electrons) in it. At the time he was also investigating the nature of

Figure 12.1 J. J. Thomson at work.

the particles in cathode rays (produced when an electrically charged plate is heated), and he presented his conclusions at the Royal Institution in London on 30 April 1897. He could not determine the charge and the mass of the cathode ray particles separately, but it was clear that a new particle, probably much smaller than the hydrogen atom, had been discovered. Thomson called this particle a 'corpuscle' and used this term for many years even after the name *electron* had been given to it by most other physicists. Since atoms are neutral and physicists had discovered a negatively charged part of an atom, it meant that there were both positive and negative charges in an atom. We now call this the **plum pudding model** of the atom (positive pudding with negative plums!).

Other experiments show that the electron has a mass of 9.11×10^{-31} kg (m_e) and a charge of -1.6×10^{-19} C ($-e$). Today we use the idea of the electron to explain all sorts of phenomena, including electrostatics, current electricity and electronics. Our ability to control electrons has made possible the computer on which this book is being written and also the computer on which you may be reading it!

Alpha-particle scattering and the nucleus

Early in the twentieth century, many physicists were investigating the recently discovered phenomenon of radioactivity, the process whereby unstable nuclei emit radiation. One kind of radiation they found consisted of what they called α-particles (alpha-particles). These α-particles were known to be smaller than atoms, and had relatively high kinetic energies. Hence they were useful in experiments designed to discover the composition of atoms.

In 1906, while experimenting with the passage of α-particles through a thin mica sheet, Rutherford (Figure 12.2) noticed that most of the α-particles passed straight through. This suggested to him that there might be a large amount of *empty space* in the atom, and by 1909 he had developed what we now call the **nuclear model of the atom**.

In 1911 Rutherford carried out a further series of experiments with Hans Geiger and Ernest Marsden at the University of Manchester using gold foil in place of the mica. They directed parallel beams of

Figure 12.2 Ernest Rutherford (on the right) in the Cavendish Laboratory, Cambridge, England. He had a loud voice that could disturb sensitive apparatus and so the notice was a joke aimed at him.

α-particles at a piece of gold foil only 10^{-6} m thick. Most of the α-particles went straight through. Some were deflected slightly, but about 1 in 20 000 were deflected through an angle of more than 90°, so that they appeared to bounce back off the foil. This confirmed Rutherford in his thinking about the atom: that it was mostly empty space, with most of the mass and all of the positive charge concentrated in a tiny region at the centre. This central **nucleus** only affected the α-particles when they came close to it.

Later, when describing the results, Rutherford wrote: 'It was quite the most incredible event that has happened to me in my life. It was almost as incredible as if you fired a 15 inch shell at a piece of tissue paper and it came back and hit you.' In fact, he was not quite as surprised as this might suggest, because the results confirmed the ideas he had used in designing the experiment.

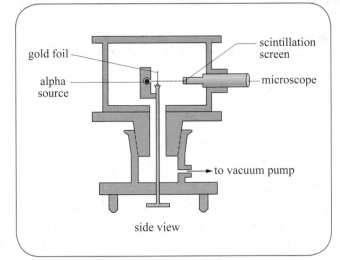

side view

Figure 12.3 The apparatus used for the α-scattering experiment. The microscope can be moved round to detect scattered radiation at different angles.

Figure 12.3 shows the apparatus used in the α-scattering experiment. Notice the following points:

- The α-particle source was encased in metal with a small aperture allowing a fine beam of α-particles to emerge.
- Air in the apparatus was pumped out to leave a vacuum; α-radiation is absorbed by a few centimetres of air.
- One reason for choosing gold was that it can be made into a very thin sheet or foil. Rutherford's foil was a few hundreds of atoms thick.
- The α-particles were detected when they struck a solid 'scintillating' material. Each α-particle gave a tiny flash of light and these were counted by the experimenters (Geiger and Marsden).
- The detector could be moved round to detect the α-particles scattered through different angles.

Geiger and Marsden had the difficult task of observing and counting the tiny flashes of light produced by individual α-particles striking the scintillation screen. They had to spend several minutes in the darkened laboratory to allow the pupils of their eyes to become dilated so that they could see the faint flashes. Each experimenter could only stare into the detector for about a minute before the strain was too much and they had to change places.

Explaining α-scattering

A very simple analogy (or model) of the experiment is shown in Figure 12.4. When you roll a ball-bearing down a slope towards the 'cymbal', it can be deflected; but even if it is rolled directly at the cymbal's centre, it does not come back but rolls over it and carries on to the other side. However, using the 'tin hat' shape, with a much narrower but higher central bulge, any ball-bearings rolled close to the centre will be markedly deflected, and those rolled directly towards it will come straight back. The shape of the cymbal represents the shape of the electric field of an atom in the 'plum pudding' model: low central intensity and spread out. The 'tin hat' represents that for the nuclear model: high central intensity and concentrated.

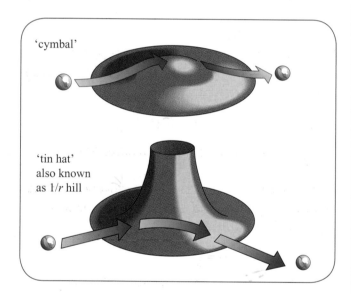

Figure 12.4 An analogy for Rutherford's experiment.

The paths of an α-particle near a nucleus are shown in Figure 12.5. Rutherford reasoned that the large deflection of the α-particle must be due to a very small charged nucleus with a very large electric field near its surface. From his experiments he calculated that the diameter of the gold nucleus was about 10^{-14} m. It has since been shown that the very large deflection of the α-particle is due to the electrostatic repulsion between the positive charge of the α-particle and the positive charge of the nucleus of the atom. The closer the path of the α-particle gets to the nucleus, the greater will be this repulsion. An α-particle making a 'head-on'

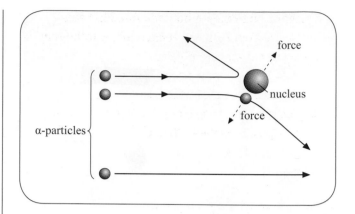

Figure 12.5 Possible paths of an α-particle near a nucleus. The nucleus and the α-particle both experience electrostatic repulsion.

collision with a nucleus was back-scattered through 180°. The α-particle and nucleus both experience an equal but opposite repulsive electrostatic force F. This force has a much greater effect on the motion of the α-particle than on the massive nucleus of gold. We can use Coulomb's law (Chapter 8) to determine the magnitude of this force:

charge on gold nucleus, $Q = +1.26 \times 10^{-17}$ C

charge on α-particle, $q = +3.20 \times 10^{-19}$ C

The equation for Coulomb's law is:

$$F = \frac{Qq}{4\pi\varepsilon_0 r^2}$$

Substituting the values for Q and q, at a typical separation of 10^{-14} m the force F is given by:

$$F = \frac{1.26 \times 10^{-17} \times 3.20 \times 10^{-19}}{4\pi \times 8.85 \times 10^{-12} \times (10^{-14})^2} \approx 360 \, \text{N}$$

This is a very large force on such tiny particles, but it lasts for a very short time of about 10^{-20} s.

SAQ

1 Rutherford's scattering experiments were done in an evacuated container. Explain why was this necessary.

> Answer

2 In Rutherford's experiment, α-particles were directed at a thin gold foil. A small fraction of the α-particles were back-scattered through 180°.

Describe and explain how the fraction back-scattered would change if each of the following changes was (separately) made.

a A thicker foil was used.

b Faster α-particles were used.

c A silver foil was used – a silver nucleus has less positive charge than a gold nucleus.

> Answer

A simple atom model

After Rutherford had presented his findings, the nuclear model of the atom gained rapid acceptance. This was partly because it helped chemists to explain the phenomenon of chemical bonding (the way in which atoms bond together to form molecules). Subsequently, the proton was discovered. It had a positive charge, equal and opposite to that of the electron. However, its mass was too small to account for the entire mass of the atom and it was not until the early 1930s that this puzzle was solved by the discovery of the neutron, an uncharged particle with a similar mass to that of the proton.

This suggests a model for the atom like the one shown in Figure 12.6.

- Protons and neutrons make up the nucleus of the atom.
- The electrons move around the nucleus in a cloud, some closer to and some further from the centre of the nucleus.

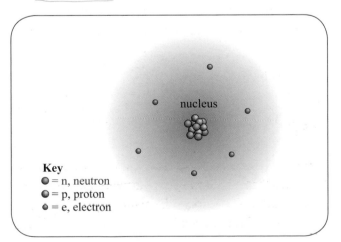

Key
- = n, neutron
- = p, proton
- = e, electron

Figure 12.6 A simple model of the atom. If the nucleus was drawn to scale, it would be invisible (and the electrons are even smaller!).

From this model it looks as though all matter, including ourselves, is mostly empty space. For example, if we scaled up the hydrogen atom so that the nucleus was the size of a 1 cm diameter marble, the orbiting electron would be a grain of sand some 800 m away!

The scale of things

It is useful to have an idea of the approximate sizes of typical particles:

- radius of proton ~ radius of neutron ~ 10^{-15} m
- radius of nucleus ~ 10^{-15} m to 10^{-14} m
- radius of atom ~ 10^{-10} m
- size of molecule ~ 10^{-10} m to 10^{-6} m.

(Some molecules, such as large protein molecules, are very large indeed – compared to an atom!)

The radii of nuclear particles are often quoted in femtometres (fm), where 1 fm = 10^{-15} m.

Nuclear density

We can picture a proton as a small, positively charged sphere. Knowing its mass and radius, we can calculate its density:

mass of proton $m_p = 1.67 \times 10^{-27}$ kg

radius of proton $r = 0.80$ fm $= 0.80 \times 10^{-15}$ m

(In fact, the radius of the proton is not very accurately known; it is probably between 0.80×10^{-15} m and 0.86×10^{-15} m.)

$$\text{volume of proton} = \tfrac{4}{3}\pi r^3$$
$$= \tfrac{4}{3}\pi \times (0.80 \times 10^{-15})^3$$
$$= 2.14 \times 10^{-45}\,\text{m}^3 \approx 2.1 \times 10^{-45}\,\text{m}^3$$

$$\text{density} = \frac{\text{mass}}{\text{volume}}$$

$$\text{density} = \frac{1.67 \times 10^{-27}}{2.14 \times 10^{-45}} \approx 7.8 \times 10^{17}\,\text{kg m}^{-3}$$

So the proton has a density of roughly 10^{18} kg m^{-3}. This is also the density of an atomic nucleus, because nuclei are made of protons and neutrons held closely together.

Compare the density of nuclear material with that of water whose density is 1000 kg m^{-3} – the nucleus is 10^{15} times as dense. Nuclear matter the size of a tiny grain of sand will have a mass of about a million tonnes! This is a consequence of the fact that the nucleus occupies only a tiny fraction of the volume of an atom. The remainder is occupied by the cloud of orbiting electrons whose mass makes up less than one-thousandth of the atomic mass.

SAQ

3 Gold has a density of $19\,700\,\mathrm{kg\,m^{-3}}$. 193 g of gold contains the Avogadro number of atoms. Use this information to estimate the volume of a gold atom, and hence its radius. State any assumptions you make. ($N_A = 6.02 \times 10^{23}\,\mathrm{mol^{-1}}$.)

> Hint

> Answer

Nucleons and electrons

We will start this section with a summary of the particles mentioned so far (Table 12.1). All nuclei, except the lightest form of hydrogen, contain protons and neutrons, and each nucleus is described by the number of protons and neutrons that it contains.

- Protons and neutrons in a nucleus are collectively called **nucleons**. For example, in a nucleus of gold, there are 79 protons and 118 neutrons, giving a total of 197 nucleons altogether.
- The total number of nucleons in a nucleus is called the **nucleon number** (or mass number) A.
- The nucleon number is equal to the sum of the number of neutrons in the nucleus, the **neutron number** N, and the number of protons, the **proton number** (or atomic number) Z, i.e.

$$A = N + Z$$

Particle	Relative mass (proton = 1)*	Charge†
proton (p)	1	$+e$
neutron (n)	1	0
electron (e)	0.0005	$-e$
alpha-particle (α)	4	$+2e$

Table 12.1 Summary of the particles that we have met so far in this chapter. The α-particle is in fact a helium nucleus (with two protons and two neutrons).

*The numbers given for the masses are approximate.

†$e = 1.60 \times 10^{-19}\,\mathrm{C}$.

Any nucleus of an atom can be represented by the symbol for the element along with the nucleon number and proton number as shown below:

$$\begin{matrix}\text{nucleon number} \\ \text{proton number}\end{matrix}\text{element symbol} \qquad {}^{A}_{Z}X$$

oxygen ${}^{16}_{8}O$ \qquad gold ${}^{197}_{79}Au$ \qquad uranium ${}^{235}_{92}U$

A specific combination of protons and neutrons in a nucleus is called a **nuclide**.

The proton and nucleon numbers of some common elements are shown in Table 12.2.

You can see from Table 12.2 that, as the nuclei get heavier, so the ratio of the number of neutrons to the number of protons gets larger. For example, for light elements such as hydrogen, helium, carbon and oxygen this ratio is 1, for iron it is 1.15 and for uranium it has risen to 1.59. After this it starts to fall again for the artificial elements with $Z > 92$. A graph of neutron number against proton number for the naturally occurring elements is shown in Figure 12.7.

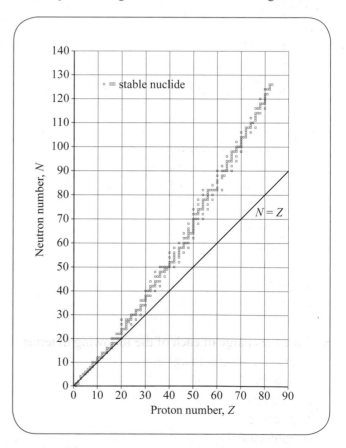

Figure 12.7 A graph of neutron number N against proton number Z for the naturally occurring elements.

Element	Nucleon number A	Proton number Z	Element	Nucleon number A	Proton number Z
hydrogen	1	1	bromine	79	35
helium	4	2	silver	107	47
lithium	7	3	tin	120	50
beryllium	9	4	iodine	130	53
boron	11	5	caesium	133	55
carbon	12	6	barium	138	56
nitrogen	14	7	tungsten	184	74
oxygen	16	8	platinum	195	78
neon	20	10	gold	197	79
sodium	23	11	mercury	202	80
magnesium	24	12	lead	206	82
aluminium	27	13	bismuth	209	83
chlorine	35	17	radium	226	88
calcium	40	20	uranium	238	92
iron	56	26	plutonium	239	94
nickel	58	28	americium	241	95

Table 12.2 Proton and nucleon numbers of some nuclides.

SAQ

4 Table 12.2 shows the proton and nucleon numbers of several nuclei. Determine the number of neutrons in each of the following nuclei shown in the table:

   a nitrogen
   b bromine
   c silver
   d gold
   e mercury.

[Answer]

5 State the charge of each of the following in terms of the elementary charge e:

   a proton
   b neutron
   c nucleus
   d molecule
   e α-particle.

[Answer]

Isotopes

Although atoms of the same element may be identical chemically, their nuclei may be slightly different. The number of protons in the nucleus of an atom determines what element it is; helium always has 2 protons, carbon 6 protons, oxygen 8 protons, neon 10 protons, radium 88 protons, uranium 92 protons and so on.

However, the number of neutrons in the nuclei for a given element can vary. Take neon as an example. Three different naturally occurring forms of neon are:

$$^{20}_{10}\text{Ne} \qquad ^{21}_{10}\text{Ne} \qquad ^{22}_{10}\text{Ne}$$

The first has 10 neutrons in the nucleus, the second 11 neutrons and the third 12 neutrons. These three types of neon nuclei are called **isotopes** of neon. Each isotope has the same number of protons (for neon this is 10) but a different number of neutrons. The word 'isotope' comes from the Greek *isotopos* (same place), because all isotopes of the same element have the same place in the Periodic Table of elements.

> Isotopes are nuclei of the same element with a different number of neutrons but the same number of protons.

Any atom is electrically neutral (it has no net positive or negative charge), so the number of electrons surrounding the nucleus must equal the number of protons in the nucleus of the atom. If an atom gains or loses an electron, it is no longer electrically neutral and is called an **ion**.

For an atom, the number of protons (and hence the number of electrons) determines the chemical properties of the atom. The number of protons and the number of neutrons determine the nuclear properties. It is important to realise that, since the number of protons, and therefore the number of electrons, in isotopes of the same element are identical, they will all have the same chemical properties but very different nuclear properties.

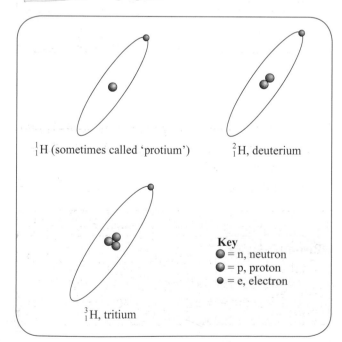

Figure 12.8 The isotopes of hydrogen.

Hydrogen has three important isotopes, $^1_1$H, $^2_1$H (deuterium) and $^3_1$H (tritium) (Figure 12.8). $^1_1$H and deuterium occur naturally, but tritium has to be made. Deuterium and tritium form the fuel of many fusion research reactors. Hydrogen is the most abundant element in the Universe (Figure 12.9), because it consists of just one proton and one electron, and this is the simplest structure possible for an atom.

The relative atomic masses of isotopes will also be different. There are differences too in some of their physical properties, such as density and boiling point. For example, heavy water, water containing deuterium, has a boiling point of 104 °C under normal atmospheric pressure.

Table 12.3 gives details of some other commonly occurring isotopes.

(Extension)

Figure 12.9 The Horsehead Nebula in Orion. The large coloured regions are expanses of dust and gas, mostly hydrogen, that are ionised by nearby stars so that they emit light. The dark 'horse head' is where the areas of gas and dust remain in atomic form and block out the light from behind.

Element	Nucleon number A	Proton number Z	Neutron number N
hydrogen	1	1	0
	2	1	1
carbon	12	6	6
	14	6	8
oxygen	16	8	8
	18	8	10
neon	20	10	10
	21	10	11
potassium	39	19	20
	40	19	21
strontium	88	38	50
	90	38	52
caesium	135	55	80
	137	55	82
lead	206	82	124
	208	82	126
radium	226	88	138
	228	88	140
uranium	235	92	143
	238	92	146

Table 12.3 Some commonly occurring isotopes.

SAQ

6 Uranium has atomic number 92. Two of its common isotopes have nucleon numbers 235 and 238. Determine the number of neutrons for these isotopes. [Answer]

7 There are seven naturally occurring isotopes of mercury with nucleon numbers (relative abundances) of 196 (0.2%), 198 (10%), 199 (16.8%), 200 (23.1%), 201 (13.2%), 202 (29.8%) and 204 (6.9%).
   a Determine the proton and neutron numbers for each isotope.
   b Determine the average relative atomic mass (equivalent to the 'average nucleon number') of naturally occurring mercury. [Answer]

8 Group the following imaginary elements A–H into isotopes and name them using the Periodic Table in the back of the book (Appendix A). [Answer]

	A	B	C	D	E	F	G	H
Proton number	20	23	21	22	20	22	22	23
Nucleon number	44	50	46	46	46	48	50	51

9 A nucleus of strontium has a nucleon number of 90 and a proton number of 38. Describe the structure of the strontium nucleus. [Answer]

10 An element has several isotopes.

    a State how their nuclei differ.

    b In what ways are their nuclei the same?

        (Answer)

Forces in the nucleus

As you know from earlier in this chapter, there are two kinds of particle in the nucleus of an atom: protons, which each carry positive charge $+e$; and neutrons, which are uncharged. It is therefore quite surprising that the nucleus holds together at all. You would expect the electrostatic repulsions from all those positively charged protons to blow it apart. The fact that this does not happen is very good evidence for the existence of an *attractive* force between the nucleons. This is called the **strong nuclear force**. It only acts over very short distances (10^{-14} m), and it is what holds the nucleus together.

We can get an idea of the strength of the strong nuclear force by thinking about two other forces, the electrostatic and gravitational forces.

Consider two protons, adjacent to each other in a nucleus (Figure 12.10). They are separated by two proton radii, about 1.6×10^{-15} m. They repel each other because each has charge $+e$, equal to $+1.6 \times 10^{-19}$ C. We can calculate the electrostatic repulsive force between the protons using Coulomb's law:

$$F = \frac{Qq}{4\pi\varepsilon_0 r^2}$$

$$= \frac{(1.6 \times 10^{-19})^2}{4\pi \times 8.85 \times 10^{-12} \times (1.6 \times 10^{-15})^2} \approx 90\,\text{N}$$

This is a force that tends to push the protons apart.

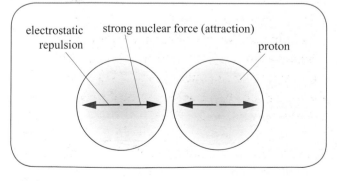

electrostatic repulsion   strong nuclear force (attraction)

proton

Figure 12.10 The forces between two protons in a nucleus.

Can the attractive gravitational force between two protons of mass 1.67×10^{-27} kg balance this repulsive force? We can calculate this force using Newton's law of gravitation:

$$F = \frac{GMm}{r^2}$$

$$= \frac{6.67 \times 10^{-11} \times (1.67 \times 10^{-27})^2}{(1.6 \times 10^{-15})^2} \approx 7.3 \times 10^{-35}\,\text{N}$$

You can see that the gravitational force is about 10^{36} times smaller than the electrostatic force and so cannot possibly balance it out. We conclude that there must be another attractive force between the protons, and that its value must be at least 90 N when two protons are separated by 1.6×10^{-15} m. This is the strong nuclear force.

Diluting the protons

In small nuclei the strong nuclear force from all the nucleons reaches most of the others in the nucleus, but as we go on adding protons and neutrons the balance becomes much finer. The longer-range electrostatic force affects the whole nucleus, but the short-range strong nuclear force of any particular nucleon only affects those nucleons around it – the rest of the nucleus is unaffected. In a large nucleus the nucleons are not held together so tightly, and this can make the nucleus unstable. The more protons there are in a nucleus, the greater the electric forces between them, and we need a few extra neutrons to help 'keep the protons apart'. This is why heavy nuclei have more neutrons than protons.

The variation of neutron number with proton number is shown in Figure 12.7. You can see that for light elements these two numbers are the same, but they become very different for heavy elements. Adding more neutrons helps to keep the nucleus stable, but when the number of protons is greater than 83, adding more neutrons is not enough. Elements with a proton number greater than 83 are less stable.

Most atoms that make up our world have stable nuclei; that is, they do not change as time goes by, which is quite fortunate really! However, some are less stable and give out radiation. Whether or not an atom is unstable depends on the numbers of protons and neutrons in its nucleus. Hydrogen-1 (1p), helium-4 (2p, 2n), carbon-12 (6p, 6n) and oxygen-16

(8p, 8n) are all stable – but add or subtract neutrons and the situation changes.

For example, add a neutron to helium-4 and you get helium-5, a very unstable nucleus – it undergoes radioactive decay. (There is much more about radioactive decay in Chapter 14.)

SAQ

11 State which of the following forces act between protons in a nucleus and which act between neutrons.
- gravitational
- electrostatic
- strong nuclear

Answer

Fundamental particles?

Chemistry is very complicated because there are literally billions of different molecules that can exist. The discovery of the Periodic Table simplified things because it suggested that there were roughly 92 different elements whose atoms could be arranged to make these various molecules. The idea that atoms are made up of just three types of particle (protons, neutrons and electrons) seemed to simplify things still more, and scientists were very happy with it because it seemed to provide a very simple explanation of a complex world. Protons, neutrons and electrons were thought of as **fundamental particles**, which could not be subdivided further.

However, in the middle decades of the twentieth century, physicists discovered many other particles that did not fit this pattern. They gave them names such as pions, kaons, muons, etc., using up most of the letters of the Greek alphabet.

These new particles were found in two ways:
- by looking at cosmic rays, which are particles that arrive at the Earth from outer space
- by looking at the particles produced by high-energy collisions in particle accelerators.

Figure 12.11 shows the tracks of particles detected in an accelerator experiment. A particle has entered from the left and then struck another particle just to the right of the centre. Four new particles fly out from the point of impact.

This detector is placed in a strong magnetic field so that charged particles will follow curved paths (because of the *Bev* force). Uncharged particles

Figure 12.11 Particle tracks in a bubble chamber detector.

travel in straight lines. Measuring the curvature of the tracks allows the charge and mass of the particles to be deduced. The spiral tracks arise from electrons and positrons, which lose energy as they follow a curved path.

The discovery of new particles with masses different from those of protons, neutrons and electrons suggested that these were not fundamental particles. Various attempts were made to tidy up this very confusing picture.

In principle, we can never know for certain whether a particle such as the electron is truly fundamental; the possibility will always remain that a physicist will discover some deeper underlying structure.

Families of particles

Today, sub-atomic particles are divided into two families:

- **Hadrons** such as protons and neutrons. These are all particles that are affected by the strong nuclear force.
- **Leptons** such as electrons. These are particles that are unaffected by the strong nuclear force.

The word *hadron* comes from a Greek word meaning *bulky*, while *lepton* means *light* (in mass). It is certainly true that protons and neutrons are bulky compared to electrons.

Physicists are still experimenting with hadrons in the hope of finding answers to some fundamental questions about this family of particles. The Large Hadron Collider (Figure 12.12) at the CERN laboratory in Geneva illustrates the fact that particle accelerators have become bigger and bigger as scientists have sought to look further and further into the fundamental nature of matter.

Figure 12.12 One of the particle detectors of the Large Hadron Collider (LHC), as it was about to be installed. This gives an idea of the scale of the experiment. The entire collider is 27 km in circumference.

Inside hadrons

To sort out the complicated picture of the hadron family of particles, Murray Gell-Mann in 1964 proposed a new model. He suggested that they were made up of just a few different particles, which he called **quarks**. (A similar idea was proposed at the same time by George Zweig; he called his particles 'aces', but it didn't stick.)

Figure 12.13 shows icons used to represent three quarks, together with the corresponding *antiquarks*. These are called the up (u), down (d) and strange (s) quarks. Gell-Mann's idea was that each hadron was made up of two or three quarks, held together by the strong nuclear force. For example:

- A proton is made up of two up quarks and a down quark; proton = (u u d).
- A neutron is made up of one up quark and two down quarks; neutron = (u d d).
- A pi$^+$ meson is made up of an up quark and a down antiquark; pi$^+$ meson = (u $\bar{\text{d}}$).
- A phi meson is made up of a strange quark and an antistrange quark; phi meson = (s $\bar{\text{s}}$).

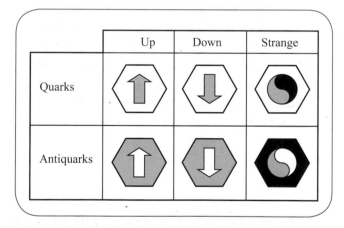

Figure 12.13 Icons representing three 'flavours' of quark, *up*, *down* and *strange*, and their antiquarks.

Antiquarks are shown with a 'bar' on top of the letter for the quark. Antiquarks are needed to account for the existence of antimatter. This is matter that is made of antiparticles; when a particle meets its antiparticle, they annihilate each other, leaving only photons of energy. You will learn about one antiparticle, the positron or antielectron, in Chapter 14.

Particle properties

Quark theory accounts for the properties of hadrons, including their electric charge and their mass. It does this by identifying some basic properties of quarks. These are *charge Q, baryon number B* and *strangeness S*. Table 12.4 shows values of these for the three flavours of quark we have looked at so far.

You should not worry too much about the meanings of these properties. You should understand the idea of electric charge (although it may surprise you to see particles whose charge is a fraction of the electron charge *e*), but the meanings of baryon number and strangeness are beyond the scope of this book. The idea of strangeness was introduced when a particle (called the lambda) was discovered that decayed far more slowly than expected. It was suggested that it must have an unfamiliar property called 'strangeness' to account for this, and this name was later transferred to one of the quarks from which it is made. (The lambda particle consists of one up quark, one down quark and one strange quark.)

It is important to appreciate two things:
- The properties of a hadron are the sum of the properties of the quarks of which it is made. So, for example, a proton (u u d) has charge:

$$Q = (+\tfrac{2}{3}) + (+\tfrac{2}{3}) + (-\tfrac{1}{3}) = +1$$

- The quantities of charge, baryon number and strangeness are all conserved when particles interact with each other.

Three other quarks (and their antiquarks) are needed to complete this picture. These are the *charm* (c), *top* (t) and *bottom* (b) quarks. The properties of these quarks are expressed in terms of charm, topness and bottomness. Their icons are shown in Figure 12.14. Physicists believe that these can account for all of the hadrons that have been observed to exist.

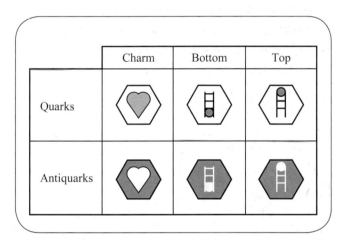

Figure 12.14 Icons representing three 'flavours' of quark, *charm*, *bottom* and *top*, and their antiquarks.

Quark (flavour)	Charge Q (in units of e)	Baryon number B	Strangeness S
up (u)	$+\tfrac{2}{3}$	$+\tfrac{1}{3}$	0
down (d)	$-\tfrac{1}{3}$	$+\tfrac{1}{3}$	0
strange (s)	$-\tfrac{1}{3}$	$+\tfrac{1}{3}$	-1

Table 12.4 Q, B and S values for three quarks. The antiquarks have opposite values.

Now try Worked example 1.

Worked example 1

The K$^+$ meson consists of one up quark and one antistrange quark. Determine the charge Q, baryon number B and strangeness S of this particle.

Step 1 Write down what the K$^+$ meson is made of and their associated Q, B and S values.

$$K^+ \text{ meson} = (u\,\bar{s})$$

For an up quark: $Q = +\frac{2}{3}$ $B = +\frac{1}{3}$ $S = 0$

An antiquark has opposite values for Q, B and S.

For an antistrange quark: $Q = +\frac{1}{3}$ $B = -\frac{1}{3}$ $S = +1$

Step 2 Now determine the individual values of Q, B and S for the K$^+$ meson.

Charge $Q = (+\frac{2}{3}) + (+\frac{1}{3}) = +1$

Baryon number $B = (+\frac{1}{3}) + (-\frac{1}{3}) = 0$

Strangeness $S = (0) + (+1) = +1$

SAQ

12 A neutron consists of two down quarks and one up quark. Show that this gives the neutron zero electric charge.

Answer

13 The proton and the neutron are hadrons. Determine their values of baryon number and strangeness.

Answer

14 A sigma-plus hadron (Σ^+) has the quark structure (u u s). Name these three quarks, and determine the Q, B and S values of the Σ^+.

Answer

Evidence for quarks

No-one has ever detected an isolated quark – that is, a quark on its own. It seems that they are always tied up in twos or threes, forming hadrons. So can we be sure that they really exist? The evidence from electron diffraction suggests that they do exist.

Electron diffraction is a technique used to study matter on the atomic and sub-atomic scale. Electrons are accelerated to high velocities and directed at a target containing the particles of interest. The electrons behave like waves and are diffracted by the particles in the target. (This is an example of wave–particle duality, which you studied in Chapter 19 of *Physics 1*.) The pattern of the diffracted electrons can be analysed to determine the size and shape of the diffracting particles.

High-energy electron beams have been used to show up the structure of the atomic nucleus. Nuclei are imperfect spheres, as one would expect; they are made up of protons and neutrons, packed tightly together.

To investigate individual protons, electrons must be accelerated to even higher energies. This is because their wavelength λ is related to their momentum p by the de Broglie relationship

$$\lambda = \frac{h}{p}$$

where h is the Planck constant (6.63×10^{-34} J s). (Recall that, to observe the maximum diffraction effect, the wavelength must be comparable to the dimensions of the diffracting object.) The results of such experiments show that protons do appear to have internal structure, and the diffraction pattern suggests that the electrons are being scattered by particles with charges that are a fraction of e. This is experimental confirmation that protons (and other hadrons) are not fundamental particles.

That leaves the question: can we say that quarks are fundamental particles? Or, if we could probe them closely, would we find that quarks were made up of something even more fundamental? At present, nobody knows.

Summary

Glossary

- The α-particle scattering experiment provides evidence for the existence of a small, massive and positively charged nucleus at the centre of the atom.

- Most of the mass of an atom is concentrated in its nucleus.

- The nucleus consists of protons and neutrons, and is surrounded by a cloud of electrons.

- The number of protons and neutrons in the nucleus of an atom is called its nucleon number A.

- The number of protons in the nucleus of an atom is called its proton number (or atomic number) Z.

- Isotopes are nuclei of the same element with a different number of neutrons but the same number of protons.

- Different isotopes (or nuclides, if referring to the nucleus only) can be represented by the notation $^A_Z X$, where X is the chemical symbol for the element.

- The strong nuclear force acts between nucleons; it is attractive and very short-ranged.

- The electrostatic force acts between protons in the nucleus and is balanced by the strong force; the gravitational force between nucleons is very small.

- Hadrons (e.g. the neutron) are particles that consist of quarks and hence are affected by the strong nuclear force. Leptons (e.g. the electron) are particles that are unaffected by the strong nuclear force.

- All hadrons consist of quarks (up, down, strange, charm, bottom and top) and their antiquarks. Quarks are now thought to be fundamental particles.

- In all hadron interactions, the quantities of charge Q, baryon number B, strangeness S, charm, bottomness and topness are all conserved.

Questions

1 Describe what conclusions can be drawn about the structure of the atom from Rutherford's experiment in which α-particles are scattered by gold nuclei. Explain how and why the experiment differs when high-speed electrons are fired at nuclei. [Total 7]

OCR Physics A2 (2824) January 2005

Answer

2 The figure below shows the path of an alpha particle (α-particle) $^4_2$He being deflected through an angle of 30° as it passes a nucleus **N** in a thin gold foil.

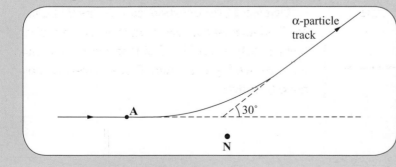

α-particle track

A

30°

N

continued

   a Copy the diagram and draw on arrows to represent:

     i the direction of the electrostatic force on the α-particle when it is at **A** [1]

     ii the direction of the maximum electrostatic force on the nucleus **N** during the passage of the α-particle. [1]

   b The incident α-particle has kinetic energy 8.0×10^{-13} J and mass 6.7×10^{-27} kg. Show that:

     i its initial speed is 1.5×10^{7} m s^{-1} [2]

     ii the magnitude of its initial momentum is 1.0×10^{-19} kg m s^{-1}. [1]

   c Imagine a proton moving initially along the same path as the α-particle with the same kinetic energy.

     i Show that the initial momentum of the proton is 5.0×10^{-20} kg m s^{-1}. [2]

     ii The proton is deflected through about 15° as it passes the gold nucleus. State qualitatively <u>two</u> ways in which the movement of the nucleus differs in this case from the movement caused by the α-particle. [2]

   d Calculate the magnitude of the electrostatic force between the proton at the point **A** and the gold nucleus $^{197}_{79}$Au. The distance **AN** is 7.5×10^{-13} m. [4]

OCR Physics A2 (2824) June 2003 [Total 13]

> Hint

> Answer

3 **a** An ion of lithium-7 ($^{7}_{3}$Li) has a charge $+1.6 \times 10^{-19}$ C. For this ion, state the number of:

     i protons [1]

     ii neutrons [1]

     iii electrons. [1]

   b One of the isotopes of iron is iron-55 ($^{55}_{26}$Fe).

     i Explain the term *isotopes*. [1]

     ii Determine the number of iron-55 nuclei in a sample of mass 30 µg. [3]

     iii In a particular reaction of the iron-55 nucleus, one proton and two neutrons are removed from the nucleus. Describe the new nucleus produced in such a reaction. [2]

[Total 9]

> Hint

> Answer

4 **a** Give one example of:

     i a hadron [1]

     ii a lepton. [1]

   b Using the simple quark model, state the constituents of a proton and a neutron. [2]

   c In a particle accelerator two protons collide with sufficient energy to produce a positive pion (π^{+}) according to the nuclear equation:

$$\text{proton} + \text{proton} \longrightarrow \text{proton} + \text{neutron} + \pi^{+}$$

     i Name all quantities conserved in such a reaction. [3]

     ii Determine the baryon number B of the π^{+} particle. [3]

[Total 10]

> Hint

> Answer

Chapter 13

Nuclear physics

e-Learning

Objectives

Nuclear processes

Radioactivity was discovered at the end of the nineteenth century. The next decades saw an increasing understanding of radioactivity as just one of several nuclear processes, along with nuclear fission and nuclear fusion. The second half of the twentieth century saw increasing applications of these processes, in nuclear power and nuclear weapons (see Figure 13.1), so that people talked of 'the nuclear age'.

These processes were predicted following Einstein's development of his Special Theory of Relativity, with his famous equation $\Delta E = \Delta mc^2$. In this chapter, we will look at fission and fusion processes as sources of energy and see how Einstein's equation can explain the release of energy that occurs during these reactions.

Figure 13.1 Our understanding of nuclear physics has proved to be a mixed blessing. Nuclear weapons dominated global politics for much of the twentieth century.

Nuclear fission

In Nature, we find nuclei with proton numbers Z up to 92 (uranium). However, the most massive of these, beyond $Z = 83$, are unstable, and are gradually decaying away. In Chapter 14, we will look in more detail at the nature of this radioactive decay.

However, there is another way in which massive, unstable nuclei such as uranium and plutonium can become more stable. They can split apart into two, more stable fragments; this process is called **nuclear fission**. Usually, fission occurs when a neutron collides with a large, unstable nucleus; this is **induced nuclear fission** (Figure 13.2). The neutron is absorbed, making the nucleus even more unstable, so that the nucleus then splits into two nuclei. Several neutrons are also released in such a fission reaction. (These neutrons may go on to cause the fission of other large nuclei. A chain reaction is set up; use is made of this in nuclear power stations and in nuclear explosions – see the section 'Nuclear power' on page 201.)

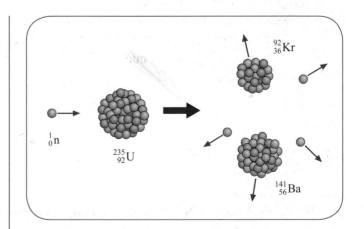

Figure 13.2 In induced nuclear fission, a neutron ($^1_0$n) is absorbed by a uranium-235 nucleus ($^{235}_{92}$U), causing it to become unstable, so that it splits into two large fragments. In the process, neutrons are released.

We can represent nuclear fission by nuclear equations. Here is the equation for the fission shown in Figure 13.2:

$$^1_0n + \, ^{235}_{92}U \longrightarrow \, ^{92}_{36}Kr + \, ^{141}_{56}Ba + 3^1_0n$$

(^1_0n represents a neutron. A proton may be represented by ^1_1p or ^1_1H.)

In words, this describes what happens when a single neutron ^1_0n collides with a uranium nucleus $^{235}_{92}U$. Fission occurs, resulting (in this case) in isotopes of krypton and barium, and three neutrons are also released. In the reaction, energy is released as kinetic energy of the fragments and the neutrons, and as gamma radiation. Fission may result in a different pair of isotopes; two, three or four neutrons may be released.

There is an intermediate stage in fission which we can include in the equation. The uranium-235 nucleus captures the neutron and, for a short time, becomes an unstable uranium-236 nucleus. We can show this as follows:

$$^1_0n + \, ^{235}_{92}U \longrightarrow \, ^{236}_{92}U^* \longrightarrow \, ^{92}_{36}Kr + \, ^{141}_{56}Ba + 3^1_0n$$

For these equations to be balanced, we require that both the proton number and the nucleon number are conserved. The total number of protons (representing positive charge) must be the same on both sides of the equation, because we cannot create or destroy charge in a nuclear reaction. Similarly, the total number of nucleons must be the same on both sides. We can check like this:

- for Z

  $0 + 92 = 36 + 56 + (3 \times 0)$

  [l.h.s. = r.h.s. = 92]

- for A

  $1 + 235 = 92 + 141 + (3 \times 1)$

  [l.h.s. = r.h.s. = 236]

SAQ

1 Show that the following nuclear decay equation is correctly balanced:

$$^{235}_{92}U + \, ^1_0n \longrightarrow \, ^{138}_{54}Xe + \, ^{95}_{38}Sr + 3^1_0n$$

Answer

2 In a nuclear reactor, a nucleus of uranium $^{238}_{92}U$ may capture a neutron ^1_0n and become a nucleus of plutonium $^{239}_{94}Pu$. Electrons are released. Write a balanced equation for this reaction, and deduce how many electrons are released. (An electron is represented as $^0_{-1}e$.)

Answer

3 In a nuclear fission event, the large nucleus usually splits into two unequal fragments; sometimes two neutrons are released, sometimes three or four. Complete the following equations by ensuring that both proton number and nucleon number are conserved. (In **b**, the missing element is an isotope of krypton, Kr.)

a $\quad ^{239}_{94}Pu + \, ^1_0n \longrightarrow \, ^{145}_{56}Ba + \, ^{93}_{38}Sr + \, ?$

b $\quad ^{239}_{94}Pu + \, ^1_0n \longrightarrow \, ^{147}_{58}Ce + \, ? + 3^1_0n$

Answer

4 A light nucleus can become unstable if it is bombarded with nuclear radiation. Copy and complete the equation below to find the particle released when a nucleus of $^{14}_7N$ captures an α-particle ^4_2He:

$$^{14}_7N + \, ^4_2He \longrightarrow \, ^{17}_8O + \, ?$$

Answer

Nuclear fusion

Massive nuclei tend to be unstable, but they can become more stable through the process of fission. In a similar way, light nuclei can become more stable by joining together in the process of **nuclear fusion**. As a general rule, middle-sized nuclei tend to be the most stable. This will be discussed in more detail in the next section.

Figure 13.3 shows two light nuclei, both isotopes of hydrogen, fusing to form a helium nucleus. The equation for this is:

$$^2_1H + \, ^1_1H \longrightarrow \, ^3_2He$$

Note that, as before, both proton number Z and nucleon number A are conserved.

Often in fusion reactions, the result is not a single particle, but two or more. For example:

$$^2_1H + \, ^2_1H \longrightarrow \, ^3_1H + \, ^1_1H$$

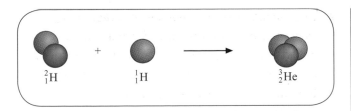

Figure 13.3 In nuclear fusion, two light nuclei join together to make a more stable nucleus.

In this fusion reaction, energy is released as kinetic energy of the tritium nucleus $^3_1$H and the proton $^1_1$H. Such reactions are the source of energy that keeps stars shining for billions of years. Extreme conditions, such as those that exist in the Sun, are required for fusion to happen.

- The temperature of the Sun's core is of the order of 15 million kelvin. So the hydrogen nuclei have a great deal of kinetic energy.
- The density of the Sun's core is about $150\,000\,\mathrm{kg\,m^{-3}}$, implying that the hydrogen nuclei are squashed closely together.

Both high energy and high density are required for the hydrogen nuclei to be able to overcome the electrostatic repulsion between them, so that they can fuse.

It is hoped that in the future we will have fusion reactors for generating electricity. Prototype reactors, such as the Joint European Torus (JET) at Culham in Oxfordshire (Figure 13.4), attempt to reproduce the conditions found inside the Sun but on a small scale.

Figure 13.4 The JET at the Culham Laboratory in Oxfordshire is a European experiment to solve some of the problems associated with maintaining controlled nuclear fusion as a source of energy.

Results suggest that controllable fusion reactions may one day be within our technological grasp.

SAQ

5 Complete the following equation for a fusion reaction in which *three* particles result:

$$^3_2\mathrm{H} + ^3_2\mathrm{H} \longrightarrow ^4_2\mathrm{He} + ?$$

> Answer

6 In one of the fusion reactions that occur in the Sun, the most stable isotope of carbon, $^{12}_6$C, is formed from the fusion of a proton with a nucleus of an isotope of nitrogen, $^{15}_7$N. Write a balanced nuclear equation for this reaction. Identify the other new element that is formed.

> Answer

Explaining fission and fusion

In both fission and fusion, unstable nuclei become more stable. Energy is released. In order to explain these processes, we need to be able to say where this energy comes from. One answer lies in the origins of the nuclei we are considering. Take, for example, uranium. The Earth's crust contains uranium. In some places, it is sufficiently concentrated to make it worth while extracting it for use as the fuel in fission reactors (Figure 13.5). This uranium has been part of the Earth since it was formed, 4500 million years ago.

The Earth formed from a swirling cloud of dust and gas, at the same time that the Sun itself was

Figure 13.5 Uranium, the fuel used in nuclear reactors, comes from mines such as the Ranger mine in Australia's Northern Territory.

forming. These materials condensed under the force of gravitational attraction. But where did they come from in the first place? It is believed that heavy elements (such as uranium) were formed in supernovae. At some time in the distant past, an ageing star collapsed and then blew itself apart in an explosion of awesome scale. At the very high temperatures that resulted, there was sufficient energy available for light nuclei to fuse to form the heaviest nuclei, which we now find if we dig in the Earth's crust. It is this energy, from an ancient stellar explosion, that is released when a large nucleus undergoes fission.

Mass and energy

We can extend this explanation by asking: 'How can we calculate the amount of energy released in fission or fusion?' To find the answer to this, we need to think first about the masses of the particles involved.

We will start by considering a stable nucleus, $^{12}_{6}$C. This consists of six protons and six neutrons. Fortunately for us, because we have a lot of this form of carbon in our bodies, this is a very stable nuclide. This means that the nucleons are bound tightly together by the strong nuclear force. It takes a lot of energy to pull them apart.

Figure 13.6 shows the results of an imaginary experiment in which we have done just that. On the left-hand side of the balance is a single $^{12}_{6}$C nucleus. On the right-hand side are six protons and six neutrons, the result of dismantling the nucleus. The surprising thing is that the balance is tipped to the right. The separate nucleons have *more* mass than the nucleus itself. This means that the law of

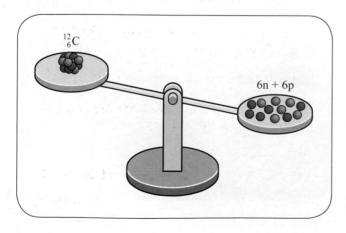

Figure 13.6 The mass of a nucleus is less than the total mass of its component protons and neutrons.

conservation of mass has been broken. We have violated what was thought to be a fundamental law of Nature, something that was held to be true for hundreds of years. How can this be?

Notice that, in dismantling the $^{12}_{6}$C nucleus, we have had to do work. The nucleons attract one another with nuclear forces and these are strong enough to make the nucleus very stable. So we have put energy into the nucleus to pull it apart. Where has this energy gone?

At the same time, we have the mystery of the appearing mass. There is more mass when we have pulled the nucleons apart than when they are bound together.

You probably already know that these two problems, disappearing energy and appearing mass, can be solved together. We say that 'energy has turned into mass'. If we let the separate protons and neutrons recombine to make a $^{12}_{6}$C nucleus, the extra mass will disappear and the missing energy will be released. This 'mass–energy conversion' explains where the energy comes from in nuclear fusion.

A better way to express this is to treat mass and energy as aspects of the same thing. Rather than having separate laws of conservation of mass and conservation of energy, we can combine these two. The total amount of mass and energy together in a system is constant. There may be conversions from one to the other, but the total amount of 'mass–energy' remains constant.

Einstein's mass–energy equation

If we are saying that the total amount of 'mass–energy' in a closed system remains constant, we need to know how to change mass (in kg) to energy (in J). Albert Einstein produced his famous mass–energy equation, which allows us to do this. The change in energy ΔE equivalent to the change in mass Δm is given by:

$$\Delta E = \Delta mc^2$$

where c is the speed of light in free space. The value of c is approximately $3.0 \times 10^8\ \mathrm{m\,s^{-1}}$, but its precise value has been fixed as $c = 299\,792\,458\ \mathrm{m\,s^{-1}}$.

Note: The symbol Δ means 'a change in' a quantity; hence ΔE means a change in energy E, and Δm means a change in mass m.

According to Einstein's equation:

- the mass of a system *increases* when energy is supplied to it
- energy is released from a system when its mass *decreases*.

Now, if we know the total mass of particles before a nuclear reaction and their total mass after the reaction, we can work out how much energy is released. Table 13.1 gives the relative masses of the particles shown in Figure 13.6, together with their masses in kg. The relative mass of the particles is expressed in **unified atomic mass unit** u, where $1\,u \approx 1.66 \times 10^{-27}\,kg$. This is defined as $\frac{1}{12}$th of the mass of an atom of carbon isotope $^{12}_{6}C$. (It is very convenient to measure atomic and nuclear masses in u.)

Particle	Relative mass/u	Mass/10^{-27} kg
^1_1p	1.007276	1.672623
^1_0n	1.008665	1.674929
$^{12}_6C$ nucleus	11.996706	19.926483

Table 13.1 Masses of some particles. It is worth noting that the mass of the neutron is slightly larger than the proton, but they are both approximately 1 u.

Nuclear masses are measured to a high degree of precision using mass spectrometers (see Chapter 9), often to seven or eight significant figures.

We can use the mass values in kg to calculate the mass that is released as energy when nucleons combine to form a nucleus. So for our particles in Figure 13.6, we have:

$$\text{mass before} = (6 \times 1.672623 + 6 \times 1.674929) \times 10^{-27}\,kg$$
$$= 20.085312 \times 10^{-27}\,kg$$

$$\text{mass after} = 19.926483 \times 10^{-27}\,kg$$

$$\text{mass difference } \Delta m$$
$$= (20.085312 - 19.926483) \times 10^{-27}\,kg$$
$$= 0.158829 \times 10^{-27}\,kg$$

When six protons and six neutrons combine to form the nucleus of carbon-12, there is a very small loss of mass Δm, known as the **mass defect**.

The mass defect of a nucleus is equal to the difference between the total mass of the individual, separate nucleons and the mass of the nucleus.

The loss in mass implies that energy is released in this process. The energy released ΔE is given by Einstein's mass–energy equation. Therefore:

$$\Delta E = \Delta mc^2$$
$$= 0.158829 \times 10^{-27} \times (3.0 \times 10^8)^2$$
$$\approx 1.43 \times 10^{-11}\,J$$

This may seem like a very small amount of energy, but it is a lot on the scale of an atom. For comparison, the amount of energy released in a chemical reaction involving a single carbon atom would typically be of the order of $10^{-18}\,J$, more than a million times smaller.

Now look at Worked example 1.

Worked example 1

Use the data below to determine the minimum energy required to split a nucleus of oxygen-16 ($^{16}_8O$) into its separate nucleons. Give your answer in joules (J) and in electronvolts (eV).

$$\text{mass of proton} = 1.007276\,u$$
$$\text{mass of neutron} = 1.008665\,u$$
$$\text{mass of } {}^{16}_8O \text{ nucleus} = 15.994915\,u$$
$$1\,u = 1.66 \times 10^{-27}\,kg$$
$$c = 3.0 \times 10^8\,m\,s^{-1}$$

Step 1 Find the difference Δm in kg between the mass of the oxygen nucleus and the mass of the individual nucleons. The $^{16}_8O$ nucleus has 8 protons and 8 neutrons.

$$\Delta m = \text{final mass} - \text{initial mass}$$
$$\Delta m = (8 \times 1.007276 + 8 \times 1.008665) - 15.994915$$
$$= +0.132613\,u$$

There is an increase in the mass of this system because external energy is supplied.

$$\Delta m = 0.132613 \times 1.66 \times 10^{-27} \approx 2.20 \times 10^{-28}\,kg$$

Step 2 Use Einstein's mass–energy equation to determine the energy supplied.

$$\Delta E = \Delta mc^2$$
$$\Delta E = 2.20 \times 10^{-28} \times (3.0 \times 10^8)^2 \approx 1.98 \times 10^{-11}\,J$$

continued

197

Step 3 Now convert the energy into electronvolts; you should recall from *Physics 1* that 1 eV is the energy gained or lost by an electron in moving through 1 V, so that $1\,\text{eV} = 1.60 \times 10^{-19}\,\text{J}$.

$$\Delta E = \frac{1.98 \times 10^{-11}}{1.60 \times 10^{-19}} \approx 1.24 \times 10^8\,\text{eV} \quad (124\,\text{MeV})$$

Mass–energy conservation

Einstein pointed out that his equation $\Delta E = \Delta mc^2$ applied to *all* energy changes, not just nuclear processes. So, for example, it applies to chemical changes, too. If we burn some carbon, we start off with carbon and oxygen. At the end, we have carbon dioxide and energy. If we measure the mass of the carbon dioxide, we find that it is very slightly less than the mass of the carbon and oxygen at the start of the experiment. Some of the original mass is now 'seen' as energy. A better way to express this is to say that 'mass–energy' is conserved. In a chemical reaction such as this, the change in mass is very small, less than a microgram if we start with 1 kg of carbon and oxygen. Compare this with the change in mass that occurs during the fission of 1 kg of uranium, mentioned above. The change in mass in a chemical reaction is a much, much smaller proportion of the original mass, which is why we don't notice it.

Here is another surprising consequence of mass–energy conservation. If you take a ride upwards in a lift, your gravitational potential energy (GPE) increases. If you could measure your mass with sufficient precision, you would find that it is greater at the top of the building than at the bottom. Energy has been transferred to you to get you to the top of the building, and this appears as an increase in your mass.

For a person of mass 60 kg who travels in a lift to the top of a 30 m high building:

increase in GPE, $\Delta E = mgh$
$$= 60 \times 9.81 \times 30.0$$
$$= 1.77 \times 10^4\,\text{J}$$

increase in mass, $\Delta m = \dfrac{\Delta E}{c^2}$

$$\Delta m = \frac{1.77 \times 10^4}{(3.0 \times 10^8)^2} \approx 2.0 \times 10^{-13}\,\text{kg}$$

This is a very tiny mass increase indeed, but it really does happen!

SAQ

7　The Sun releases vast amounts of energy. Its power output is $4.0 \times 10^{26}\,\text{W}$. Estimate by how much its mass decreases each second because of this energy loss.

> Hint

> Answer

8　a　Calculate the energy released if a ^4_2He nucleus is formed from separate protons and neutrons. The masses of the particles are given in Table 13.2.

　　b　Calculate also the energy released per nucleon.

> Answer

Particle	Mass/10^{-27} kg
^1_1p	1.672623
^1_0n	1.674929
^4_2He	6.644661

Table 13.2 Masses of some particles.

9　Use the mass values given in Table 13.3 to explain why the fusion reaction

$$^4_2\text{He} + {}^4_2\text{He} \longrightarrow {}^8_4\text{Be}$$

is unlikely to occur, unless some extra energy is supplied to the ^4_2He particles.

> Answer

Particle	Mass/u*
^4_2He	4.001506
^8_4Be	8.003111

Table 13.3 Relative masses of some particles in atomic mass units (u).

*$1\,\text{u} \approx 1.66 \times 10^{-27}\,\text{kg}$

Binding energy and stability

We can now begin to see why some nuclei are more stable than others. If a nucleus is formed from separate nucleons, energy is released. In order to pull the nucleus apart, energy must be put in; in other words, work must be done against the strong nuclear force which holds the nucleons together. The more energy involved in this, the more stable is the nucleus.

> The minimum energy needed to pull a nucleus apart into its separate nucleons is known as the **binding energy** of the nucleus.

Take care: This is *not* energy stored in the nucleus; on the contrary, it is the energy that must be put in to the nucleus in order to pull it apart. In the example of $^{12}_{6}C$ discussed above, we calculated the binding energy from the mass difference between the mass of the $^{12}_{6}C$ nucleus and the masses of the separate protons and neutrons.

In order to compare the stability of different nuclides, we need to consider the binding energy per nucleon. We can determine the binding energy per nucleon for a nuclide as follows:

- Determine the mass defect for the nucleus.
- Use Einstein's mass–energy equation to determine the binding energy of the nucleus by multiplying the mass defect by c^2.
- Divide the binding energy of the nucleus by the number of nucleons to calculate the binding energy per nucleon.

Now look at Worked example 2.

Worked example 2

Calculate the binding energy per nucleon for the nuclide $^{56}_{26}Fe$.

$$\text{mass of neutron} = 1.675 \times 10^{-27}\,\text{kg}$$

$$\text{mass of proton} = 1.673 \times 10^{-27}\,\text{kg}$$

$$\text{mass of } ^{56}_{26}Fe \text{ nucleus} = 9.288 \times 10^{-26}\,\text{kg}$$

Step 1 Determine the mass defect.

number of neutrons $= 56 - 26 = 30$

mass defect
$$= (30 \times 1.675 \times 10^{-27} + 26 \times 1.673 \times 10^{-27})$$
$$\quad - 9.288 \times 10^{-26}$$
$$= 8.680 \times 10^{-28}\,\text{kg}$$

Step 2 Determine the binding energy of the nucleus.

$$\text{binding energy} = \Delta m c^2$$
$$= 8.680 \times 10^{-28} \times (3.0 \times 10^{8})^2$$
$$= 7.812 \times 10^{-11}\,\text{J}$$

Step 3 Determine the binding energy per nucleon.

binding energy per nucleon
$$= \frac{7.812 \times 10^{-11}}{56}$$
$$\approx 14 \times 10^{-13}\,\text{J} \quad (8.7\,\text{MeV})$$

Figure 13.7 shows the binding energy per nucleon for stable nuclei, including the value for $^{56}_{26}Fe$ (shown as a red dot) from Worked example 2. This is a graph plotted against the nucleon number A. The greater the value of the binding energy per nucleon, the more tightly bound are the nucleons that make up the nucleus.

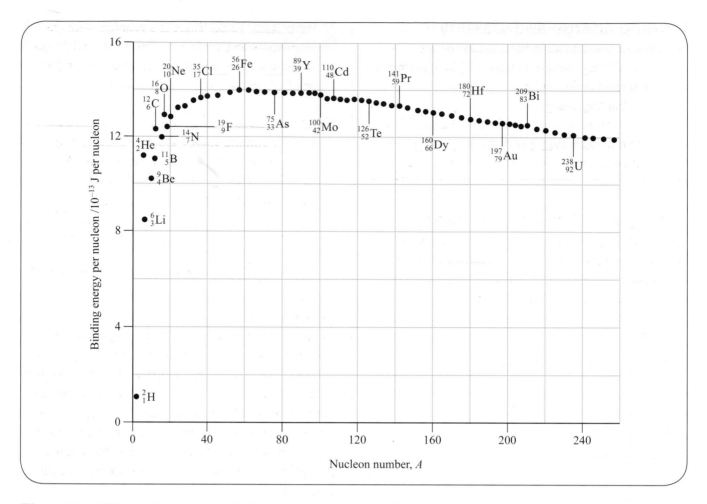

Figure 13.7 This graph shows the binding energy per nucleon for a number of nuclei. The nucleus becomes more stable as binding energy per nucleon increases.

If you examine this graph, you will see that the general trend is for light nuclei to have low binding energies per nucleon. For nuclides with $A > 20$ approximately, there is not much variation in binding energy per nucleon.

The greatest value of binding energy per nucleon is found for $^{56}_{26}$Fe. This isotope of iron requires the most energy per nucleon to dismantle it into separate nucleons; hence iron-56 is the most stable isotope in Nature.

Notice the anomalous position of $^{4}_{2}$He, which lies off the main curve of the graph. This nucleus (two protons and two neutrons, the same as an α-particle) is very stable. Other common stable nuclei include $^{12}_{6}$C and $^{16}_{8}$O, which can be thought of as three and four α-particles bound together (Figure 13.8).

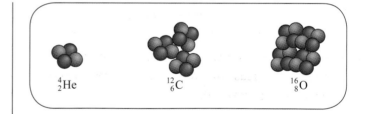

Figure 13.8 More stable nuclei are formed when 'α-particles' are bound together. In $^{12}_{6}$C and $^{16}_{8}$O, the 'α-particles' do not remain separate, as shown here; rather, the protons and neutrons are tightly packed together.

SAQ

10 Explain why hydrogen $^{1}_{1}$H does not appear on the graph shown in Figure 13.7.

Answer

11 The mass of a $^{8}_{4}$Be nucleus is 1.33×10^{-26} kg. A proton and a neutron have a mass of about 1.67×10^{-27} kg. For the nucleus of $^{8}_{4}$Be determine:

a the mass defect in kg

b the binding energy (in J and eV)

c the binding energy per nucleon (in J and eV).

Hint

Answer

Binding energy, fission and fusion

We can use the binding energy graph to help us decide which nuclear processes – fission, fusion, radioactive decay (Chapter 14) – are likely to occur (Figure 13.9).

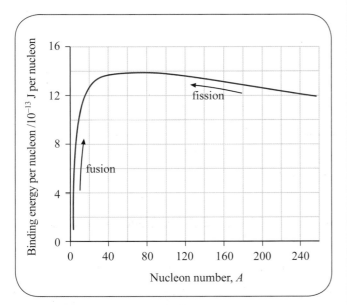

Figure 13.9 Both fusion and fission are processes that tend to increase the binding energy per nucleon of the particles involved.

● *Fission*

When a massive nucleus splits, it forms two smaller fragments. For uranium, we have $A = 235$, and the typical fragments have $A = 140$ and 95. If we look at the binding energy curve, we see that these two fragments have greater binding energy per nucleon than the original uranium nucleus. Hence, if the uranium nucleus splits in this way, energy will be released.

● *Fusion*

In a similar way, if two light nuclei fuse, the final binding energy per nucleon will be greater than

the original value. There is a problem with the anomalous value for $^{4}_{2}$He. This makes it difficult for two of these nuclei to fuse; you worked this out from the particles' masses in SAQ 9.

SAQ

12 Use the binding energy graph to suggest why fission is unlikely to occur with 'light nuclei' ($A < 20$), and why fusion is unlikely to occur for heavier nuclei ($A > 40$).

Answer

Extension

Nuclear power

In the UK, nuclear power stations (Figure 13.10) supplied about 20% of the nation's electricity supply in 2008. This fraction is gradually decreasing but may start to rise again when a new generation of stations is constructed. Nuclear power can be thought of as 'green' because it does not produce the greenhouse gas carbon dioxide. However, it does result in the production of hazardous wastes which are difficult to deal with.

Most nuclear power stations use uranium as their fuel; alternative nuclear fuels are plutonium and thorium. Note that it is only certain isotopes of these elements that can undergo fission (they are described as *fissile*). These materials are all stores of energy which can be released through the process of fission. In order for this to happen, a **chain reaction** must

Figure 13.10 Sizewell B power station in Suffolk, UK. This is a pressurised water reactor (PWR).

be established. Think about the process of induced fission (Figure 13.2):

- A single neutron strikes a uranium nucleus.
- The neutron is absorbed, creating a larger, unstable nucleus.
- This highly unstable nucleus splits into two unequal halves and a number of neutrons (two, three or four) are released.

These neutrons may go on to induce the fission of other uranium nuclei. If at least one neutron from each fission event goes on to cause another, we have a chain reaction (Figure 13.11). In a nuclear bomb, the reaction escalates so that more and more neutrons fly around inside the uranium, causing a very rapid release of energy. A more controlled reaction goes on inside a nuclear power reactor, so that energy is released at the required rate. To understand how this is done, we need to look at the construction of a nuclear reactor.

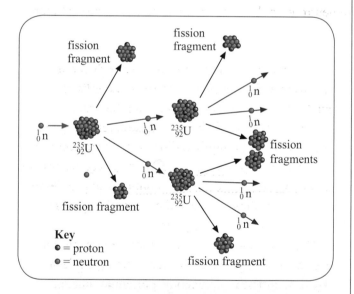

Key

- = proton
- = neutron

Figure 13.11 A nuclear chain reaction. The number of neutrons increases exponentially.

Inside a fission reactor

Figure 13.12 shows the basic components of a nuclear power station. The uranium fuel is in the reactor core. It releases energy so that the core gets hot; this heat is transferred by the fluid coolant to a boiler, where steam is generated. The steam turns a turbine which turns a generator to produce electricity.

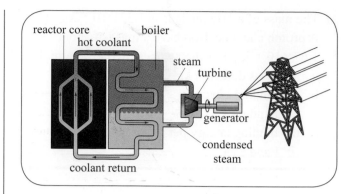

Figure 13.12 Outline of a nuclear power station.

It is the reactor core that makes this different from a fossil-fuel power station.

The core has several components, arranged as shown in Figure 13.13. The fuel rods (or fuel elements) are positioned vertically. A **coolant** can flow between them, removing the heat produced by fission. The fuel rods are surrounded by a material called the **moderator**; there are also **control rods** which can move up and down in the core.

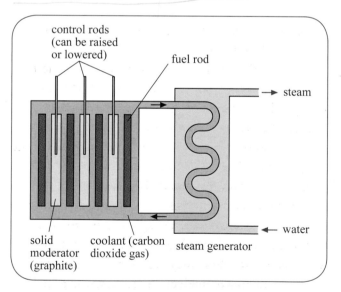

Figure 13.13 Diagram of a gas-cooled reactor.

The moderator has a vital function. The neutrons released in fission are very energetic. They are described as 'fast neutrons'. They move so rapidly that they are unlikely to interact with uranium nuclei. The moderator is a material such as graphite. As the fast neutrons pass through, they are slowed down without being absorbed. (The neutrons make inelastic collisions with the carbon atoms of the moderator.)

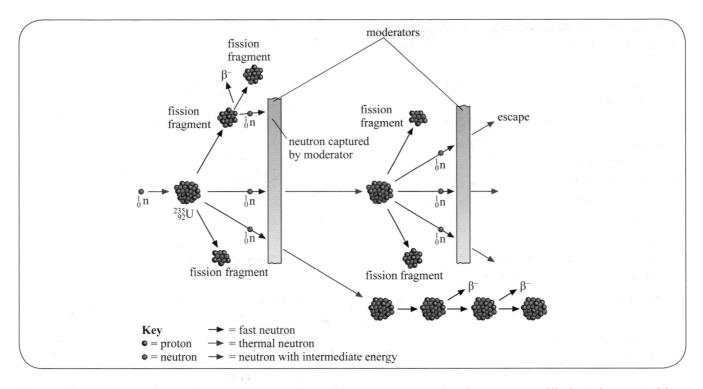

Figure 13.14 The moderator in a reactor core slows down neutrons so that they are more likely to interact with uranium nuclei.

Once they are moving more slowly, they are known as 'thermal neutrons' and there is a much greater chance that they will cause induced fission of more uranium nuclei. (In some reactors, the coolant itself also plays the role of moderator.) The mean kinetic energy of a thermal neutron is equal to $\frac{3}{2}kT$, where k is the Boltzmann constant and T is the thermodynamic temperature of the reactor core. The typical mean speed of a thermal neutron is about $3\,\mathrm{km\,s^{-1}}$.

The control rods are made of a neutron-absorbing material such as boron. To slow down or stop the chain reaction, they are lowered into the core. To speed up the reaction, they are partially withdrawn.

Figure 13.14 summarises the main reactions that can happen in the reactor core. Apart from $^{235}_{92}\mathrm{U}$ nuclei, fuel rods also contain $^{238}_{92}\mathrm{U}$. Neutrons with intermediate kinetic energies can be captured by uranium-238 nuclei. They then undergo two decays to become plutonium-239. Plutonium has a half-life of $24\,000$ years and is extremely toxic. It is one of the most dangerous waste products obtained from reactors.

Nuclear waste

Figure 13.14 shows the origins of nuclear waste. When a fraction of the uranium-235 has been split,

the chain reaction stops because fewer than one neutron per fission event reaches another fissile nucleus. The fuel rods now contain the fission fragments that result from the fission reaction, and these are usually highly radioactive. Some decay rapidly, causing the spent fuel rods to become hot, so that they must be cooled for months after use. Some decay more slowly, so that their radiation poses a hazard for thousands of years.

Notice also in Figure 13.14 that some neutrons are absorbed by uranium nuclei which then decay (by beta emission) to become plutonium nuclei. Plutonium is a hazardous material and is another reason why spent fuel is difficult to deal with.

Various approaches have been developed to cope with the increasing amounts of radioactive waste produced by nuclear power stations. It may be stored in containers on the surface where it can be monitored. Alternatively, it may be buried deep underground, but this arouses concerns that containers may leak, polluting underground water courses (see Figure 13.15). Any approach has its problems which can add greatly to the cost of generating electricity from nuclear sources.

Figure 13.15 This underground tunnel in New Mexico, USA, is 650 metres below the surface in 900 metre thick salt beds. It has been developed as a repository for waste from the development and production of nuclear weapons.

SAQ

13 Outline the roles of the moderator and coolant in a nuclear reactor. [Answer]

14 a   If all of the nuclei in 1.0 kg of uranium-235 undergo fission, its mass decreases by 0.90 g. Calculate the energy released.

  b   The average UK citizen consumes electricity at an average rate of about 1.0 kW. Estimate the typical lifetime consumption and compare this with your answer to **a**. [Answer]

Summary

[Glossary]

- Nuclear reactions can be represented by balanced nuclear equations. In any such reaction, the following quantities are conserved:
  - proton number Z
  - nucleon number A
  - 'mass–energy'.

- In an induced nuclear fission, a heavy nucleus (e.g. $^{235}_{92}U$) absorbs a neutron and splits into lighter fragments and two or more fast neutrons.

- In nuclear fusion, light nuclei (e.g. $^{2}_{1}H$) join to form a more massive one. In stars, high temperatures and pressures are needed to achieve this.

- Atomic and nuclear masses are often expressed using the unified atomic mass unit u, where $1\,u \approx 1.66 \times 10^{-27}\,kg$.

- Einstein's mass–energy equation $\Delta E = \Delta mc^2$ relates mass changes to energy changes.

- The mass defect is equal to the difference between the mass of the separate nucleons and the nucleus.

- The binding energy of a nucleus is the minimum energy required to break up the nucleus into separate nucleons.

- The binding energy per nucleon indicates the relative stability of different nuclides.

- The variation of binding energy per nucleon shows that energy is released when light nuclei undergo fusion and when heavier nuclei undergo fission, because these processes increase the binding energy per nucleon and hence result in more stable nuclides.

- Fissile materials are used as fuel in nuclear power stations and in nuclear bombs.

- The core of a nuclear reactor contains fuel rods, control rods and moderator.

- Waste materials from nuclear reactors are highly radioactive and pose a threat to the environment.

Questions

1 This question is about nuclear fission of uranium-235.
   a i State what is meant by a *thermal neutron*. [1]
     ii State the importance of thermal neutrons in relation to the fission of uranium-235. [1]
   b A $^{235}_{92}$U nucleus undergoes fission, producing nuclei of $^{146}_{57}$La and $^{87}_{35}$Br. The binding energies per nucleon of these nuclides are shown below.

Nuclide	Binding energy per nucleon/MeV
$^{235}_{92}$U	7.6
$^{146}_{57}$La	8.2
$^{87}_{35}$Br	8.6

   Use information from the table to calculate how much energy in MeV is released when a $^{235}_{92}$U nucleus undergoes fission. [3]

OCR Physics A2 (2825/04) June 2007 [Total 5]

Answer

2 This question is about the nucleus of uranium-235 ($^{235}_{92}$U) which has a mass of 3.89×10^{-25} kg.
   a State the number of protons and neutrons in this nucleus. [1]
   b The radius r of a nucleus is given by the equation:

   $$r = 1.41 \times 10^{-15} A^{\frac{1}{3}}$$

   where A is the nucleon number of the nucleus.
   Determine the density of the $^{235}_{92}$U nucleus. [3]
   c Explain why the total mass of the nucleons is different from the mass of the $^{235}_{92}$U nucleus. [2]
   d Without calculations, explain how you can determine the binding energy per nucleon for the uranium-235 nucleus from its mass and the masses of a proton and a neutron. [4]

[Total 10]

Answer

Hint

3 When a helium nucleus ($^4_2$He) is produced by hydrogen fusion, 28.4 MeV of energy is released.
   Calculate how much energy is released when 1.00 kg of $^4_2$He nuclei is produced. Give your answer in joules. [3]

OCR Physics A2 (2825/04) January 2005 [Total 3]

Answer

Chapter 14

Radioactivity

e-Learning

Objectives

Discovering radioactivity

You should be familiar with the three types of radiation, α, β and γ, that are emitted by radioactive materials such as uranium and radium. Although they are around us all the time, they were not discovered until 1896. The fact that these radiations are invisible meant that people were unaware of them.

The French physicist Henri Becquerel (Figure 14.1) is credited with the discovery of radioactivity. He had been looking at the properties of uranium compounds when he noticed that they affected photographic film – he realised that they were giving out radiation all the time and he performed several ingenious experiments to shed light on the phenomenon.

Becquerel won the Nobel prize for his work. However, he was not the only scientist working in this area at the time. In Glasgow, Lord Kelvin was performing similar experiments and coming to very similar conclusions. Indeed, without knowing it, they presented their findings to scientific meetings on the same evening, in Paris and Edinburgh. The Nobel prize committee decided that Becquerel had arrived at a greater understanding earlier than Kelvin, so he won the prize.

In fact, much of Becquerel's work had been carried out 40 years earlier by another Frenchman, Claude Niepce de Saint-Victor. It was the early days of photography, and Niepce was experimenting

Figure 14.1 Henri Becquerel, the discoverer of radioactivity, in his laboratory. His father and grandfather had been professors of physics in Paris before him.

with different chemical substances in photographic film. He observed that uranium salts blackened film in the same way that light did. However, the world of science was not ready to accept the idea of 'invisible rays', and his findings were taken no further. Becquerel's discovery came shortly after Röntgen's discovery of X-rays, so invisible rays were in vogue and many physicists and chemists were enthusiastic in following up Becquerel's work.

Radiation from radioactive substances

There are three types of radiation that are emitted by radioactive substances: alpha (α), beta (β) and gamma (γ) radiations come from the unstable nuclei of atoms. Nuclei consist of protons and neutrons, and if the balance between these two types of particles is too far to one side, the nucleus may emit α or β radiation as

a way of achieving greater stability. Gamma radiation is usually emitted after α or β decay, to release excess energy from the nuclei.

In fact, there are two types of β radiation. The more familiar is beta-minus (β^-) radiation, which is simply an electron, with negative charge of $-e$. However, there are also many unstable nuclei that emit beta-plus (β^+) radiation. This radiation is in the form of **positrons**, similar to electrons in terms of mass but with positive charge of $+e$. Positrons are a form of *antimatter*. When a positron collides with an electron, they annihilate each other. Their mass is converted into electromagnetic energy in the form of two gamma photons (Figure 14.2).

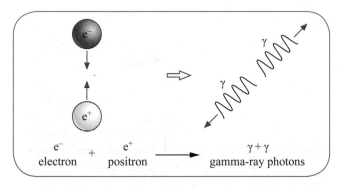

Figure 14.2 Energy is released in the annihilation of matter and antimatter.

Table 14.1 shows the basic characteristics of the different types of radiation. The masses are given relative to the mass of a proton; charge is measured in units of e, the elementary charge.

Note the following points:

- α and β radiation are particles of matter. A γ-ray is a photon of electromagnetic radiation, similar to an X-ray. (X-rays are produced when electrons are decelerated; γ-rays are produced in nuclear reactions.)
- An α-particle consists of two protons and two neutrons; it is a nucleus of helium-4. A β^- particle is simply an electron and a β^+ particle is a positron.

- The mass of an α-particle is nearly 10 000 times that of an electron and it travels at roughly one-hundredth of the speed of an electron.

Discovering neutrinos

There is a further type of particle which we need to consider. These are the **neutrinos**. When β decay was first studied, it was realised that β-particles were electrons coming from the *nucleus* of an atom. There are no electrons in the nucleus (they 'orbit' outside the nucleus), so the process was pictured as the decay of a neutron to give a proton and an electron.

It was noticed that β-particles were emitted with a *range* of speeds – some travelled more slowly than others. It was deduced that some other particle must be carrying off some of the energy and momentum released in the decay. This particle is now known as the *antineutrino* (or, more correctly, the electron antineutrino), with symbol $\bar{\nu}$. The decay equation for β^- decay is written as:

$$\text{beta-minus } (\beta^-) \text{ decay: } {}_{0}^{1}\text{n} \longrightarrow {}_{1}^{1}\text{p} + {}_{-1}^{0}\text{e} + \bar{\nu}$$

Note that both nucleon number A and proton number Z are conserved in this decay. Neutrinos are bizarre particles. They have very little mass (much less than an electron) and no electric charge, which makes them very difficult to detect. The Austrian physicist Wolfgang Pauli predicted their existence in 1930, long before they were first detected in 1956.

In β^+ decay, a proton decays to become a neutron and an *electron neutrino* (symbol ν) is released:

$$\text{beta-plus } (\beta^+) \text{ decay: } {}_{1}^{1}\text{p} \longrightarrow {}_{0}^{1}\text{n} + {}_{+1}^{0}\text{e} + \nu$$

Radiation	Symbol	Mass (relative to proton)	Charge	Typical speed
α-particle	$\alpha, {}_{2}^{4}\text{He}$	4	$+2e$	'slow' ($10^6\,\text{m s}^{-1}$)
β^- particle	$\beta, \beta^-, \text{e}^-, {}_{-1}^{0}\text{e}$	$\frac{1}{1840}$	$-e$	'fast' ($10^8\,\text{m s}^{-1}$)
β^+ particle	$\beta^+, \text{e}^+, {}_{+1}^{0}\text{e}$	$\frac{1}{1840}$	$+e$	'fast' ($10^8\,\text{m s}^{-1}$)
γ-ray	γ	0	0	speed of light ($3 \times 10^8\,\text{m s}^{-1}$)

Table 14.1 The basic characteristics of ionising radiations.

Fundamental families

Electrons and neutrinos both belong to a family of fundamental particles called **leptons**. These are particles that do not feel the strong nuclear force. (Recall from Chapter 12 that particles that experience the strong force are hadrons, and that these are made up of fundamental particles called quarks.)

So we have two families of fundamental particles, quarks and leptons. How can we understand β decay in terms of these particles?

Consider first β^- decay, in which a neutron decays. A neutron consists of three quarks (up, down, down or u d d). It decays to become a proton (u u d). Comparing these shows that one of the down quarks has become an up quark. In the process, it emits a β-particle and an antineutrino:

$$d \longrightarrow u + {}_{-1}^{0}e + \bar{\nu}$$

In β^+ decay, a proton decays to become a neutron. In this case, an up quark becomes a down quark:

$$u \longrightarrow d + {}_{+1}^{0}e + \nu$$

Fundamental forces

The nucleus is held together by the strong nuclear force, acting against the repulsive electrostatic or Coulomb force between protons. This force explains α decay, when a positively charged α-particle flies out of the nucleus, leaving it with less positive charge.

However, the strong force cannot explain β decay. Instead, we have to take account of a further force within the nucleus, the **weak interaction**, also known as the weak nuclear force. This is a force that acts on both quarks and leptons. The weak interaction is responsible for β decay.

SAQ

1   The equation ${}_{1}^{1}p \longrightarrow {}_{0}^{1}n + {}_{+1}^{0}e + \nu$ represents β^+ decay. Use the equation to explain why the neutrino ν can have no charge and very little mass.

Answer

Balanced equations

In Chapter 13, we saw how the nuclear processes of fission and fusion can be represented by balanced equations. The same is true for radioactive decay processes. As for all equations representing nuclear processes, both nucleon number and proton number are conserved.

The nucleus before the decay is often referred to as the *parent* nucleus and the new nucleus after the decay is known as the *daughter* nucleus.

Worked example 1 and Worked example 2 show how both nucleon number A and proton number Z are conserved.

Worked example 1 – α decay

Radon is a radioactive gas that decays by α emission to become polonium. Here is the equation for the decay of one of its isotopes radon-222:

$$^{222}_{86}\text{Rn} \longrightarrow {}^{218}_{84}\text{Po} + {}^{4}_{2}\text{He}$$

Show that A and Z are conserved.

Compare the nucleon and proton numbers on both sides of the equation:

nucleon number A $222 = 218 + 4$
proton number Z $86 = 84 + 2$

In α decay, A decreases by 4 and Z decreases by 2.

In this case, radon-222 is the parent nucleus and polonium-218 is the daughter nucleus.

Worked example 2 – β decay

A carbon-14 nucleus (parent) decays by β emission to become an isotope of nitrogen (daughter). Here is the equation that represents this decay:

$$^{14}_{6}\text{C} \longrightarrow {}^{14}_{7}\text{N} + {}^{0}_{-1}e + \bar{\nu}$$

Show that both nucleon number and proton number are conserved.

continued

Compare the nucleon and proton numbers on both sides of the equation:

nucleon number A $14 = 14 + 0$
proton number Z $6 = 7 - 1$

(Note that the antineutrino does not contribute to these equations, since it has no charge and negligible mass.)

In β^- decay, A remains the same and Z increases by 1.

SAQ

2   Study of the decay equations given in Worked example 1 and Worked example 2, and write balanced equations for the following:
   a A nucleus of radon-220 ($^{220}_{86}$Rn) decays by α emission to form an isotope of polonium, Po.
   b A nucleus of a sodium isotope ($^{25}_{11}$Na) decays by β emission to form an isotope of magnesium, Mg.

   Hint

   Answer

3   Copy and complete the following equations.
   a The decay by β^- of a nucleus of argon:

   $$^{41}_{18}\text{Ar} \longrightarrow \text{K} + ? + ?$$

   b The decay by β^+ of a nucleus of oxygen:

   $$^{15}_{8}\text{O} \longrightarrow \text{N} + ? + ?$$

   Answer

Energy released in radioactive decay

Unstable nuclei may emit α- and β-particles with large amounts of kinetic energy. We can use Einstein's mass–energy equation $\Delta E = \Delta mc^2$ to explain the origin of this energy. Take for example the decay of a nucleus of uranium-238. It decays by emitting an α-particle and changes into an isotope of thorium:

$$^{238}_{92}\text{U} \longrightarrow ^{234}_{90}\text{Th} + ^{4}_{2}\text{He}$$

Energy is released spontaneously from this decay because there is a decrease in the mass of the system. That is, the combined mass of the thorium nucleus

and the α-particle is less than the mass of the uranium nucleus. According to Einstein's mass–energy equation, this difference in mass Δm is equivalent to the energy released as kinetic energy of the products. Using the most accurate values available:

mass of $^{238}_{92}$U nucleus $= 3.95283 \times 10^{-25}$ kg

total mass of $^{234}_{90}$Th nucleus and α-particle ($^{4}_{2}$He)
$= 3.95276 \times 10^{-25}$ kg

change in mass $\Delta m = (3.95276 - 3.95283) \times 10^{-25}$ kg
$= -7.0 \times 10^{-30}$ kg

The minus sign shows a decrease in mass, hence, according to the equation $\Delta E = \Delta mc^2$, energy is released in the decay process:

energy released $= 7.0 \times 10^{-30} \times (3.0 \times 10^8)^2$
$\approx 6.3 \times 10^{-13}$ J

This is an enormous amount of energy for a single decay. One mole of uranium-238, which has 6.02×10^{23} nuclei, has the potential to emit total energy equal to about 10^{11} J.

We can calculate the energy released in all decay reactions, including β decay, using the same ideas as above.

SAQ

4   A nucleus of beryllium $^{10}_{4}$Be decays into an isotope of boron by β^- emission. The chemical symbol for boron is B.
   a Write a nuclear decay equation for the nucleus of beryllium-10.
   b Calculate the energy released in this decay and state its form.
   mass of $^{10}_{4}$Be nucleus $= 1.66238 \times 10^{-26}$ kg
   mass of boron isotope $= 1.66219 \times 10^{-26}$ kg
   mass of electron $= 9.10956 \times 10^{-31}$ kg

   Hint

   Answer

Properties of ionising radiation

Radiation affects the matter it passes through by causing ionisation. Both α- and β-particles are fast-moving charged particles, and if they collide with or pass close to atoms, they may knock or

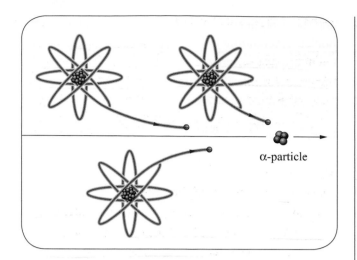

Figure 14.3 As an α-particle passes through a material, it causes ionisation of atoms. A single 0.5 MeV α-particle can ionise about 50 000 air molecules before it stops.

drag electrons away from the atoms (Figure 14.3). The resulting atoms are said to be *ionised*, and the process is called ionisation. In the process, the radiation loses some of its kinetic energy. After many ionisations, the radiation loses all of its energy and no longer has any ionising effect.

Alpha-radiation is the most strongly ionising, because the mass and charge of an α-particle are greater than those of a β-particle, and it usually travels more slowly. This means that an α-particle interacts more strongly with any atom that it passes,

and so it is more likely to cause ionisation. Beta-particles are much lighter and faster, and so their effect is less. Gamma-radiation also causes ionisation, but not as strongly as α- and β-particles, as γ-rays are not charged.

SAQ

5 a Explain why you would expect β-particles to travel further through air than α-particles.

b Explain why you would expect β-particles to travel further through air than through metal.

Answer

Electric and magnetic fields

Because α-, β- and γ-radiations have different charges, or no charge, they behave differently in electric and magnetic fields. This can be used to distinguish one kind of radiation from another.

Figure 14.4 shows the effect of a uniform electric field created by charged parallel plates. A mixture of α-, β- and γ-radiations is passing through the gap between two parallel plates; the electric field in this space is uniform (Chapter 8). Since α- and β-particles are charged, they are attracted to the plate that has the opposite charge to their own. Beta-particles are deflected more than α-particles, since their mass is so much less. Gamma-rays are undeflected since they are uncharged.

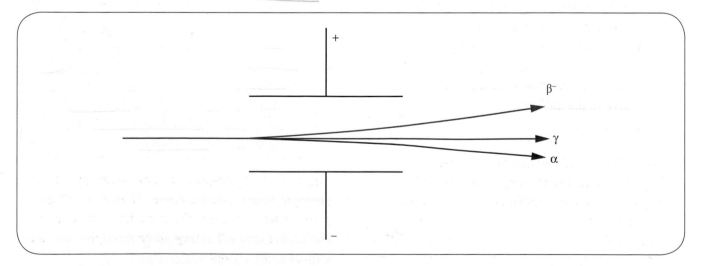

Figure 14.4 Alpha, beta-minus and gamma-radiations may be separated using an electric field. (The track of a β⁺ particle will be a mirror image of that of a β⁻ particle.)

Figure 14.5 shows the effect of a magnetic field. In this case, the deflecting force on the particles is at right angles to their motion. Fleming's left-hand rule (Chapter 9) gives the direction of the force on the moving particles; remember that beta-particles moving to the right constitute a conventional current towards the left.

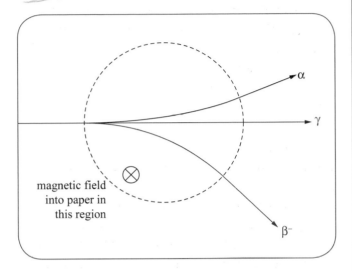

Figure 14.5 A magnetic field may also be used to separate alpha, beta-minus and gamma radiations.

SAQ

6 a Some radioactive substances emit α-particles having two different speeds. Draw a diagram similar to Figure 14.4 to show how these particles would move in a uniform electric field. Label your diagram to show the tracks of the faster and slower α-particles.

b A radioactive substance emits β-particles with a range of speeds. Add to the diagram you drew in **a** to show how these particles would behave in the uniform electric field.

 Answer

7 Copy Figure 14.5 and add to it the track of a β⁺ particle with the same speed as that of the β⁻ particle shown. Explain how you deduced the track that it would follow.

Answer

Radiation penetration

Safety note
When working with radioactive sources, it is essential to follow the relevant safety regulations, which your teacher will explain to you.

Alpha-radiation

Because α-radiation is highly ionising, it cannot penetrate very far into matter. A cloud chamber can be used to show the tracks of α-particles in air (Figure 14.6). The tracks are very dense, because of the dense concentration of ions produced, and they extend for only a few centimetres into the air. By the time the α-particles have travelled this far, they have lost virtually all of their kinetic energy. The α-particle, which is a nucleus of helium-4, grabs two drifting electrons in the air and becomes a neutral atom of helium gas.

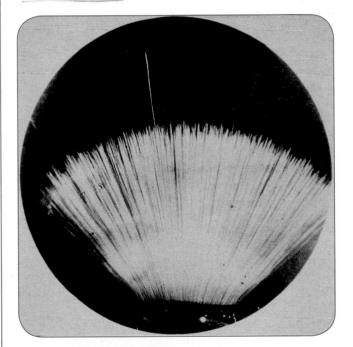

Figure 14.6 Alpha-particle tracks show up in this photograph of a cloud chamber. Notice that all the particles travel roughly the same distance through the air, indicating that they all have roughly the same initial kinetic energy.

Alpha-particles can also be detected by a solid-state detector, or by a Geiger–Müller (GM) tube with a thin end-window (Figure 14.7) connected to an electronic counter. By moving the source back and forth in front of the detector, it is simple to show that the particles only penetrate 5 or 6 cm of air. Similarly, with the source close to the detector, it can be shown that a single sheet of paper is adequate to absorb all of the α-radiation.

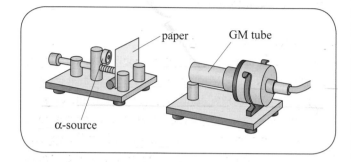

Figure 14.7 Alpha radiation can be absorbed by a single sheet of paper.

Beta-radiation

A Geiger–Müller tube can detect β-radiation. The source is placed close to the tube, and different materials are positioned between source and tube. Paper has little effect; a denser material such as aluminium or lead is a more effective absorber. A few millimetres of aluminium will almost completely absorb β-radiation.

Gamma-radiation

Since γ-radiation is the least strongly ionising, it is the most penetrating. Lead can be used to absorb γ-rays. The intensity of the radiation decreases gradually as it passes through the lead. In principle, an infinite thickness of lead would be needed to absorb the radiation completely; in practice, a couple of centimetres of lead will reduce the intensity by half and 10 cm will reduce the intensity to a safe level in most situations.

The different penetrating properties of α-, β- and γ-radiations are summarised in Figure 14.8.

- α-radiation is absorbed by a thin sheet of paper
- β-radiation is absorbed by a few millimetres of metal
- γ-radiation is absorbed by a few centimetres of lead, or several metres of concrete.

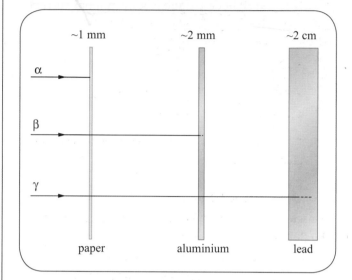

Figure 14.8 A summary of the penetrating powers of α-, β- and γ-radiations. The approximate thickness of the material is also shown.

SAQ

8 Explain why the most strongly ionising radiation (α-particles) are the least penetrating, while the least ionising (γ-rays) are the most penetrating.

Answer

9 A smoke detector (Figure 14.9) uses a source of α-radiation to detect the presence of smoke in the air. Find out how the smoke detector works and suggest why an α-source is more suitable for this than a β- or γ-source.

Answer

Extension

Figure 14.9 A smoke detector that uses the absorption of α-radiation as the principle of its operation.

Randomness and decay

Listen to a counter connected to a Geiger–Müller tube that is detecting the radiation from a weak source, so that the count rate is about one count per second. Each count represents the detection of a single α-particle or a β-particle or a γ-ray photon. You will notice that the individual counts do not come regularly. The counter beeps or clicks in a random, irregular manner. If you try to predict when the next clicks will come, you are unlikely to be right.

You can see the same effect if you have a ratemeter, which can measure faster rates (Figure 14.10). The needle fluctuates up and down. Usually a ratemeter has a control for setting the 'time constant' – the time over which the meter averages out the fluctuations. Usually this can be set to 1 s or 5 s. The fluctuations are smoothed out more on the 5 s setting.

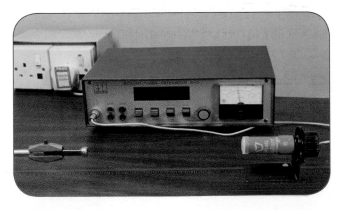

Figure 14.10 The time constant of this ratemeter can be adjusted to smooth out rapid fluctuations in the count rate.

So it is apparent that radioactive decay is a random, irregular phenomenon. But is it completely unpredictable? Well, not really. We can measure the average rate of decay. We might measure the number of counts detected in 1000 s, and then calculate the average number per second. We cannot be sure about the average rate, either, because the number of counts in 1000 s will fluctuate, too. So all of our measurements of radioactive decay are inherently uncertain and imprecise.

Spontaneous decay

Radioactive decay occurs within the unstable nucleus of an atom. A nucleus emits radiation and becomes the nucleus of an atom of a different element. This is a *spontaneous* process, which means that we cannot predict, for a particular nucleus, when it will happen. If we sit and stare at an individual nucleus, we cannot see any change that will tell us that it is getting ready to decay. And if it doesn't decay in the first hour when we are watching it, we cannot say that it is any more likely to decay in the next hour. What is more, we cannot affect the probability of an individual nucleus decaying, for example by changing its temperature.

This is slightly odd, because it goes against our everyday experience of the way things around us change. We observe things changing. They gradually age, die, rot away. But this is not how things are on the scale of atoms and nuclei. Many of the atoms of which we are made have existed for billions of years, and will still exist long after we are gone. The nucleus of an atom does not age.

If we look at a very large number of atoms of a radioactive substance, we will see that the number of undecayed nuclei gradually decreases. However, we cannot predict when an *individual* nucleus will decay. Each nucleus 'makes up its own mind' when to decay, independently from its neighbours. This is because neighbouring nuclei do not interact with one another (unlike neighbouring atoms). The nucleus is a tiny fraction of the size of the atom, and the nuclear forces do not extend very far outside the nucleus. So one nucleus cannot affect a neighbouring nucleus by means of the nuclear force. Being inside a nucleus is a bit like living in a house in the middle of nowhere; you can just see out into the garden, but everything is darkness beyond, and the next house is 1000 km away.

The fact that individual nuclei decay spontaneously, and independently of their neighbours and of environmental factors, accounts for the random pattern of clicks that we hear from a Geiger counter and the fluctuations of the needle on the ratemeter.

To summarise, nuclear decay is *spontaneous* because:

- the decay of a particular nucleus is not affected by the presence of other nuclei
- the decay of nuclei cannot be affected by chemical reactions or external factors such as temperature and pressure

and it is *random* because:

- it is impossible to predict when a particular nucleus in a sample is going to decay
- each nucleus in a sample has the same chance of decaying per unit time

Decay constant, λ

Because we cannot say when individual nuclei will decay, we have to start thinking about very large numbers of nuclei. Even a tiny speck of radioactive material will have more than 10^{15} nuclei. Then we can talk about the average number of nuclei that we expect to decay in a particular time interval; in other words, we can find out the *average* decay rate. Although we cannot make predictions for individual nuclei, we can say that certain types of nuclei are more likely to decay than others. For example, a nucleus of carbon-12 is stable; carbon-14 decays gradually over thousands of years; carbon-15 nuclei last, on average, a few seconds.

So, because of the spontaneous nature of radioactive decay, we have to make measurements on very large numbers of nuclei and then calculate averages. One quantity we can determine is the probability that an individual nucleus will decay in a particular time interval. For example, suppose we observe one million

nuclei of a particular radioisotope. After one hour, 200 000 have decayed. Then the probability that an individual nucleus will decay in 1 h is 0.2 or 20%, since 20% of the nuclei have decayed in this time. (Of course, this is only an approximate value, since we might repeat the experiment and find that only 199 000 decay because of the random nature of the decay. The more times we repeat the experiment, the more reliable our answer will be.)

We can now define the **decay constant**.

> The probability that an individual nucleus will decay per unit time interval is called the decay constant, λ.

For the example above, we have:

decay constant $\lambda = 0.20 \, \text{h}^{-1}$

Note that, because we are measuring the probability of decay per unit time interval, λ has units of h^{-1} (or s^{-1}, day^{-1}, year^{-1}, etc.).

Activity, A

The **activity** of a source is defined as follows:

> The activity A of a radioactive sample is the rate at which nuclei decay or disintegrate.

Activity is measured in decays per second (or h^{-1}, day^{-1}, etc.). An activity of one decay per second is one becquerel (1 Bq):

$1 \, \text{Bq} = 1 \, \text{s}^{-1}$

Clearly, the activity of a sample depends on the decay constant λ of the isotope under consideration. The greater the decay constant (the probability that an individual nucleus decays per unit time interval), the greater is the activity of the sample. It also depends on the number of undecayed nuclei N present in the sample. For a sample of N undecayed nuclei, we have:

$A = \lambda N$

We can also think of the activity as the number of α- or β-particles emitted from the source per unit time. Hence, we can also write the activity A as:

$$A = \frac{\Delta N}{\Delta t}$$

where ΔN is equal to the number of emissions (or decays) in a small time interval of Δt.

Now look at Worked example 3 and Worked example 4.

Worked example 3

A radioactive source emits β-particles. It has an activity of 2.8×10^7 Bq. Estimate the number of β-particles emitted in a time interval of 2.0 minutes. State one assumption made.

Step 1 Write down the quantities given in SI units.

$$A = 2.8 \times 10^7 \, \text{Bq} \qquad \Delta t = 120 \, \text{s}$$

Step 2 Determine the number of β-particles emitted.

$$A = \frac{\Delta N}{\Delta t}$$

$$\Delta N = 2.8 \times 10^7 \times 120 = 3.36 \times 10^9 \approx 3.4 \times 10^9$$

We have assumed that the activity remains constant over a period of 2.0 minutes.

Worked example 4

A sample consists of 1000 undecayed nuclei of a nuclide whose decay constant is $0.20 \, \text{s}^{-1}$. Determine the initial activity of the sample. Estimate the activity of the sample after 1.0 s.

Step 1 Since activity $A = \lambda N$, we have:

$$A = 0.20 \times 1000 = 200 \, \text{s}^{-1} = 200 \, \text{Bq}$$

continued

Step 2 After 1.0 s, we might expect 800 nuclei to remain undecayed.

The activity of the sample would then be:

$$A = 0.2 \times 800 = 160 \, \text{s}^{-1} = 160 \, \text{Bq}$$

(In fact, it would be slightly higher than this. Since the rate of decay decreases with time all the time, less than 200 nuclei would decay during the first second.)

Count rate

Although we are often interested in finding the activity of a sample of radioactive material, we cannot usually measure this directly. This is because we cannot easily detect *all* of the radiation emitted. Some will escape past our detectors, and some may be absorbed within the sample itself. A Geiger–Müller (GM) tube placed in front of a radioactive source therefore only detects a fraction of the activity. The further it is from the source, the smaller the count rate. Therefore, our measurements give a received **count rate** R that is significantly lower than the activity A. If we know how efficient our detecting system is, we can deduce A from R. If the level of background radiation is significant, then it must be subtracted to give the *corrected* count rate.

SAQ

10 A sample of carbon-15 initially contains 500 000 undecayed nuclei. The decay constant for this isotope of carbon is $0.30 \, \text{s}^{-1}$. Determine the initial activity of the sample.

Answer

11 A small sample of radium gives a received count rate of 20 counts per minute in a detector. It is known that the counter detects only 10% of the decays from the sample. The sample contains 1.5×10^9 undecayed nuclei. Determine the decay constant of this form of radium.

Answer

12 A radioactive sample is known to emit α-, β- and γ-radiations. Suggest four reasons why the count rate measured by a Geiger counter placed next to this sample would be lower than the activity of the sample.

Answer

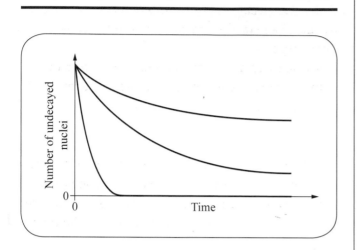

Figure 14.11 Some radioactive materials decay faster than others.

Decay graphs and equations

The activity of a radioactive substance gradually diminishes as time goes by. The atomic nuclei emit radiation and become different substances. The pattern of radioactive decay is an example of a very important pattern found in many different situations, a pattern called exponential decay. Figure 14.11 shows the decay graphs for three different isotopes, each with a different rate of decay.

Although the three graphs look different, they all have something in common – their shape. They are curved lines having a special property. If you know what is meant by the **half-life** of a radioisotope, then you will understand what is special about the shape of these curves.

> The half-life $t_{\frac{1}{2}}$ of a radioisotope is the mean time taken for half of the active nuclei in a sample to decay.

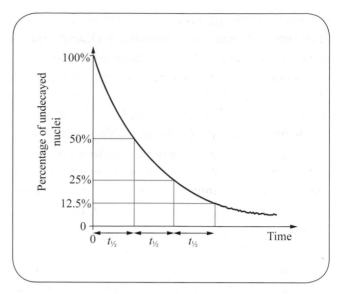

Figure 14.12 All radioactive decay graphs have the same characteristic shape.

In a time equal to one half-life, the activity of the sample will also halve. This is because activity is proportional to the number of undecayed nuclei ($A \propto N$). It takes the same amount of time again for half of the remainder of the nuclei to decay, and a third half-life for half of the new remainder to decay (Figure 14.12).

In principle, the graph never reaches zero; it just gets closer and closer. In practice, when only a few undecayed nuclei remain, it will cease to be a smooth curve and will eventually reach zero. We use the idea of half-life, because we cannot say when a sample will have completely decayed.

If you have already studied Chapter 11, you will have met this form of graph before. It is an exponential decay graph, with the same pattern of decrease as the discharge of a capacitor in a C–R circuit. We will shortly look at the exponential equations that we can use to calculate the activity of a decaying sample.

Determining half-life

If you are to determine the half-life of a radioactive substance in the laboratory, you need to choose something that will not decay too quickly or too slowly. In practice, the most suitable isotope is protactinium-234, which decays by emitting β-radiation. This is produced in a bottle containing a solution of a uranium compound (uranyl(VI) nitrate) (Figure 14.13). By shaking the bottle, you can separate the protactinium into the top layer of solvent in the bottle. The counter allows you to measure the decay of the protactinium.

After recording the number of counts in consecutive 10-second intervals over a period of a few minutes, you can then draw a graph, and use it to find the half-life of protactinium-234.

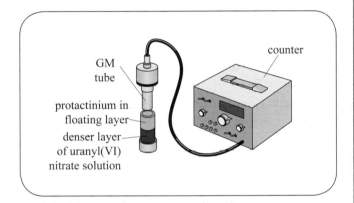

Figure 14.13 Practical arrangement for observing the decay of protactinium-234.

Mathematical decay

We can write an equation to represent the graph shown in Figure 14.12. If we start with N_0 undecayed nuclei, then the number N that remain undecayed after time t is given by:

$$N = N_0 e^{-\lambda t}$$

In this equation, λ is the decay constant, as before. Note that you must take care with units. If λ is in s^{-1},

then the time t must be in s. (You should recognise the form of this equation from our study of capacitor discharge in Chapter 11.)

As before, the symbol e represents the number e = 2.71828…, a special number in the same way that π is a special number. You will need to be able to use the e^x key on your calculator to solve problems involving e.

The activity A of a sample is proportional to the number of undecayed nuclei N. Hence the activity of the sample decreases exponentially:

$$A = A_0 e^{-\lambda t}$$

Usually we measure the corrected count rate R in the laboratory rather than the activity or the number of undecayed nuclei. Since the count rate is a fraction of the activity, it too decreases exponentially with time:

$$R = R_0 e^{-\lambda t}$$

Now look at Worked example 5 and Worked example 6.

Worked example 5

Suppose we start an experiment with 1.0×10^{15} undecayed nuclei of an isotope for which λ is equal to $0.02\,s^{-1}$. Determine the number of undecayed nuclei after 20 s.

Step 1 In this case, we have $N_0 = 1.0 \times 10^{15}$, $\lambda = 0.02\,s^{-1}$ and $t = 20\,s$. Substituting in the equation gives:

$$N = 1.0 \times 10^{15} e^{(-0.02 \times 20)}$$

Step 2 First calculate the expression in brackets; then use the e^x key and multiply by 1.0×10^{15}.

$$N = 1.0 \times 10^{15} e^{-0.40}$$

$$N = 6.7 \times 10^{14}$$

Worked example 6

A sample initially contains 1000 undecayed nuclei of an isotope whose decay constant $\lambda = 0.10\,\text{min}^{-1}$. Draw a graph to show how the sample will decay over a period of 10 min.

Step 1 We have $N_0 = 1000$ and $\lambda = 0.10\,\text{min}^{-1}$. Hence, we can write the equation for this decay:

$$N = 1000\,e^{-(0.10 \times t)}$$

Step 2 Calculate values of number N of undecayed nuclei at intervals of 1.0 min (60 s); this gives Table 14.2 and the graph shown in Figure 14.14.

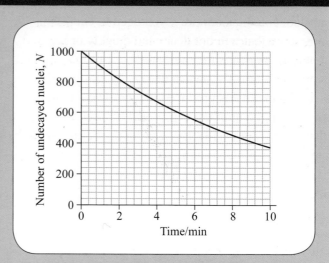

Figure 14.14 Radioactive decay graph.

t/min	0	1.0	2.0	3.0	4.0	5.0
N	1000	905	819	741	670	607
t/min	6.0	7.0	8.0	9.0	10.0	
N	549	497	449	407	368	

Table 14.2

SAQ

13 The isotope nitrogen-13 has a half-life of 10 min. A sample initially contains 8.0×10^{10} undecayed nuclei.

   a Write down an equation to show how the number undecayed, N, depends on time, t.

   b Determine how many nuclei will remain after 10 min, and after 20 min.

   c Determine how many nuclei will decay during the first 30 min.

   [Answer]

14 A sample of an isotope for which $\lambda = 0.10\,\text{s}^{-1}$ contains 5.0×10^9 undecayed nuclei at the start of an experiment. Determine:

   a the number of undecayed nuclei after 50 s

   b its activity after 50 s.

   [Answer]

15 The value of λ for protactinium-234 is $9.63 \times 10^{-3}\,\text{s}^{-1}$. Table 14.3 shows the number of undecayed nuclei, N, in a sample.

   Copy and complete Table 14.3. Draw a graph of N against t, and use it to find the half-life $t_{\frac{1}{2}}$ of protactinium-234.

t/s		0	20	40	60	80	100	120	140
N		400	330						

Table 14.3

   [Answer]

Carbon-dating

Archaeologists and geologists use the fact that particular isotopes decay at known rates to find the ages of various materials, including rocks, bone and wood. In particular, **carbon-dating** is used to find out how much time has elapsed since a piece of living material died (Figure 14.15).

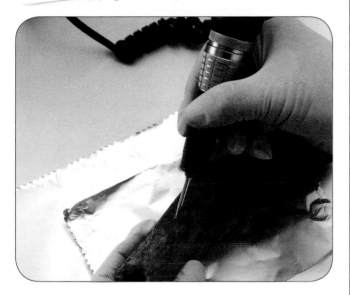

Figure 14.15 A small sample is cut from a bone, thought to be medieval, for use in carbon-dating.

All living materials contain carbon atoms. Plants take in carbon (as CO_2) from the atmosphere; animals eat plants, and so on. Atmospheric carbon is mainly the common, non-radioactive isotope carbon-12, but a tiny fraction is carbon-14. This is formed in the atmosphere when cosmic rays strike nitrogen-14 nuclei. There is a (roughly) constant fraction of carbon-14 in living tissue but, once the organism dies, the radioactive isotope decays gradually and the fraction decreases.

The half-life of the carbon-14 isotope is 5730 ± 40 years. By measuring the fraction of carbon-14 nuclei in dead material, the time since death can be determined. This is known as carbon-dating. There are several problems with this technique for determining half-life:

- Material that died recently will show little change in carbon-14 content, so the technique cannot be used on material that is less than a century old.

- Modern living tissue may contain a reduced fraction of carbon-14 because we have burned so much fossil fuel, which contains little of the radioactive isotope.

- The number of carbon-14 nuclei as a fraction of all the carbon present is very small (just one part in 10^{12}) so activities are small (less than 14 counts per minute for a 1 gram sample).

- There is a small uncertainty in the half-life of carbon-14.

Sensitive techniques are used to determine the amount of carbon-14 present. Today, a mass spectrometer is likely to be used, instead of trying to measure decay rates (Figure 14.16).

Figure 14.16 A mass spectrometer at Oxford University, used for carbon-dating of samples.

SAQ

16 Carbon-14 is the radioactive isotope used by archaeologists for carbon-dating of dead organic matter. It has a decay constant of $1.21 \times 10^{-4}\,\mathrm{year}^{-1}$. In laboratory tests, a standard sample of fresh material gives a corrected count rate of $200\,\mathrm{min}^{-1}$. Calculate how this count rate will decrease at 1000-year intervals over a period of $10\,000$ years. Draw a graph of count rate against time, and use it to determine the age of a sample that gives a corrected count rate of $116\,\mathrm{min}^{-1}$.

Hint

Answer

219

Decay constant and half-life

A radioactive isotope that decays rapidly has a short half-life $t_{\frac{1}{2}}$. Its decay constant must be large, since the probability per unit time of an individual nucleus decaying must be high. What is the connection between the decay constant and the half-life?

In a time equal to one half-life $t_{\frac{1}{2}}$, the number of undecayed nuclei is halved. Hence the equation:

$$N = N_0 e^{-\lambda t}$$

becomes:

$$\frac{N}{N_0} = e^{-(\lambda \times t_{\frac{1}{2}})} = \frac{1}{2}$$

Therefore:

$$e^{(\lambda \times t_{\frac{1}{2}})} = 2$$
$$\lambda t_{\frac{1}{2}} = \ln 2 \approx 0.693$$
(remember if $e^x = y$, then $x = \ln y$)

The half-life of an isotope and the decay constant are inversely proportional to each other. That is:

$$\lambda = \frac{0.693}{t_{\frac{1}{2}}}$$

Thus if we know either $t_{\frac{1}{2}}$ or λ, we can calculate the other. For a nuclide with a very long half-life, we might not wish to sit around waiting to measure the half-life; it is easier to determine λ by measuring the activity (and using $A = \lambda N$), and then determine $t_{\frac{1}{2}}$.

Note that the units of λ and $t_{\frac{1}{2}}$ must be compatible; for example, λ in s^{-1} and $t_{\frac{1}{2}}$ in s.

SAQ

17 Figure 14.17 shows the decay of a radioactive isotope of caesium, $^{134}_{55}\text{Cs}$. Use the graph to determine the half-life of this nuclide in years, and hence find the decay constant in year^{-1}.

> Answer

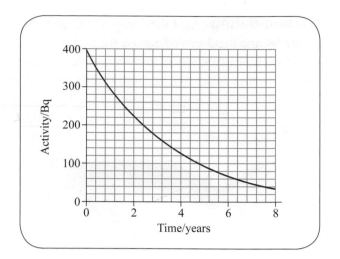

Figure 14.17 Decay graph for a radioactive isotope of caesium – see SAQ 17.

18 The decay constant of a particular isotope is known to be $3.0 \times 10^{-4}\,\text{s}^{-1}$. Determine how long it will take for the activity of a sample of this substance to decrease to one-eighth of its initial value.

> Answer

19 The isotope $^{16}_{7}\text{N}$ decays with a half-life of 7.4 s.
  a Calculate the decay constant for this nuclide.
  b A sample of $^{16}_{7}\text{N}$ initially contains 5000 nuclei. Determine how many will remain after a time of:
  i 14.8 s
  ii 20.0 s.

> Answer

20 A sample contains an isotope of half-life $t_{1/2}$.
  a Show that the fraction f of the number of undecayed nuclei left in the sample after a time t is given by the equation:

  > Hint

  $$f = \left(\frac{1}{2}\right)^n$$

  where $n = t/t_{1/2}$
  b Calculate the fraction f after each of the following times:
  i $t_{1/2}$ **iii** $2.5 t_{1/2}$
  ii $2 t_{1/2}$ **iv** $8.3 t_{1/2}$.

> Answer

21 Compare and contrast the decay of radioactive nuclei and the decay of charge on a capacitor in a C–R circuit.

Answer

Summary

Glossary

- There are three types of ionising radiation produced by radioactive substances: α-particles, β-particles and γ-rays.

- The most strongly ionising, and hence the least penetrating, is α-radiation. The least strongly ionising is γ-radiation.

- Because of their different charges, masses and speeds, they can be identified by the effect of an electric or magnetic field.

- The weak interaction between quarks is responsible for β decay. There are two types of β decay: β^- and β^+.

- In β^- decay, an electron is emitted along with an antineutrino $\bar{\nu}$. A down quark in the nucleus changes into an up quark:

$$d \longrightarrow u + {}_{-1}^{0}e + \bar{\nu}$$

- In β^+ decay, a positron is emitted along with a neutrino ν. An up quark in the nucleus changes into a down quark:

$$u \longrightarrow d + {}_{+1}^{0}e + \nu$$

- Electrons, positrons and neutrinos are all leptons.

- Nuclear decay is a spontaneous and random process. This unpredictability means that count rates tend to fluctuate, and we have to measure average quantities.

- The half-life $t_{\frac{1}{2}}$ of a radioisotope is the mean time taken for half of the active nuclei in a sample to decay.

- The decay constant λ is the probability that an individual nucleus will decay per unit time interval.

- The decay constant and half-life are related by the equation:

$$\lambda t_{\frac{1}{2}} = \ln 2 \quad \text{or} \quad \lambda t_{\frac{1}{2}} = 0.693$$

- We can represent the exponential decrease of a quantity by an equation of the form

$$x = x_0 e^{-\lambda t}$$

where x can be activity A, count rate R or number of undecayed nuclei N.

Questions

1 This question is about the ways in which a gold isotope might undergo spontaneous decay.
Data:

Name	Symbol	Mass/u
gold-192	$^{192}_{79}\text{Au}$	191.92147
platinum-192	$^{192}_{78}\text{Pt}$	191.91824
mercury-192	$^{192}_{80}\text{Hg}$	191.92141
electron	$^{0}_{-1}\text{e}$	0.00055

A student suggests that $^{192}_{79}\text{Au}$ should undergo either β^+ or β^- decay.

  a Write nuclear equations for each of these suggested reactions. [2]
  b Deduce whether either of these reactions can take place. [5]
  c Calculate the maximum kinetic energy, in joules, of any emitted β-particle. [4]

OCR Physics A2 (2825/04) January 2006   [Total 11]

Hint

Answer

2 A uranium-236 nucleus, $^{236}_{92}\text{U}$, undergoes fission, producing nuclei of zirconium-100, $^{100}_{40}\text{Zr}$, and tellurium-131, $^{131}_{52}\text{Te}$.

  a Write a nuclear equation to represent this fission reaction. [1]
  b Each of the product nuclei is a β^- emitter.
    i State the change, if any, in the nucleon number and the proton number caused by a β^- emission. [1]
    ii The β^- decay of zirconium-100 is followed by three more β^- decays before the product nucleus is stable.
    State the nucleon number and the proton number of the resulting stable nucleus. [1]

OCR Physics A2 (2825/04) January 2007   [Total 3]

Hint

Answer

3 a The activity A of a sample of a radioactive nuclide is given by the equation:

$$A = \lambda N$$

<u>Define</u> each of the terms in the equation. [3]

  b A 1000 MW coal-fired power station burns 7.0×10^6 kg of coal in one day. Two parts per million of the mass of the coal is $^{238}_{92}\text{U}$. The uranium remains in the residue left after the coal is burnt. The uranium nuclide $^{238}_{92}\text{U}$ decays by α-particle emission with a half-life of 4.5×10^9 years to an isotope of thorium.

continued

i Write down the proton number Z of thorium and the nucleon number A for this isotope of thorium. [1]

ii Calculate the mass of uranium produced in the residue in one day. [1]

iii Hence show that the number of uranium atoms in this mass of uranium is 3.5×10^{25}. [1]

iv Calculate the activity of this mass of uranium. Give a suitable unit with your answer. (1 year $= 3.2 \times 10^7$ s.) [3]

c To drive the turbines in the power station superheated steam at 450 K is required. Cold water enters the boilers at 290 K. Suggest and explain <u>two</u> reasons why it is <u>not</u> possible to use the formula:

$$E = mc\Delta\theta$$

to calculate the total energy used to transform the cold water into superheated steam. In the formula E is the energy absorbed by a mass m of water, c is the specific heat capacity of water and $\Delta\theta$ is its change in temperature. [3]

OCR Physics A2 (2824) June 2007 [Total 12]

4 The radioactive nickel nuclide $^{63}_{28}\text{Ni}$ decays by β-particle emission with a half-life of 120 years.

a A copper nucleus is produced as the result of this decay. State the number of nucleons in the copper nucleus which are:

i protons [1]

ii neutrons. [1]

b Show that the decay constant of the nickel nuclide is $1.8 \times 10^{-10}\,\text{s}^{-1}$. (1 year $= 3.2 \times 10^7$ s.) [1]

c A student designs an electronic clock powered by the decay of nuclei of $^{63}_{28}\text{Ni}$. One plate of a capacitor of capacitance 1.2×10^{-12} F is to be coated with this isotope. As a result of this decay, the capacitor becomes charged. The capacitor is connected across the terminals of a small neon lamp, as shown in Figure 1.

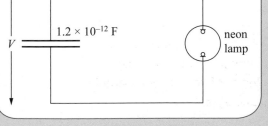

Figure 1

continued

When the capacitor is charged to 90 V, the neon gas inside the lamp becomes conducting, causing it to emit a brief flash of light and discharging the capacitor. The charging starts again. Figure 2 shows how the voltage V across the capacitor varies with time.

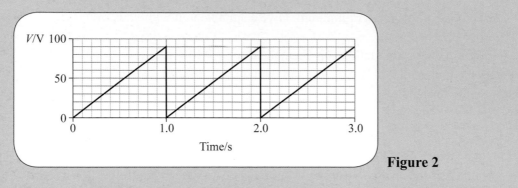

Figure 2

i   Show that the maximum charge stored on the capacitor is 1.1×10^{-10} C. [2]

ii   When a nickel atom emits a β-particle, a positive charge of 1.6×10^{-19} C is added to the capacitor plate. Show that the number of nickel nuclei that must decay to produce 1.1×10^{-10} C is about 7×10^8. [2]

iii   The neon lamp is to flash once every 1.0 s. Using your answer to **b**, calculate the number of nickel atoms needed in the coating on the plate. [3]

iv   State, giving a reason, whether or not you would expect the clock to be accurate within 1% one year after manufacture. [1]

OCR Physics A2 (2824) January 2006 [Total 11]

Answer

5   This question is about the decay of an isotope of bismuth, $^{212}_{83}$Bi.

a

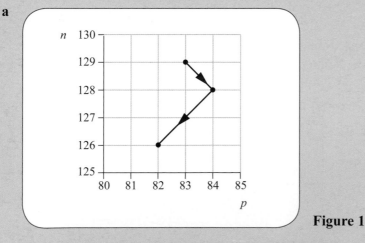

Figure 1

Figure 1 shows a small region of the chart of neutron number n against proton number p. An isotope of bismuth, Bi, decays to an isotope of lead, Pb, in two stages along the path shown by the two arrows on Figure 1.

Complete the nuclear equations which describe these two decays.

i $^{212}_{83}\text{Bi} \longrightarrow\ ^{?}_{84}\text{Po}\ +\ ?$ [2]

ii $^{?}_{84}\text{Po} \longrightarrow\ ^{?}_{82}\text{Pb}\ +\ ?$ [2]

continued

b Imagine that you are given a sample of $^{212}_{83}$Bi mounted on a stand. You are asked to verify experimentally that the two decays in **a i** and **ii** occur. Outline briefly the experiment that you would perform. [4]

c The decay constant for $^{212}_{83}$Bi is $0.0115\,\mathrm{min}^{-1}$.

   i Show that the initial activity of a sample containing $1.00 \times 10^{-9}\,\mathrm{g}$ of the isotope is about $3 \times 10^{10}\,\mathrm{min}^{-1}$. [3]

   ii Calculate the half-life of the isotope in minutes. [1]

   iii Assume that only one decay in a million is detected in an experiment to measure the half-life. Copy the axes shown in Figure 2 and plot a graph of the count rate against time that you would expect to observe. [1]

Hint

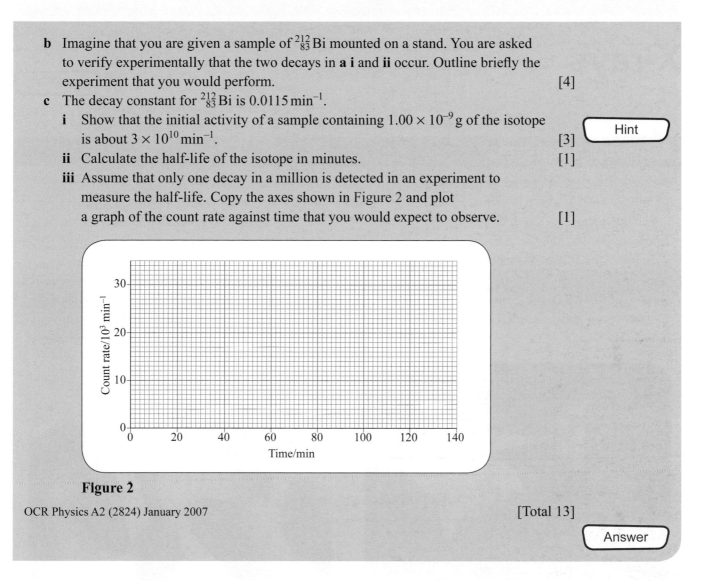

Figure 2

OCR Physics A2 (2824) January 2007

[Total 13]

Answer

Chapter 15

X-rays

Objectives

Medical diagnosis

When you are unwell, you may have external symptoms such as a rash or unusual skin colour which the doctor can use to diagnose your illness. Alternatively, you may be required to report on your internal symptoms – aches, pains and so on. The human body is opaque to light, so how can a doctor know what is going on inside you? Figure 15.1 shows an early use of technology to see inside the body.

Figure 15.1 This electrical medical lamp from 1869 allowed the doctor to see more clearly into the patient's throat.

Although light does not penetrate the human body, other electromagnetic radiations do. The best known are X-rays, good for showing up bones (Figure 15.2) and the subject of this chapter.

The chapters that follow will look at the physics behind other medical diagnostic techniques, including the use of radioactive substances, magnetic resonance and ultrasound.

These techniques are often described as *non-invasive*. This is because they do not involve cutting the patient open to discover what is wrong. Nor do they involve inserting surgical instruments into any of the body's orifices. Both of these are procedures that can allow infections to enter the body. Any damage to the body may take time to heal and can lead to permanent scarring.

Figure 15.2 A radiographer and a doctor examine X-ray images of a patient's leg at a hospital in Uganda.

The nature and production of X-rays

X-rays are a form of electromagnetic radiation. They belong to the short-wavelength, high-frequency end of the electromagnetic spectrum, beyond ultraviolet radiation (Figure 15.3). They have wavelengths in the range 10^{-8} m to 10^{-13} m and are effectively the same as gamma rays (γ-rays), the difference being in the way they are produced:

- X-rays are produced when fast-moving electrons are rapidly decelerated. As the electrons slow down, their kinetic energy is transformed to photons of electromagnetic radiation.

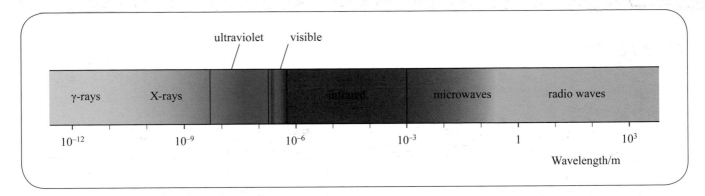

Figure 15.3 The electromagnetic spectrum; X-rays and γ-rays lie at the high-frequency, short-wavelength end of the spectrum.

- γ-rays are produced by radioactive decay. Following alpha (α) or beta (β) emission, a gamma photon is often emitted by the decaying nucleus (see Chapter 14).

The X-rays used in medical applications are usually described as *soft X-rays*, because their energy is not very great, usually less than the energies of γ-rays produced by radioactive substances.

As with all electromagnetic radiation, we can think of X-rays either as waves or as photons (see Chapter 19 of *Physics 1*). X-rays travel in straight lines through a uniform medium.

X-ray tube

Figure 15.4a shows a patient undergoing a pelvic X-ray to check for bone degeneration. The X-ray machine is above the patient; it contains the **X-ray tube** that produces the X-rays which pass down through the patient's body. Below the patient is the detection system. In this case an electronic detector is being used, but often photographic film is used in the detection system. Figure 15.4b shows the resulting image.

Figure 15.5 shows the principles of the modern X-ray tube. The tube itself is evacuated, and contains two electrodes:

- *Cathode*
  The heated filament acts as the cathode (negative) from which electrons are emitted.
- *Anode*
  The rotating anode (positive) is made of a hard metal such as tungsten. (The anode metal is often referred to as the 'target metal'.)

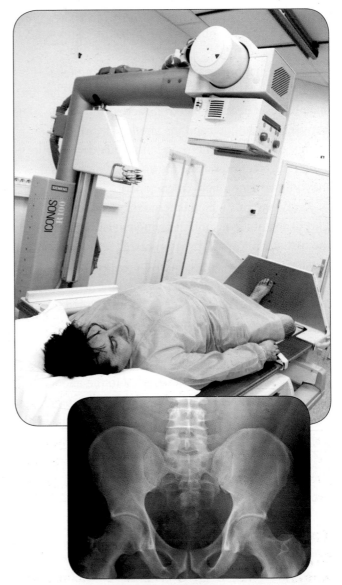

Figure 15.4 a A general-purpose X-ray system.
b A typical X-ray image produced by such a machine, showing the region around the pelvis.

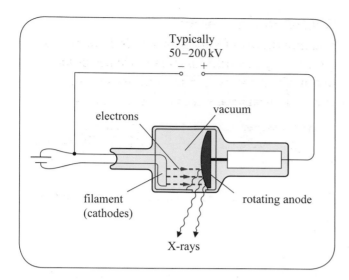

Figure 15.5 A simplified diagram of an X-ray tube.

An external power supply produces a voltage of up to 200 kV between the two electrodes. This accelerates a beam of electrons across the gap between the cathode and the anode. The kinetic energy of an electron arriving at the anode is 200 keV. When the electrons strike the anode at high speed, they lose some of their kinetic energy in the form of X-ray photons which emerge in all directions. Part of the outer casing, the window, is thinner than the rest and allows X-rays to emerge into the space outside the tube. The width of the X-ray beam can be controlled using metal tubes beyond the window to absorb X-rays. This produces a parallel-sided beam called a **collimated beam**.

Only a small fraction, about 1%, of the kinetic energy of the electrons is converted to X-rays. Most of the incident energy is transferred to the anode, which becomes hot. This explains why the anode rotates; the region that is heated turns out of the beam so that it can cool down by radiating heat to its surroundings. Some X-ray tubes have water circulating through the anode to remove this excess heat.

X-ray spectrum

The X-rays that emerge from an X-ray tube have a range of energies, as represented in the X-ray spectrum shown in Figure 15.6. The spectrum has two components, the broad background 'hump' of **braking radiation** (also known as Bremsstrahlung radiation) and a few sharp 'lines' of **characteristic radiation**. These arise from the different ways in which an individual electron loses its energy when it crashes into the anode.

An electron striking the anode loses its energy as it interacts with the electric fields of the anode nuclei. This may result in a single X-ray photon or, more usually, several photons. These all contribute to the background braking radiation.

An electron may cause a rearrangement of the electrons in an anode atom in which an electron drops from a high energy level to a lower energy level. As it does so, it emits a single photon whose energy is equal to the difference in energy levels. You should recall from Chapter 20 in *Physics 1* that this is how a line spectrum arises and the photon energies are characteristic of the atom involved. So the characteristic spectral lines of X-rays from a tungsten anode have different energies from those of a molybdenum or copper target. In practice, these characteristic X-rays are relatively unimportant in medical applications.

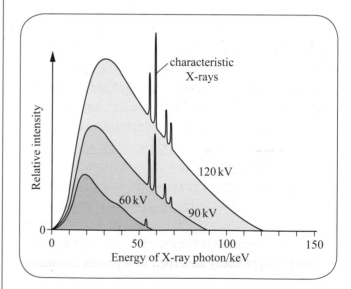

Figure 15.6 X-ray spectra for a tungsten target with accelerating voltages of 60 kV, 90 kV and 120 kV. The continuous curve shows the braking radiation while the sharp spikes are the characteristic X-rays.

SAQ

1 a Summarise the energy changes that take place in an X-ray tube.

   b An X-ray tube is operated with a potential difference of 80 kV between the cathode and the tungsten anode. Calculate the kinetic energy (in electronvolts and joules) of an electron arriving at the anode. Estimate the impact speed of such an electron (assume that the electron is non-relativistic).

     Answer

2 Determine the minimum wavelength of X-rays emitted from an X-ray tube operated at a voltage of 120 kV.

     Answer

3 Gamma radiation from a radioactive source could be used instead of X-rays to obtain images of patients' bones. Describe one advantage that X-rays have over γ-rays in a hospital setting.

     Answer

X-ray attenuation

As you can see if you look back to Figure 15.2, bones look white in an X-ray photograph. This is because they are good absorbers of X-rays, so that little radiation arrives at the photographic film to cause blackening. Flesh and other soft tissues are less absorbing, so the film is blackened. Modern X-ray systems use digital detectors instead of photographic films. The digital images are easier to process, store and transmit using computers.

X-rays are a form of ionising radiation; that is, they ionise the atoms and molecules of the materials they pass through. In the process, the X-rays transfer some or all of their energy to the material, and so a beam of X-rays is gradually absorbed as it passes through a material.

The gradual decrease in the intensity of a beam of X-rays as it passes through matter is called attenuation. We will first consider the *pattern* of attenuation of X-rays as they travel through matter, and then we will look at the *mechanisms* by which X-rays are absorbed.

Decreasing intensity

You should recall from Chapter 15 in *Physics 1* that the intensity of a beam of radiation indicates the rate at which energy is transferred across unit cross-sectional area. Intensity is defined thus:

> Intensity is the power per unit cross-sectional area.

We can determine the intensity I using the equation:

$$I = \frac{P}{A}$$

where P is power and A is the cross-sectional area normal to the radiation. The unit of intensity is W m^{-2}.

The intensity of a collimated beam of X-rays (i.e. a beam with parallel sides, so that it does not spread out) decreases as it passes through matter. Picture a beam entering a block of material. Suppose that, after it has passed through 1 cm of material, its intensity has decreased to half its original value. Then, after it has passed through 2 cm, the intensity will have decreased to one quarter of its original value (half of a half), and then after 3 cm it will be reduced to one eighth. You should recognise this pattern $(1, \frac{1}{2}, \frac{1}{4}, \frac{1}{8} \ldots)$ as a form of exponential decay.

We can write an equation to represent the attenuation of X-rays as they pass through a uniform material as follows:

$$I = I_0 e^{-\mu x}$$

where I_0 is the initial intensity (before absorption), x is the thickness of the material, I is the transmitted intensity and μ is the *attenuation* (or *absorption*) *coefficient* of the material. Figure 15.7 shows this pattern of absorption. It also shows that bone is a better absorber of X-rays than flesh; it has a higher attenuation coefficient. (The attenuation coefficient also depends on the energy of the X-ray photons.)

The unit of the attenuation coefficient μ is m^{-1} (or cm^{-1} etc.).

Now look at Worked example 1.

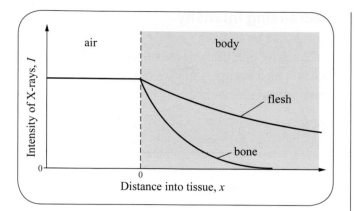

Figure 15.7 The absorption of X-rays follows an exponential pattern.

Worked example 1

The attenuation (absorption) coefficient of bone is $600\,\text{m}^{-1}$ for X-rays of energy 20 keV. A beam of such X-rays has an intensity of $20\,\text{W m}^{-2}$. Calculate the intensity of the beam after passing through a 4.0 mm thickness of bone.

Step 1 Write down the quantities that you are given; make sure that the units are consistent.

$$I_0 = 20\ \text{W m}^{-2}$$
$$x = 4.0\,\text{mm} = 0.004\,\text{m}$$
$$\mu = 600\,\text{m}^{-1}$$

Step 2 Substitute in the equation for intensity and solve. Take care to calculate the exponent (the value of $-\mu x$) first.

$$I = I_0 e^{-\mu x}$$
$$= 20 \times e^{-(600 \times 0.04)} = 20 \times e^{-2.4}$$
$$= 1.8\,\text{W m}^{-2}$$

So the intensity of the X-ray beam will have been reduced to about 10% of its initial value after passing through just 4.0 mm of bone.

Extension

Absorption mechanisms

There are three important mechanisms by which X-rays may be absorbed as they pass through matter:

- *Photoelectric effect*

  In the **photoelectric effect**, an X-ray photon with energy less than 100 keV is absorbed by one of the electrons of an atom in the target metal, so that the electron gains enough energy to escape from the atom (Figure 15.8). (You should recall from Chapter 19 in *Physics 1* that the photoelectric effect also occurs when photons of light release electrons from a metal surface. The energies of X-ray photons are much greater and so they can release electrons from deep inside atoms.)

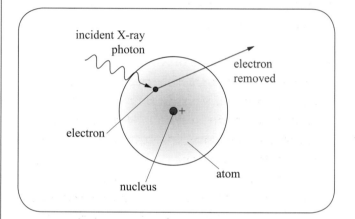

Figure 15.8 The photoelectric effect. The energy of an X-ray photon is absorbed by an electron which then escapes from the target atom.

- *Compton scattering*

  In **Compton scattering**, an X-ray photon (with energy in the range 0.5 MeV to 5.0 MeV) loses only a fraction of its energy to an atomic electron in the absorbing material (Figure 15.9). The interaction between the photon and the electron is inelastic. The scattered X-ray photon has less energy than before, and so its wavelength is greater. The Compton electron goes off in a different direction from the scattered photon, because momentum must be conserved.

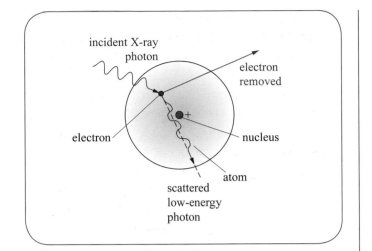

Figure 15.9 Compton scattering. The X-ray photon gives up part of its energy to an electron and is deflected in the process.

- *Pair production*

  In **pair production**, a high-energy X-ray photon (energy over 1.02 MeV) passing through the electric field of the nucleus suddenly produces an electron–positron pair; its energy appears as the mass of the electron and positron (Figure 15.10). The positron is quite soon annihilated when it collides with another electron. This process is not very important in diagnostic X-rays because the X-ray energies used are usually too low.

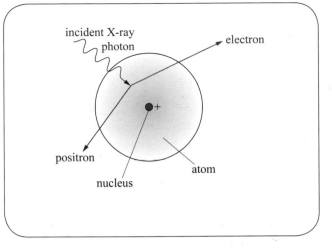

Figure 15.10 Pair production. The X-ray photon interacts with the electric field of the atomic nucleus, disappears and then materialises as an electron and a positron. The electric field of the nucleus is a catalyst for this process.

For all the three mechanisms described, the attenuation coefficient μ depends on the proton (atomic) number Z of the atom and the energy E of the incident X-ray photon. Table 15.1 summaries the three attenuation mechanisms.

Attenuation mechanism	Energy range of X-ray photons/MeV	What happens to the X-ray photon?	Relationship between μ and Z	Relationship between μ and E
photoelectric effect	< 0.1	Photon disappears and removes an electron from the atom.	$\mu \propto Z^3$	$\mu \propto \dfrac{1}{E^3}$
Compton scattering	0.5–5.0	Photon is inelastically scattered by atomic electron. The scattered photon has lower energy.	μ independent of Z	Decreases slowly with E
pair production	> 1.02	Photon disappears and produces electron–positron pair.	$\mu \propto Z^2$	Rises slowly with E

Table 15.1 A summary of the attenuation processes for X-rays passing through a material.

SAQ

4 An X-ray beam transfers 400 J of energy through 5.0 cm² each second. Calculate its intensity in W m⁻².

5 An X-ray beam of initial intensity 50 W m⁻² is incident on soft tissue of attenuation coefficient 1.2 cm⁻¹. Calculate its intensity after it has passed through a 5.0 cm thickness of tissue.

6 The data in Table 15.2 shows how the attenuation coefficient μ depends on the energy of the X-rays in bone and muscle. When making a diagnostic X-ray image, it is desirable that bone should be clearly distinguished from muscle. Use the data in Table 15.2 to explain why it would be best to use lower energy (50 keV) X-rays for this purpose.

Maximum X-ray energy	Bone: μ/cm⁻¹	Muscle: μ/cm⁻¹
4.0 MeV	0.087	0.049
250 keV	0.32	0.16
100 keV	0.60	0.21
50 keV	3.32	0.54

Table 15.2 See SAQ 6.

Improving X-ray images

The X-ray systems in use in hospitals and clinics today are highly developed pieces of technology. They do not simply show bones against a background of soft tissue. They can also show very fine detail in the soft tissue, including the arrangement of blood vessels.

Radiographers (the people in charge of X-ray systems) have two main aims:
- to reduce as much as possible the patient's exposure to harmful X-rays – to do this, they use sensitive detectors
- to improve the **contrast** of the image, so that the different tissues under investigation show up clearly in the image.

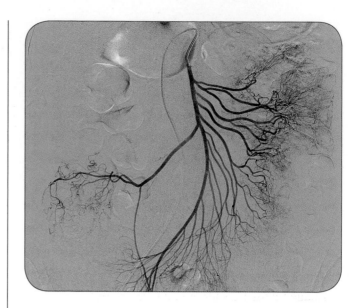

Figure 15.11 An X-ray image of blood vessels branching out from an artery carrying oxygenated blood to the intestines.

Figure 15.11 shows a remarkably detailed X-ray image of blood vessels in the human abdomen.

Detection systems

A radiographer may choose to record the X-ray image on film or digitally.

X-rays are only weakly absorbed by photographic film, so, historically, patients had to be exposed to long and intense doses of X-rays. Today, *intensifier screens* are used. These are sheets of a material that contains a phosphor, a substance that emits visible light when it absorbs X-ray photons. The film is sandwiched between two intensifier screens. Each X-ray photon absorbed results in several thousand light photons, which then blacken the film. This reduces the patient's exposure by a factor of 100–500.

In digital systems, **image intensifiers** are used (Figure 15.12). The incoming X-rays strike a phosphor screen, producing visible light photons. These then release electrons (by the photoelectric effect) from the photocathode. The electrons are accelerated and focused by the positively charged anode so that they strike a screen, which then gives out visible light. The image on this screen can be viewed via a television camera. At the same time, the image can be stored electronically. Digital systems have the advantage that images can be easily stored, shared and viewed.

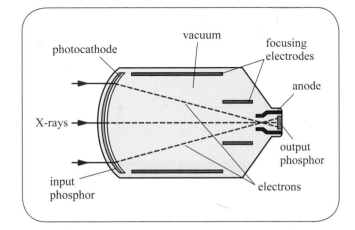

Figure 15.12 An X-ray image intensifier.

Image intensifiers are particularly useful in a technique called *fluoroscopy*. A continuous X-ray beam is passed through the patient onto a fluorescent screen where a real-time image is formed. Using an image intensifier ensures that the patient is not exposed to dangerous levels of X-rays over a long period.

Improving contrast

As we have seen, different tissues show up differently in X-ray images. In particular, bone can readily be distinguished from soft tissue such as muscle because it is a good absorber of X-rays. However, it is often desirable to show up different soft tissues that absorb X-rays equally. In order to do this, **contrast media** are used.

A contrast medium is a substance such as iodine or barium which is a good absorber of X-rays. The patient may swallow a barium-containing liquid (a 'barium meal'), or have a similar liquid injected into the tissue of interest. This tissue is then a better absorber of X-rays and its edges show up more clearly on the final image.

Figure 15.13 shows an X-ray image of the intestine of a patient who has been given a barium meal. The large pale areas show where the barium has accumulated. Other parts of the intestine have

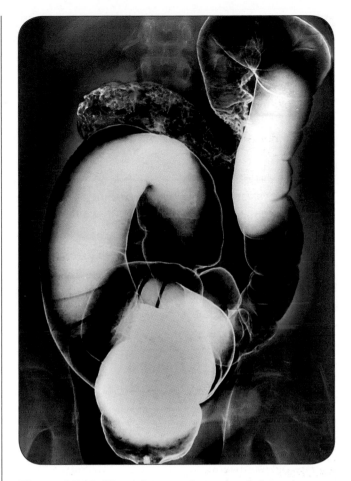

Figure 15.13 X-ray image of a patient's intestine after taking a barium meal. Barium shows up as pale in this image, which has also been artificially coloured to highlight features of interest.

become smeared with barium, and this means that the outline of the tissue shows up clearly.

Contrast media are elements with high values of atomic number Z. This means that their atoms have many electrons with which the X-rays interact, so they are more absorbing. The attenuation mechanism is mainly the photoelectric effect, for which the attenuation coefficient is proportional to the cube of the proton number ($\mu \propto Z^3$). Soft tissues mostly consist of compounds of hydrogen, carbon and oxygen (low Z values), while bone has the heavier elements calcium and phosphorus – see Table 15.3.

Substance	Elements (Z values)	Average Z
soft tissue	H (1), C (6), O (8)	7
bone	H (1), C (6), O (8), P (15), Ca (20)	14
contrast media	I (53), Ba (56)	55

Table 15.3 Proton (atomic) numbers of the constituents of different tissues, and of contrast media.

SAQ

7 When low-energy X-rays are used, the attenuation coefficient μ is (roughly) proportional to the cube of the proton (atomic) number Z of the absorbing material. The main attenuation mechanism at low energies is the photoelectric effect. Use the data in Table 15.3 to show that bone absorbs X-rays eight times as strongly as muscle.

Answer

Computerised axial tomography

A conventional X-ray image has an important limitation. Because an X-ray is essentially a two-dimensional shadow image, it shows the bones, organs, etc. at different depths within the body superimposed on each other. For example, in Figure 15.14, it is difficult to distinguish the bones of the front and back of the ribcage. This can be overcome by taking several images at different angles. An experienced radiographer can then study these images and deduce what is going on inside the patient.

An ingenious technique for extending this approach was invented by Geoffrey Hounsfield and his colleagues at EMI in the UK in 1971. They developed the **computerised axial tomography** scanner (CAT scanner or CT scanner). Figure 15.15 illustrates the principle of a modern scanner.

- The patient lies in a vertical ring of X-ray detectors.
- The X-ray tube rotates around the ring, exposing the patient to a fan-shaped beam of X-rays from all directions.
- Detectors opposite the tube send electronic records to a computer.

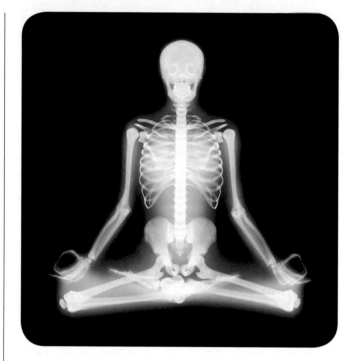

Figure 15.14 Computer-generated X-ray image of a person in a yoga position. This shows the difficulty of distinguishing one bone from another when they overlap.

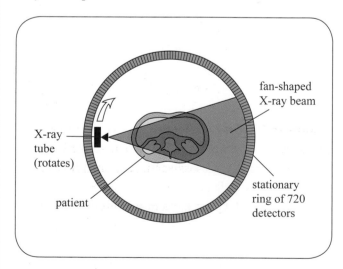

Figure 15.15 Operation of a modern CAT scanner. The X-ray tube rotates around the patient while the detectors are stationary.

- The computer software builds up a three-dimensional image of the patient.
- The radiographer can view images of 'slices' through the patient on the computer screen.

CAT scanners have undergone many developments since they were first invented. In a fifth-generation scanner, the patient's bed slides slowly through the ring of detectors as the X-ray tube rotates. The tube thus traces out a spiral path around the patient, allowing information to be gathered about the whole body.

Figure 15.16 shows a child undergoing a CAT scan. On the monitor you can see a cross-section of the patient's head.

This technique is called *computerised axial tomography* because it relies on a computer to control the scanning motion and to gather and manipulate the data to produce images; because the X-ray tube rotates around an axis; and because it produces images of slices through the patient – the Greek word *tomos* means *slice*.

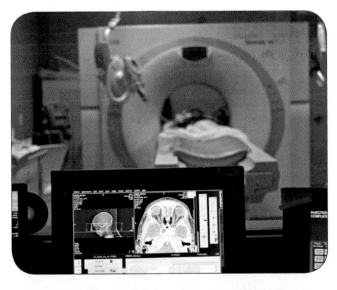

Figure 15.16 A boy undergoes a CAT scan in an investigation of an eye condition. The larger image on the monitor shows a cross-section through his head.

Advantages of a CAT scan

Although single X-ray images still have many uses (and they can be made very quickly), CAT scans have a number of advantages:

- They produce images that show three-dimensional relationships between different tissues.
- They can distinguish tissues with quite similar densities (attenuation coefficients).

So, for example, a CAT scan can show up the precise position, shape and size of a tumour. This allows it to be precisely targeted in treatment with high-energy X-rays or γ-rays.

However, it is worth noting that a CAT scan involves using X-rays and any exposure to ionising radiation carries a risk for the patient. A single scan can expose the patient to a radiation dose equal to several years' worth of background radiation. (This is not a problem with MRI scans, discussed in Chapter 16.)

SAQ

8 Suggest why a patient may be asked to hold his or her breath during a CAT scan.

Answer

9 A patient with an injury to the skull, perhaps as a result of a road accident, is likely to undergo a CAT scan. Explain why a CAT scan is preferable to a conventional X-ray in a case like this.

Answer

Summary

Glossary

- X-rays are short-wavelength, high-frequency electromagnetic radiation, produced when electrons are decelerated.

- There are three main mechanisms by which X-rays are absorbed as they pass through matter: the photoelectric effect, Compton scattering and pair production.

- The intensity of an X-ray beam is the power transmitted per unit cross-sectional area.

- The intensity of a collimated X-ray beam decreases exponentially according to the equation $I = I_0 e^{-\mu x}$, where μ is the attenuation coefficient of the medium. μ has units m^{-1} (or cm^{-1} or mm^{-1}).

- X-ray images can be improved using image intensifiers and contrast media (such as barium or iodine).

- A computerised axial tomography scanner (CAT scanner) produces three-dimensional X-ray images of a patient.

Questions

1 Full-body CAT scans produce detailed 3-D information about a patient and can identify cancers at an early stage in their development.

   a Describe how a CAT scan image is produced, referring to the physics principles involved. [7]

   b State and explain <u>two</u> reasons why full-body CAT scans are not offered for regular checking of healthy patients. [3]

OCR Physics A2 (2825/02) June 2007   [Total 10]

Answer

2 The diagram below shows a simplified X-ray tube.

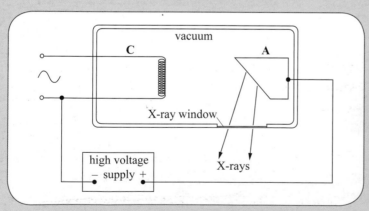

Explain briefly, with reference to the parts labelled **C** and **A**:
- how X-rays are generated
- the energy conversions that occur. [7]

OCR Physics A2 (2825/02) June 2005   [Total 7]

Hint

Answer

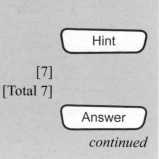

continued

3 In order to take an X-ray photograph, the X-ray beam is passed through an aluminium filter to remove low energy X-ray photons before reaching the patient.

a The average linear attenuation coefficient for X-rays that penetrate the aluminium is $250\,m^{-1}$. The intensity of an X-ray beam after travelling through 2.5 cm of aluminium is $347\,W\,m^{-2}$.

Show that the intensity incident on the aluminium is about $2\times10^5\,W\,m^{-2}$. [3]

Hint

b The X-ray beam at the filter has a circular cross-section of diameter 0.20 cm. Calculate the power of the X-ray beam emerging from the aluminium filter. Assume that the beam penetrates the aluminium filter as a parallel beam. [2]

c The total power of X-rays generated by an X-ray tube is 18 W. The efficiency of conversion of kinetic energy of the electrons into X-ray photon energy is 0.15%.

i Calculate the power of the electron beam. [2]

ii Calculate the velocity of the electrons if the rate of arrival of electrons is $7.5\times10^{17}\,s^{-1}$. Relativistic effects may be ignored. [2]

OCR Physics A2 (2825/02) June 2005 [Total 9]

Answer

4 The table below shows data for the intensity of a parallel beam of X-rays after penetration through varying thicknesses of a material.

Intensity/MW m^{-2}	Thickness/mm
0.91	0.40
0.69	0.80
0.52	1.20
0.40	1.60
0.30	2.00
0.23	2.40
0.17	2.80

a Plot a graph of transmitted X-ray intensity against thickness of absorber. [3]

b i Find the thickness that reduces the intensity of the incident beam by one half. [1]

ii Use your answer to **b i** to calculate the linear attenuation coefficient μ. Give the unit for your answer. [4]

Hint

OCR Physics A2 (2825/02) January 2006 [Total 8]

Answer

5 Describe the use of a contrast medium, such as barium, in the imaging of internal body structures. Your answer should include:

● how an image of an internal body structure is produced from an X-ray beam
● an explanation of the use of a contrast medium
● examples of the types of structure that can be imaged by this process. [8]

OCR Physics A2 (2825/02) January 2006 [Total 8]

Answer

Chapter 16

Diagnostic methods in medicine

e-Learning

Objectives

Using radioisotopes

As we saw in the last chapter, X-rays are used to diagnose problems in a patient because they can be generated *outside* the body and then directed through the patient's body to produce an image. An alternative approach is to place a source of radiation *inside* the patient and use the radiation that emerges from inside the body to produce an image.

An example of this approach is where a patient undergoes a bone scan (to see whether there is cancerous tissue in their bones). The patient is given an injection containing the radioactive substance. They then have a few hours in which to relax while the material circulates around their body. Next, they are placed in a machine called a gamma camera (Figure 16.1) which detects γ-rays coming from inside their body. The result is an image showing points in the body where the radioisotope has accumulated (Figure 16.2). After the scan, the patient must take care to flush the toilet twice after use and to avoid kissing other people – this is because the radioisotope is still active for several hours and it is present in their saliva and urine.

In this chapter, we will look in detail at some ways in which radioisotopes (also known as radionuclides) are used for diagnosis. Radioisotopes are also used in treatment, where the radiation they produce is used to destroy harmful tissue, particularly cancerous tumours.

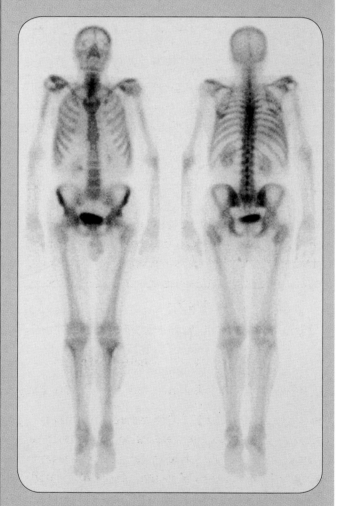

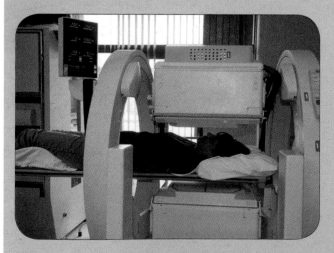

Figure 16.1 A female patient undergoing a bone scan in a gamma camera. There are two detectors, one above the patient and one below.

Figure 16.2 Bone scan images of a healthy patient. The radionuclide has been taken up by the patient's bones; there is a lot of it in the bladder also.

Choosing a radionuclide

All radioactive substances decay, some more quickly than others. There are several hundred different radionuclides which are found in Nature or which can be created in a nuclear reactor or a small *lin*ear particle *ac*celerator (linac). So which ones are suitable for medical purposes?

The radionuclide is put into the patient's body and its radiation detected. This requires that the substance chosen should be a gamma emitter. (An alpha or beta source is not suitable because the body will absorb the α- or β-particles. These types of radiation are also extremely lethal inside the body because of their strong ionising properties.)

The radionuclide should also have a short half-life. There are two reasons for this.

1 It will give out its radiation quickly, so that only a small amount is needed to form an image in the gamma camera.

2 Any radionuclide that remains in the patient will soon decay away, ensuring that they are not exposed to hazardous levels of radiation.

The problem then is that, if a hospital buys a batch of a short-lived radioisotope, it has bought something that is rapidly decaying away. What can be done to stop it decaying before the hospital has time to make use of it?

One solution is illustrated by a radioisotope called *technetium-99m*. This is an isotope of the element technetium (Tc) with nucleon number 99. Tc-99m is produced when molybdenum-99 undergoes β decay. This happens in two stages:

$$^{99}_{42}\text{Mo} \longrightarrow {}^{99}_{43}\text{Tc}^{m} + {}^{0}_{-1}\text{e} + \bar{\nu} \quad \text{half-life 67 h}$$

$$^{99}_{43}\text{Tc}^{m} \longrightarrow {}^{99}_{43}\text{Tc} + \gamma \quad \text{half-life 6 h}$$

$$^{99}_{43}\text{Tc} \text{ decays by } \beta \text{ emission} \quad \text{half-life } 2.1 \times 10^5 \text{ years}$$

The 'm' indicates that $^{99}_{43}\text{Tc}^{m}$ is **metastable**, that is, it remains in an energetic state for some time before decaying by γ emission. Each γ-ray photon has an energy of 140 keV. How does this solve the hospital's problem? The nuclear medicine department of the hospital buys a supply of Mo-99, which is produced in a nuclear reactor. The Mo-99 then produces Tc-99m at a predictable rate, and this can then be extracted for use with patients.

Figure 16.3 shows the system used for the extraction ('elution') of Tc-99m from the container of Mo-99. A saline solution is passed through the container, and this dissolves out the Tc-99m.

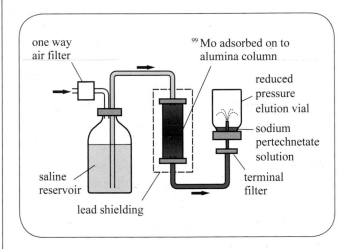

Figure 16.3 A simplified diagram of a technetium-99m generator. It is designed to minimise the risk that the technician will be exposed to radiation. An evacuated collection vial on the output side draws saline from the reservoir through the column. Here the saline dissolves the technetium to form a solution of sodium pertechnetate.

Radiopharmaceuticals

To ensure that the radioisotope reaches the correct organ, it must be converted into a **radiopharmaceutical**. This means that it is chemically combined with other elements to produce a substance which will be taken up by the tissue of interest. For example, for a bone scan, Tc-99 m is combined with a phosphorus-containing compound and the patient injected with a dose of activity about 600 MBq. This is taken up by bone tissue, particularly cancerous tissue where there is a high rate of metabolism as new cells are being formed.

Because radiopharmaceuticals are designed to target particular organs or tissues in the body, they are often described as **tracers**.

A summary of a few radioisotopes used by hospitals and their diagnostic use is given in Table 16.1.

Radioisotope	Uses
fluorine-18 ($^{18}_{9}$F)	bone imaging
technetium-99m ($^{99}_{43}$Tc^m)	bone growth blood circulation in lung, brain and liver function of heart and liver
iodine-123 ($^{123}_{53}$I)	function of thyroid function of kidney
xenon-133 ($^{133}_{54}$Xe)	function of lung

Table 16.1 Some radioisotopes used in hospitals and their uses.

SAQ

1 Mo-99 is used to produce Tc-99m. The half-life of molybdenum-99 is 67 h.

  a Explain why a hospital will require supplies of this substance to be delivered each week.

  b Explain why it would be inconvenient if the half-life of Mo-99 was much longer than 67 h, and if it was much shorter than 67 h.

  Answer

The gamma camera

It is over 50 years since the gamma camera (Figure 16.1) was first invented, and it is now the major imaging device used in diagnostic nuclear medicine. It detects γ-ray photons coming from sources such as technetium-99m inside the patient.

Inside the camera is a single, very large crystal of sodium iodide with about 0.5% of thallium iodide, typically between 400 and 500 mm in diameter and 9–12 mm thick. This crystal is a scintillator; that is, a gamma photon incident on this material may produce a flash of visible light in the crystal.

Figure 16.4 shows how the gamma camera constructs an image of the patient's insides from these flashes of light.

- The gamma photons pass upwards through the **collimator**. The collimator consists of a honeycomb of cylindrical tubes in a lead plate. The scintillator detects only photons travelling along the axis of these tubes. It therefore cuts out any γ-rays travelling at an angle to the scintillator.

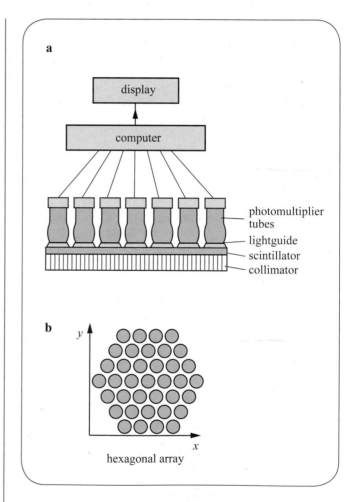

Figure 16.4 a The structure of a gamma camera. **b** The arrangement of photomultipliers.

- The beam of gamma photons then strikes the scintillator crystal, where each photon produces a flash of light. About 10% of the incident γ-ray photon energy is converted into visible light.
- The light is detected by one or more of the **photomultiplier tubes** which produce an electrical pulse for each photon of light they receive. The photomultipliers are arranged in a hexagonal array over the surface of the crystal. Figure 16.5 shows a single photomultiplier tube.
- The incident gamma photon strikes the scintillator crystal to produce photons of visible light. A single light photon releases a single electron from the photocathode by the process of photoelectric effect. This electron is accelerated to the +100 V electrode (dynode) and on impact releases two or three 'secondary' electrons. This process is repeated at each electrode and soon there is an avalanche of electrons. These eventually give rise to an electrical pulse at the last electrode. Thus a single electrical pulse is produced by a single photon of light incident on the photocathode.
- The electrical signals from the photomultipliers are processed electronically by a computer to produce a high-quality image on a screen. The output from each photomultiplier corresponds to a single point or pixel on the screen.

Uses of the gamma camera

A gamma camera is used in a bone scan. This is an example of a static study, in which a single image is produced a suitable time after the injection of the tracer.

Another use is in situations where it is desired to see the progress of the tracer through the body. An example is a kidney scan (a renogram – see Figure 16.6). The patient is given a radiopharmaceutical which will pass through their system and be excreted by the kidneys. A series of images of the kidneys are made over a period of time to see the process of excretion as it happens. This is an example of a dynamic study.

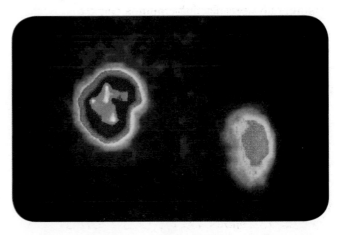

Figure 16.6 A gamma camera image of a patient's kidneys. The image, called a scintigram, has been coloured to show how the intensity of the γ-rays varies. The kidney on the left is functioning normally while the one on the right has very limited blood flow through it.

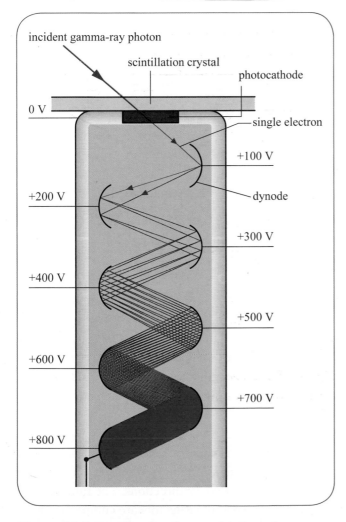

Figure 16.5 Details of a photomultiplier tube.

SAQ

2 A gamma camera can be adjusted by changing the collimator.

   a The collimator is changed to one with lead tubes of larger diameter. Explain why this will allow a shorter exposure time, but will give a less well-defined image.

   b If the collimator is changed to one with lead tubes of longer length, more γ-rays will be cut out as they cannot pass through to the scintillator crystal. How will this affect the exposure time and the definition of the image?

> Answer

Positron emission tomography

PET scanning is another technique which uses the fact that gamma rays can emerge from a source inside the body. The name is an abbreviation of **positron emission tomography**. As with CAT scanning, the word *tomography* implies that images of slices through the body can be obtained (using computer manipulation of the image data).

The radiopharmaceuticals used in a PET scan contain radioisotopes that emit positrons; that is, they are β^+ emitters. An example is fluorine-18, which decays like this:

$$^{18}_{9}F \longrightarrow \, ^{18}_{8}O + \, ^{0}_{+1}e + \gamma + \nu$$

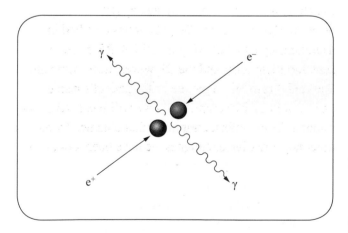

Figure 16.7 Positron–electron annihilation. The masses of the positron e⁺ and electron e⁻ appear as the energy of the two gamma photons.

However, it is not the gamma photon emitted in this decay that we are interested in. Rather, it is the positron $^{0}_{+1}e$ that is useful. Once emitted, it soon collides with an electron and the two are annihilated. Their mass is released as energy in the form of two gamma photons. These are emitted at 180° to each other (see Figure 16.7). In PET scanning, it is these two gamma photons that are detected.

PET scanner

A PET scanner looks similar to a CAT scanner but, of course, it is detecting γ-rays, not X-rays. The principle is illustrated in Figure 16.8.

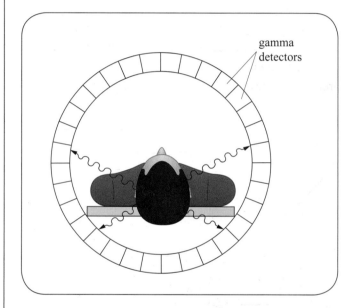

Figure 16.8 A patient undergoing a PET scan. In this case, γ-rays emitted by the tracer in the brain are being detected.

The patient is injected with a positron-emitting radiopharmaceutical, in this case a form of glucose (sugar) tagged with fluorine-18. This tends to accumulate in tissues with a high rate of respiration. In this case, we imagine that the doctors are looking at brain function, so the tracer will be taken up most by active cells in the brain.

The patient is surrounded by a ring of gamma detectors (similar to those in a gamma camera). These detect pairs of γ-rays coming from inside the patient and travelling in *opposite* directions. The times at which they arrive at the detectors are compared and from this the position at which they were emitted can be determined. Because gamma photons travel at the speed of light, the time interval that must be measured is very small.

Gradually, a three-dimensional image of the distribution of radioactive tracer in the patient is built up and, from this, any abnormal functioning can be deduced. An image of a slice through the patient can be viewed on a computer screen.

Uses of PET scanning

PET scanning is an important diagnostic tool, in particular for showing up cancerous tissue. However, it has also proved very useful in showing up aspects of normal bodily functions, such as brain activity. Figure 16.9 shows scans of a person's brain when they were reading aloud and then silently. Different areas of the brain are active in these apparently similar situations.

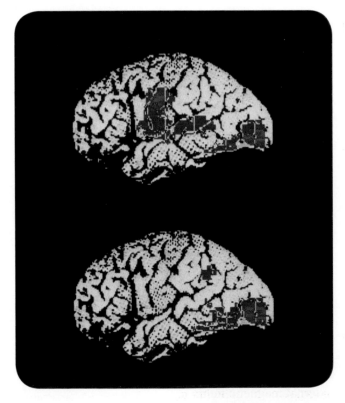

Figure 16.9 Artificially coloured PET scans of a human brain when the subject was reading aloud (top) and silently (bottom). Reading aloud requires extra areas of the brain to be active in order to control the mouth and tongue and to listen to the sounds produced.

SAQ

3 Fluorine-18 is a β^+-emitting radioisotope commonly used in PET scanning. Its half-life is 110 minutes. Suggest why this makes it a good choice for this purpose.

      Answer

4 Tomography is a type of imaging.
   a Describe how tomography differs from conventional imaging.
   b Describe how a PET scan forms a tomographic image.

      Answer

Extension

Magnetic resonance imaging

Magnetic resonance imaging, or MRI, is another technique from nuclear medicine. However, it does not rely on nuclides that are radioactive; rather, it relies on the fact that some atomic nuclei behave like tiny magnets in an external magnetic field.

(MRI was originally known as *nuclear magnetic resonance imaging*, but the word 'nuclear' was dropped because it was associated in patients' minds with bombs and power stations. To emphasise: MRI does not involve radioactive decay, fission or fusion.)

As in CAT scanning, PET scanning and the gamma camera, MRI scanning involves electromagnetic radiation, in this case radio frequency (RF) electromagnetic waves. The patient lies on a bed in a strong magnetic field (Figure 16.10), RF waves are sent into their body, and the RF waves that emerge are detected. From this, a picture of the patient's insides can be built up by computer. As we will see, MRI gives rather different information from that obtained by the other non-invasive techniques we have been looking at.

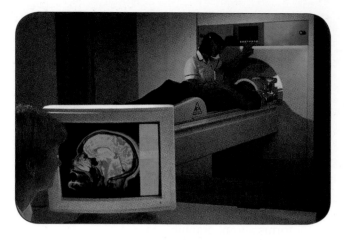

Figure 16.10 A patient undergoing an MRI scan of the brain. This is a form of tomography; the display shows different 'slices' through the patient's brain.

Principles of nuclear magnetic resonance

The nuclei of certain atoms have a property called **spin**, and this causes them to behave as tiny magnets in a magnetic field. In MRI, it is usually the nuclei

of hydrogen atoms that are studied, since hydrogen atoms are present in all tissues. A hydrogen nucleus is a proton, so we will consider protons from now on.

A proton has positive charge. Because it spins, it behaves like a tiny magnet with N and S poles. Figure 16.11a shows a number of protons aligned randomly.

When a very strong external magnetic field is applied, the protons respond by lining up in the field (just as plotting compasses line up to show the direction of a magnetic field). Most line up with their N poles facing the S pole of the external field, a low energy state; a few line up the other way round, which is an unstable, higher energy state (Figure 16.11b).

A proton does not align itself directly along the external field. In practice, its magnetic axis rotates around the direction of the external field (Figure 16.12), just like the axis of a spinning top. This rotation or gyration action is known as **precession**.

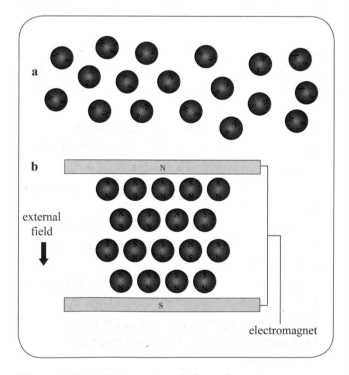

Figure 16.11 How protons behave in a strong magnetic field. **a** Protons are randomly directed when there is no external magnetic field. **b** Because protons are magnetic, a strong external magnetic field causes most of them to align themselves with the field.

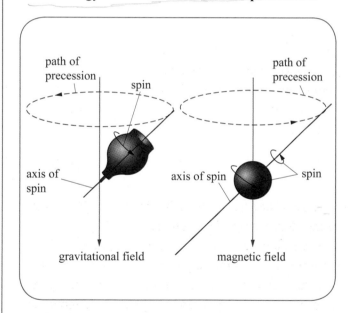

Figure 16.12 A spinning top (left) rotates about its axis; at the same time, its axis precesses about the vertical, which is the direction of the gravitational field. In a similar way, a proton (right) spins and its axis of rotation precesses about the direction of the external magnetic field.

The angular frequency of precession is called the **Larmor frequency** ω_0, and depends on the individual nucleus and the magnetic flux density B_0 of the magnetic field:

$$\omega_0 = \gamma B_0$$

So, the stronger the external field, the faster the protons precess about it. The quantity γ is called the gyromagnetic ratio for the nucleus in question and is a measure of its magnetism. (Note that the Larmor frequency is measured in radians per second. This means that, strictly speaking, it is not a frequency.)

For protons, γ has the approximate value $2.68 \times 10^8 \, \mathrm{rad\,s^{-1}\,T^{-1}}$. To determine the frequency f_0 of the precessing nuclei, we can use the equation

$$\omega_0 = 2\pi f_0$$

Therefore:

$$f_0 = \frac{\gamma B_0}{2\pi}$$

In an MRI scanner, the external magnetic field is very strong, of the order of 1.5 T (thousands of times the strength of the Earth's field). The precession frequency f_0 is

$$f_0 = \frac{2.68 \times 10^8 \times 1.5}{2\pi} = 6.4 \times 10^7 \, \mathrm{Hz} = 64 \, \mathrm{MHz}$$

This frequency lies in the radio frequency (RF) region of the electromagnetic spectrum.

You should recall that **resonance** requires a system with a natural frequency of vibration; when it is stimulated with energy of the same frequency, it absorbs energy. In MRI, protons precessing about the strong external field are exposed to a burst or pulse of RF waves whose frequency equals the frequency of precession. Each proton absorbs a photon of RF energy and flips up into the higher energy state; this is nuclear magnetic resonance (Figure 16.13).

Now we come to the useful bit. The RF waves are switched off and the protons gradually relax into their lower energy state. As they do so, they release their excess energy in the form of RF waves. These can be detected, and the rate of *relaxation* tells us something about the environment of the protons.

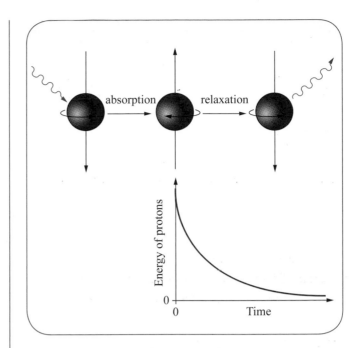

Figure 16.13 In nuclear magnetic resonance, a spinning nucleus is flipped into a higher energy state when it absorbs a photon of RF energy; then it relaxes back to its lower energy state.

In Figure 16.13, you can see that the relaxation of the protons follows an exponential decay pattern. Curves like this are characterised by two **relaxation times**:

- T_1, the spin–lattice relaxation time, where the energy of the spinning nuclei is transferred to the surrounding 'lattice' of nearby atoms;
- T_2, the spin–spin relaxation time, where the energy is transferred to other spinning nuclei.

These relaxation times depend on the environment of the nuclei. For biological materials, it depends on their water content:

- Water and watery tissues (e.g. cerebrospinal fluid) have relaxation times of several seconds.
- Fatty tissues (e.g. white matter in the brain) have shorter relaxation times, several hundred milliseconds.
- Cancerous tissues have intermediate relaxation times.

This means that different tissues can be distinguished by the different rates at which they release energy after they have been forced to resonate. That is the basis of medical applications of nuclear magnetic resonance.

SAQ

5 Protons precess at a frequency of 42.6 MHz in an external field of magnetic flux density 1.0 T.

    a Determine the frequency at which will they precess in a field of magnetic flux density 2.5 T.

Hint

    b State the frequency of RF radiation that will cause the protons to resonate in this stronger magnetic field.

Answer

6 Figure 16.14 shows how the amplitude of RF waves coming from watery tissue varies after resonance. Copy the graph and add lines and labels to show the graphs you would expect to see for cancerous and fatty tissues.

Answer

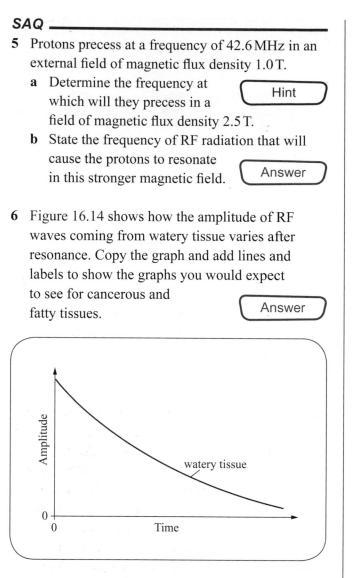

Figure 16.14 See SAQ 6.

MRI scanner

Figure 16.15 shows the main components of MRI scanner. The main features are:

- A large superconducting magnet which produces the external magnetic field (up to 2.0 T) needed to align the protons. Superconducting magnets are cooled to 4.2 K (−269 °C) using liquid helium.
- An RF coil that transmits RF pulses into the body.
- An RF coil that detects the signal emitted by the relaxing protons.
- A set of gradient coils. (For clarity, only one pair of gradient coils in shown in Figure 16.14.) These

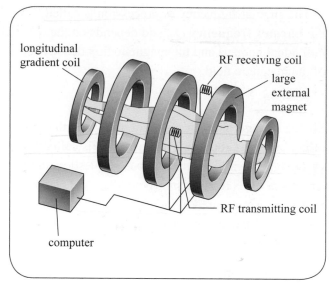

Figure 16.15 The main components of an MRI scanner.

produce an additional external magnetic field that varies across the patient's body. These coils are arranged such that they alter the magnitude of the magnetic flux density across the length, depth and width of the patient. This ensures that the Larmor frequency of the nuclei within the patient will be slightly different for each part of the body. This means that only a small volume of the body is at exactly the right field value for resonance and so the computer can precisely locate the source of the RF signal within the patient's body and construct an image.

- A computer that controls the gradient coils and RF pulses, and which stores and analyses the received data, producing and displaying images.

Procedure

The patient lies on a bed which is moved into the bore of the electromagnet. The central imaging section is about 0.9 m long and 0.6 m in diameter. The magnetic field is very uniform, with variations smaller than 50 parts per million in its strength. The gradient field is superimposed on this fixed field. An RF pulse is then transmitted into the body, causing protons to flip (resonate). Then the receiving coils pick up the relaxation signal and pass it to the computer.

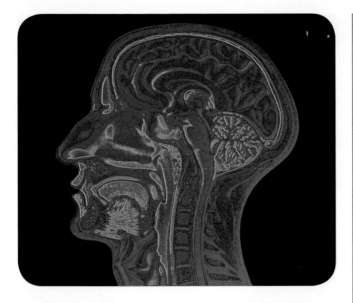

Figure 16.16 MRI scan through a healthy human head. Different tissues, identified by their different relaxation times, are coloured differently.

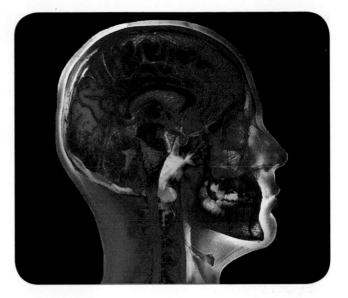

Figure 16.17 A combined CAT scan and MRI scan, showing how the tissues revealed by MRI relate to the bone structure shown by X-rays.

The result is an image like the one shown in Figure 16.16. This image has been coloured to show up the different tissues, which are identified by their different relaxation times.

Advantages and disadvantages of MRI

MRI has several advantages compared to other scanning techniques:

- It does not use ionising radiation which causes a hazard to patients and staff.
- There are no moving mechanisms, just changing currents and magnetic fields.
- The patient feels nothing during a scan (although the gradient coils are noisy as they are switched), and there are no after-effects.
- MRI gives better soft-tissue contrast than a CAT scan, although it does not show bone as clearly.
- Computer images can be generated showing any section through the volume scanned, or as a three-dimensional image.

One disadvantage of MRI is that any metallic objects in the patient, such as surgical pins, can become heated. Also, heart pacemakers can be affected, so patients with such items cannot undergo MRI scans. Loose steel objects must not be left in the room as these will be attracted to the magnet, and the room must be shielded from external radio fields.

Figure 16.17 shows how an MRI scan can be combined with a CAT scan to show detail of both bone and soft tissue, allowing medical staff to see how the two are related. Compare this with Figure 16.16.

SAQ

7 An MRI scan might be considered a safer procedure than a CAT scan.
   a Explain why it might be considered to be safer.
   b Why might a CAT scan be chosen in preference to an MRI scan?
   c Explain why MRI is described as *non-invasive*.

Answer

Summary

- Medical tracers such as technetium-99m are used to diagnose the function of organs.

- A gamma camera detects gamma radiation coming from the medical tracer in the body and deduces its position.

- The main components of a gamma camera are: collimator, scintillator crystal, photomultiplier tubes and computer.

- In PET scanning, a β^+ emitter is used as a tracer; γ-rays produced as the positrons annihilate with electrons are used to determine the position of the tracer.

- In MRI scanning, spinning, precessing protons are forced to resonate using radio frequency pulses. RF radiation from relaxing protons is used to obtain diagnostic information about internal organs, particularly soft tissues.

- The main components of an MRI scanner are: superconducting magnet, RF transmitter coil, RF receiver coil, set of gradient coils and computer.

Questions

1 a State <u>one</u> application of technetium-99m as a tracer.   [1]

  b Technetium-99m nuclei are produced when radioactive nuclei of molybdenum-99 emit β-particles.

    i Complete the nuclear reactions below:

$$^{99}_{42}\text{Mo} \longrightarrow \,^{99}_{?}\text{Tc}^{m} + \,^{0}_{-1}\text{e} + \,?$$

$$^{99}_{43}\text{Tc}^{m} \longrightarrow \,^{99}_{43}\text{Tc} + \,?$$

Hint

     [2]

    ii Suggest why technetium-99m is suitable as a tracer.   [2]

    iii Molybdenum-99 has a half-life of 67 h. The initial activity of a sample of molybdenum is 600 MBq. For this sample of molybdenum, calculate:

      1 the decay constant in s^{-1} [1]

      2 the initial mass in grams of the sample   [3]

      3 the activity of the sample after 30 h.   [2]

Hint

        [Total 11]

Answer

2 This question is about magnetic resonance imaging (MRI).

  a Explain what is meant by:

    i the Larmor frequency ω_0 of nuclei   [2]

    ii relaxation time of nuclei.   [3]

  b Describe <u>two</u> advantages of MRI compared with a CAT scan.   [2]

  c Outline some of the main components of an MRI scanner.   [5]

        [Total 12]

Answer

continued

3 a The diagram below shows the key components of a gamma camera.

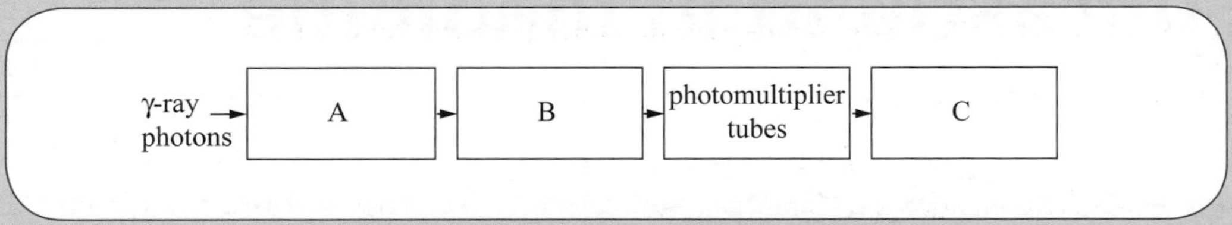

γ-ray photons $\rightarrow$ | A | $\rightarrow$ | B | $\rightarrow$ | photomultiplier tubes | $\rightarrow$ | C |

Name each component A, B and C and state its function.   [6]

b A photomultiplier tube has 10 electrodes known as dynodes. An electron emitted from the photocathode is accelerated towards the first dynode. On impact, it produces, on average, three 'secondary' electrons. These are accelerated towards the second dynode and the whole process is repeated. An electrical pulse lasting for 2.0 ns at the tenth dynode is produced. Calculate:

i   the total number of electrons at the tenth dynode as a result of a single electron impacting the first dynode   [2]

ii the average current from the last dynode.   [3]

[Total 11]

Hint

Hint

Answer

Chapter 17

Using ultrasound in medicine

e-Learning

Objectives

Family photos

Ultrasound scanning is routinely used to check the condition of a baby in the womb (Figure 17.1). There do not seem to be any harmful side-effects associated with this procedure, and it can provide useful information on the baby's development. Indeed, for many children, their first appearance in the family photo album is in the form of an ante-natal (before birth) scan!

This technique has many other uses in medicine. It can be used to detect gallstones or kidney stones (two very painful complaints), so men as well as women may experience this type of scan.

The technique of ultrasound scanning is rather similar to the way in which sailors use echosounding and echolocation to detect the seabed and shoals of fish. Ultrasound waves are directed into the patient's body. These waves are partially reflected at the boundaries between different tissues and the reflected waves are detected and used to construct the image.

In this chapter, we will look at the principles of ultrasound scanning and we will also look at another technique in which ultrasound is used to measure the rate of blood flow in the body.

Figure 17.1 An expectant mother undergoes an ultrasound scan. The image of her baby is built up by computer and appears on the monitor.

Working with ultrasound

Ultrasound is any sound wave that has a frequency above the upper limit of human hearing. This is usually taken to imply frequencies above 20 kHz (20 000 Hz), although the limit of hearing decreases with age to well below this figure. In medical applications, the typical frequencies used are in the megahertz range.

Sound waves are longitudinal waves. They can only pass through a material medium; they cannot pass through a vacuum. The speed of sound (and hence of ultrasound) depends on the material. In air, it is approximately $330\,\mathrm{m\,s^{-1}}$; it is higher in solid materials. A typical value for body tissue is $1500\,\mathrm{m\,s^{-1}}$. Using the wave equation $v = f\lambda$, we can calculate the wavelength of 2.0 MHz ultrasound waves in tissue:

$$\lambda = \frac{v}{f} = \frac{1500}{2.0 \times 10^6}$$

$$\lambda = 7.5 \times 10^{-4}\,\mathrm{m} \approx 1\,\mathrm{mm}$$

This means that 2.0 MHz ultrasound waves will be able to distinguish detailed features whose dimensions are of the order of 1 mm. Higher-frequency waves have shorter wavelengths and these are used to detect smaller features inside the body.

Producing ultrasound

Like audible sound, ultrasound is produced by a vibrating source. The frequency of the source is the same as the frequency of the waves it produces. In ultrasound scanning, ultrasonic waves are produced by a device in which a varying electrical voltage is used to generate ultrasound. The same device also acts as a detector. This device is known as a **transducer**; this is a general term used to describe any device that changes one form of energy into another.

At the heart of the transducer is a **piezoelectric crystal**. This is a crystal that has a useful property: when a voltage is applied across it in one direction, it shrinks slightly – see Figure 17.2a. When the voltage is reversed, it expands slightly. So an alternating voltage with frequency f causes the crystal to contract and expand at the same frequency f. We say that the voltage induces a strain in the crystal. In the best piezoelectric substances, the maximum value of strain is about 0.1%; in other words, the crystal's width changes by about 0.1%.

In a piezoelectric transducer, an alternating voltage is applied across the crystal, which then acts as the vibrating source of ultrasound waves. A brief pulse of ultrasound waves is sent into the patient's body; the transducer then receives an extended pulse of reflected ultrasound waves.

Detecting ultrasound

The transducer also acts as the detector of reflected ultrasound waves. It can do this because the piezoelectric effect works in reverse: a varying stress applied to the crystal produces a varying e.m.f. across the crystal – see Figure 17.2b. To maximise the effect, the frequency of the waves must match the resonant frequency of the crystal. The optimum size of the crystal is half the wavelength ($\frac{\lambda}{2}$) of the ultrasound waves.

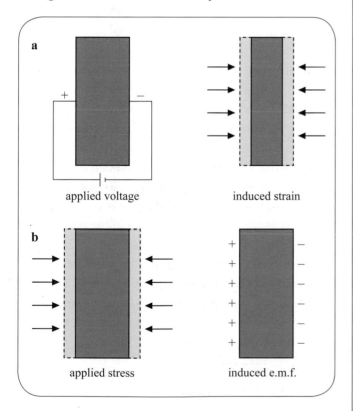

Figure 17.2 The piezoelectric effect. **a** An applied voltage causes a piezoelectric crystal to contract or expand. **b** An applied stress causes an induced e.m.f. across the crystal.

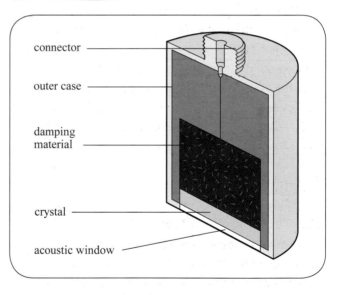

Figure 17.3 A section through an ultrasound transducer.

Figure 17.3 shows the construction of a piezoelectric ultrasound transducer. Note the following features:

- The crystal is now usually made of polyvinylidene difluoride. Previously, quartz and lead zirconate titanate were used.
- The outer case supports and protects the crystal.

- At the base is the acoustic window made from a material that is a good transmitter of ultrasound.
- Behind the crystal is a large block of damping material (usually epoxy resin). This helps to stop the crystal vibrating when a pulse of ultrasound has been generated. This is necessary so that the crystal is not vibrating when the incoming, reflected ultrasound waves reach the transducer.

SAQ

1 Quartz is an example of a piezoelectric material. The speed of sound in quartz is $5700\,\mathrm{m\,s^{-1}}$.
   a Calculate the wavelength of ultrasound waves of frequency 2.1 MHz in a quartz crystal. | Hint |
   b If the crystal is to be used in an ultrasound transducer, its thickness must be half a wavelength. Calculate the thickness of the transducer. | Answer |

2 Piezoelectric crystals have many applications other than in ultrasound scanning. For example, they are used:
   a in gas lighters (to produce a spark)
   b in inkjet printers (to break up the stream of ink into droplets)
   c in guitar pickups (to connect the guitar to an amplifier)
   d in the auto-focus mechanism of some cameras (to move the lens back and forth).
   For each of these examples, state whether the piezoelectric effect is being used to convert mechanical energy to electrical energy or the other way round. | Answer |

Echosounding

The principle of an ultrasound scan is to direct ultrasound waves into the body. These pass through various tissues and are partially reflected at each

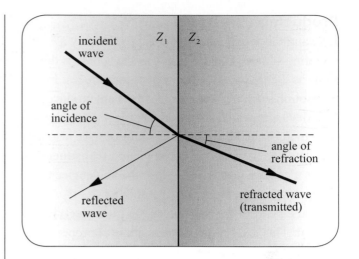

Figure 17.4 An ultrasound wave is both refracted and reflected when it strikes the boundary between two different materials.

boundary where the wave speed changes. The reflected waves are then detected and used to construct an internal image of the body.

Figure 17.4 shows what happens when a beam of ultrasound reaches a boundary between two different media. The beam is partially refracted (so that the transmitted beam has changed direction) and partially reflected. This diagram should remind you of the way in which a ray of light is refracted and reflected when it strikes the boundary between two media. It is the change in speed which causes the refraction of a wave.

For ultrasound, we are interested in the fraction of the incident intensity of ultrasound that is reflected at the boundary. This depends on the **acoustic impedance** Z of each material. This quantity depends on the density ρ and the speed of sound c in the material. Acoustic impedance is defined as follows:

acoustic impedance = density × speed of sound

$$Z = \rho c$$

The unit of acoustic impedance Z is $\mathrm{kg\,m^{-2}\,s^{-1}}$.

Material	Density $\rho/\mathrm{kg\,m^{-3}}$	Speed of sound $c/\mathrm{m\,s^{-1}}$	Acoustic impedance $Z/10^6\ \mathrm{kg\,m^{-2}\,s^{-1}}$
air	1.3	330	0.0004
water	1000	1500	1.50
Biological			
blood	1060	1570	1.66
fat	925	1450	1.34
soft tissue (average)	1060	1540	1.63
muscle	1075	1590	1.71
bone (average; adult)	1600	4000	6.40
Transducers			
barium titanate	5600	5500	30.8
lead zirconate titanate	7650	3790	29.0
quartz	2650	5700	15.1
polyvinylidene difluoride	1780	2360	4.20

Table 17.1 Ultrasound properties of some materials important in medical scanning.

Table 17.1 shows values of ρ, c and Z for some materials that are important in medical ultrasonography.

Calculating reflected intensities

When an ultrasound beam reaches the boundary between two materials, the greater the *difference* in acoustic impedances, the greater the fraction of the ultrasound waves that is reflected. For normal incidence (i.e. angle of incidence = 0°) the ratio of the reflected intensity I_r to the incident intensity I_0 is given by:

$$\frac{I_r}{I_0} = \frac{(Z_2 - Z_1)^2}{(Z_2 + Z_1)^2}$$

or

$$\frac{I_r}{I_0} = \left(\frac{Z_2 - Z_1}{Z_2 + Z_1}\right)^2$$

where Z_1 and Z_2 are the acoustic impedances of the two materials (see Figure 17.4). The ratio $\dfrac{I_r}{I_0}$ indicates the fraction of the intensity of the beam that is reflected.

Now look at Worked example 1.

Worked example 1

A beam of ultrasound is normally incident on the boundary between muscle and bone. Use Table 17.1 to determine the fraction of its intensity reflected.

Step 1 Write down the values of Z_1 (for muscle) and Z_2 (for bone).

$$Z_1 = 1.71 \times 10^6\ \mathrm{kg\,m^{-2}\,s^{-1}}$$
$$Z_2 = 6.40 \times 10^6\ \mathrm{kg\,m^{-2}\,s^{-1}}$$

Step 2 Substitute these values in the equation for $\dfrac{I_r}{I_0}$; note that we can use this equation because we know that the angle of incidence = 0°.

$$\frac{I_r}{I_0} = \frac{(Z_2 - Z_1)^2}{(Z_2 + Z_1)^2}$$

$$= \frac{(6.40 - 1.71)^2}{(6.40 + 1.71)^2}$$

$$= 0.33$$

Note also that we can ignore the factor of 10^6 in the Z values because this is a factor common to all the values, so they cancel out.

So 33% of the intensity of ultrasound will be reflected at the muscle–bone boundary.

Comparing acoustic impedances

A big change in acoustic impedance gives a large fraction of reflected intensity. Inspection of Table 17.1 shows that:

- a very large fraction ($\frac{I_r}{I_0} \approx 99.95\%$) of the incident ultrasound will be reflected at an air–tissue boundary

- a large fraction will be reflected at a tissue–bone boundary (as shown in Worked example 1)
- very little will be reflected at a boundary between soft tissues including fat and muscle.

This means that bone shows up well in an ultrasound scan, but it is difficult to see different soft tissues (Figure 17.5). Another problem is that the patient's skin is in contact with air, and 99.95% of the ultrasound will be reflected before it has entered the body. To overcome this, the transducer must be 'coupled' to the skin using a gel whose impedance matches that of the skin. This process of **impedance matching** explains why the patient's skin is smeared with gel before a scan.

The acoustic impedance of the gel is typically $1.65 \times 10^6 \, \text{kg} \, \text{m}^{-2} \, \text{s}^{-1}$ and that of skin is $1.71 \times 10^6 \, \text{kg} \, \text{m}^{-2} \, \text{s}^{-1}$. With gel between the skin and the transducer, the percentage of the intensity reflected is 0.03%.

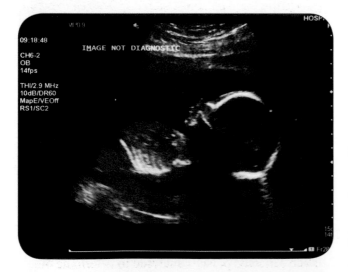

Figure 17.5 Ultrasound scan of a fetus at 20 weeks; the baby's skin is clearly visible, as are its bony skull and ribs.

The poor match of impedance between air and tissue means that ultrasound cannot penetrate the lungs. The operator must take care to avoid any bubbles of gas in the intestines. Bones are also difficult to see through. For an ultrasound scan of the heart, the probe must be directed through the gap between two ribs.

SAQ

3 Calculate the acoustic impedance of brain tissue. (Density = $1025 \, \text{kg} \, \text{m}^{-3}$, speed of sound = $1540 \, \text{m} \, \text{s}^{-1}$.)

[Answer]

4 Determine the fraction of the intensity of an ultrasound beam that is reflected when a beam is incident normally on a boundary between water and fat. (Use values from Table 17.1.)

[Answer]

5 The ultrasound image shown in Figure 17.5 clearly shows the baby's skin and some bones. Explain why these show up clearly while softer organs inside its body do not.

[Answer]

6 Explain why ultrasound cannot readily be used to examine the brain. Suggest an alternative scanning technique(s) that can be used for this.

[Answer]

Ultrasound scanning

There are several different types of ultrasound scan which are used in practice. To illustrate the basic principles, we will concentrate on the A-scan and the B-scan.

A-scan

This is the simplest type of scan. A pulse of ultrasound is sent into the body and the reflected 'echoes' are detected and displayed on an oscilloscope or computer screen as a voltage against time graph.

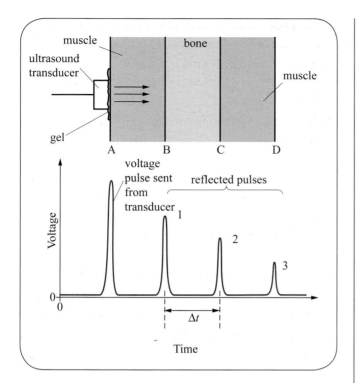

Figure 17.6 An A-scan. Information about the depth of reflecting tissues can be obtained from the positions of the spikes along the time axis; their relative amplitudes can indicate the nature of the reflecting surfaces.

A pulse generator controls the ultrasound transducer. It is also connected to the time base of the oscilloscope. Simultaneously, the pulse generator triggers a pulse of ultrasound which travels into the patient and starts a trace on the screen. Each partial reflection of the ultrasound is detected and appears as a spike on the screen (Figure 17.6).

In Figure 17.6, the pulses 1, 2 and 3 are reflected at the various boundaries. Pulse 1 is the reflection at the muscle–bone boundary at B. Pulse 2 is the reflection at the bone–muscle boundary at C. The time Δt is the time taken for the ultrasound to travel *twice* the thickness of the bone. Finally, pulse 3 is the reflection at the muscle–air boundary at D. The thickness of the bone can be determined from this A-scan.

time interval between pulses 1 and 2 = Δt

$$\text{thickness of bone} = \frac{\text{distance travelled by ultrasound}}{2}$$

$$\text{thickness of bone} = \frac{c\Delta t}{2}$$

where c is the speed of the ultrasound in the bone (see Worked example 2).

Because ultrasound waves are gradually attenuated as they pass through the body (their energy is absorbed so that their amplitude and intensity decrease), the echoes from tissues deeper in the body are weaker and must be amplified.

A-scans are used for some straightforward procedures such as measuring the thickness of the eye lens.

Worked example 2

In a particular A-scan, similar to Figure 17.6, the time interval between pulses 1 and 2 is $12\,\mu s$. The speed of ultrasound in bone is about $4000\,m\,s^{-1}$. Determine the thickness of the bone.

Step 1 Determine the distance travelled by the ultrasound in the time interval of $12\,\mu s$.

$$\text{distance} = \text{speed} \times \text{time}$$

$$\text{distance} = 4000 \times 12 \times 10^{-6} = 4.8 \times 10^{-2}\,m$$

Step 2 Calculate the thickness of the bone.

The ultrasound wave has to travel twice the thickness of the bone. Hence:

$$\text{thickness of bone} = \frac{4.8 \times 10^{-2}}{2}$$

$$= 2.4 \times 10^{-2}\,m\ (2.4\,cm)$$

B-scan

In a B-scan, a detailed image of a cross-section through the patient is built up from many A-scans. The ultrasound transducer is moved across the patient's body in the area of interest. Its position and orientation are determined by small sensors attached to it.

Each reflected pulse is analysed to determine the depth of the reflecting surface (from the time of echo) and the nature of the surface (from the amplitude of the reflected wave). A two-dimensional image is then built up on a screen by positioning dots to represent the position of the reflecting surfaces and

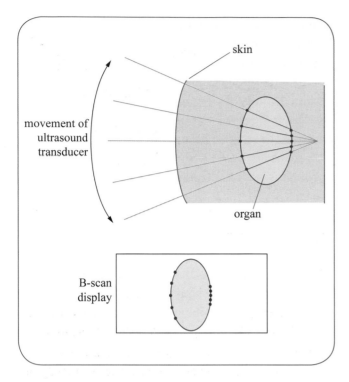

Figure 17.7 In a B-scan, dots are produced on the screen rather than the pulses as in the A-scan. By moving the transducer, a series of dots on the screen trace out the shape of the organ being examined.

with brightness determined by the intensity of the reflection, brighter dots indicating more reflected ultrasound (see Figure 17.7).

Figure 17.8 shows the result of a typical B-scan. Because it takes several seconds for the scanner to move across the body, problems can arise if the organs of interest are moving – this gives a blurred image.

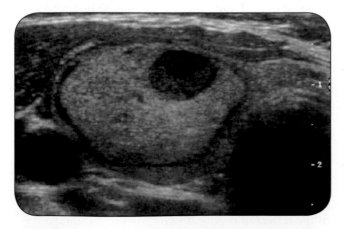

Figure 17.8 An ultrasonic B-scan of an abnormal thyroid gland.

7 Two consecutive peaks in an ultrasound A-scan are separated by a time interval of 0.034 ms. Calculate the distance between the two reflecting surfaces. (Assume that the speed of sound in the tissue between the two surfaces is 1540 m s^{-1}.)

Answer

8 Explain why an ultrasound B-scan is used to examine a fetus rather than X-rays.

Answer

Doppler ultrasound

The patient in Figure 17.9 is undergoing a different medical application of ultrasound scanning. The doctor is holding an ultrasound probe against her neck to examine the blood flow in a major artery. This relies on the **Doppler effect**.

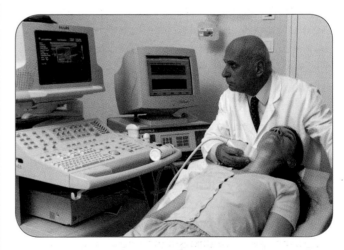

Figure 17.9 Ultrasound examination of the carotid artery in the neck, a form of Doppler ultrasonography.

The Doppler effect occurs when waves are emitted, reflected or detected by a moving object. In this case, we will consider a moving reflector – the iron-rich blood cells moving along an artery. When a pulse of ultrasound waves is sent along the artery, they are partially reflected back by the cells. The reflected waves have a slightly different wavelength and frequency, an example of the Doppler effect.

Why does this happen? If the reflecting surface is stationary, nothing unusual happens – the reflected waves are a mirror image of the incident waves, so that their wavelength is unaltered. However, if the reflector is moving away from the source, things are different. Each reflected wave is reflected from a slightly different position, slightly further away from the source. The result is that the string of reflected waves is slightly longer than the incident waves. In other words, the reflected waves are longer – they have an increased wavelength. Because their speed is unaffected, their frequency must decrease.

The greater the speed of the receding reflector, the greater the decrease in the frequency of the ultrasound waves. It follows that the speed of the receding reflector can be deduced from the change in frequency of the waves. (Note that an approaching reflector will increase the frequency of the ultrasound waves.)

Doppler ultrasonography is used to study the movement of a patient's blood along blood vessels (veins and arteries). It can show up the pulsing movement of the blood as the heart beats. More importantly, it can show whether the blood is moving smoothly (the blood moves at a uniform speed throughout the blood vessel) or whether there is turbulence (blood flows at different speeds in different regions of the vessel). This can be a sign of blockages developing, or of weakening of the walls of the vessel.

Kidney transplant patients are monitored using Doppler ultrasound to determine whether blood is flowing normally through their new organ. The technique is also used in the diagnosis of faulty heart valves.

SAQ

9 Doppler ultrasound can be used to monitor the action of the heart as it beats. At any instant, some areas of the heart will be moving towards the ultrasound probe while others will be moving away from the probe. How will the wavelength and frequency of ultrasound waves be affected when they reflect from a surface that is moving towards the probe? Explain your answer.

Answer

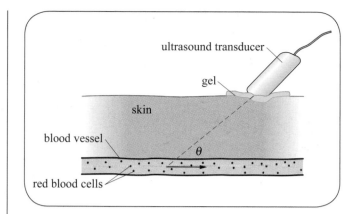

Figure 17.10 For SAQ 10.

10 Figure 17.10 shows an ultrasound transducer pointing towards a blood vessel.

The frequency of the ultrasound waves emitted by the transducer is f. The detected ultrasound waves have a higher frequency because of the Doppler effect. The change in the frequency Δf of the waves is given by the equation:

$$\Delta f = \frac{2fv\cos\theta}{c}$$

where v is the speed of the blood, θ is the angle between the incident ultrasound and the direction of the blood flow and c is the speed of the ultrasound in blood.

A transducer emitting ultrasound at frequency 6.0 MHz detects a change in frequency of 0.85 kHz when the angle between the emitted waves and the blood vessel is 58°. The speed of ultrasound in blood is 1500 m s^{-1}. The diameter of the blood vessel is 1.2 mm.

Determine the speed v of the blood flow in the vessel and the rate of flow of blood (in m^3 s^{-1}) through the vessel.

Answer

Extension

Summary

Glossary

- Ultrasound is a longitudinal mechanical wave with a frequency greater than 20 kHz.

- Ultrasound transducers use the piezoelectric effect to generate and detect ultrasound waves.

- The acoustic impedance Z of a material depends on its density ρ and the speed c of sound:
  $Z = \rho c$.

- The fraction of the intensity of an ultrasound wave reflected at a boundary is given by

$$\frac{I_r}{I_0} = \frac{(Z_2 - Z_1)^2}{(Z_2 + Z_1)^2} \qquad \text{or} \qquad \frac{I_r}{I_0} = \left(\frac{Z_2 - Z_1}{Z_2 + Z_1}\right)^2$$

- To transfer a high proportion of the intensity of an ultrasound pulse into the patient's body, an impedance-matching gel must be used with acoustic impedance almost the same as that of the skin.

- In ultrasound scanning, an A-scan uses a single pulse to determine the depth and nature of reflecting surfaces. A B-scan builds up a two-dimensional image from multiple A-scans.

- In the Doppler effect, the wavelength and frequency of a wave are altered on reflection by a moving surface. The frequency of a wave decreases for a receding source and increases for an approaching source.

- The Doppler effect can be used to determine the speed of blood in arteries.

Questions

1   a   Define *acoustic impedance* of a material and show it has unit $\text{kg m}^{-2}\text{s}^{-1}$.   [2]

   b   The acoustic impedance of air, gel and skin are $430\,\text{kg m}^{-2}\text{s}^{-1}$, $1.6\times10^6\,\text{kg m}^{-2}\text{s}^{-1}$ and $1.7\times10^6\,\text{kg m}^{-2}\text{s}^{-1}$ respectively.

     i   Calculate the fraction of intensity of the ultrasound that penetrates the air–skin boundary and the gel–skin boundary.   [6]

     ii   Explain why gel is smeared on the skin and the transducer before an ultrasound scan.   [2]

Hint

[Total 10]

Answer

2   a   Describe the principles of the production of a short pulse of ultrasound using a piezoelectric transducer.   [5]

continued

b The diagram below shows a trace on a cathode-ray oscilloscope (CRO) of an ultrasound reflection from the front edge and rear edge of a fetal head.

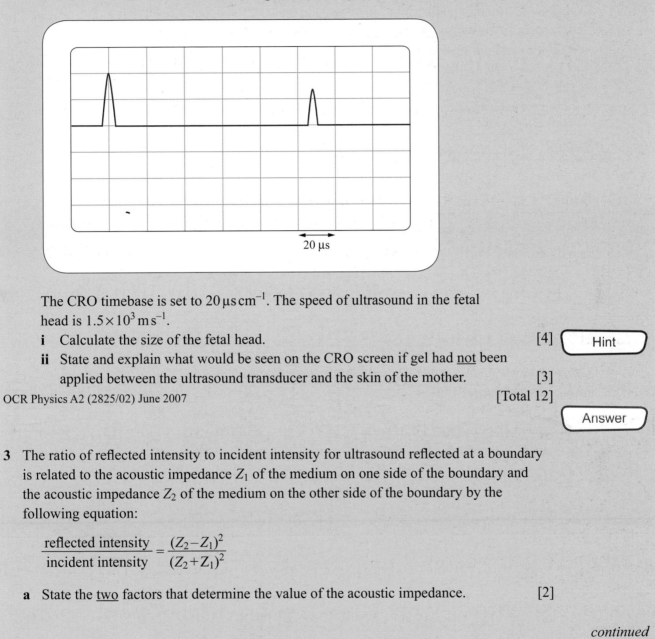

20 µs

The CRO timebase is set to $20\,\mu\text{s cm}^{-1}$. The speed of ultrasound in the fetal head is $1.5 \times 10^3\,\text{m s}^{-1}$.

i Calculate the size of the fetal head. [4]

ii State and explain what would be seen on the CRO screen if gel had <u>not</u> been applied between the ultrasound transducer and the skin of the mother. [3]

OCR Physics A2 (2825/02) June 2007 [Total 12]

Hint

Answer

3 The ratio of reflected intensity to incident intensity for ultrasound reflected at a boundary is related to the acoustic impedance Z_1 of the medium on one side of the boundary and the acoustic impedance Z_2 of the medium on the other side of the boundary by the following equation:

$$\frac{\text{reflected intensity}}{\text{incident intensity}} = \frac{(Z_2 - Z_1)^2}{(Z_2 + Z_1)^2}$$

a State the <u>two</u> factors that determine the value of the acoustic impedance. [2]

continued

b An ultrasound investigation was used to identify a small volume of substance in a patient. It is suspected that this substance is either blood or muscle.

   During the ultrasound investigation, an ultrasound pulse of frequency 3.5×10^6 Hz passed through soft tissue and then into the small volume of unidentified substance. A pulse of ultrasound reflected from the front surface of the volume was detected 26.5 μs later. The ratio of the reflected intensity to incident intensity for the ultrasound pulse reflected at this boundary was found to be 4.42×10^{-4}. The table below shows data for the acoustic impedances of various materials found in a human body.

Medium	Acoustic impedance Z/kg m^{-2} s^{-1}
air	4.29×10^2
blood	1.59×10^6
water	1.50×10^6
brain tissue	1.58×10^6
soft tissue	1.63×10^6
bone	7.78×10^6
muscle	1.70×10^6

   i Use appropriate data from the table to identify the unknown medium. You must show your reasoning. [4]
   ii Calculate the depth at which the ultrasound pulse was reflected if the speed of ultrasound in soft tissue is 1.54 km s^{-1}. [2]
   iii Calculate the wavelength of the ultrasound in the soft tissue. [2]

OCR Physics A2 (2825/02) June 2005 [Total 10]

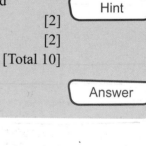

Chapter 18

The nature of the universe

e-Learning

Objectives

The cosmological principle

Looking out at a clear night sky, you might see a few hundred stars if you were lucky. You might also see the Moon and, if you knew where to look, a planet or two. The naked-eye view from the Earth allows us to see just a tiny fraction of the universe in which we live.

The universe is all the matter and energy which we can observe, or which we might in principle be able to observe. Here, we use the word 'observe' rather than 'see' because there is much out there that we cannot see with our eyes or through telescopes – cold objects that do not emit much visible light but emit other forms of electromagnetic radiation outside the visible part of the electromagnetic spectrum.

Figure 18.1 A view of several distant galaxies, taken by the Hubble Space Telescope. Many of these galaxies appear blue because they are young; blue light is characteristic of stars forming.

Today's telescopes allow us to observe far beyond our local region of the universe and across the entire spectrum. Figure 18.1 shows a view of distant galaxies taken by the Hubble Space Telescope.

All observations have to be interpreted. Is that speck of light in the night sky a star or a planet? Why does a certain star's position in the sky seem to wobble very slightly? Does that pattern of stars really represent an ancient hero called Orion? Some interpretations are better than others, but every idea about the nature of the universe must be tested by further observations.

Fortunately for us, it seems that distant regions of the universe are not very different from our own region. The light from distant galaxies is not a different kind of light; faraway stars seem similar to those nearby. This makes it easier to understand the universe as a whole, and so we can hope to develop ideas about the structure of the universe and how it has developed.

The idea that the universe has the same large-scale structure when observed from any point within it is known as the **cosmological principle**. This important principle has three facets:

- The universe is *homogeneous*. This means that on a large scale the universe is the same at all places – its density is the same everywhere.
- The universe is *isotropic*. This means that the universe is the same in all directions. Strong support for this comes from the cosmic microwave background radiation, which has the same intensity in all directions (see Chapter 19).
- The laws of physics are *universal*. This means that the same tried and tested laws of physics on the Earth can be applied to other places in the universe.

continued

This principle allows us to make observations of parts of the universe and then extrapolate them to the whole universe. If this were not the case – if distant regions consisted entirely of clusters of black holes orbiting under a previously unknown force – we would find it hard to develop any general theories of the universe.

In this chapter, you will learn a bit about scientists' current view of the nature of the universe, based on observations. Then, in Chapter 19, we will look at ideas about how the universe has evolved and come to be as it is today, and how it may end up.

The life of stars

What is out there? There are many billions of galaxies, each a large cluster of billions of stars, held together by their mutual gravitational attraction. If there are about 10^{11} stars in the average galaxy and about 10^{11} galaxies in the universe, that makes a grand total of about 10^{22} stars in the universe. Such vast numbers are beyond out everyday imaginings. Spread amongst the galaxies are electromagnetic radiation, of various sorts, fast-moving particles and clouds of dust.

Our own galaxy is the Milky Way. Our Sun is just one star in this galaxy, part way out along one of its spiral arms (Figure 18.2). The solar system consists of the Sun together with everything held within its gravitational field – the eight planets, the minor planets, natural planetary satellites such as the Moon, comets, asteroids and so on.

Figure 18.2 A spiral galaxy very similar to the Milky Way.

Most stars live for a very long time – millions or even billions of years. We do not have scientific records going back that far, so we have to rely on the fact that we can see vast numbers of stars. We must assume that those that we see represent stars at all stages of their lives. This means that we can deduce the life history of stars from the evidence gathered over the last century or two. (This is a bit like observing the population of a town. You would see smaller people and bigger ones, and it would not take you long to deduce how people grow up, get older and die.)

The birth, life and death of the Sun

We will start by focusing on the Sun since it is a fairly ordinary star. Then we will consider how the life cycles of other stars might differ.

Stars like the Sun form from clouds of interstellar dust and gas. The main elements are the gases hydrogen and helium, together with small amounts of other elements such as iron, silicon and carbon. This is material that is scattered thinly throughout the galaxy. Where it is denser, its own gravity causes material to pull together and contract to form a denser mass. This has a stronger pull, so that more matter is pulled in, and so on. This process is known as **gravitational collapse**.

Although space is very cold, the interstellar dust and gas heats up as it collapses. This is because it is losing gravitational potential energy and gaining kinetic energy. The particles collide with each other, sharing out their energy and getting hotter in the process. In effect, they form a gas whose internal energy is increasing. (Recall that, in Chapter 7, in the section 'Temperature and molecular kinetic energy', we saw that the internal energy of a gas is directly proportional to its thermodynamic temperature.)

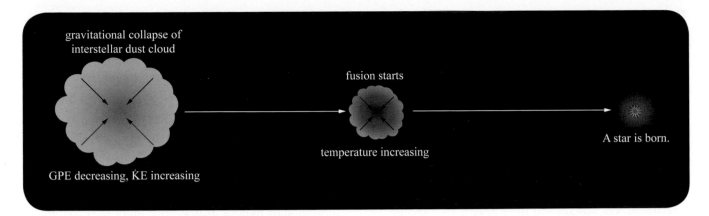

gravitational collapse of
interstellar dust cloud

fusion starts

A star is born.

temperature increasing

GPE decreasing, KE increasing

Figure 18.3 Stages in the formation of a star.

At the centre of this collapsing dust and gas cloud, the material becomes very hot and dense. A star is forming – see Figure 18.3 and Figure 18.4. When its temperature is high enough ($\sim 10^7$ K), fusion reactions start, with hydrogen nuclei fusing to form helium nuclei and nuclei of other light elements. The fusion of hydrogen into helium is known as **hydrogen burning**, represented by the following nuclear equation:

$$4\,^1_1\text{H} \longrightarrow \,^4_2\text{He} + 2\,^0_{+1}\text{e} + 2\nu$$

The chance of four hydrogen nuclei interacting to produce a helium nucleus is almost zero. The equation above is really a summary of the proton–proton cycle:

$$^1_1\text{H} + \,^1_1\text{H} \longrightarrow \,^2_1\text{H} + \,^0_{+1}\text{e} + \nu$$

$$^1_1\text{H} + \,^2_1\text{H} \longrightarrow \,^3_2\text{He} + \gamma$$

$$^3_2\text{He} + \,^3_2\text{He} \longrightarrow \,^4_2\text{He} + 2\,^1_1\text{H}$$

(In these equations, γ is a gamma-ray photon and ν is a neutrino.) The fusion reactions release energy as mass is converted into energy in accordance with Einstein's mass–energy equation $\Delta E = \Delta mc^2$. This increases the temperature of the stellar material even more rapidly than if the collapse was entirely due to gravitational forces. Once this happens, the star will glow for millions or billions of years.

A star reaches a steady temperature when the power released by fusion reactions is equal to the power radiated away from the star. The star has a stable size because of equilibrium between the attractive gravitational forces and outward forces due to **radiation pressure** from the photons released by the star fusion reactions.

The gravitational collapse of the interstellar dust and gas results in a spinning star with a small fraction of the material ($< 1\%$) orbiting around the star. Again, gravity is at work, pulling matter together to form planets, planetary satellites and the other objects that orbit the star.

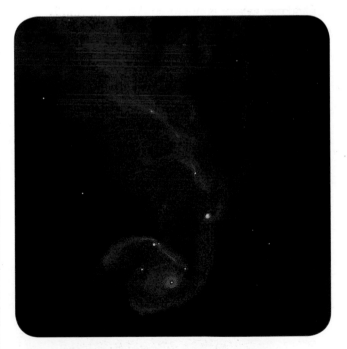

Figure 18.4 A computer simulation of star formation. It is impossible to photograph such an event as the material is cold and dark, but this image generated by a computer model shows how it might look. Several stars are forming from a cloud of interstellar matter.

The ageing Sun

The Sun is thought to have existed for about 4.5 billion years, as has the Earth. It is likely to go on shining for at least as long again, but eventually its store of hydrogen fuel will start to run low. The description below describes the evolution of the Sun or of any star with a mass less than about 3 solar masses.

As the temperature and pressure of the innermost parts of a star increase, more complex fusion reactions can occur and these produce other elements such as carbon, silicon and iron. Figure 18.5 shows the typical structure of the core of an ageing star.

As the rate of fusion reactions slows down, the core of the star starts to collapse under gravitational attraction. The thin shell of helium nuclei surrounding the core of the star start to fuse to produce beryllium, carbon and oxygen nuclei. A thin layer of the hydrogen shell surrounding the helium-rich core becomes sufficiently hot to fuse hydrogen nuclei again. The increased power production from the helium shell causes the outer shell of the star to expand due to radiation pressure. The size of the star increases and its surface temperature drops. It becomes a **red giant**. When our Sun becomes a red giant, it will engulf the closest planets – Mercury, Venus and possibly Earth. Figure 18.6 gives an idea of the relative sizes of a Sun-like star and a red giant.

The core continues to collapse. Its density and temperature increase. The helium nuclei in the outer shell reach a temperature of about 10^8 K and start to fuse together at a phenomenal rate. In a process known as the *helium flash*, the material surrounding the core is ejected away as a **planetary nebula** (Figure 18.7). Note that the term 'planetary nebula' can be misleading – it has nothing to do with the formation of planets as was once thought.

A bright central core is left behind. This remnant is known as a **white dwarf**. It gradually cools and dims over a period of millions of years. Here are some characteristics of a white dwarf:

- No fusion of hydrogen occurs in a white dwarf. It glows because photons produced by fusion reactions in the past are still leaking away from it.
- It is very dense. A teaspoon of white dwarf material will have a mass of 5 tonnes.
- As the material of the star becomes more compressed, electrons are no longer attached to individual atoms but move freely throughout the star in the state of matter called plasma.

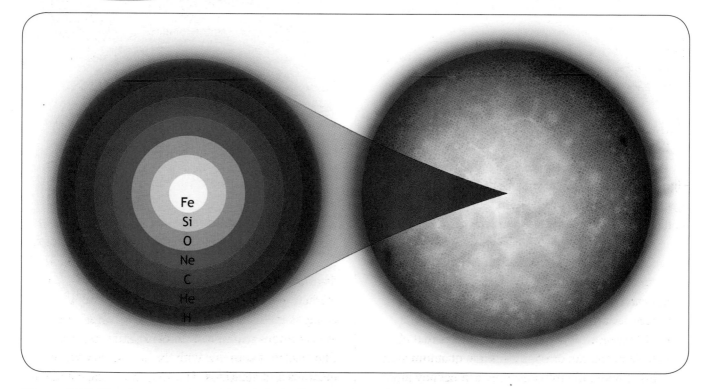

Figure 18.5 The tiny core of an old star shows layers where elements are made by fusion reactions.

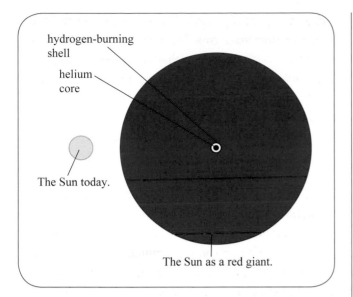

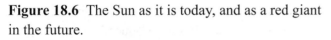

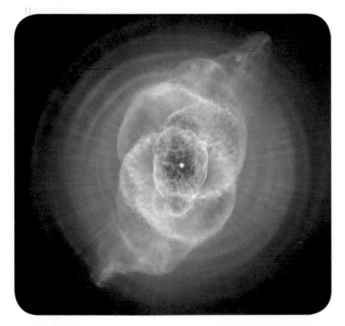

Figure 18.6 The Sun as it is today, and as a red giant in the future.

Figure 18.7 The Cat's Eye nebula lies around 3600 light years from Earth in the constellation Draco. At the centre, you can see a white dwarf.

- A white dwarf is prevented from further gravitational collapse by **electron degeneracy pressure** (also known as **Fermi pressure**). This comes about as follows. There is a law called Pauli's exclusion principle which states that no two electrons can exist in the same quantum state. (This is why only two electrons can occupy any energy level in an atom.) As gravity tries to cause the star to collapse further, a limit is reached when further collapse would require two or more electrons to exist in the same quantum state.

- The maximum mass of a white dwarf is about 1.4 solar masses. This upper limit for the mass of a white dwarf is known as the **Chandrasekhar limit,** named after the Indian-American astrophysicist Subrahmanyan Chandrasekhar who first predicted this in 1930 (Figure 18.8).

Figure 18.8 Subrahmanyan Chandrasekhar (1910–1995), Indian-US astrophysicist. Chandrasekhar's main work was in showing that the fate of a star is dependent on its mass.

More massive stars

A star that is more massive than the Sun (typically, more than 3 solar masses) behaves differently. Approaching the end of its life, it swells to become a **super red giant**. When it collapses to form a white dwarf, provided its mass is still more than 1.4 solar masses, its gravity is strong enough to cause it to collapse even further. The gravitational pressures are enormous and overcome the Fermi pressure. The electrons combine with the protons to produce neutrons and neutrinos. The neutrinos escape and the central core of the star is now made entirely of closely packed neutrons. The outer shells surrounding the neutron core collapse violently and rebound against the solid neutron core. This generates a shockwave which explodes the surface layers of the star as a **supernova**. A supernova blasts off heavier elements like carbon, oxygen, and iron into the galaxy. These become incorporated into future stellar systems. In fact, the carbon in our bodies and the oxygen we breathe originated from explosive supernovae.

Supernova events are rather rare – they only occur about once every 50 years in our galaxy. However, they are very bright, so bright that for a few days they can outshine an entire galaxy. A supernova has the intensity equivalent to about 10^{11} stars. This means that quite distant supernovae can be readily observed.

What remains of the core of the star depends on its mass.

- For lighter stars, the core is entirely made up of neutrons, as described above. The result is a **neutron star,** a remnant with an extremely high density, roughly $10^{18}\,\mathrm{kg\,m^{-3}}$.
- For even heavier stars, the supernova leaves a neutron star that is so massive that it continues to collapse inwards under its own gravity to form a **black hole**.

A black hole forms when matter collapses almost to a point (a singularity). The gravitational field within a few kilometres of the point is so strong that not even light can escape from it – that is why it appears black. While we cannot see a black hole, we can see its effects. For example, some stars seem to be orbiting around an invisible partner, which is probably a black hole.

Now look at Worked example 1.

Worked example 1

The density of a particular neutron star is $2.0\times10^{17}\,\mathrm{kg\,m^{-3}}$ and it has a mass of $6.0\times10^{30}\,\mathrm{kg}$. Calculate the radius of this neutron star.

Step 1 Write down the information given.

density $\rho = 2.0\times10^{17}\,\mathrm{kg\,m^{-3}}$
mass $m = 6.0\times10^{30}\,\mathrm{kg}$

Step 2 Use the equation for density to calculate the volume of the star.

$$\rho = \frac{m}{V}$$

$$V = \frac{m}{\rho} = \frac{6.0\times10^{30}}{2.0\times10^{17}}$$

$$= 3.0\times10^{13}\,\mathrm{m^3}$$

Step 3 Now calculate the radius of the star using

$$V = \frac{4}{3}\pi r^3$$

$$\frac{4}{3}\pi r^3 = 3.0\times10^{13}$$

$$r = \sqrt[3]{\frac{3\times3.0\times10^{13}}{4\pi}} \approx 1.9\times10^4\,\mathrm{m}$$

The radius of the neutron star is about 19 km. Compare this with the radius of our Sun, which is 700 000 km.

Figure 18.9 summarises the possible life-histories of stars.

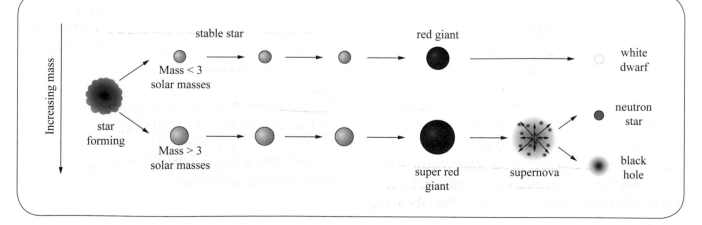

Figure 18.9 The life-history of a star depends on its mass.

SAQ

1 a In Figure 18.9, which part shows the life-history of the Sun?

b Explain why the Sun will never become a black hole.

2 a When a star forms, what force causes a cloud of dust and gas to collapse inwards?

b State the force that causes planets to form around a new star.

c State the force that causes a massive neutron star to become a black hole.

3 A neutron star consists of a vast number of neutrons, closely packed together.

a Use the following data to determine the density of a neutron. *Hint*

mass of neutron = 1.7×10^{-27} kg

radius of neutron = 1.3×10^{-15} m

b A particular neutron star has a mass of 4.0×10^{30} kg. Using your answer to part **a**, estimate the radius of the neutron star.

c The material of a neutron star consists of spherical neutrons with small gaps between them. Explain whether this means that your answer to part **b** is an underestimate or an overestimate.

d The mass of the Sun is 2.0×10^{30} kg; its radius is 7.0×10^{8} m. Explain why the neutron star's radius is so different from that of the Sun. *Answer*

Measuring the universe

In science, we generally use SI units. However, because of the vast scale of the universe, other units have come into use which can give a better impression of the distances involved. We will look at three of these units, their definitions, and their relationships to the metre, the SI unit of distance.

For measuring distances in our solar system, it is convenient to use the **astronomical unit** (AU). For example, the planet Uranus is 19.2 AU from the Sun.

The astronomical unit (AU) is the average distance of the Earth from the Sun.

$$1\,AU = 1.496 \times 10^{11}\,m \approx 1.5 \times 10^{11}\,m$$

It is useful to remember that the distance to the Sun is approximately 150 million km.

For measuring distances between stars in our galaxy, astronomers tend to use **light-years** (ly), which is a much bigger distance.

The light-year (ly) is the distance travelled by light through a vacuum in one year.

$$1\,ly \approx 9.46 \times 10^{15}\,m \approx 9.5 \times 10^{15}\,m$$

We can easily determine the light-year by multiplying the speed of light in a vacuum ($3.0 \times 10^{8}\,m\,s^{-1}$) by the time of one year in seconds (see SAQ 4). The distance to the nearest star from the Sun is about 4.2 ly. The radius of the solar system is roughly 2.0 ly.

For measuring distances between stars and galaxies, astronomers tend to use the **parsec** (pc). The parsec is defined from a technique that astronomers have used to measure the distance to other stars nearby in our galaxy. These stars show **parallax**; that is, their *apparent* position against the background of other, more distant stars alters when they are observed at different times during the year. This is a consequence of the Earth's orbiting around the Sun. Figure 18.10 shows the Earth at opposite ends of its orbit (E_1 and E_2). If the star 61 Cygni is observed from these two positions, it is observed to move through an angle $2p$. The angle p is called the *parallax* of the star, and it is such a small angle that it is measured in seconds of arc.

There are 60 arc seconds in a minute of arc, and 60 arc minutes in a degree. Hence:

$$1\ \text{arc second} = \frac{1}{3600}\ \text{degrees}$$

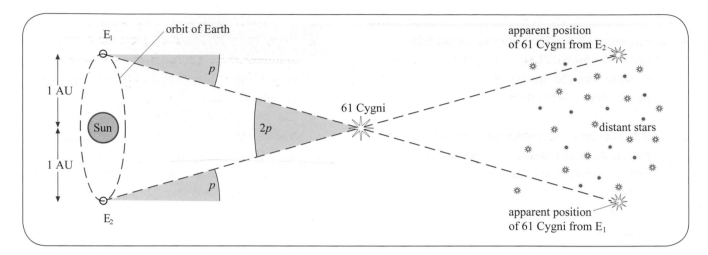

Figure 18.10 Measuring the parallax p of a nearby star.

The term parsec comes from the words *par*allax and *sec*ond.

> The parsec is defined as the distance that gives a parallax angle of 1 arc second.

Clearly, stars with smaller values of p are at greater distances, so:

$$\text{distance (pc)} = \frac{1}{\text{parallax (arc seconds)}}$$

or

$$d \text{ (pc)} = \frac{1}{p \text{ (arc second)}}$$

For 61 Cygni, $p = 0.3$ arc seconds, so its distance from the Sun is $1/0.3 = 3.3$ pc.

From the definition of the parsec, it can be shown that (as in Worked example 2):

$$1 \text{ pc} \approx 3.1 \times 10^{16} \text{ m} \approx 3.3 \text{ ly}$$

Worked example 2

Show that a parsec (1 pc) is equal to 3.1×10^{16} m.

Step 1 For a star at a distance of 1 pc, we can draw a triangle similar to Figure 18.10. The side of the triangle opposite to the star has a length of 1 AU – see Figure 18.11. *continued*

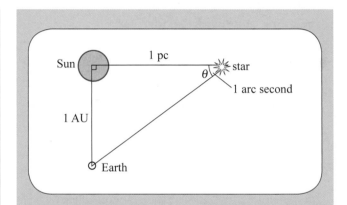

Figure 18.11 This triangle defines the parsec; note that it is *not* drawn to scale – the page would have to be at least 1 km wide.

Step 2 Use the triangle to determine the parsec.

$$1 \text{ AU} = 1.496 \times 10^{11} \text{ m}$$

$$\theta = 1 \text{ arc second} = 1/3600 \text{ degrees}$$

$$\tan \theta = \frac{1 \text{ AU}}{1 \text{ pc}}$$

$$1 \text{ pc} = \frac{1 \text{ AU}}{\tan \theta} = \frac{1.496 \times 10^{11}}{\tan (1/3600)}$$

$$\approx 3.1 \times 10^{16} \text{ m}$$

SAQ

4   Given that the speed of light in a vacuum is $c = 299\,792\,458\,\text{m s}^{-1}$ and that 1 year = 365.25636 days, show that 1 light-year is approximately $9.46 \times 10^{15}\,\text{m}$.

Answer

5   The nearest star (other than the Sun) is Proxima Centauri. It has a parallax of 0.76 seconds of arc. Calculate its distance from Earth:
    a   in parsecs
    b   in light-years
    c   in metres.

Answer

6   The Moon's average distance from the Earth is $4.0 \times 10^5\,\text{km}$. What is this distance in astronomical units (AU)?

Answer

7   The distance d of a star can be determined from its parallax p. Table 18.1 shows details of some of the brightest stars in our night sky. The parallax p is in arc seconds and the distance d is in light years.

a   Copy Table 18.1 and complete the last two columns of the table as follows: Calculate d in pc using the conversion 1 pc = 3.3 ly; then calculate $p \times d$.

b   Explain significance of the last column.

Answer

Star	p/arc sec	d/ly	d/pc	p×d/pc arc sec
Altair	0.20	16		
Arcturus	0.090	36		
Capella	0.073	45		
Sirius	0.38	8.7		
Vega	0.12	26		

Table 18.1 See SAQ 7.

Extension

Olbers' paradox

Isaac Newton (1642–1727) suggested that the universe must be infinitely large and roughly uniform in its composition. In other words, the universe has stars scattered throughout it and it goes on for ever, in all directions. He thought it must be infinite because he realised that a finite universe would collapse under the pull of its own gravity. An infinite universe has no centre and so it would not collapse. (In a finite universe, every star is pulled towards the centre of gravity of the universe; in an infinite universe, every star is pulled equally in all directions so that there is no resultant force on it.)

This idea was challenged in 1826 by Heinrich Olbers. He pictured a universe that was:
- infinite
- uniform
- static.

'Static' means neither expanding nor contracting. He had the idea that, if we lived in such a universe,

the sky would always be brightly lit, even at night. He argued this by saying that, in no matter what direction you looked, your line of sight would eventually reach a star. So every point in the sky would be lit by a star. Although the most distant stars are very dim, there must be large numbers of them, which would compensate for their dimness. The universe would be full of starlight and the surface of the Earth would be as hot as the surface of a star.

There is another mathematical argument which also suggests that the night sky ought to be bright. In an infinite universe with an infinite number of stars:
- the number of stars increases with the square of the distance. (Imagine a sphere of radius r sprinkled with stars. The number of stars in this shell will be proportional to the surface area of the shell; that is $4\pi r^2$.)

continued

- the intensity of light from these stars decreases according to the inverse square with distance. These two effects cancel each other and hence the night sky ought to be bright!

Because we know that the sky at night is dark, Olbers said that at least one of his assumptions about the universe must be incorrect. It must be finite or non-uniform or expanding/contracting, or some combination of these.

This is **Olbers' paradox**:

> For an infinite, uniform and static universe, the night sky should be bright because of light received in all directions from stars.

Olbers' paradox is an example of how big conclusions (in this case, about the nature of the universe) can be drawn from simple observations. Before Olbers, everyone knew that the night sky is dark, but no-one had realised what that observation can tell us about the nature of the universe.

In the next section, we will look at evidence that was gathered in the early twentieth century which helped to give an answers to Olbers' paradox.

The expanding universe

Edwin Hubble (Figure 18.12) was an American astronomer working in the early decades of the twentieth century. This was a time when big telescopes were being constructed, which allowed many thousands of distant and dim galaxies to be observed. Hubble photographed many galaxies and made a catalogue of them, classifying them according to their different shapes. He also became expert in measuring the distances to galaxies.

Figure 18.12 Edwin Hubble in front of the 2.5 m telescope at Mount Wilson Observatory. He was the first astronomer to measure the distance to another galaxy, confirming the existence of galaxies beyond our own.

These modern telescopes were fitted with spectrometers which made it possible to record the spectra of light from individual stars or galaxies. The lines in the spectra can be interpreted to identify the elements present in the star. (Every atom of a particular element produces a line spectrum and the wavelengths of the lines are characteristic of the element; see Chapter 20 in *Physics 1*.)

Another American, Vesto Slipher, had noticed an interesting phenomenon when he looked at the spectra of other galaxies. Although they showed the same *pattern* of lines (indicating that the same elements were present as in our own galaxy), the lines were slightly out of position. The entire spectrum was shifted, either towards the red end of the spectrum or towards the blue end. For most galaxies, the lines were shifted towards the red end of the spectrum. In other words, their wavelengths were slightly increased by an amount called the **redshift**. Figure 18.13 shows spectra for four galaxies with increasing redshifts. You can see that each line in the spectrum has been progressively shifted to longer wavelengths and that the effect is greater for some galaxies than for others.

Slipher explained these redshifts in terms of the Doppler effect (see Chapter 17). Electromagnetic waves (such as light) emitted by a source that is moving away from the observer are stretched out, increasing their wavelength from λ to $\lambda + \Delta\lambda$ – see Figure 18.14. The faster the source is receding, the greater the redshift. The speed of recession v of a galaxy (or other source) can be deduced from the fractional change in wavelength. We can show that:

$$\frac{\Delta\lambda}{\lambda} = \frac{v}{c}$$

where c is the speed of light. Note that this only tells us the component of the galaxy's velocity along the line joining the galaxy to the observer, i.e. directly away from or towards the observer. The galaxy may have another component of velocity at right angles to this, across the observer's field of view. The equation above is known as the **Doppler equation** and can only be applied to a galaxy travelling slowly compared with the speed of light (that is, $v \ll c$).

Slipher's measurements made it possible to calculate the speed of recession of galaxies beyond our own, and the technique was also applied to determine the motion of individual stars in our own galaxy. (A few galaxies were found to have blueshifts; characteristic wavelengths in their spectra were found to be shortened, indicating that they are moving towards us.)

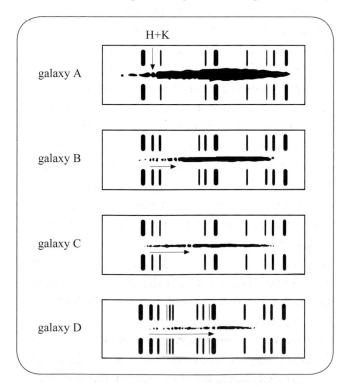

Figure 18.13 Redshifts in the spectra from distant galaxies. The upper and lower traces are reference spectra, for comparison. The arrows indicate how a pair of lines (H+K) are redshifted by different amounts.

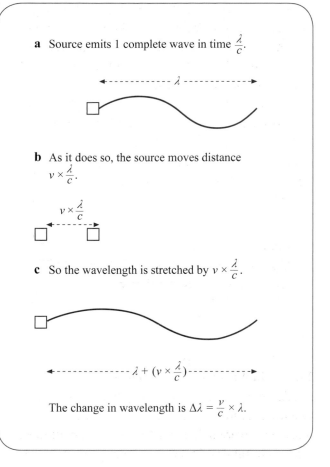

a Source emits 1 complete wave in time $\frac{\lambda}{c}$.

b As it does so, the source moves distance $v \times \frac{\lambda}{c}$.

c So the wavelength is stretched by $v \times \frac{\lambda}{c}$.

The change in wavelength is $\Delta\lambda = \frac{v}{c} \times \lambda$.

Figure 18.14 Explaining the Doppler origin of the redshift. The wavelength increases by an amount equal to the distance moved by the source as it emits one wave.

Hubble's law

Hubble's great achievement was to combine his measurements of the distances of the galaxies with measurements of their speeds of recession, deduced from their redshifts. He plotted a graph showing the recessional speed v of each galaxy against its distance x from us. A more up-to-date version of this is shown in Figure 18.15. The pattern is clear. The greater the distance x to a galaxy, the greater its speed of recession v:

speed of recession of galaxy $\propto$ distance of galaxy

$$v \propto x$$

This relationship is known as Hubble's law. We can write it as an equation:

$$v = H_0 x$$

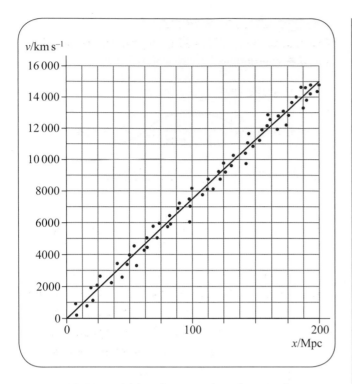

Figure 18.15 Hubble's law graph, using modern values of measurements of recessional speed v and distance x. The gradient of the graph is equal to the Hubble constant.

where the constant of proportionality H_0 is known as the **Hubble constant**. The measured value of H_0 is:

$$H_0 \approx 70\,\text{km s}^{-1}\,\text{Mpc}^{-1}$$

This shows that a galaxy that is 1 megaparsec (Mpc) distant from the Earth will have a speed of recession of $70\,\text{km s}^{-1}$; at $2\,\text{Mpc}$, v will be $2\times70 = 140\,\text{km s}^{-1}$, and so on.

The implication of Hubble's law is that the universe is expanding; the galaxies are moving away from each other.

Interpreting Hubble's law

At first sight, it might appear that Hubble had shown that all the galaxies are moving away from the Earth, and that this means that we are at the centre of the universe. However, we are not so special! Figure 18.16 shows why.

We picture galaxies A–H, equally spaced in an expanding universe. After a time interval Δt, the whole

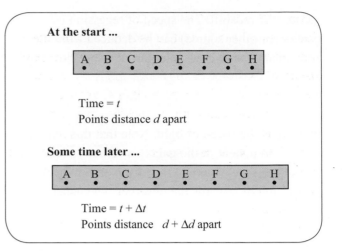

Figure 18.16 The fabric of space is represented by the strip and the galaxies by the dots. An expanding universe carries all galaxies apart from each other.

strip of universe has expanded. An observer at A will conclude that all the other galaxies have moved away from him, with the distance to H having increased the most. At the same time, an observer at H will conclude that all of the galaxies are moving away from him. Equally, an observer at D will see galaxies A–C moving away to the left and E–H moving away to the right. For each observer, all galaxies are receding and the further the galaxy, the faster it is receding.

This is an example of the cosmological principle (see page 261). Each observer will observe the same effect. There is no special place in the universe from which you could observe anything different.

SAQ

8 A distant galaxy has a redshift of 0.085. Calculate its speed of recession.

9 A green line in the spectrum of calcium has a wavelength of 527.0 nm when measured in a (stationary) laboratory on Earth. In the spectrum of a distant star, its wavelength is found to be 526.3 nm. State what you can deduce about the motion of the star. Support your answer with a numerical value.

The birth of the universe

Hubble's law implies that, at present, the universe is expanding. What does this suggest about the past history of the universe? The fact that $v \propto x$ suggests that, at some time in the past, all of the galaxies must have been concentrated together in a very small space.

You can picture this as a movie of the history of the universe. As we watch today, the galaxies are moving further and further apart. Run the film backwards and they move closer and closer together.

Hubble's graph was the first evidence that the universe might have started from a **Big Bang**. The universe is believed to have originated from a very hot explosion from which space and time evolved. Since the Big Bang, all the galaxies have been moving apart. The gradient of the Hubble's law graph can tell us about how long ago this event happened. If the gradient is steep (H_0 large), it suggests that galaxies are moving fast and that the universe must therefore be relatively young. If the gradient is less steep (H_0 small), the universe must be older. If the rate of expansion of the universe has been constant, we can conclude that:

$$\text{age of universe} \approx \frac{1}{\text{Hubble constant}}$$
$$\approx \frac{1}{H_0}$$

Changing units

To use this relationship to estimate the age of the universe, we need to convert H_0 to SI units. Distances to galaxies are large so they are often given in mega-parsecs or light-years rather than metres. However, it is useful to be able to convert these to metres.

Since $1\,\text{pc} \approx 3.1 \times 10^{16}\,\text{m}$, we have
$1\,\text{Mpc} \approx 3.1 \times 10^{22}\,\text{m}$.

Now we can convert the units of the Hubble constant to SI units; note that we have to include a factor of 10^3 to change km s^{-1} to m s^{-1}.

$$70\,\text{km s}^{-1}\,\text{Mpc}^{-1} = \frac{70 \times 10^3\,\text{m s}^{-1}}{3.1 \times 10^{22}\,\text{m}}$$
$$= 2.26 \times 10^{-18}\,\text{s}^{-1} \approx 2.3 \times 10^{-18}\,\text{s}^{-1}$$

The units reduce to s^{-1}. (This should not be written as Hz, as it is not a frequency.)

The age of the universe

Now that we have H_0 in SI units, we can deduce the age of the universe:

$$\text{age of universe} \approx \frac{1}{H_0}$$

$$\text{age of universe} = \frac{1}{2.26 \times 10^{-18}} \approx 4.43 \times 10^{17}\,\text{s}$$

Since there are roughly $3.16 \times 10^7\,\text{s}$ in one year, we have:

$$\text{age of universe} \approx \frac{4.43 \times 10^{17}}{3.16 \times 10^7} \approx 14 \times 10^9\,\text{years}$$

So we conclude that the universe is roughly 14 billion years old. Remember that this is based on the assumption that the universe has been expanding at a steady rate over this time. It also depends on the accuracy of the various measurements which contribute to the Hubble's law graph.

Because nothing can move faster than the speed of light, it follows that we can only observe the universe up to a distance of 14 billion light years from us. This gives us an upper limit on the observable size of the universe.

Efforts have been made over the last 50 years to refine these measurements and to find other ways of approaching the question. You can check using the internet to see the current range of possible values for H_0 and the implications these have for the age of the universe.

Now we can re-visit Olbers' paradox and reconsider the model of the universe which he started from. The Big Bang model (also known as the standard model) of an expanding universe suggests:

- The universe is not static – it is expanding.
- The universe is (probably) not infinite.
- The finite age of the universe and the finite speed of light means that light from the most distant galaxies has yet to reach us.
- As distant galaxies recede, their light is red-shifted. This means that it is less energetic and so dimmer.

In this chapter, we have considered only some of the experimental evidence for the idea that the universe is expanding following a Big Bang. In Chapter 19, we will look at the nature of the Big Bang and how the universe may change in the future.

SAQ

10 One experiment to estimate the Hubble constant gives a value of $78\,\text{km}\,\text{s}^{-1}\,\text{Mpc}^{-1}$.

  a Determine a value for the Hubble constant in s^{-1}. ($1\,\text{pc} = 3.1 \times 10^{16}\,\text{m}$.)

  b Estimate the age of the universe both in seconds and in years. [Answer]

11 Figure 18.15 is a Hubble's law graph, plotted using recently obtained data. Use it to estimate the age of the universe. [Answer]

Summary

[Glossary]

- The cosmological principle suggests that the universe is uniform; there are no 'special places' in the universe. This principle is based on a universe that is homogeneous and isotropic and in which the laws of physics are universal.

- The universe contains matter in the form of stars, clustered into galaxies, and electromagnetic radiation.

- The solar system consists of the Sun and all the objects (planets, comets, etc.) held in its gravitational field.

- Stars form when clouds of interstellar gas and dust contract under the pull of their own gravity.

- The Sun will evolve to become a red giant and then a planetary nebula and a white dwarf. A more massive star will become a super red giant and then a supernova and either a neutron star or a black hole, depending on its initial mass.

- Astronomical distances may be measured in astronomical units (AU), light-years (ly) or parsecs (pc).

  $$1\,\text{AU} \approx 1.5 \times 10^{11}\,\text{m} \qquad 1\,\text{ly} \approx 9.5 \times 10^{15}\,\text{m} \qquad 1\,\text{pc} \approx 3.1 \times 10^{16}\,\text{m}$$

- Olbers' paradox: For an infinite, uniform and static universe, the night sky should be bright because of light received in all directions from stars. (The paradox is resolved because the universe is neither static nor infinite.)

- Redshift is related to speed of recession by the Doppler equation:

  $$\frac{\Delta\lambda}{\lambda} = \frac{v}{c}$$

- Hubble's law: speed of recession of a galaxy $\propto$ distance of galaxy. An equation for Hubble's law is:

  $$v = H_0 x$$

- The age of the universe is related to the Hubble constant H_0 by the equation:

  $$\text{age} \approx \frac{1}{H_0}$$

- The SI unit for the Hubble constant is s^{-1}.

Questions

1 a Explain why a star like the Sun does not collapse as a result of its own
   gravitational field. [2]

   b Describe some of the characteristics of a red giant and suggest why it emits
   greater power than a star like the Sun. [4]

   c Describe the evolution of a star that is much more massive than our Sun. [5]

   d Explain why a white dwarf is technically not a star. [2]

   [Total 13]

   Answer

2 The graphs below show the variation of intensity with wavelength for part of the
   Sun's spectrum and for the same part of the spectrum from a distant star.

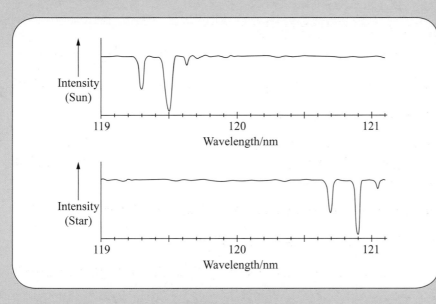

   a Explain how the star's motion causes corresponding minima of intensity to
   occur at different wavelengths. [2]

   b Use the graphs to calculate the velocity of the star. [4]

   OCR Physics A2 (2825/01) January 2006 [Total 6]

   Answer

3 a Explain briefly how the composition of a star is determined. [2]

   b The distances to nearby stars may be determined by *parallax*, and are often
   quoted in *parsecs*.

   i Explain the meaning of the term *parallax*. [2]

   ii Explain how the *parsec* is defined. A diagram may be helpful. [2]

   OCR Physics A2 (2825/01) June 2003 [Total 6]

   Answer

continued

4 a Explain how Olbers' paradox and the work of Hubble on the motions of galaxies provide evidence for a finite universe. [6]

b The Hubble constant H_0 is given by the equation:

$$H_0 = \frac{v}{r}$$

where v is the speed of recession of a galaxy and r is the distance from the observer to the galaxy.

  i Some observations indicate a value for the Hubble constant $H_0 = 70\,\text{km}\,\text{s}^{-1}\text{Mpc}^{-1}$. Convert this value into s^{-1}. [3]

  ii Hence estimate the age of the universe. [1]

  iii Use your answer to **ii** to estimate the maximum observable size for the universe. [2]

c State an assumption you have made in answering **b**. [1]

OCR Physics A2 (2825/01) January 2004 [Total 13]

Hint

Answer

5 a What is meant by *stellar parallax*? [2]

b The first recorded stellar parallax had a value of 0.314 arc seconds.

  i Calculate the distance of the star from Earth, giving your answer in parsecs. [2]

  ii What is this distance in metres? [1]

OCR Physics A2 (2825/01) June 2007 [Total 5]

Answer

Chapter 19

The evolution of the universe

e-Learning

Objectives

The standard model of the universe

Edwin Hubble's work and subsequent improved measurements established the fact that we live in an expanding universe. This gave cosmologists the idea that the universe emerged from a hot **Big Bang**. (Cosmology is the study of the nature and origin of the universe.) This is not simply an intelligent guess, based on the fact that the galaxies are moving apart according to Hubble's law; there is a lot more to it than that.

The hot Big Bang model has become established as the leading theory of the evolution of the universe, so that it is now known as the **standard model of the universe**. It is comparable to the standard model of fundamental particles (quarks and leptons) and four fundamental forces, which we looked at in Chapter 12. Indeed, these two models have been developed in parallel. For physicists, it has been somewhat surprising to discover that ideas about the tiniest particles and their interactions have been vital in developing theories of the largest possible thing, the universe.

How does a theory like the hot Big Bang theory become established? It has had to compete with other theories (such as the steady-state model) over several decades. Cosmologists have had to make mathematical models that take account of what we know about the fundamental particles and forces of Nature. Each model must be tested to see if it gives a realistic picture of the universe as we see it today.

In this chapter, we will look in detail at the Big Bang theory and consider what it can tell us about the past and future of the universe.

Back to the beginning

Today, we see that the galaxies are moving apart. We deduce that, at some time in the past, they were all packed closely together. In fact, because of the nature of gravity, we can deduce that all of the matter that we now see in the universe (Figure 19.1) must have been packed into an infinitely small space – a point or singularity.

This implies that the age of the universe is finite – as we saw in Chapter 18, it has probably existed for between 13 and 14 billion years. We cannot know what existed before the Big Bang. Perhaps the universe emerged from some other universe. Unfortunately, because all of the matter and energy in the universe was crushed into a single point, no 'fossil' evidence can have survived to tell us about its past history, before the Big Bang.

In fact, we cannot know what happened during the first 10^{-43} s after the Big Bang. This length of time

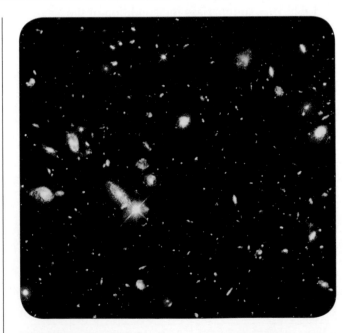

Figure 19.1 A Hubble Space Telescope (HST) image showing a huge number of very distant galaxies some 13 billion light-years from the Earth.

is known as the Planck time and is thought to be the shortest interval into which time can be divided. Our current knowledge of physics is inadequate in explaining the universe up to the Planck time. (Physicists have not been able to create the extreme conditions of the early universe in their particle accelerators.) Cosmologists believe that, at that time, the four separate forces we know about today – gravitational, electromagnetic, weak nuclear and strong nuclear – were all unified.

The evolving universe

When scientists talk about the 'evolution' of the universe, they simply mean the stages in its development as it has expanded since the Big Bang. (This is not the same as the evolution of a biological species, which involves competition between individuals.)

We will look first at the current picture of the different steps in the evolution of the universe, and then we will consider the evidence that supports this. Figure 19.2 shows an artist's impression of eight stages in the history of the universe. At the left is the Big Bang and at the right is the universe as we see it today.

Table 19.1 summarises the condition of the universe at each of the stages represented in Figure 19.2.

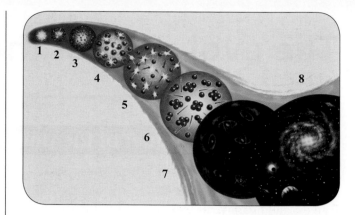

Figure 19.2 Eight stages in the history of the universe. Definitely not to scale!

From Table 19.1, you can see that the history of the universe is a story of expansion, cooling and condensing. The universe started off infinitely hot and has been cooling down ever since. As it has cooled and expanded, its particles have gradually slowed down and joined up to form larger particles and eventually stars and galaxies.

- After 10^{-6} s, the universe consisted of a 'soup' of quarks and leptons (e.g. electrons), rushing about too fast to combine to form hadrons.
- After 10^{-3} s, the quarks had slowed down enough to start combining in twos and threes to form hadrons. Most of the mass of the universe was created throughout the first second of its existence

Stage	Time from Big Bang	Temperature/K	Nature of universe
1	0 s	infinite	Infinitesimally small, infinitely dense – a point. All four fundamental forces are unified.
2, 3	10^{-6} s	10^{14}	Quark and lepton 'soup'.
4, 5	10^{-3} s	10^{12}	Quarks combine to form hadrons such as protons, neutrons, etc.
6	10^2 s	10^7	'Primordial' helium nuclei form by fusion (but too cool for further fusion reactions).
7	3×10^5 y	10^4	Atoms form as electrons combine with nuclei. The universe becomes transparent so that electromagnetic radiation in the form of photons moves freely through universe.
8	10^6 y to present	10^3 to 2.7	Matter clumps together to form gas clouds, dust, stars, galaxies. The universe is saturated with electromagnetic radiation with a characteristic temperature of 2.7 K.

Table 19.1 Stages in the evolution of the universe; stage numbers refer to Figure 19.2.

through a process called *pair production*. In the hot conditions of the early universe, pairs of high-energy photons were able to interact and produce particle–antiparticle pairs such as electrons and positrons:

$$\gamma + \gamma \longrightarrow {}_{-1}^{0}e + {}_{+1}^{0}e$$

- The creation of matter by the process of pair production stopped by a time of about 1 s, when the temperature had dropped to $\sim 6 \times 10^9$ K.
- After 10^2 s (that is, 100 s after the Big Bang), protons and neutrons fused together to form helium nuclei (and a small quantity of lithium and beryllium nuclei). As the temperature dropped below about 10^7 K, fusion stopped. At the end of this period, about 25% of the matter in the universe was helium nuclei, the rest being hydrogen nuclei with small traces of nuclei of the elements beryllium and lithium.

Now we have to think in timescales of years.

Figure 19.3 George Gamow (1904–1968) predicted the universe's temperature to be about 3 K (−270 °C) in his famous paper *The origin of chemical elements*.

- After 300 000 years or so, atoms started to form, as protons (hydrogen nuclei) and helium nuclei grabbed electrons. The universe consisted mainly of hydrogen and helium atoms with photons of electromagnetic radiation moving around the spaces in between.
- Subsequently gravity became the dominant force and we have the story of star and galaxy formation, as discussed in Chapter 18.
- The expansion of the universe led to cooling. The present temperature of the universe, about 2.7 K, was predicted in 1948 by George Gamow (Figure 19.3).

Figure 19.4 shows another way of representing the history of the universe, as a temperature against time graph. Notice that both scales are logarithmic (each division represents a change in the power of 10).

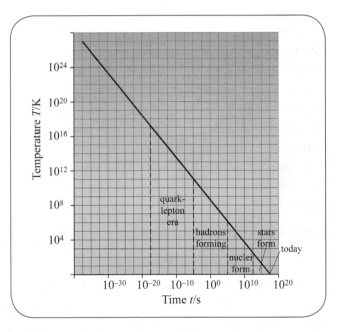

Figure 19.4 This graph shows how the temperature of the universe has decreased since the Big Bang.

Evidence for the standard model

We have already looked in depth at the evidence (from redshifts) that the universe is expanding. This is the first of three major pieces of evidence for the hot Big Bang model, but it doesn't confirm any of the detail given above. Here are the other two pieces of evidence.

Firstly, when astronomers look at the most distant galaxies, they are looking back in time. When they look at the most distant galaxies, they are looking at galaxies that formed less than a billion years after the Big Bang. The stars in these young galaxies are found to consist almost entirely of hydrogen and helium, with a small amount of lithium and beryllium (the third and fourth elements in the Periodic Table). The standard model predicts that only these four light elements were able to form in the first years of the universe's life. (Heavier elements formed much later, in the supernova explosions of the first generation of stars to die.)

A further piece of evidence for the hot Big Bang theory comes from the temperature of the universe today. When microwave detectors are sent into space, they can detect the electromagnetic radiation which pervades space. Figure 19.5 shows one of the satellites that has done this work.

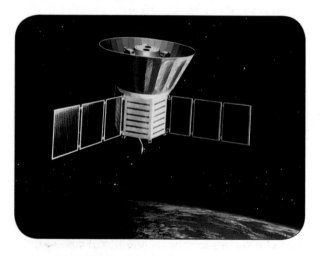

Figure 19.5 The Cosmic Background Explorer satellite (COBE) which measured the microwave background radiation reaching us from all directions in space.

The radiation detected is in the microwave region of the electromagnetic spectrum and is known as the **cosmic microwave background radiation**. It corresponds to a very low temperature, just 2.7 K (as predicted by George Gamow). The radiation can be detected in all directions in space, and is almost perfectly uniform. That is, the intensity of the microwaves at a particular wavelength is the same in all directions. This confirms the isotropic nature of the universe and backs up the cosmological principle.

What is this radiation? Recall that, 300 000 years after the Big Bang, matter had formed into atoms.

These were well separated, so that photons of energy moving between them could travel significant distances without being absorbed. In the billions of years since then, the universe has expanded vastly, so that the temperature of these photons has dropped close to absolute zero. So the microwave background radiation represents the cooled remnants of radiation that first started to travel around the universe roughly 13 billion years ago.

Why does an expanding universe result in cooler photons? Think of electromagnetic waves rather than photons. The universe has expanded because space itself is expanding. This has had the effect of stretching the waves as they move through space. Stretched waves have longer wavelengths, and longer wavelength radiation corresponds to a lower temperature.

There is another way to think about the cosmic microwave background radiation. A hot object like the Sun, whose surface temperature is about 5000 K, emits intense electromagnetic waves in the visible region. An object at a temperature of 2.7 K, in this case the universe, will emit electromagnetic waves intensely in the microwave region of the spectrum. Figure 19.6 shows the radiation profile for the universe at a temperature of 2.7 K.

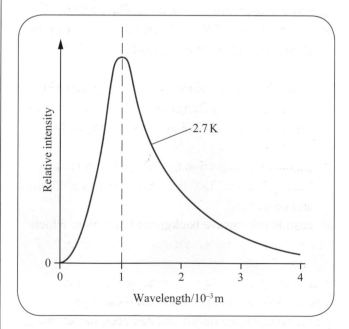

Figure 19.6 The electromagnetic radiation energy profile for the universe at a temperature of 2.7 K. The spectrum peaks at a wavelength of about 1.0 mm, corresponding to microwaves.

It is significant that the microwave background is not perfectly uniform. Experiments have detected slight variations in its density, as shown in the map (Figure 19.7). These 'ripples', which are very slight (about one part in 100 000), show us that, 300 000 years after the Big Bang, the universe was not quite uniform. Matter was very slightly more concentrated in some areas than in others, and these concentrations eventually formed the nuclei of today's galaxies. It was a triumph of scientific measurement to be able to map out such tiny variations in the background temperature of space.

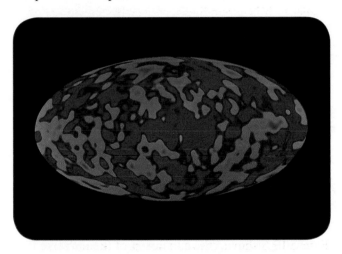

Figure 19.7 COBE's map of variations in the microwave background radiation. The average temperature is 2.725 K; pink and red areas are up to 30 μK warmer, blue areas are similarly cooler.

So the three major pieces of evidence supporting the standard (hot Big Bang) model of the universe are:
- galaxies receding (and therefore an expanding universe)
- chemical composition of early galaxies (mostly hydrogen with ~25% helium and traces of lithium and beryllium)
- cosmic microwave background radiation, which corresponds to a temperature of the universe of about 2.7 K.

Periodically, cosmologists come up with other theories which attempt to explain these three phenomena, but so far no-one has been successful in knocking down the standard model of the universe.

SAQ

1 Put these events in the history of the universe in order, starting with earliest:
- atomic nuclei form
- stars form
- the Big Bang
- quarks and leptons exist freely
- today
- atoms form
- protons form

Answer

2 Look at Figure 19.4, the graph that shows how the universe's temperature has decreased since it formed. From the graph, deduce:
   a the average temperature of the universe 10^{-10} s after the Big Bang
   b the time taken after the Big Bang for the temperature to drop to 10^4 s
   c the typical temperature of the universe when nuclei were forming.

Answer

Extension

The future of the universe

You might guess from the graph of Figure 19.4 that the universe will go on expanding and cooling for ever. It has cooled to 2.7 K and it will cool still further. Will this process go on for ever? In fact, the hot Big Bang theory cannot tell us for certain what will be the ultimate fate of the universe. Figure 19.8 shows two possibilities.

As we have said, the universe may continue to expand forever (Figure 19.8a). The rate of expansion (gradient of Figure 19.8a) decreases with time, but is still finite after infinite time. This will happen if there is insufficient matter in the universe. Gravitational force cannot provide the necessary deceleration to slow down the expansion of the universe. This is described as an **open universe**.

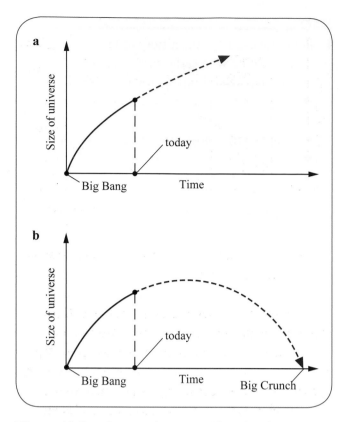

Figure 19.8 a Open universe. **b** Closed universe.

Alternatively, if there is enough matter in the universe so that gravity is strong enough, the expansion of the universe may come to a halt and go into reverse (Figure 19.8b). As it shrinks, it will eventually go backwards through all the stages of the hot Big Bang, ending in a 'Big Crunch'. This is described as a **closed universe**.

In between lies a third possibility, in which the universe expands forever, but the rate of expansion tends to zero after infinite time. This is called a **flat universe**.

The geometry of the universe

Einstein suggested that the presence of matter caused the structure of space itself to 'warp'. This can help us to picture the difference between open, flat and closed universes.

Figure 19.9 shows his idea. In a closed universe, space is curved round on itself. In an open universe, the warping results in a universe that goes on forever. The geometry of a flat universe is, unsurprisingly, flat.

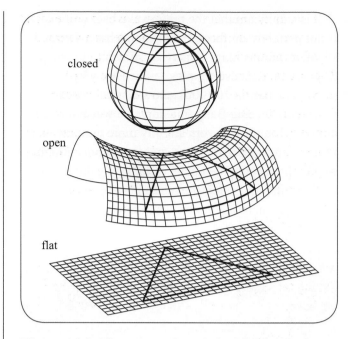

Figure 19.9 The geometries of closed, open and flat universes.

Which future?

How can we tell which future lies in store for the universe? This depends on the strength of gravity – is gravity strong enough to pull back on all the galaxies, eventually stopping the expansion of the universe that has been in progress for the last 13 billion years? That depends on how much matter there is in the universe and how thinly the matter is spread.

- In a low-density universe, gravitational force is too weak to stop it expanding forever.
- In a high-density universe, gravitational force will be strong enough to halt and then reverse its expansion.

You can see that there must be a **critical density** ρ_0 above which the universe will head back to a Big Crunch; below the critical density, the universe will expand for ever, ending up as an infinite, dark, cold space.

The fate of the universe can be summarised as follows:

- *Density of universe* $> \rho_0$: Gravitational forces eventually halt the expansion of matter and reverse the process towards a Big Crunch. The universe is closed.
- *Density of universe* $< \rho_0$: Gravitational forces cannot halt the expansion of matter. The universe expands forever. The universe is open.

- *Density of universe* $= \rho_0$: The universe will expand forever but the rate of expansion tends to zero after infinite time. The universe is flat.

The critical density depends on the strength of gravity, i.e. on the universal gravitational constant, G, and on the Hubble constant, H_0. A universe with a high value of H_0 has galaxies that are moving apart rapidly, and so it will require a high density of matter to pull them back.

The critical density is given by the equation:

$$\rho_0 = \frac{3H_0^2}{8\pi G}$$

The gravitational constant G is $6.67 \times 10^{-11}\,\mathrm{N\,m^2\,kg^{-2}}$. Taking the Hubble constant H_0 to be $2.3 \times 10^{-18}\,\mathrm{s^{-1}}$ we have:

$$\rho_0 = \frac{3 \times (2.3 \times 10^{-18})^2}{8\pi \times 6.67 \times 10^{-11}}$$

$$\rho_0 \approx 9.5 \times 10^{-27}\,\mathrm{kg\,m^{-3}}$$

This is a very small density. In fact, a proton has a mass of about 1.7×10^{-27} kg, so this value corresponds only to a few protons per cubic metre.

Does the universe have a density as low as this?

The answer to this could be 'yes'. Remember that most of the universe is empty space; only a tiny fraction is made up of galaxies. Measurements suggest that the density of the universe is close to the critical value. This suggests that our universe lies between the two possibilities shown in Figure 19.8, as shown in Figure 19.10. It is neither open nor closed but flat. There is no reason why our universe should have a density close to the critical value. Its density could be orders of magnitude less than ρ_0 or it could be much greater. The fact that it is close to the critical value has encouraged cosmologists to suggest that its value is exactly equal to ρ_0 so that we do, indeed, live in a flat universe.

Experiments continue to try to make a more accurate measurement of the density of the universe to test this idea. It is not easy to do – estimates must be made of the number of galaxies, their average number of stars, the typical sizes of stars and so on.

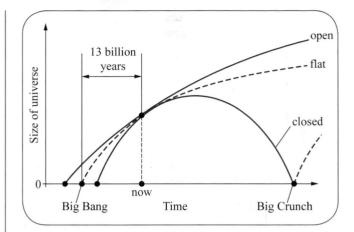

Figure 19.10 Many cosmologists now think that we live in a 'flat' universe.

There is also the major problem that not all the matter in the universe is observable. We can see distant galaxies because stars are hot and glow. We can detect radio waves and X-rays from other objects in space. However, cosmologists now believe that most of the mass of the universe consists of **dark matter**. This is matter that emits or reflects little electromagnetic radiation, making it very difficult to detect. We know that it is there because we can observe its gravitational pull on distant galaxies.

There have been several suggestions as to the nature of dark matter. It may consist of neutrinos – uncharged particles that interact only weakly with other matter. An individual neutrino has only a tiny mass, but they do saturate the universe. Other less familiar particles have been postulated to account for the effects of dark matter such as WIMPs and axions. Alternatively, there may be large amounts of mass in the form of dwarf stars that we cannot see.

There is also the possibility that the fate of the universe will be determined by the presence of **dark energy**, a form of energy thinly distributed throughout the universe and which may be causing the expansion of the universe to accelerate.

New observations and theories are published with great frequency and you can learn about them in the media. The fact that new and very contradictory theories are being developed to predict the ultimate fate of the universe shows that this is an area where much remains to be discovered – and that's one of the things that makes Physics an exciting subject for study!

SAQ

3 Our universe may end in a 'Big Crunch'. Put the following events in order, leading up to the Big Crunch.

- atoms lose their electrons
- quarks and leptons exist freely
- atomic nuclei disintegrate
- galaxies merge together
- today
- the Big Crunch
- hadrons disintegrate into quarks
- universe starts to contract

> Answer

4 Fred lives in a universe that is 10 billion years old and has a density of $2.5 \times 10^{-25}\,\mathrm{kg\,m^{-3}}$. The value of G in Fred's universe is $1.0 \times 10^{-12}\,\mathrm{N\,m^2\,kg^{-2}}$. What will be the ultimate fate of his universe?

> Answer

Summary

> Glossary

- The standard (hot Big Bang) model of the universe suggests that the universe has a finite age.

- Since the Big Bang, the universe has expanded and cooled, so that matter and radiation have gradually separated and matter has coalesced.

- Evidence for the Big Bang comes from the cosmic microwave background radiation whose current temperature is about 2.7 K.

- The universe may be open, flat or closed, depending on its density relative to the critical density.

- The critical density is given by the equation:

$$\rho_0 = \frac{3H_0{}^2}{8\pi G}$$

- The density of the universe is close to (and may be exactly equal to) the critical value, so that our universe may be flat.

Questions

1 a Outline the evolution of the universe from the Big Bang to the formation of the first atoms. [6]

b State <u>one</u> feature of the cosmic microwave background radiation and explain how it provides evidence for the Big Bang theory. [2]

OCR Physics A2 (2825/01) January 2007 [Total 8]

> Answer

2 a What is meant by the *cosmological principle*? [2]

b The ultimate fate of the universe is not yet clear. On the graph, the size of the universe is represented from the Big Bang B to the present day P. The graph has been extended into the future by the dotted line (_ _ _ _ _ _).

continued

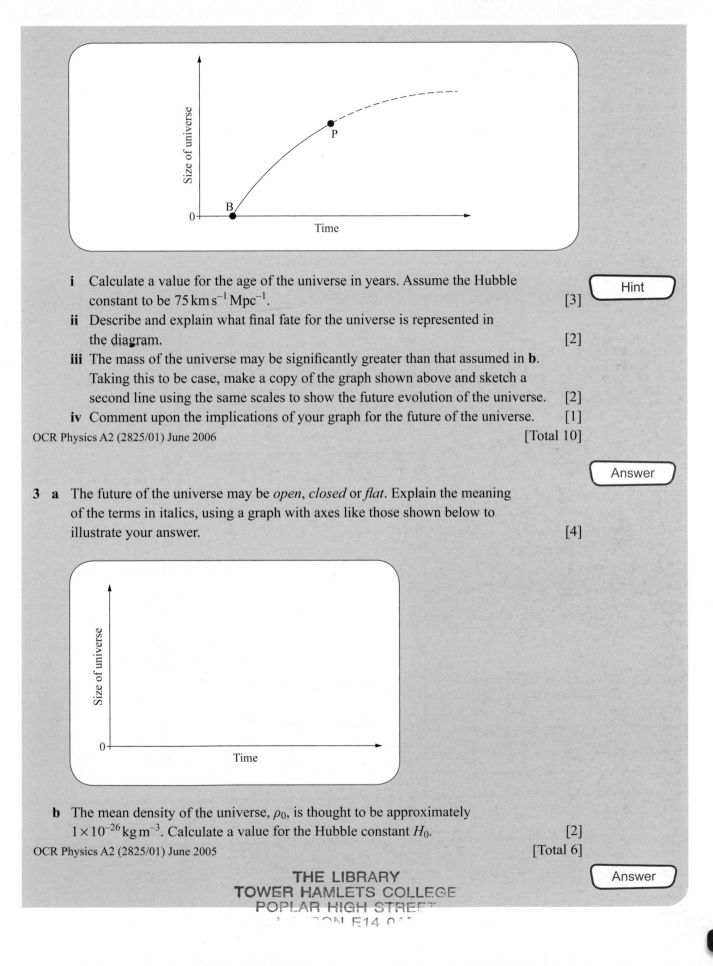

i Calculate a value for the age of the universe in years. Assume the Hubble constant to be $75\,\mathrm{km\,s^{-1}\,Mpc^{-1}}$. [3]

ii Describe and explain what final fate for the universe is represented in the diagram. [2]

iii The mass of the universe may be significantly greater than that assumed in **b**. Taking this to be case, make a copy of the graph shown above and sketch a second line using the same scales to show the future evolution of the universe. [2]

iv Comment upon the implications of your graph for the future of the universe. [1]

OCR Physics A2 (2825/01) June 2006 [Total 10]

> Hint

> Answer

3 a The future of the universe may be *open*, *closed* or *flat*. Explain the meaning of the terms in italics, using a graph with axes like those shown below to illustrate your answer. [4]

b The mean density of the universe, ρ_0, is thought to be approximately $1 \times 10^{-26}\,\mathrm{kg\,m^{-3}}$. Calculate a value for the Hubble constant H_0. [2]

OCR Physics A2 (2825/01) June 2005 [Total 6]

> Answer

The Periodic Table

Key

atomic symbol
name
atomic (proton) number

Example: **H** hydrogen 1

Main Table

Group 1	Group 2											Group 3	Group 4	Group 5	Group 6	Group 7	Group 0
H hydrogen 1																	**He** helium 2
Li lithium 3	**Be** beryllium 4											**B** boron 5	**C** carbon 6	**N** nitrogen 7	**O** oxygen 8	**F** fluorine 9	**Ne** neon 10
Na sodium 11	**Mg** magnesium 12											**Al** aluminium 13	**Si** silicon 14	**P** phosphorus 15	**S** sulfur 16	**Cl** chlorine 17	**Ar** argon 18
K potassium 19	**Ca** calcium 20	**Sc** scandium 21	**Ti** titanium 22	**V** vanadium 23	**Cr** chromium 24	**Mn** manganese 25	**Fe** iron 26	**Co** cobalt 27	**Ni** nickel 28	**Cu** copper 29	**Zn** zinc 30	**Ga** gallium 31	**Ge** germanium 32	**As** arsenic 33	**Se** selenium 34	**Br** bromine 35	**Kr** krypton 36
Rb rubidium 37	**Sr** strontium 38	**Y** yttrium 39	**Zr** zirconium 40	**Nb** niobium 41	**Mo** molybdenum 42	**Tc** technetium 43	**Ru** ruthenium 44	**Rh** rhodium 45	**Pd** palladium 46	**Ag** silver 47	**Cd** cadmium 48	**In** indium 49	**Sn** tin 50	**Sb** antimony 51	**Te** tellurium 52	**I** iodine 53	**Xe** xenon 54
Cs caesium 55	**Ba** barium 56	**La** lanthanum 57	**Hf** hafnium 72	**Ta** tantalum 73	**W** tungsten 74	**Re** rhenium 75	**Os** osmium 76	**Ir** iridium 77	**Pt** platinum 78	**Au** gold 79	**Hg** mercury 80	**Tl** thallium 81	**Pb** lead 82	**Bi** bismuth 83	**Po** polonium 84	**At** astatine 85	**Rn** radon 86
Fr francium 87	**Ra** radium 88	**Ac** actinium 89	**Rf** rutherfordium 104	**Db** dubnium 105	**Sg** seaborgium 106	**Bh** bohrium 107	**Hs** hassium 108	**Mt** meitnerium 109	**Ds** darmstadtium 110	**Rg** roentgenium 111							

Elements with atomic numbers 112–116 have been reported but not fully authenticated

Lanthanides

Ce cerium 58	**Pr** praseodymium 59	**Nd** neodymium 60	**Pm** promethium 61	**Sm** samarium 62	**Eu** europium 63	**Gd** gadolinium 64	**Tb** terbium 65	**Dy** dysprosium 66	**Ho** holmium 67	**Er** erbium 68	**Tm** thulium 69	**Yb** ytterbium 70	**Lu** lutetium 71

Actinides

Th thorium 90	**Pa** protactinium 91	**U** uranium 92	**Np** neptunium 93	**Pu** plutonium 94	**Am** americium 95	**Cm** curium 96	**Bk** berkelium 97	**Cf** californium 98	**Es** einsteinium 99	**Fm** fermium 100	**Md** mendelevium 101	**No** nobelium 102	**Lr** lawrencium 103

Appendix B

Data, formulae and relationships

Some of the prefixes used in the SI System

Prefix	pico	nano	micro	milli	centi	kilo	mega	giga	tera
Symbol	p	n	μ	m	c	k	M	G	T
Value	10^{-12}	10^{-9}	10^{-6}	10^{-3}	10^{-2}	10^{3}	10^{6}	10^{9}	10^{12}

Data

Values are given to three significant figures, except where more significant figures are useful.

speed of light in a vacuum	c	$3.00 \times 10^{8}\,\mathrm{m\,s^{-1}}$
permittivity of free space	ε_0	$8.85 \times 10^{-12}\,\mathrm{C^2\,N^{-1}\,m^{-2}}$ $(\mathrm{F\,m^{-1}})$
elementary charge	e	$1.60 \times 10^{-19}\,\mathrm{C}$
Planck constant	h	$6.63 \times 10^{-34}\,\mathrm{J\,s}$
gravitational constant	G	$6.67 \times 10^{-11}\,\mathrm{N\,m^2\,kg^{-2}}$
Avogadro constant	N_A	$6.02 \times 10^{23}\,\mathrm{mol^{-1}}$
molar gas constant	R	$8.31\,\mathrm{J\,mol^{-1}\,K^{-1}}$
Boltzmann constant	k	$1.38 \times 10^{-23}\,\mathrm{J\,K^{-1}}$
electron rest mass	m_e	$9.11 \times 10^{-31}\,\mathrm{kg}$
proton rest mass	m_p	$1.673 \times 10^{-27}\,\mathrm{kg}$
neutron rest mass	m_n	$1.675 \times 10^{-27}\,\mathrm{kg}$
alpha particle rest mass	m_α	$6.646 \times 10^{-27}\,\mathrm{kg}$
acceleration of free fall	g	$9.81\,\mathrm{m\,s^{-2}}$

Conversion factors

unified atomic mass unit	$1\,\mathrm{u} = 1.661 \times 10^{-27}\,\mathrm{kg}$
electronvolt	$1\,\mathrm{eV} = 1.60 \times 10^{-19}\,\mathrm{J}$
	$1\,\mathrm{day} = 8.64 \times 10^{4}\,\mathrm{s}$
	$1\,\mathrm{year} \approx 3.16 \times 10^{7}\,\mathrm{s}$
	$1\,\mathrm{light\ year} \approx 9.5 \times 10^{15}\,\mathrm{m}$

Mathematical equations

arc length $= r\theta$

circumference of circle $= 2\pi r$

area of circle $= \pi r^2$

curved surface area of cylinder $= 2\pi r h$

volume of cylinder $= \pi r^2 h$

surface area of a sphere $= 4\pi r^2$

volume of sphere $= \frac{4}{3}\pi r^3$

Pythagoras' theorem: $a^2 = b^2 + c^2$

For small angle θ: $\sin\theta \approx \tan\theta \approx \theta$ and $\cos\theta \approx 1$

$\lg(AB) = \lg(A) + \lg(B)$

$\lg\left(\frac{A}{B}\right) = \lg(A) - \lg(B)$

$\ln(x^n) = n\ln(x)$

$\ln(e^{kx}) = kx$

Formulae and relationships

Unit G481 Mechanics

$F_x = F\cos\theta$

$F_y = F\sin\theta$

$a = \dfrac{\Delta v}{\Delta t}$

$v = u + at$

$s = \frac{1}{2}(u + v)t$

$s = ut + \frac{1}{2}at^2$

$v^2 = u^2 + 2as$

$F = ma$

$W = mg$

$\text{moment} = Fx$

$\text{torque} = Fd$

$\rho = \dfrac{m}{V}$

$\rho = \dfrac{F}{A}$

$W = Fx\cos\theta$

$E_k = \frac{1}{2}mv^2$

$E_p = mgh$

$\text{efficiency} = \dfrac{\text{useful energy output}}{\text{total energy output}} \times 100\%$

$F = kx$

$E = \frac{1}{2}Fx$

$E = \frac{1}{2}kx^2$

$\text{stress} = \dfrac{F}{A}$

$\text{strain} = \dfrac{x}{L}$

$\text{Young modulus} = \dfrac{\text{stress}}{\text{strain}}$

Unit G482 Electrons, waves and photons

$\Delta Q = I\Delta t$

$I = Anev$

$W = VQ$

$V = IR$

$R = \dfrac{\rho L}{A}$

$R = R_1 + R_2 + \dots$

$\dfrac{1}{R} = \dfrac{1}{R_1} + \dfrac{1}{R_2} + \dots$

$P = VI$

$P = I^2 R$

$P = \dfrac{V^2}{R}$

$W = VIt$

$\text{e.m.f.} = V + Ir$

$V_{out} = \dfrac{R_2}{R_1 + R_2} \times V_{in}$

$v = f\lambda$

$\lambda = \dfrac{ax}{D}$

$d\sin\theta = n\lambda$

$E = hf$

$E = \dfrac{hc}{\lambda}$

$hf = \phi + KE_{max}$

$\lambda = \dfrac{h}{mv}$

Unit G484 The Newtonian world

$$F = \frac{\Delta p}{\Delta t}$$

$$v = \frac{2\pi r}{T}$$

$$a = \frac{v^2}{r}$$

$$F = \frac{mv^2}{r}$$

$$F = -\frac{GMm}{r^2}$$

$$g = \frac{F}{m}$$

$$g = -\frac{GM}{r^2}$$

$$T^2 = \left(\frac{4\pi^2}{GM}\right)r^3$$

$$f = \frac{1}{T}$$

$$\omega = \frac{2\pi}{T} = 2\pi f$$

$$a = -(2\pi f)^2 x$$

$$x = A\cos(2\pi f\, t)$$

$$v_{max} = (2\pi f)A$$

$$E = mc\Delta\theta$$

$$pV = NkT$$

$$pV = nRT$$

$$E = \frac{3}{2}kT$$

Unit G485 Fields, particles and frontiers of physics

$$E = \frac{F}{Q}$$

$$F = \frac{Qq}{4\pi\varepsilon_0 r^2}$$

$$E = \frac{Q}{4\pi\varepsilon_0 r^2}$$

$$E = \frac{V}{d}$$

$$F = BIL\sin\theta$$

$$F = BQv$$

$$\phi = BA\cos\theta$$

induced e.m.f. $= -$ rate of change of magnetic flux linkage

$$\frac{V_s}{V_p} = \frac{n_s}{n_p}$$

$$Q = VC$$

$$W = \frac{1}{2}QV$$

$$W = \frac{1}{2}CV^2$$

time constant $= CR$

$$x = x_0 e^{-\frac{t}{CR}}$$

$$C = C_1 + C_2 + \ldots$$

$$\frac{1}{C} = \frac{1}{C_1} + \frac{1}{C_2} + \ldots$$

$$A = \lambda N$$

$$A = A_0 e^{-\lambda t}$$

$$N = N_0 e^{-\lambda t}$$

$$\lambda t_{1/2} = 0.693$$

continued

289

$$\Delta E = \Delta mc^2$$

$$I = I_0 e^{-\mu x}$$

$$Z = \rho c$$

$$\frac{I_r}{I_0} = \frac{(Z_2 - Z_1)^2}{(Z_2 + Z_1)^2}$$

$$\frac{\Delta \lambda}{\lambda} = \frac{v}{c}$$

$$\text{age of universe} \approx \frac{1}{H_0}$$

$$\rho_0 = \frac{3H_0{}^2}{8\pi G}$$

Answers to SAQs

Chapter 1

1 a B
   b A

2 a $10 \, \text{kg m s}^{-1}$
   b $5.0 \times 10^5 \, \text{kg m s}^{-1}$
   c $1.82 \times 10^{-23} \, \text{kg m s}^{-1} \approx 1.8 \times 10^{-23} \, \text{kg m s}^{-1}$

3 Momentum before = momentum after = $-0.5 \, \text{kg m s}^{-1}$
   (i.e. to the left).

4

Type of collision	Momentum	Kinetic energy	Total energy
perfectly elastic	conserved	conserved	conserved
inelastic	conserved	not conserved	conserved

5 a $+10 \, \text{kg m s}^{-1}$; $-6 \, \text{kg m s}^{-1}$
   b $-6 \, \text{kg m s}^{-1}$; $+10 \, \text{kg m s}^{-1}$
   c Yes.
   b KE before = KE after = $4.5 \, \text{J} + 12.5 \, \text{J} = 17 \, \text{J}$

6 a

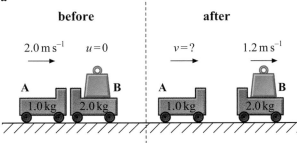

   b $0.40 \, \text{m s}^{-1}$, in reverse direction.

7 a He has given momentum to the spanner, and so gains momentum in the opposite direction.
   b $200 \, \text{s}$ (about $3.3 \, \text{min}$)

8 Change in momentum of ball = $1.08 \, \text{kg m s}^{-1}$;
   change in KE = $0.162 \, \text{J}$.
   The wall has gained momentum.

9 a The star has zero momentum before it explodes. After the explosion, matter flies off in all directions – equal amounts of momentum are created in all directions, so their (vector) sum is zero. Momentum is conserved.
   b You give downward momentum to Earth; as you slow down, so does the Earth; as you start to fall back down, the Earth starts to 'fall' back up towards you. At all times, your momentum is equal and opposite to that of the Earth, so combined momentum is zero, i.e. conserved.

10 $0.60 \, \text{m s}^{-1}$

11 $1.6 \, \text{m s}^{-1}$

Chapter 2

1 a $1.4 \times 10^4 \, \text{kg m s}^{-1}$
   b $933 \, \text{N} \approx 930 \, \text{N}$

2 a $60 \, \text{kg m s}^{-1}$ (or $60 \, \text{N s}$)
   b In the direction of the kicking force.

3 $50 \, \text{N}$ (bouncing: greater force because of greater change in momentum).

4 $1.4 \times 10^3 \, \text{N s}$

5 a $7.5 \, \text{N s}$
   b $2.4 \, \text{N s}$
   c $5.1 \, \text{N s}$

6 acceleration = $0.33 \, \text{m s}^{-2}$; $v = u + at = 14 \, \text{m s}^{-1}$

7 $1.77 \times 10^3 \, \text{N} \approx 1.8 \, \text{kN}$

8 a $1.0 \times 10^7 \, \text{kg m s}^{-1}$
   b $1.0 \times 10^6 \, \text{N}$

9 a $8.0 \, \text{ms}$
   b $1.8 \, \text{N s}$

10 a $1.2 \times 10^3 \, \text{N s}$
   b $1200 \, \text{kg m s}^{-1}$; $7.5 \, \text{m s}^{-1}$
   c $s = ut + \frac{1}{2} at^2$ gives $s = 67.5 \, \text{m}$

11 a $2.4 \, \text{m s}^{-1}$; $2.88 \times 10^3 \, \text{J} \approx 2.9 \times 10^3 \, \text{J}$
   b $0.020 \, \text{m s}^{-2}$; $144 \, \text{m}$; $2.88 \times 10^3 \, \text{J} \approx 2.9 \times 10^3 \, \text{J}$
   c work done = change in kinetic energy (or work done = energy transfer)

Chapter 3

1 a $30°$
   b i $180°$
     ii $\frac{3.5}{12} \times 360° = 105°$

2 a $0.52 \, \text{rad}$, $1.57 \, \text{rad}$, $1.83 \, \text{rad}$
   b $28.6°$, $43.0°$, $180°$, $90°$
   c $\frac{\pi}{6} \, \text{rad}$, $\frac{2\pi}{3} \, \text{rad}$, $\frac{3\pi}{2} \, \text{rad}$, $4\pi \, \text{rad}$

3 The magnitude of the velocity remains the same. (The speed is constant.)

4 a $0 \, \text{m s}^{-1}$
   b $0.4 \, \text{m s}^{-1}$

5 a Gravitational pull of Earth on Moon.
   b Frictional force of road on wheels.
   c Tension in string supporting the pendulum.

6 No frictional force between wheels and road. If driver turns steering wheel, car will carry straight on.

7 Speed and kinetic energy are scalar quantities; the others are all vectors. Speed is constant; velocity has constant magnitude but direction is changing (it is tangential to the circle); kinetic energy is constant; momentum has constant magnitude but direction is changing (tangential to the circle); centripetal force has constant magnitude but direction is changing (radial force); centripetal acceleration behaves in the same way as centripetal force.

8 5.08×10^3 s (84.6 min)

9 $3.46 \,\text{m s}^{-1} \approx 3.5 \,\text{m s}^{-1}$

10 a 184 kN
   b $7.71 \times 10^3 \,\text{m s}^{-1}$
   c 5500 s
   d 15.7 times

11 a $9.42 \,\text{m s}^{-1} \approx 9.4 \,\text{m s}^{-1}$
   b $178 \,\text{m s}^{-2} \approx 180 \,\text{m s}^{-2}$
   c 71 N

12 a $2.43 \times 10^4 \,\text{m s}^{-1} \approx 24 \,\text{km s}^{-1}$
   b $2.57 \times 10^{-3} \,\text{m s}^{-2}$
   c 1.64×10^{21} N

13 Tension in the string must have a vertical component to balance the weight of the conker.

14 In level flight, lift balances the weight. During banking, the vertical component of lift is less than the weight, so the aeroplane loses height unless lift can be increased.

15 The normal contact force of the wall of the slide has a horizontal component, which provides the centripetal force. If you are going fast, you need a bigger force, so the horizontal component must be greater. This happens when you move up the curve of the wall of the slide.

Chapter 4

1 a 6.7×10^{-9} N
   b 1.0×10^{-8} N
   c 1.2×10^5 N

2 About 10^{-6} N. Weight greater than this by factor of 10^9.

3 2.8 N (or 0.3 kg on scales). Measurable with bathroom scales, though hard to achieve accuracy.

4 a i $1.6 \,\text{N kg}^{-1}$
     ii $272 \,\text{N kg}^{-1} \approx 270 \,\text{N kg}^{-1}$
   b Only a very thin atmosphere on the Moon because the gases can escape the weak gravity.

5 a $2.8 \times 10^{-3} \,\text{N kg}^{-1}$
   b 2.1×10^{20} N; $2.8 \times 10^{-3} \,\text{m s}^{-2}$

6 $25.0 \,\text{N kg}^{-1}$

7 Field strength due to Sun at Earth = $5.93 \times 10^{-3} \,\text{N kg}^{-1}$.
Field strength due to Moon at Earth = $3.42 \times 10^{-5} \,\text{N kg}^{-1}$.
So the Sun exerts a greater pull per kilogram on seawater.

8 a 1.7×10^{-8} N
   b 8.34×10^{-8} N $\approx 8.3 \times 10^{-8}$ N

9 Closer to the Moon. The point will be 3.42×10^5 km from the centre of the Earth.

10 $7.8 \times 10^3 \,\text{m s}^{-1}$

11 a Plot T^2 against r^3, which gives a straight line through the origin. (Alternatively, determine the average value of T^2/r^3, which is $3.06 \times 10^{-16} \,\text{s}^2 \,\text{m}^{-3}$.)
   b 1.9×10^{27} kg
   c 1.8×10^8 m

12 The satellite will gradually slow (its kinetic energy will decrease) and spiral down towards the Earth's surface. Small thruster rockets are normally used to give the satellite an occasional push to maintain its speed and height above the Earth.

13 20 600 km

14 Minimum time delay = 0.24 s; signals travel perhaps 30% slower in cables, but distance much shorter.

Chapter 5

1 *Free:* pendulum in clock; cymbal *after* being struck. *Forced:* wing beat of mosquito; shaking of building *during* earthquake.

2 Curved.

3 Amplitude 10 cm, period 120 ms, frequency 8.3 Hz.

4 a Half an oscillation.
   b Different frequencies means that the term *phase difference* is meaningless.

5 The pendulum bob is the mass at the end of the pendulum. The equilibrium position is where the mass is hanging vertically downwards. The restoring force is a component of the weight.

6 The person has mass. When they have lost contact with the trampoline, the force acting on the person is constant and equal to the weight; it is not proportional to the displacement of the person.

7 a 0.02 m   b 0.40 s
   c $0.31 \,\text{m s}^{-1}$ d $5.0 \,\text{m s}^{-2}$

8 At the extreme left of the oscillation (i.e. maximum negative displacement), the acceleration is positive (towards the right).

9 Gradient = 0, so $v = 0 \,\text{m s}^{-1}$.

10 a $0 \,\text{cm s}^{-1}$ b $47 \,\text{cm s}^{-1}$
   c $0 \,\text{cm s}^{-2}$

11 a 0.5 s   **b** 2.0 Hz

    c $4\pi\,\text{rad}\,\text{s}^{-1} \approx 13\,\text{rad}\,\text{s}^{-1}$

12 a 0.20 m

    b 0.40 s

    c 2.5 Hz

    d $15.7\,\text{rad}\,\text{s}^{-1} \approx 16\,\text{rad}\,\text{s}^{-1}$

    e −0.10 m

    f $0\,\text{m}\,\text{s}^{-1}$

    g $3.1\,\text{m}\,\text{s}^{-1}$

13 a

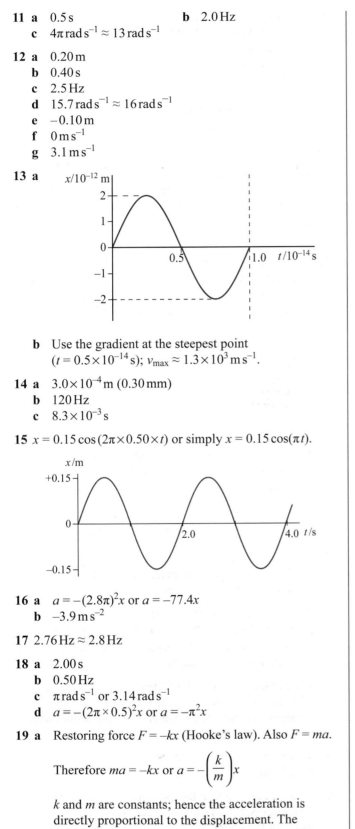

    b Use the gradient at the steepest point $(t = 0.5 \times 10^{-14}\,\text{s})$; $v_{max} \approx 1.3 \times 10^3\,\text{m}\,\text{s}^{-1}$.

14 a $3.0 \times 10^{-4}\,\text{m}$ (0.30 mm)

    b 120 Hz

    c $8.3 \times 10^{-3}\,\text{s}$

15 $x = 0.15\cos(2\pi \times 0.50 \times t)$ or simply $x = 0.15\cos(\pi t)$.

16 a $a = -(2.8\pi)^2 x$ or $a = -77.4x$

    b $-3.9\,\text{m}\,\text{s}^{-2}$

17 $2.76\,\text{Hz} \approx 2.8\,\text{Hz}$

18 a 2.00 s

    b 0.50 Hz

    c $\pi\,\text{rad}\,\text{s}^{-1}$ or $3.14\,\text{rad}\,\text{s}^{-1}$

    d $a = -(2\pi \times 0.5)^2 x$ or $a = -\pi^2 x$

19 a Restoring force $F = -kx$ (Hooke's law). Also $F = ma$.

    Therefore $ma = -kx$ or $a = -\left(\dfrac{k}{m}\right)x$

    k and m are constants; hence the acceleration is directly proportional to the displacement. The motion is s.h.m.

    b $(2\pi f)^2 = \dfrac{k}{m}$ or $\left(\dfrac{2\pi}{T}\right)^2 = \dfrac{k}{m}$

    Therefore $T = 2\pi\sqrt{\dfrac{m}{k}}$

20 a Gravitational potential energy.

    b Gravitational potential energy has changed to kinetic energy by the midpoint of the oscillation; then kinetic energy changes back to gravitational potential energy again.

21

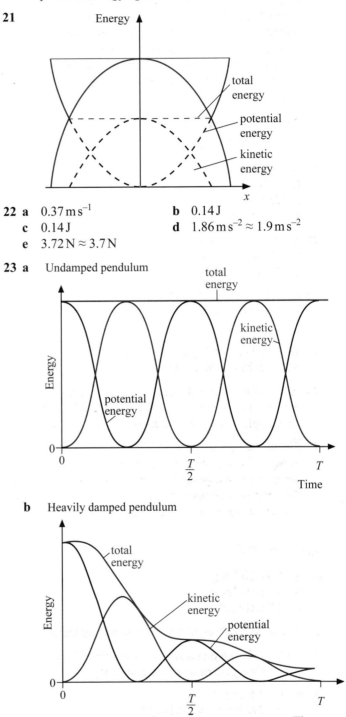

22 a $0.37\,\text{m}\,\text{s}^{-1}$ **b** 0.14 J

    c 0.14 J   **d** $1.86\,\text{m}\,\text{s}^{-2} \approx 1.9\,\text{m}\,\text{s}^{-2}$

    e $3.72\,\text{N} \approx 3.7\,\text{N}$

23 a Undamped pendulum

    b Heavily damped pendulum

    The kinetic energy and the potential energy will decrease with time. Hence the total energy will also decrease. Eventually the oscillations die out completely. All the energy of the pendulum has been transferred to the surroundings (as heat).

24 Some examples of useful and of problematic resonance:

Example	Useful/problem?	What is resonating?
Buildings in earthquake	Problem	Mechanical structure forced by energy from waves of earthquake.
Components in engines	Problem	At certain rates of rotation, parts of an engine may resonate mechanically; the resonance is driven by the energy output of the engine. This can lead to components cracking or disintegrating, with dangerous consequences.
Positive feedback in amplification systems (gives high-pitched squealing sound)	Problem	Microphone held too close to loudspeaker that is emitting waves of the same frequency as the microphone is tuned to, so the waves from the loudspeaker force the amplifier to resonate.
Tuned radio	Useful	Electric signal in circuit forced by incoming radio waves.
Microwave cooker	Useful	Water molecules forced by microwaves.
Magnetic resonance in atoms	Useful	Nuclei in atoms behave as magnets; they can be made to resonate by electromagnetic waves. Each nucleus resonates at a different frequency, so the structures of molecules can be determined.

Chapter 6

1 *Solid:* small spacing, well ordered in a lattice structure, no motion except lattice vibrations.
Liquid: small spacing but some gaps, less well ordered, motion fairly slow.
Gas: large spacing, no order, faster and random motion.

2 $\frac{1}{2}MV^2 = \frac{1}{2}mv^2$

$\frac{v}{V} = \sqrt{\frac{M}{m}}$

Since $M \gg m$, it follows that $v \gg V$.

3 **a** Takes energy (implying work and time) to separate all the molecules to form steam.
b Much greater energy required to separate all the molecules (to form gas) than to create some disorder but not separate (to form liquid).
c Increases the rate of evaporation from its tongue. Energy required for evaporation means that it cools down.

4 **a** 273 K, 293 K, 393 K, 773 K, 250 K, 73 K
b −273 °C, −253 °C, −173 °C, 27 °C, 100 °C, 227 °C

5

Temperature /°C	Resistance /Ω	Temperature /K
10	3120	283
50	3600	323
75	3900	348
100	4200	373
150	4800	423
220	5640	493
260	6120	533

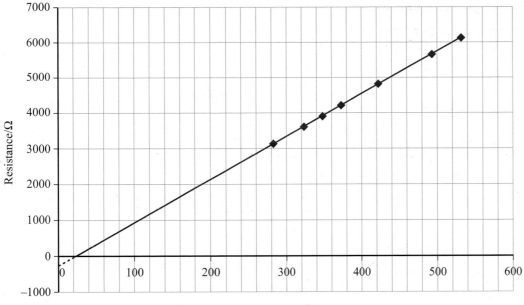

The graph, when extrapolated backwards, cuts the axis at about 20 K. At 0 K the copper atoms are not moving, so the electrons can travel freely through the metal. There are no electron–atom collisions and hence the resistance is zero at this temperature (it can't be negative).

6   1.67 MJ ≈ 1.7 MJ

7   Copper (just).

8   $435 \, \mathrm{J \, kg^{-1} \, K^{-1}} \approx 440 \, \mathrm{J \, kg^{-1} \, K^{-1}}$

9   At higher temperatures, energy escapes more quickly, so the temperature rises more slowly.

10 Systematic; can be removed (in principle) by insulation.

11 $5700 \, \mathrm{J \, kg^{-1} \, K^{-1}}$. Biggest source of error will be energy loss due to poor insulation. There will also be an error because we have ignored the specific heat capacity of the beaker.

12 **a**   AB: solid; BC: solid and liquid; CD: liquid
    b   Increasing in all sections from A to B, B to C, and C to D.
    c   Greater when a solid: CD has a steeper slope than AB, so it takes less energy to heat the liquid through 1 K than the solid.

13 660 J. When a solid melts, only about one bond per atom/molecule is broken. On boiling, several remaining bonds are broken, requiring more energy.

Chapter 7

1   **a** 6.02×10^{23} atoms
    b   4.5 mol; 2.71×10^{24} atoms
    c 5.0×10^{25} atoms

2   **a** 3.9×10^{-25} kg
    b   **i** 8.5×10^{-5} moles
          ii 5.1×10^{19} atoms

3   Typical relative atomic mass = 10, so 1 kg contains 100 moles, or 6×10^{25} atoms $\sim 10^{26}$. (Note that for heavier elements such as iron, relative atomic mass ~ 60 and number of atoms $\sim 10^{25}$ per kg.)

4   $192 \, \mathrm{kPa} = 1.92 \times 10^5 \, \mathrm{Pa} \approx 1.9 \times 10^5 \, \mathrm{Pa}$

5   6400 kPa

6   150 K; −123 °C

7   **a**   With V fixed, if T increases, so does p (because pV/T is constant).
    b   With p fixed, if T decreases, so does V.

8   **a**   Volume.
    b $p \propto T$, or p/T = constant, or $p = \text{constant} \times T$

9   1200 K

10 **a**   3.57 mol ≈ 3.6 mol
    b $8.0 \times 10^{-2} \, \mathrm{m^3} = 80 \, \mathrm{dm^3}$

11 $0.20 \, \mathrm{m^3}$

12 $0.10 \, \mathrm{m^3}$

13 385 K (= 112 °C)

14 **a**   166 g ≈ 170 g
    b   2.65 kg ≈ 2.7 kg

15 6.2×10^{-21} J

16 242 K; −31 °C

17 Temperature is proportional to (average speed)^2. So, if average speed doubles, temperature increases by a factor of $2^2 = 4$.

18 a Halved.
b Stays the same.

19 Mean KE = 6.1×10^{-21} J; O_2: 480 m s^{-1}; N_2: 510 m s^{-1}

20 Internal energy = $E = N_A \times (\frac{3}{2}kT)$; $\frac{\Delta E}{\Delta T} = \frac{3}{2}(N_A k) = \frac{3}{2}R$

Chapter 8

1 a Diagram **i** shows positive charges repelling.
b Diagram **iii** shows negative charges repelling.
c Diagram **ii** shows opposite charges attracting.

2

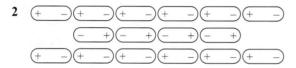

3 The field strength is greatest at the top/pointed part of the building. The electric field lines are closest together here.

4

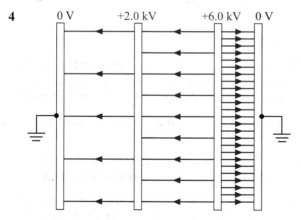

5 5000 V m^{-1} or N C^{-1}.

6 a 160 000 V
b 0.08 mm
c 400 MV

7 a

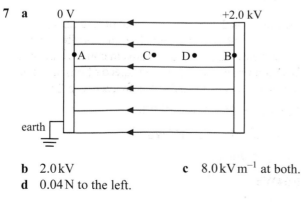

b 2.0 kV   **c** 8.0 kV m^{-1} at both.
d 0.04 N to the left.

8 a 5.0×10^4 V m^{-1} or N C^{-1} **b** 0.10 N

9 8.8×10^{17} m s^{-2}

10

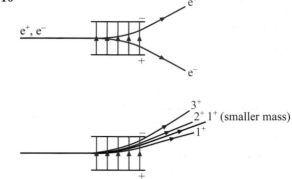

Ions with a greater mass will show smaller deflection. Ions with greater mass will have greater deflection.

11 a 2.9×10^5 V m^{-1}
b 0.072 N
c 4.32×10^5 V m^{-1} ≈ 4.3×10^5 V m^{-1} (towards negative sphere)

12 1.8×10^{-5} C

13 Electrostatic force 230 N; gravitational force 1.9×10^{-34} N. This answer tells us that gravitational attraction is nowhere near enough to balance the electric repulsion. Therefore, some other force must hold the protons together. (In fact, it is the *strong nuclear force*, which is covered in Chapter 12.)

Chapter 9

1 current flowing into page   current flowing out of page, strength doubled

2

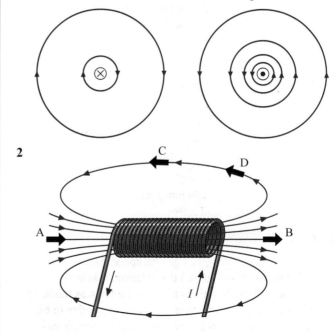

3 Pair **a** will repel, pair **b** will attract.

4 **a** No force.
b Force into the plane of the paper.
c Force down the page.

5 6.0×10^{-3} N (6.0 mN)

6 7.8×10^{-3} T

7 **a** 2.0 N
b Pivoted along one edge.
c Greater torque provided by: increasing current, increasing number of turns in coil, increasing length of side in field, pivoting by centre of coil and have magnets either side, having magnets all round the circle through which the coil turns, increasing field strength.

8 **a** 0.375 N ≈ 0.38 N
b 0.265 N ≈ 0.27 N
c 0 N.
Both **a** and **b** are into the plane of the paper.

9

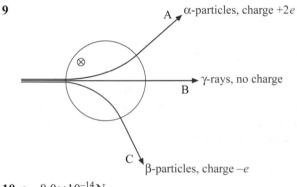

A α-particles, charge $+2e$

B γ-rays, no charge

C β-particles, charge $-e$

10 **a** 8.0×10^{-14} N
b 5.66×10^{-14} N $\approx 5.7 \times 10^{-14}$ N

11 Since the particles have opposite charges, they experience a force in opposite directions.

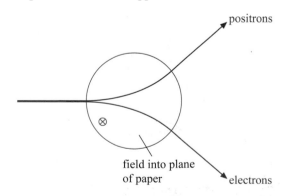

positrons

field into plane of paper

electrons

12 Out of the plane of the photograph.

13 All have same mass, charge and speed. When J. J. Thomson discovered the electron, this is what convinced him that his beam of particles was made up of just one type of particle, i.e. all the particles in his beam were identical (same mass, same charge) and moving at the same speed.

14 **a** Circular path will have smaller radius.
b Electrons will circle in the opposite direction.
c Circular path will have smaller radius.
d Electrons will spiral around field lines because they will have a constant component of velocity in the direction of the field lines.

15 **a** 1.6×10^{-16} J, 1.87×10^{7} m s^{-1} $\approx 1.9 \times 10^{7}$ m s^{-1}
b $10\,000$ V m^{-1}, 1.6×10^{-15} N
c No field in horizontal plane.
5.3×10^{-9} s
d 1.76×10^{15} m s^{-2} $\approx 1.8 \times 10^{15}$ m s^{-2}, 9.4×10^{6} m s^{-1}
e 26.6°
f 25.0 cm
g Deflection decreased; deflection increased.
h 5.34×10^{-4} T $\approx 5.3 \times 10^{-4}$ T into the page.

16 **a** The magnetic force is towards the positive plate and the electric force is towards the negative plate.
b $BQv = EQ$; therefore $v = \dfrac{E}{B}$. The charge Q does not feature in the equation.
c 5.0×10^{3} m s^{-1}
d Magnetic force > electric force; the ion travels in an upward *curved* path (towards the positive plate) and hence misses the slit S.

Chapter 10

1 The rotating magnet changes the magnetic flux linking the coil, hence an e.m.f. is induced. The induced current in the coil will light the lamp connected to the dynamo.

2 Current flows from A to B and from C to D, so X is positive.

3 Left wingtip positive. It is negative in the Southern Hemisphere because the field direction is reversed.

4 Magnetic flux = BA. A stronger magnet means greater flux linking the coil and hence a greater induced e.m.f. Faster movement means more flux cut/linked per second and more current generated, or larger e.m.f.

5 The wire is moved parallel to the field, hence only small components cut due to slight curvature at edges of field.

6 Frequency is determined by speed of rotation (so to keep constant, must be geared). E.m.f. is affected by magnet strength, number of turns in coil, size of coil. Would normally be affected by speed of rotation, but in this case that has to be fixed as frequency is fixed.

7 2.25×10^{-5} Wb $\approx 2.3 \times 10^{-5}$ Wb

8 1.44×10^{7} Wb $\approx 1.5 \times 10^{7}$ Wb

9 7.9×10^{-6} Wb

10 0.54 Wb

11 Rate of change in area = Lv;
rate of change of flux = $B \times (Lv) = BLv$.

12 6.0 mV

13 0.60 V

14 0.33 T

15 a 5.0×10^{-3} Wb
b 0.050 V

16 a Stop pushing implies no change in flux linkage, so no current is generated. Therefore, no magnetic poles are formed and no work is done; there is no movement.
b Pull away implies that flux is decreased in the flux linkage, but end of solenoid near to magnet becomes a south pole, so the poles attract each other, and work has to be done to pull magnet and coil apart.

17

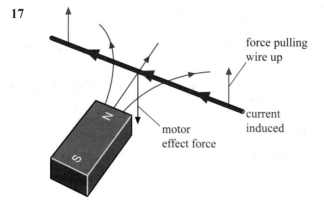

18 a There is a sudden *increase* in the flux linkage for the coil, so there is an induced e.m.f.
b There is no change in the flux linking the coil. The motion is parallel to the field.
c Magnet leaves coil, there is a *decrease* in the flux linking the coil and hence the e.m.f. is in reverse (negative) direction. The induced current is the opposite direction (Lenz's law). Peak e.m.f. is greater because magnet moving faster (acceleration due to gravity), the rate of change of flux linkage is greater.

19 Have to do work against motor effect force from induced current when lights are on.

20

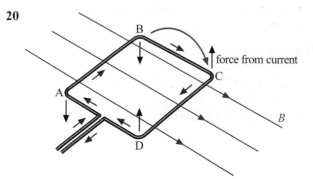

21 Alternating current. Usually, a bar magnet rotates inside a fixed coil. As the N pole passes one side of the coil, the current flows one way. Then the S pole passes, and the current reverses.

22 B greater means greater flux, hence $\dfrac{\Delta(N\phi)}{\Delta t}$ is greater; therefore $E \propto B$.

A greater means greater flux, hence $\dfrac{\Delta(N\phi)}{\Delta t}$ is greater; therefore $E \propto A$.

N greater means greater flux linkage, hence $\dfrac{\Delta(N\phi)}{\Delta t}$ is greater; therefore $E \propto N$.
f greater means rate of change of flux linkage is greater, hence $\dfrac{\Delta(N\phi)}{\Delta t}$ is greater; therefore $E \propto f$.

23 For d.c. supply, the flux linkage is constant – there is no change in the flux, and hence no induced e.m.f.

24 a Step-up: 15 : 5 = 3.
b Step-down: 4 : 8 = 0.5.
c Step-up: 30 V; step-down: 5.0 V.

25 32 000

Chapter 11

1 3300 μC, 3.3×10^{-3} C

2 2.0×10^{-6} F, 2.0 μF, 2.0×10^{6} pF

3 0.050 A (50 mA)

4

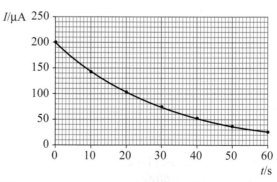

Charge = area under graph ≈ 5.1 mC
Capacitance ≈ 6.0×10^{-4} F (600 μF)

5 a 6.25×10^{-2} J ≈ 6.3×10^{-2} J
b 6.3×10^{-8} J
c 5.29 J ≈ 5.3 J

6 Charge is the same for both capacitors (2.0×10^{-2} C). Energy stored is greater in the 100 μF capacitor (2.0 J compared to 1.0 J).

7 a 0.72 J
b 0.02 s

8 a 1.8 C, 8.1 J
b 810 W
c 180 A
d 0.025 Ω

9 Gradient $= \dfrac{V}{Q} = \dfrac{1}{C}$

10 a 1.0×10^{-3} F (1 mF)

b

Q/mC	V/V	Area of strip ΔW/ mJ	Sum of areas W/mJ
1.0	1.0	0.5	0.5
2.0	2.0	1.5	2.0
3.0	3.0	2.5	4.5
4.0	4.0	3.5	8.0

c The graph is a parabola.

11 a $200\,\mu$F
b 4.0×10^{-3} C (4000 μC)

12 Two $20\,\mu$F and one $10\,\mu$F connected in parallel; or five $10\,\mu$F connected in parallel.

13 $100\,\mu$F

14 a $C_{\text{total}} = \dfrac{C}{2}$

b $C_{\text{total}} = \dfrac{C}{n}$

c $C_{\text{total}} = 2C$
d $C_{\text{total}} = nC$

15 a $\dfrac{1}{G_{\text{total}}} = \dfrac{1}{G_1} + \dfrac{1}{G_2}$

b $G_{\text{total}} = G_1 + G_2$

16 a $33.3\,\mu$F
b $300\,\mu$F
c $66.7\,\mu$F
d $150\,\mu$F

17 a Four in parallel.
b Four in series.
c Two in series with two in parallel.

18 Maximum: in parallel, 900 pF.
Minimum: in series, 60 pF.

19 $4.0\,\mu$F

20 a $40\,\mu$F
b 0.40 C
c 2.0×10^3 J

21 a $25\,\mu$F
b 4.0×10^{-3} C (4000 μC)
c 160 V
d 8.0×10^{-2} J (80 mJ)

22 8.0×10^{-5} A (80 μA), 4.0×10^{-4} C (400 μC)

23 a

Point	A	B	C	D	E
I/μA	2.2	1.7	1.2	0.9	0.7
t/s	10	20	30	40	50

b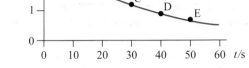

24 2.7×10^{-3} C (2.7 mC)

25 2.8 V

26 a 5.00×10^{-4} A (500 μA)
b $I = 5.0 \times 10^{-4} \times e^{-t/200}$ A

c

Time t /s	0	100	200	300	400	500
Current I /10^{-6}A	500	303	184	112	68	41

d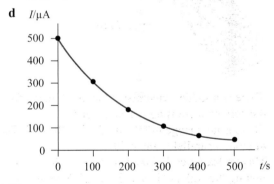

27 22 ms

28 a 8.0×10^{-5} A (80 μA)
b 2.96×10^{-5} A $\approx 3.0 \times 10^{-5}$ A (30 μA)
c 2.4 s
d $\approx 2400\,\mu$F
e 4.8 s; $\approx 2400\,\mu$F

29 a 0.50 mA
b 0.27 mA
c 50 s

30 a 50 s
b $Q = 600 \times e^{-(0.02 \times t)}\,\mu$C
$I = 12 \times e^{-(0.02 \times t)}\,\mu$A
$V = 6.0 \times e^{-(0.02 \times t)}$ V
c 3.6×10^{-6} A (3.6 μA)

Chapter 12

1 If there were air molecules in the container, the α-particles would scatter off them as well and distort the results.

2 a More back-scattered, because greater chance of close approach to gold nucleus.
  b Fewer back-scattered, because their inertia would tend to carry them forward.
  c Fewer back-scattered, because the repulsive force would be less. (Note: gold and silver atoms occupy roughly the same volume.)

3 Volume $= 1.6 \times 10^{-29} \, m^3$; radius $\sim 1.6 \times 10^{-10} \, m$ (assuming little empty space between atoms).

4 a 7
  b 44
  c 60
  d 118
  e 122

5 a $+e$
  b No charge.
  c $+Ze$, where Z is the proton number.
  d No charge.
  e $+2e$

6 143 and 146 neutrons.

7 a Proton number 80 for all.
    Neutron numbers 116, 118, 119, 120, 121, 122, 124.
  b 200.6

8 They are grouped into isotopes as follows:
  A and E; C; D, F and G; B and H.
  $A = {}^{44}_{20}Ca$ isotope of calcium
  $B = {}^{50}_{23}V$ isotope of vanadium
  $C = {}^{46}_{21}Sc$ isotope of scandium
  $D = {}^{46}_{22}Ti$ isotope of titanium
  $E = {}^{46}_{20}Ca$ isotope of calcium
  $F = {}^{48}_{22}Ti$ isotope of titanium
  $G = {}^{50}_{22}Ti$ isotope of titanium
  $H = {}^{51}_{23}V$ isotope of vanadium

9 There are 38 protons and 52 neutrons in the nucleus.

10 a There are different numbers of neutrons in the nuclei.
   b There is the same number of protons in each nucleus.

11 Protons: gravitational, electrostatic, strong nuclear.
   Neutrons: gravitational, strong nuclear.

12 For (u d d), $Q = (+\frac{2}{3}) + (-\frac{1}{3}) + (-\frac{1}{3}) = 0$.

13 For both proton and neutron: $B = +1$, $S = 0$.

14 Quarks are up, up and strange: $Q = +1$, $B = 1$, $S = -1$.

Chapter 13

1 ${}^{235}_{92}U + {}^{1}_{0}n \longrightarrow {}^{138}_{54}Xe + {}^{95}_{38}Sr + 3{}^{1}_{0}n$
  For A $235 + 1 = 138 + 95 + (3 \times 1)$ is correct
  For Z $92 + 0 = 54 + 38 + (3 \times 0)$ is correct

2 ${}^{235}_{92}U + {}^{1}_{0}n \longrightarrow {}^{239}_{94}Pu + 2{}^{0}_{-1}e$
  Two electrons are released.

3 a $2{}^{1}_{0}n$
  b ${}^{90}_{36}Kr$

4 ${}^{1}_{1}H$ (or ${}^{1}_{1}p$)

5 $2{}^{1}_{1}H$

6 ${}^{15}_{7}N + {}^{1}_{1}H \longrightarrow {}^{12}_{6}C + {}^{4}_{2}He$
  Helium is also formed.

7 $4.4 \times 10^{9} \, kg$

8 a $4.5 \times 10^{-12} \, J$
  b $1.1 \times 10^{-12} \, J$

9 The mass of the product (${}^{8}_{4}Be$) is *greater* than the initial mass, so energy is required rather than given out in this reaction.

10 It is a single nucleon and hence does not have binding energy.

11 a $6.00 \times 10^{-29} \, kg$
   b $5.40 \times 10^{-12} \, J$, $3.38 \times 10^{7} \, eV$
   c $6.75 \times 10^{-13} \, J$, $4.22 \times 10^{6} \, eV$

12 Fission for $A < 20$ is unlikely because the products would have a smaller binding energy per nucleon. The reaction would require an input of external energy. Similarly, fusion for $A > 40$ is unlikely for the same reason.

13 Moderator: slows down fast neutrons to thermal speeds so that they will have a greater chance of interacting with the fissile nuclei. Coolant: transfers heat energy from the core to the boiler.

14 a $8.1 \times 10^{13} \, J$
   b (Lifetime $= 80 \, years = 2.5 \times 10^{9} \, s$) so $2.5 \times 10^{12} \, J$, a few per cent of **a**.

Chapter 14

1 Charge is balanced in the equation (proton on left, positron on right); similarly, proton and neutron masses are almost the same, a small mass is left over for the positron, but virtually zero mass for the neutrino.

2 a ${}^{220}_{86}Rn \longrightarrow {}^{216}_{84}Po + {}^{4}_{2}He$
  b ${}^{25}_{11}Na \longrightarrow {}^{25}_{12}Mg + {}^{0}_{-1}e + \bar{v}$

3 a ${}^{41}_{18}Ar \longrightarrow {}^{41}_{19}K + {}^{0}_{-1}e + \bar{v}$
  b ${}^{15}_{8}O \longrightarrow {}^{15}_{7}N + {}^{0}_{+1}e + v$

4 **a** $^{10}_{4}\text{Be} \longrightarrow ^{10}_{5}\text{B} + ^{0}_{-1}\text{e} + \bar{\nu}$

b 8.9×10^{-14} J; the energy is released as kinetic energy of the products.

5 **a** A β-particle is smaller and travels faster.

b Air is much less dense; also metal may 'poach' β-particles (electrons) for conduction.

6 **a, b**

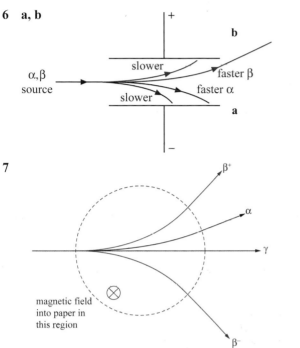

7

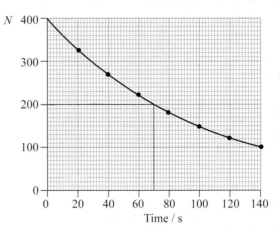

The β⁺ particle track curves in the opposite direction as it has opposite charge to the β⁻ particle (but same mass and speed). The directions are consistent with Fleming's left-hand rule.

8 Most strongly ionising implies many more collisions occur, so there is greater loss of momentum and therefore less penetration.

9 The α-particles are detected by an electronic circuit. When smoke enters the device, the α-particles are absorbed. The circuit then switches on the alarm. Alpha radiation is most suitable because it is the most strongly ionising and so it is more likely to be absorbed by smoke. Also the range of the alpha particles is so small that they are unlikely to constitute a hazard to the user.

10 $150\,000\,\text{s}^{-1}$, or $150\,000\,\text{Bq}$

11 $2.2 \times 10^{-9}\,\text{s}^{-1}$

12 Count rate is less than activity because:

i γ-rays are not always detected (weakly ionising)

ii the counter is inefficient

iii some radiation is absorbed within the sample before reaching the detector

iv the detector is directional, so some radiation will move away from the detector rather than towards it.

13 **a** $N = N_0 e^{-\lambda t}$

b 4.0×10^{10}, 2.0×10^{10}

c 7.0×10^{10}

14 **a** $3.37 \times 10^7 \approx 3.4 \times 10^7$

b $3.4 \times 10^6\,\text{Bq}$

15

t/s	0	20	40	60	80	100	120	140
N	400	330	272	224	185	153	126	104

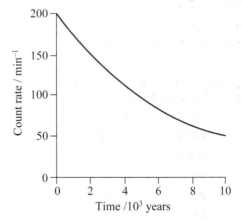

Half-life is about 70 s.

16 Count rate is $59.6\,\text{min}^{-1}$ at 10 000 years.

Age of sample = 4500 years.

17 2.3 years, 0.30 year⁻¹

18 $6.93 \times 10^3 \approx 6900\,\text{s}$

19 **a** $0.094\,\text{s}^{-1}$

b **i** 1250

ii 768 (approximately)

20 **a** $N = N_0 e^{-\lambda t}$; $\dfrac{N}{N_0} = f = e^{-(\ln 2/t_{1/2})t} = e^{-\ln 2(t/t_{1/2})}$; $f = (e^{-0.693})^{t/t_{1/2}}$; $f = (\frac{1}{2})^{t/t_{1/2}}$

b **i** 0.50

ii 0.25

iii $0.177 \approx 0.18$

iv $3.17 \times 10^{-3} \approx 0.0032$

21 *Similarities*

Both decay exponentially.

Reference to equations:

$N = N_0 e^{-\lambda t}$ and $Q = Q_0 e^{-t/CR}$

Differences

The charge Q remaining on a capacitor after a certain time t can be predicted *exactly*.

The number N of undecayed nuclei left after a certain time t shows *statistical variation* – a graph of N against t has random fluctuations because the decay of radioactive nuclei is random and spontaneous (see sketch below).

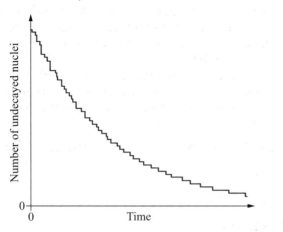

Chapter 15

1 a Electrical energy from supply transferred to energy of electron beam (100%).

Energy of electron beam transferred to internal energy of anode (~99%) and energy of X-ray photons (~1%).

b $80\,\text{keV}$, $1.28 \times 10^{-14}\,\text{J} \approx 1.3 \times 10^{-14}\,\text{J}$, $1.68 \times 10^{8}\,\text{m s}^{-1} \approx 1.7 \times 10^{8}\,\text{m s}^{-1}$

2 Photon energy $E = \dfrac{hc}{\lambda} = V \times e$

Wavelength $\lambda = 1.04 \times 10^{-11}\,\text{m} \approx 1.0 \times 10^{-11}\,\text{m}$

3 X-rays can be switched on and off as desired; gamma sources continue to emit even when not in use. Also, the activity of gamma sources decay with time, are more dangerous to handle, etc.

4 $8.0 \times 10^{5}\,\text{W m}^{-2}$

5 $0.12\,\text{W m}^{-2}$

6 Consider the ratio of attenuation coefficients for bone : muscle. This is approximately 6 for $50\,\text{keV}$ X-rays, so bone is a much better absorber at this energy than is muscle. At $4.0\,\text{MeV}$, the ratio is less than 2, so bone and muscle will not appear very different on the image. (You could also calculate the fraction of X-rays absorbed by, say, $1\,\text{cm}$ of tissue. At $4.0\,\text{MeV}$, only a small fraction is absorbed, so the X-ray image will be flooded with unabsorbed X-rays.)

7 The ratio $\dfrac{Z_{\text{bone}}}{Z_{\text{soft tissue}}} \approx 2$. Since attenuation coefficient $\mu \propto Z^3$, the ratio $\dfrac{\mu_{\text{bone}}}{\mu_{\text{soft tissue}}} = 2^3 = 8$.

8 Breathing causes movement of the body so that organs or bones of interest may move in the X-ray beam as the image is processed.

9 The skull has bone all round. In a conventional X-ray, the beam must pass through both sides of the skull and this makes it difficult to see the inner tissue. In a CAT scan, the inner tissue shows up more clearly and any damage to the skull bones can be pinpointed accurately.

Chapter 16

1 a The half-life is approx 3 days; after a week, the rate of production of Tc-99m will have dropped by a factor of more than $2^2 = 4$.

b Much longer: It would decay very slowly, so a much larger amount would be required to produce Tc-99m at a useful rate.

Much shorter: It would decay much faster, so that new supplies would be required every day, or more frequently.

2 a With larger diameter tubes, more γ-rays will get through. However, each tube will represent a larger area of the patient and so less detail will be seen. (The image will be blurred.)

b γ-rays that are at a slight angle will be absorbed by the collimator. This means that a longer exposure time will be needed in order to receive the same number of X-rays. However, each tube will represent a smaller area of the patient and so the definition will be better.

3 110 minutes is long enough for the tracer to pass around the patient's body. Because it decays fairly quickly (in the course of a few hours), a small dose will give a measurable amount of radiation, and little will remain undecayed in the patient after the treatment is finished.

4 a In conventional imaging, a single image is produced from radiation that has passed through the patient. In tomography, multiple images produced by radiation at different angles are combined in a computer. From this data, images can be constructed of 'slices' through the patient's body – a 3D image.

b In PET scanning, the gamma camera can detect the point of origin in the patient of each pair of X-rays. Thus a 3D picture can be built up of the distribution of the tracer. A computer can then show images of slices through the patient, hence 'tomography'.

5 a $106.5\,\text{MHz}$

b This is also their resonant frequency ($106.5\,\text{MHz}$).

6

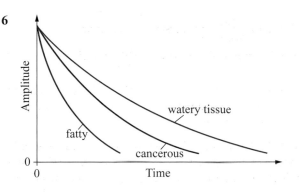

7 a MRI uses non-ionising RF electromagnetic radiation, whereas CAT scanning uses X-rays, which are a form of ionising radiation.
   b CAT scans show up bone, which is poorly imaged by MRI.
   c The patient's body does not have to be cut open; nor do any instruments have to be inserted into the body.

Chapter 17

1 a 2.7×10^{-3} m (2.7 mm)
   b 1.35×10^{-3} m ≈ 1.4 mm

2 a Mechanical to electrical.
   b Electrical to mechanical.
   c Mechanical to electrical.
   d Electrical to mechanical.

3 1.58×10^{6} kg m^{-2} s^{-1} $\approx 1.6 \times 10^{6}$ kg m^{-2} s^{-1}

4 3.2×10^{-3} (0.32%)

5 There is a big change in acoustic impedance when ultrasound passes from fluid into skin, and from tissue into bone. These surfaces therefore give strong reflections. Other soft tissues have similar values of acoustic impedance and so reflections are very weak.

6 The brain is surrounded by solid bone which reflects ultrasound. Little penetrates the brain and hence the signal is very weak.

7 0.026 m (26 mm)

8 X-rays are ionising radiation and hence are damaging to the fetus. Ultrasound carries very little risk because it is not a form of ionising radiation. (The intensity used must not cause heating of the baby's tissues.)

9 Waves reflected by a reflector moving towards the source are 'squashed up' and so their wavelength is reduced. This increases their frequency (because their speed is constant).

10 0.20 m s^{-1}, 2.27×10^{-7} m^3 s^{-1} $\approx 2.3 \times 10^{-7}$ m^3 s^{-1}

Chapter 18

1 a The Sun's mass is relatively low so it follows the track ending with red giant and white dwarf.
   b The mass of the Sun is too small for its gravity to be strong enough to produce a black hole.

2 a Gravity (the gravitational attraction of each particle pulling on all the other particles).
   b Gravity.
   c Gravity.

3 a 1.8×10^{17} kg m^{-3}
   b 1.7×10^{4} m
   c The density of the neutron star will be less than that of a neutron. Hence its volume and radius will be greater than calculated in part **b**; the answer to **b** is an underestimate.
   d The neutron star is made of closely packed neutrons; the Sun is a plasma of protons, neutrons and electrons with a density 10^{14} times less than that of a neutron star.

4 1 ly = 299 792 458 $\times$ 365.25636 $\times$ 24 $\times$ 60 $\times$ 60 $\approx 10^{16}$ m

5 a 1.3 pc
   b 4.3 ly
   c 4.1×10^{16} m

6 2.7×10^{-3} AU

7 a

Star	p/arc sec	d/ly	d/pc	p×d/pc arc sec
Altair	0.20	16	4.85	0.97
Arcturus	0.090	36	10.9	0.98
Capella	0.073	45	13.6	0.99
Sirius	0.38	8.7	2.64	1.00
Vega	0.12	26	7.88	0.95

   b Since $d = 1/p$, the product of d in parsec and p in arc second must be equal to one. That is: $pd = 1$.

8 2.55×10^{7} m s^{-1} $\approx 2.6 \times 10^{7}$ m s^{-1}

9 Redshift $= 1.33 \times 10^{-3}$ so component of velocity along line of sight $= 4.0 \times 10^{5}$ m s^{-1}. This is the component of the star's velocity *towards* the observer (because the wavelength is reduced); it may have another component at right angles to this.

10 a 2.52×10^{-18} s^{-1} $\approx 2.5 \times 10^{-18}$ s^{-1}
   b 3.97×10^{17} s $= 1.26 \times 10^{10}$ y ≈ 13 billion years

11 Gradient of graph $= H_0 = 75$ km s^{-1} Mpc^{-1}
   $= 2.42 \times 10^{-18}$ s^{-1}
   Age of universe $\approx 1/$gradient (gradient in unit s^{-1}) $=$
   4.13×10^{17} s $= 13.1 \times 10^{9}$ y ≈ 13 billion years.

Chapter 19

1
- the Big Bang
- quarks and leptons exist freely
- protons form
- atomic nuclei form
- atoms form
- stars form
- today

2 (All answers are approximate.)
   a 10^{14} K
   b 10^{10} s
   c 10^5 K

3
- today
- universe starts to contract
- galaxies merge together
- atoms lose their electrons
- atomic nuclei disintegrate
- hadrons disintegrate into quarks
- quarks and leptons exist freely
- the Big Crunch

4 $H_0 = 3.2 \times 10^{-18}$ s^{-1}; $\rho_0 = 1.2 \times 10^{-24}$ kg m^{-3}; density is greater than this, so universe is closed and will collapse to a Big Crunch.

Glossary

absolute zero The temperature at which a system has minimum internal energy; equivalent to $-273.15\,°C$.

acoustic impedance Acoustic impedance Z is the product of the density ρ of a substance and the speed c of sound in that substance ($Z = \rho c$). Unit: $kg\,m^{-2}\,s^{-1}$.

activity The rate of decay or disintegration of nuclei in a radioactive sample.

amplitude The maximum displacement of a particle from its equilibrium position.

angular displacement The angle through which an object moves in a circle.

angular frequency The rate of change of angle expressed in radian per second. Angular frequency $\omega = \dfrac{2\pi}{T}$

astronomical unit The average distance of the Earth from the Sun.

Avogadro constant The number of particles in one mole of any substance ($6.02 \times 10^{23}\,mol^{-1}$), denoted N_A.

Big Bang An event that describes a very hot explosion from which space and time evolved – the beginning of the universe.

binding energy The minimum external energy required to separate all the neutrons and protons of a nucleus.

black hole A remnant of a massive star formed as a result of matter collapsing to a point (singularity). The density of a black hole is so intense that even light cannot escape from it.

Boyle's law The pressure exerted by a fixed mass of gas is inversely proportional to its volume, provided the temperature of the gas remains constant.

braking radiation X-rays produced when electrons are decelerated (also called Bremsstrahlung radiation).

capacitance The ratio of charge stored by a capacitor to the potential difference across it.

carbon-dating A technique used to date relics using the carbon-14 isotope.

centripetal force The net force acting on an object moving in a circle; it is always directed towards the centre of the circle.

chain reaction An exponential growth of a fission reaction caused by the increasing flux of neutrons causing fission.

Chandrasekhar limit The maximum mass of a white dwarf – about 1.4 solar masses.

characteristic radiation Very intense X-rays produced in an X-ray tube having specific wavelengths that depend on the target metal.

Charles' law The volume occupied by a gas at constant pressure is directly proportional to its thermodynamic (absolute) temperature.

closed system A system of interacting objects where there are no external forces.

closed universe A model of the universe in which gravitational force is strong enough to halt its expansion and reverse the process towards a Big Crunch.

collimated beam A parallel-sided beam of radiation.

collimator A device for producing a parallel beam of radiation.

Compton scattering An interaction between an X-ray photon and an electron in which the photon is scattered with a longer wavelength.

computerised axial tomography A technique where X-rays are used to image slices of the body in order to produce a computerised 3-D image.

conservation of momentum In a closed system, when bodies interact, the total momentum in any specified direction remains constant.

contrast In a high-contrast image, there is a big difference in brightness between bright and dark areas.

contrast media Materials such as barium that easily absorb X-rays. A contrast medium is used to reveal the outlines or edges of soft tissues in an X-ray image.

control rods Rods of a neutron-absorbing material used to reduce the rate of a nuclear chain reaction.

coolant A substance used to transfer thermal energy from the core of a nuclear reactor.

cosmic microwave background radiation Electromagnetic radiation in the microwave region of the spectrum that corresponds to a temperature of the universe of 2.7 K.

cosmological principle A principle that states that the universe has the same large-scale structure when observed from any point in the universe.

Coulomb's law Any two point charges exert an electrical force on each other that is proportional to the product of their charges and inversely proportional to the square of the distance between them.

count rate The number of particles (beta or alpha) or gamma-ray photons detected per unit time by a Geiger–Müller tube. Count rate is always a fraction of the activity of a sample.

critical density The density of the universe that will give rise to a flat universe, given by the equation:

$$\rho_0 = \frac{3H_0^2}{8\pi G}$$

damped Describes an oscillatory motion where the amplitude decreases with time due to energy losses.

dark energy A form of energy thinly distributed throughout the universe and which may be causing the expansion of the universe to accelerate.

dark matter Matter that emits or reflects little electromagnetic radiation, making it very difficult to detect.

decay constant The constant λ for an isotope that appears in the equation $A = \lambda N$. It is equal to the probability of an isotope decaying per unit time interval.

Doppler effect The change in the frequency and wavelength of a wave caused by the relative movement between source and detector.

Doppler equation An equation that relates the fractional change in the wavelength of a wave to the speed of the source as a fraction of the speed of light:

$$\frac{\Delta\lambda}{\lambda} = \frac{v}{c}$$

electric field lines Lines used to map out electric field patterns. The arrow on a field line shows the direction of the field and the strength of the field is indicated by the closeness of the field lines.

electric field strength The force per unit positive charge at a point. Unit: $V\,m^{-1}$ or $N\,C^{-1}$.

electron degeneracy pressure Pressure created by closely packed electrons in a white dwarf due to Pauli's exclusion principle. (Also known as Fermi pressure.)

equation of state Equation for an ideal gas: $pV = nRT$ or $pV = NkT$. (Also known as the ideal gas equation.)

evaporation The process by which a liquid becomes a gas at a temperature below its boiling point.

exponential decay A quantity that has a 'constant-ratio property' with respect to time.

exponential decay graph A decaying graph that has a constant-ratio property for a given interval of time.

farad The unit of capacitance. $1\,F = 1\,C\,V^{-1}$.

Fermi pressure See electron degeneracy pressure.

flat universe A universe that expands forever, but whose rate of expansion tends to zero after infinite time.

Fleming's left-hand (motor) rule This rule is used to predict the force experienced by a current-carrying conductor placed in an external magnetic field: thu<u>m</u>b $\longrightarrow$ <u>m</u>otion, <u>f</u>irst finger $\longrightarrow$ magnetic <u>f</u>ield and se<u>c</u>ond finger $\longrightarrow$ conventional <u>c</u>urrent.

Fleming's right-hand (dynamo) rule This rule is used to predict the direction of the induced current or e.m.f. in a conductor moved at right angles to a magnetic field: thu<u>m</u>b $\longrightarrow$ <u>m</u>otion, <u>f</u>irst finger $\longrightarrow$ magnetic <u>f</u>ield and se<u>c</u>ond finger $\longrightarrow$ induced conventional <u>c</u>urrent.

frequency The number of oscillations of a particle per unit time. Unit: hertz (Hz).

fundamental particles Particles that cannot be subdivided.

geostationary orbit The orbit of an artificial satellite which has a period equal to one day so that the satellite remains above the same point on the Earth's equator. From Earth the satellite appears to be stationary.

gravitational collapse The gathering of dust and gas due to gravitational forces.

gravitational field strength The gravitational force experienced by an object per unit mass:

$$g = \frac{F}{m}$$

hadrons Particles consisting of quarks (e.g. proton, neutron).

half-life The mean time taken for half the number of active nuclei in a radioactive sample to decay.

Hubble constant The ratio of the speed v of a receding galaxy to its distance x from the observer:

$$H_0 = \frac{v}{x}$$

hydrogen burning A sequence of nuclear reactions in which four protons fuse together to produce a helium nucleus:

$$4\,^1_1H \longrightarrow\, ^4_2He + 2\,^0_{+1}e + 2\nu$$

ideal gas A gas that behaves according to the equations $pV = nRT$ and $pV = NkT$.

ideal gas equation Equation for an ideal gas: $pV = nRT$ or $pV = NkT$. (Also known as the equation of state.)

image intensifier A device used to change a low-intensity X-ray image into a bright visual image.

impedance matching The reduction in intensity of reflected ultrasound at the boundary between two substances, achieved when the two substances have similar acoustic impedances.

impulse The product of the force F and the time Δt for which it acts: impulse $= F\Delta t$.

induced nuclear fission A fission reaction started when a neutron is absorbed by a nucleus.

inelastic A collision is inelastic when the kinetic energy is not conserved; some is transferred to other forms such as heat. Momentum and total energy are always conserved.

internal energy The sum of the random distribution of kinetic and potential energies of the atoms or molecules in a system.

ion An atom with a net positive or negative charge.

isotopes Nuclei of the same element with a different number of neutrons but the same number of protons.

kinetic theory of gases A model based on the microscopic motion of atoms or molecules of a gas.

Larmor frequency The frequency of precession of nuclei in an external magnetic field.

latent heat of fusion The energy absorbed by a substance to change state from solid to liquid without any change in temperature.

latent heat of vaporisation The energy absorbed by a substance to change state from liquid to gas without any change in temperature.

Lenz's law The induced current or e.m.f. is in a direction so as to produce effects which oppose the change producing it.

leptons A group of fundamental particles that includes the electron and the neutrino.

light-year The distance travelled by light in one year. $1\,ly \approx 9.5 \times 10^{15}\,m$.

linear momentum The product of an object's mass and its velocity, $p = mv$. Momentum is a vector quantity.

magnetic flux The product of magnetic flux density normal to a circuit and the cross-sectional area of the circuit. Unit: weber (Wb).

magnetic flux density The strength of a magnetic field. Magnetic flux density B is defined as:

$$B = \frac{F}{IL}$$

where F is the force experienced by a conductor in the magnetic field, I is the current in the conductor and L is the length of the conductor in the magnetic field. (The conductor is at right angles to the field.)

magnetic flux linkage The product of magnetic flux and the number of turns. Unit: weber (Wb).

mass defect The difference between the total mass of the individual, separate nucleons and the mass of nucleus.

metastable Describes a nucleus that is in an unstable but relatively long-lived state.

moderator A material used in a nuclear reactor to slow down fast-moving neutrons so that they have a greater chance of interacting with the fissile nuclei.

natural frequency The unforced frequency of oscillation of a freely oscillating object.

neutrino An uncharged particle with almost no mass emitted during beta decay.

neutron number The number of neutrons in the nucleus of an atom.

neutron star The remnant of a massive star following a supernova.

Newton's first law An object will remain at rest or keep travelling at constant velocity unless it is acted on by an external force.

Newton's law of gravitation Any two point masses attract each other with a force that is directly proportional to the product of their masses and inversely proportional to the square of their separation.

Newton's second law The net force acting on an object is equal to the rate of change of its momentum. The net force and the change in momentum are in the same direction.

Newton's third law When two bodies interact, the forces they exert on each other are equal and opposite.

nuclear fission The splitting of a nucleus (e.g. $^{235}_{92}U$) into two large fragments and a small number of neutrons.

nuclear fusion A nuclear reaction where two light nuclei (e.g. $^{2}_{1}H$) join together to form a heavier but more stable nucleus.

nuclear model of the atom A model of the atom in which negative charges (electrons) are distributed outside a tiny nucleus of positive charge.

nucleon A particle found in an atomic nucleus, i.e. a neutron or a proton.

nucleon number The number of neutrons and protons in the nucleus of an atom (also called mass number).

nucleus The tiny central region of the atom that contains most of the mass of the atom and all of its positive charge.

nuclide A specific combination of protons and neutrons in a nucleus.

Olbers' paradox For an infinite, uniform and static universe, the night sky should be bright because of light received in all directions from stars.

open universe A model of the universe in which gravitational force cannot halt the expansion of matter. The universe will expand forever.

oscillates Another term for 'vibrates'.

oscillation A repetitive back-and-forth motion.

pair production A process where an X-ray photon produces an electron–positron pair.

parallax The apparent shifting of the position of a star relative to the background of distant stars when observed from different positions in the Earth's orbit round the Sun.

parsec The distance that gives a parallax angle of 1 arc second. $1\,pc \approx 3.1 \times 10^{16}\,m$.

perfectly elastic A collision is perfectly elastic when kinetic energy is conserved. Momentum and total energy are always conserved.

period The time taken by an object (e.g. a planet) to complete one orbit. The period is also the time taken for one complete oscillation of a vibrating object. Unit: second (s).

phase Describes the point that an oscillating mass has reached in a complete cycle.

phase difference The fraction of an oscillation between the vibrations of two oscillating particles, expressed in degrees or radians.

photoelectric effect An interaction between an X-ray photon and an electron in which the electron is removed from the atom.

photomultiplier tubes Devices used in a gamma camera to change the energy of an incident γ-ray photon into an electrical pulse.

piezoelectric crystal A material that produces an induced e.m.f. when it is compressed. Also, when a voltage is applied across it in one direction, it shrinks slightly.

planetary nebula Hot gases and dust blown away from a low-mass star as it evolves into a white dwarf. (Has nothing to do with the formation of planets!)

plum pudding model A model of the atom in which negative charges are distributed throughout a sphere of positive charge.

point mass An object with mass that is represented as a point (dot) because its size is extremely small compared with the separation between objects.

positron A positively charged particle with mass equal to that of an electron.

positron emission tomography A technique where γ-ray photons from electron–positron annihilations are detected to produce a 3D image of the body.

precession The movement of the axis of a spinning object (proton) around another axis.

proton number The number of protons in the nucleus of an atom (also called atomic number).

quarks Fundamental particles that make up hadrons such as the proton and the neutron.

radian An alternative unit for measuring angles. 2π radians $= 360°$ or π radians $= 180°$.

radiation pressure An outward pressure created by the photons produced from fusion reactions in a star.

radiopharmaceutical A substance tagged with a radioisotope and which targets a specific organ or tissue in the body.

red giant A star characterised by its cooler surface and extremely large surface area.

redshift A term used to describe the shifting of the entire spectrum of a receding source to longer wavelengths.

relaxation time The time taken for the nuclei to fall back to their lower energy state.

resonance The forced motion of an oscillator characterised by maximum amplitude when the forcing frequency matches the oscillator's natural frequency. A system absorbs maximum energy from a source when the source frequency is equal to the natural frequency of the system.

simple harmonic motion Motion of an oscillator where its acceleration is directly proportional to its displacement from its equilibrium position and is directed towards that position.

solenoid A long current-carrying coil used to generate a uniform magnetic field within its core.

specific heat capacity The energy required per unit mass of a substance to raise its temperature by $1\,K$ (or $1\,°C$). Unit: $J\,kg^{-1}\,K^{-1}$.

specific latent heat The energy required per kilogram of the substance to change its state without any change in temperature. Unit: $J\,kg^{-1}$.

speed The rate of change of the distance moved by an object:

$$\text{speed} = \frac{\text{distance}}{\text{time}}$$

Unit: $m\,s^{-1}$.

spin A quantum property of many atomic or sub-atomic particles.

standard model of the universe Another term for the Big Bang model of the universe.

strong nuclear force A fundamental (attractive) force of nature that acts between quarks.

super red giant A red giant formed towards the end of the life of a massive star.

supernova The explosion of a high-mass star that leaves a neutron star or a black hole.

tesla The SI unit for magnetic flux density. $1\,T = 1\,N\,A^{-1}\,m^{-1}$.

thermal energy Energy transferred from one object to another because of a temperature difference; another term for heat energy.

thermal equilibrium A condition when two or more objects in contact have the same temperature so that there is no net flow of energy between them.

thermodynamic scale A temperature scale where temperature is measured in kelvin (K).

time constant The time taken for the current, charge stored or p.d. to fall to $1/e$ (about 37%) when a capacitor discharges through a resistor. It is also equal to the product of capacitance and resistance.

tracers Radioactive substances used to investigate the function of organs of the body.

transducer A general term used for any device that changes one form of energy into another.

turns-ratio equation An equation relating the ratio of voltages to the ratio of numbers of turns on the two coils of a transformer:

$$\frac{V_s}{V_p} = \frac{n_s}{n_p}$$

unified atomic mass unit A convenient unit used for the mass of atomic and nuclear particles. ($1\,u$ is equal to $\frac{1}{12}$ the mass of a $^{12}_{6}C$ carbon atom.) $1\,u = 1.66 \times 10^{-27}\,kg$.

velocity The rate of change of the displacement of an object:

$$\text{velocity} = \frac{\text{change in displacement}}{\text{time}}$$

Unit: $m\,s^{-1}$. (You can think of velocity as 'speed in a certain direction'.)

weak interaction The nuclear force responsible for β decay.

white dwarf The very hot remnant of a low-mass star.

X-ray tube A device that produces X-rays when accelerated electrons hit a target metal.

Index

Italic page references are to figures and tables. Extension topics, which are to be found only on the accompanying CD-ROM, are shown in **bold**.